A LONG DAY'S DYING

CRITICAL MOMENTS IN THE DARFUR GENOCIDE

A LONG DAY'S DYING

CRITICAL MOMENTS IN THE DARFUR GENOCIDE

ERIC REEVES

Articles collected by
Ahmed Mohamedain Abdalla

Editor
Michael Brassard

CLINTON COLLEGE LIBRARY

The Key Publishing House Inc.

First Edition 2007
The Key Publishing House Inc.
Toronto, Canada
Website: www.thekeypublish.com
E-mail: info@thekeypublish.com

ISBN 0-9780431-4-6 paperback

Cover design and typesetting by Sean Tai
Cover photo © Paul Jeffery: Displaced Girl in Labado, Darfur.

Maps are used with permisson of United Nations Office for the Coordination of Humanitarian Affairs (OCHA) Sudan, ochasudan@un.org, http://ochaonline2.un.org/sudan

Pictures are used with permission from Darfur Diaspora Association (DDA) Canada, Gritty.org for Physicians for Human Rights (PHR) http://physiciansforhumanrights.org/, and Integrated Regional Information Networks (IRIN) http://www.irinnews.org/.

Printed and Bound by MCRL. This book is printed on acid-free paper suitable for recycling and made from fully sustained forest sources.

The Key Publishing promotes mutual understanding, respect and peaceful coexistence among the people of the world. We represent unique and unconventional voices whose objective is to bring ultimate peace, harmony and happiness to our human society.

Dedicated to
Ted Dagne
friend, brother, champion of Sudan

ACKNOWLEDGEMENTS

As isolating as my work habits have been, I owe my ability to persist in writing about Sudan—now for almost eight years—to those who have supported me so generously along the way. My wife Nancy and daughters Meredith and Hannah have endured in our otherwise tranquil home the all too frequent intrusion of rage and despair occasioned by Sudan's relentless suffering. I've depended upon the immensely supportive brotherhood of Ted Dagne, John Prendergast, Roger Winter, and Brian D'Silva. Wisdom, good counsel, and friendship have been offered by many, at many difficult junctures; but I would be remiss not to mention in particular Sharon Hutchinson, Jean-François Darcq, Julie Flint, Susannah Sirkin, Jerry Fowler, David Melvill, Jeb Sharp, and Sebastian Mallaby. And how to thank my many Sudanese friends? Truly too numerous to name, although Francis Deng has been especially supportive and Ahmed Mohamedain Abdalla saw this book project well along before my own time was required. Mohamed Nagi of *The Sudan Tribune* has been a steadfast believer in my work on Darfur, and I am immensely grateful for his consistent and timely publication of the analyses that make up the bulk of this volume. Huda Henry-Riyad of The Key Publishing House has supported the present project with unstinting enthusiasm, and the appearance of this book is due in no small measure to her kind efforts.

And finally there are those I can't name, even as they risked much to tell me what they felt was essential to be known. It tells all too much about the ongoing agony of Sudan that they should be so numerous.

TABLE OF CONTENTS

1

INTRODUCTION

I N FEBRUARY 2003, years of severe political and economic marginalization in the Darfur region of western Sudan culminated in the outbreak of a major insurgency campaign, directed against the vast tyranny
embodied in the ruling Khartoum junta. Outraged by government-supported ethnic violence that targeted their families and villages, rebel
groups drawing their strength from non-Arab or "African" tribal groups in
Darfur targeted military installations and police stations associated with
the brutal and widely reviled National Islamic Front (NIF) regime in
Khartoum, which had several years earlier innocuously renamed itself the
National Congress Party (NCP). Violence escalated and soon the entire
region was deeply affected by a brutal counter-insurgency war that rapidly
became genocidal in nature. Initially the war was largely concealed by
Darfur's remoteness, Khartoum's deliberate isolation of the region, and by
the singular focus of international diplomatic efforts on ending the long-
running north-south civil war. Western diplomats involved in the regional
negotiations to halt this conflict felt that Darfur would overload the agenda
with Khartoum. Thus despite the horrific accounts of human suffering
and destruction that were filtering out, it was decided that the Darfur conflict would have to wait until a final deal had been secured. It was a sur-
passingly expedient and destructive calculation.

1

Sudan, geographically the largest country in Africa, had long been ruled from Khartoum by a series of Arab-dominated governments. But the June 1989 military coup that brought the National Islamic Front (NIF) to power set in motion events that led inexorably to the military explosion of early 2003. At the same time, the conflict was from the beginning defined by the complex ethnic tensions that had intensified following the famine of 1984-85, and were exacerbated by changes in regional governance and administration imposed by the NIF in 1994. Designed to garner political support from the Arab minority of Darfur, Khartoum's political actions ensured that ethnic identity would become an increasingly salient feature of life and violence in the region.

The rebel organization that came to be known as the Sudan Liberation Army (SLA), along with the much smaller Justice and Equality Movement (JEM), launched a series of lightning military attacks, many on police stations that had for years failed to protect the insurgents and their families. The two groups drew their military strength primarily from three of the many non-Arab or "African" tribal groups of Darfur – the Fur (the largest ethnic group in Darfur), the Massaleit, and the Zaghawa. Initial military efforts by the insurgency forces were consistently successful, and culminated in April 2003 with a spectacular surprise attack on the el-Fasher air base, the primary military installation in Darfur for the Khartoum regime's Sudan Armed Forces (SAF). The insurgents destroyed a number of military aircraft on the ground, seized great quantities of military equipment, killed many soldiers, and captured an air force general.

But the consequences of these early successes were ominous. Although able to run rings around the ponderous and relatively poorly trained military forces that Khartoum had deployed to Darfur, the insurgents could not defend against the ensuing dramatic switch in military strategy. Recruiting from some of the nomadic Arab groups in Darfur, Khartoum vastly expanded militia groups that had been previously known as the *Janjaweed*, Arabic for "devil on horseback," although the word had also meant "bandit," an ambiguity that has been made much of by Khartoum. The *Janjaweed* that emerged fully in 2003, although an extension of earlier Arab militia groups that had violently preyed on African villagers for years, were a new force in the savage counter-insurgency war that Khartoum had launched. Traveling primarily on horse and camel-back, the *Janjaweed* were heavily armed by the regime and actively coordinating with its regular military forces. Indeed, as numerous human rights reports established on the basis of highly authoritative on-the-ground research, the *Janjaweed* have worked hand-in-glove with the SAF, inside a command structure that reaches to the senior ranks of the NIF military and political establishment.

Attacks on African villages typically began with aerial attacks by Antonov "bombers." In fact, the Antonov is not a bomber by design, but rather a retrofitted Russian cargo plane from which crude barrel bombs are simply rolled out the back cargo bay. Antonovs had been used relentlessly against civilians in the north-south war, which was still far from settled when the Darfur insurgency broke out. Bombs dropped from Antonovs are far too imprecise to be used against military targets. To avoid ground fire, Antonovs typically fly at altitudes over 15,000 feet. But such bombs are exquisitely suited as instruments of civilian terror. Following early morning bombing attacks on targeted villages, attacks which dispersed the terrified inhabitants, the *Janjaweed* would sweep in, shooting all in their sight. Very often they were accompanied by regular SAF forces in trucks, armored personnel carries, and other vehicles. Deadly helicopter gunships would also be deployed, killing fleeing civilians and any who might choose to resist.

Following the initial military operations, the *Janjaweed* and ground troops would engage in a systematic destruction of the livelihoods of the villagers. Homes, buildings, and mosques were burned; water wells, precious in this arid land, were poisoned with human or animal corpses; irrigation systems were destroyed; food and seed stocks were looted or burned; mature fruit trees were cut down; agricultural implements were destroyed. The *Janjaweed* and SAF would also loot cattle, a critical form of insurance against hard times in this forbidding region. In a land and agricultural economy largely without banks, cattle represent the wealth of generations. On countless occasions, African villagers saw this wealth disappear in the space of hours.

Such comprehensive destruction, clearly animated by a desire to destroy the Fur, Massaleit, and Zaghawa people as such, constituted genocide – as did the direct, ethnically-targeted murder of these people. Article 2 of the 1948 UN Convention on the Prevention and Punishment of the Crime of Genocide specifies a number of acts which, when "committed with an intent to destroy, in whole or in part, a national, ethnical, racial or religious group, as such," constitute genocide. Article 2, Clause C refers to acts,

> Deliberately inflicting on the group conditions of life calculated to bring about its physical destruction in whole or in part.

This feature of conflict in Darfur has been insufficiently recognized as genocidal in nature, and is one reason that some groups have been hesitant to use the word "genocide" to describe what has occurred there. One human rights organization, Physicians for Human Rights, has attended to this issue in very considerable detail, and devoted much research energy on the ground to establishing just how comprehensive the destruction of livelihoods has been. Their February 2005 report, *Evidence of Intentional Destruction of Livelihoods in Darfur*, powerfully documents their grim conclusions. Too often the issue of genocide in Darfur has been forced into the template of the Rwandan genocide, with distorting effects. In the long run, the greatest human mortality in Darfur will derive not directly from violence but from the violent destruction of livelihoods and the means of living.

Attacks on African villages were, and are, also typically accompanied by the brutal rape (often gang-rape) of women and girls; these violent sexual assaults also have a genocidal purpose. For the inevitable effect of rape in the traditional Muslim cultures of Darfur – all in Darfur are Muslim – is stigmatization, leading to disgrace and often ostracizing. In order to assure precisely these effects, *Janjaweed* and SAF rapists have often scarred or burned women and girls to mark them as victims of a crime that is highly unusual in traditional Darfuri society. Here we must recall that Article 2 of the UN Convention on the Prevention and Punishment of the Crime of Genocide also speaks of acts "causing serious bodily or mental harm to members of the group." The racialized use of rape as a weapon of war clearly meets the high standard of the Genocide Convention.

During the rapes, killings, and pillaging, *Janjaweed* militiamen commonly hurled derogatory racial epithets at their victims. A February 2004 report from Amnesty International, *Darfur: 'Too many people killed for no reason*,' offered many examples of the kind of language indicating genocidal intent on the part of the *Janjaweed* and their masters in Khartoum. Two examples:

A refugee farmer from the village of Kishkish reported . . . the words used by the militia: "You are Black and you are opponents. You are our slaves, the Darfur region is in our hands and you are our herders."

A civilian from Jafal confirmed [he was] told by the Janjawid: "You are opponents to the regime, we must crush you. As you are Black, you are like slaves. Then all the Darfur region will be in our hands. The government is on our side. The government plane is on our side to give us ammunition and food."

There was a terrible prescience in comments made by an African tribal leader to a UN news service in late 2003: "I believe this is an elimination of the black race."

This was violence such as Darfur had never seen, and as its ethnic character became more salient, so too did a hardening of ethnic identities. People who in earlier times would have referred to themselves as "Fur" or "Massaleit" increasingly referred to themselves as "African," as opposed to "Arab," even as generations of intermarriage and migration had made such distinctions extremely difficult.

DARFUR IS a harsh and austere land, although its people have been extraordinarily resourceful in carving out lives that are culturally rich and materially self-sustaining. Even after the Darfur region was brought within Anglo-Egyptian condominium control of Sudan following the British conquest of the last Fur sultan (1916), colonial rule entailed relatively little in the way of administration except ensuring that violence was kept low-key. Governance was by way of "native administration," through which tribal chiefs did the work of the colonial power. Development and investment in the region were almost non-existent. This remained the case long after Sudanese independence in 1956.

Darfur has dozens of tribal groupings, and distinctions within these groupings can be bewilderingly complex. A key difference is between Arab tribal groups that are cattle herders or *Baggara*, and those that are camel herders or *Abbala*. The *Abbala* are much more likely to be found in northern Darfur, and, because of their poverty, have been more susceptible to recruitment into the *Janjaweed*. African tribal groups, not only the Fur, Massaleit, and Zaghawa, but the Tunjur, Dajo, Bertig, and many others, tend to remain in permanent farming villages, growing crops of millet, sorghum, and other grains, as well as raising livestock as conditions permit. There are exceptions, and the Zaghawa in particular are well known as camel herders.

Although never an untroubled symbiosis, the relationship between African agriculturalists and Arab pastoralists had evolved over centuries in ways that permitted a number of mechanisms for conflict resolution, serving to mitigate violence and reprisals. This represented implicit recognition of the limitations of the traditional system of land tenure, or *hakura*. Even so, such mechanisms have in recent decades found themselves under increasing strain as the Sahara continues its inexorable spread southwards through the great Sahel region of northern Africa. Northern Darfur has always been the harshest, most forbidding region of the province, and it was here that a number of Arab tribal groups were without a "Dar," or homeland ("Darfur" means "homeland of the Fur"). As the land became poorer, as the valuable natural resources of Darfur – arable land and water – became scarcer, competition for these resources inevitably became more intense, and nowhere more so than in northern Darfur.

As Alex de Waal and Julie Flint reveal in their deft history of the region, *Darfur: A Short History of a Long War* [2005], ethnic violence of a highly ominous nature was in evidence for years before the insurgency began in 2003. They note on page 64 that in "October 2002, government-supported *Janjawiid* from the camps in South Darfur launched a major offensive, the first of its kind against Fur civilians." Many civilians were killed and "hundreds of villages burned." Earlier yet, in 1998, *Janjaweed* forces had attacked in Dar Massaleit, the Massaleit homeland in western Darfur, killing more than a thousand people and burning some 30 villages. De Waal and Flint make clear in their account that the *Janjaweed* were even then supported and directed by Khartoum; indeed, from the perspective of many Massaleit, the late 1990s were a turning point – the moment in which the *Janjaweed* became the primary military instrument of the Khartoum regime.

Politically, the National Islamic Front regime had also been active in cultivating favor among the Arab groups of Darfur, this as a way of expanding what was an excessively narrow political base following the June 1989 military coup. A key move in this strategy was the 1994 division of Darfur into three states: North Darfur, with a capital in el-Fasher; South Darfur, with a capital in Nyala; and West Darfur, with a capital in el-Geneina. This division, without precedent in Darfur's history, worked to weaken the Fur by denying them a political majority in any one Darfur state. In the wake of this decision Khartoum gradually took full administrative control of the province, and the growing strength of the intelligence services ensured that political dissent could be controlled.

Political marginalization and the increase of ethnically-targeted violence – as well as Khartoum's efforts throughout the 1990s to disarm African tribal groups and villages but not Arab militias – made full-scale conflict inevitable. If it was hard to anticipate how rapidly the region would become engulfed in the most hateful and destructive forms of violence against civilians, there were nonetheless terrifying reports almost from the beginning of the insurgency. And now, as ethnic violence spills deeper into Chad to the west, it is impossible not to draw the direst conclusions about the future of the region as a whole. Eastern Chad, with an ethnic mix very similar to that of Darfur – the border between Darfur and Chad is an arbitrary line in the sand – will continue to see an explosion of violence unless international security forces are introduced into the region. Khartoum has supported not only the *Janjaweed* in their brutal predations against African populations in eastern Chad, but also the rebel groups seeking to topple the government of President Idriss Déby. Chadian military forces have concentrated on protecting the garrison towns and major city of eastern Chad, Abéché, and in the process exposed both civilian populations and humanitarian operations to intolerable insecurity. The Central African Republic (CAR) is also being drawn into the conflict (there is strong evidence of Khartoum's support for rebels in CAR), with devastating consequences for civilians in the northern part of this weak and impoverished country.

As a number of senior UN officials have warned – including the Under-Secretary General for Humanitarian Affairs and the High Commissioner for Refugees – the Darfur genocide threatens to create regional instability on a massive scale. We may be witnessing a crisis that will grow in proportion to what has for years been so tragically in evidence in the Democratic Republic of the Congo. There are no encouraging signals of resolve on the part of the international community to halt the slide toward catastrophic violence.

For its part, the Khartoum security cabal is determined to retain its monopoly on Sudanese national wealth and power – the former increasingly serving as a means of consolidating the latter. Since oil exports began in August 1999, the regime has been the almost exclusive beneficiary of an enormous growth in the northern Sudanese economy. Certainly there has been no lack of investors, particularly from Asia. China has become the dominant player in Sudanese oil development, concentrated in southern Sudan, and has provided Khartoum with more than $10 billion in commercial and capital investments over the past decade. China has also been Khartoum's primary supplier of weapons, including many of the weapons that are currently being used in Darfur. But despite very significant oil wealth, nearly all of Sudan outside a sliver of the Nile River Valley has seen no benefits from this national resource. Whether we look to the eastern provinces, to the devastated south of Sudan, to the far north, or to Darfur, there is no evidence that Khartoum has used oil wealth in any but self-serving ways. Military purchases have been profligate, even as the cities of Khartoum, Omdurman, and their suburbs have seen virtually all the benefits of foreign investment and the regime's tight control of oil revenues. Lavish lifestyles in Khartoum contrast hideously with the abject poverty that dominates the lives of most Sudanese.

THE PRESENT VOLUME comprises representative "moments" from the more than 150 analyses of Darfur I have written since Fall 2003. Each was written with an eye to what I took to be the most significant developments of the moment bearing on the Darfur crisis. They address key reports from human rights and policy groups, UN offices, and aid organizations; they collate information bearing on particularly consequential humanitarian developments; they analyze security conditions on the ground in Darfur; and they assess the regional and international responses to what was quickly recognized in some quarters as "ethnic cleansing," and in less than a year as genocide. These analyses, then, form a kind of archival resource for any history of the first genocide of the 21st century, containing an extremely wide range of sources and references, as well as forceful contemporaneous moral and political judgments about inaction in the face cataclysmic human destruction. References and sources include reports from human rights organizations and operational humanitarian aid groups, as well as the analytic and advocacy work of policy "think tanks" and UN agencies. Additionally, I have made extensive use of news from a broad range of wire services, reportage from journalists for major print newspapers and news magazines, and individual accounts by those traveling in the region, frequently journalists speaking off the record. The analyses also assess, as carefully as possible, implications of the many political pronouncements by various Western and regional governments, UN officials, as well as organizations such as the Arab League, the African Union, and the Organization of the Islamic Conference.

Issues of confidentiality have posed serious challenges in my work, and create a significant problem in using this archive for historical analysis and assessment. Security conditions in Darfur are, as of this writing, deteriorating rapidly and the danger to many sources on the ground is greater than ever. The obligations of confidentiality are extraordinarily acute. At the same time, customary journalistic obligations to protect sources, many of whom have provided me with information on a confidential basis, and continue to do so, cannot be compromised. I believe I have gained widespread respect for my care in preserving confidences, and for precisely this reason receive an unusually large number of reports and accounts not publicly available, both from the ground as well as from UN, governmental, and nongovernmental sources. Because the analyses in this volume have had such wide readership, this fact in itself becomes an incentive for further confidential disclosures, particularly from those who possess information of considerable value but which hasn't been judged newsworthy by conventional news sources.

Working independently, I have inevitably confronted a wide range of methodological problems in rendering various aspects of the crisis in Darfur, and have addressed these in a number of ways. At the same time, two of the particular problems I confront suggest the advantages of working as this volume does, with both fine-grained chronological representation as well as a broader chapter organization.

For example, it is impossible to say with any certainty how many villages in Darfur have been destroyed, or even precisely how to define a village. But the consensus among my many sources within the Darfuri diaspora, those with ongoing contacts on the ground in Darfur, is that between 80 and 90% of all African villages have been destroyed. Massaleit villages have been almost entirely destroyed, even as the Massaleit people had been particular targets of ethnic violence prior to the outbreak of the insurgency in

February 2003. Earlier in the crisis the US Agency for International Development (USAID) released a series of aerial reconnaissance photographs demonstrating the extent of village destruction; but there has been no public updating of these photographs, even as village destruction proceeded remorselessly. A close reading of this volume will give some sense of where destruction has been concentrated over these many months, as well as a sense of the most salient episodes of ethnically-targeted village destruction.

Even more difficult to establish is mortality during the Darfur conflict. There is, however, a great deal of extant data, though it has not elsewhere been collated and assessed as a collective body of information bearing on deaths from violence, disease, and malnutrition. I am convinced that by the end of 2006 approximately 500,000 people had died from all causes since the outbreak of the insurgency. This figure is considerably higher than all but one of the rival mortality studies that have been published since I began to challenge figures promulgated by the UN. The *terminus a quo* for my efforts was a questioning of the official UN figure of 3,000 dead in January 2004.

My fifteen full-dress mortality assessments have been criticized in some quarters, but they have the unique advantage of attempting to make use of all the data available. Other mortality studies have been highly selective in the data and contextualizing information they analyze, and because of this selectivity arrive at significantly lower figures for global mortality, although all such figures now indicate deaths in the hundreds of thousands. Their epidemiological methodology is more "hygienic" but is unlikely to do justice to the scale of human destruction that has occurred in circumstances that do not permit the kinds of surveys required for greater certainty and smaller margins of error. For the present, I take satisfaction in the judgment of my work offered by Francesco Checchi, a London epidemiologist who has worked in Darfur for humanitarian groups. Checchi acknowledges that I may have an activist agenda but also declares that, "[Reeves] knows Darfur well," and that what I have done is "mathematically correct" and "sufficiently legitimate to establish a high-end count" (*Christian Science Monitor*, August 30, 2006).

There are some significant disadvantages to my approach, as well as some significant lacunae in my accounts. I only occasionally address the suffering and destruction endured by those Arab tribal groups in Darfur that have not joined the *Janjaweed*, indeed have struggled to remain neutral in the war. As a group they have endured some of the worst consequences of genocidal counter-insurgency warfare; global health indicators, when they can be established, suggest very high levels of morbidity and mortality. Migratory routes for these primarily nomadic pastoralists have been severed both by insecurity and by deliberate attacks on the part of various elements of the SLA and JEM. These Arab people and their suffering are largely invisible in the analyses of this volume, though it must be said there are exceedingly few humanitarian or other reports from which to draw.

Methodologically, I have of necessity been dependent upon too few sources, and have not been able to travel myself to the Darfur region, although I have traveled in southern Sudan and the Nuba Mountains. Balancing the roles of advocacy and analysis can also be extremely difficult, and at times I am sure I lean too much to the former, at least for purposes of creating an historical archive. Even so, I believe the historical record shows I have proved accurate in far too many of my predictions, though I have also erred at times, certainly with respect to the time-frame and scale for predicted developments. In such error, I have had much distinguished company.

BECAUSE THIS volume, as edited, attempts to provide a retrospective running commentary on the emerging realities of the Darfur genocide, to give a whelming sense of what could and should have been known about the ethnically-targeted destruction of non-Arab or African tribal populations in Darfur, it has of necessity been highly selective. Less than twenty percent of the body of work accumulated to date has been published here. This reflects above all the need to make reading fluent enough so that a sense of chronology remains clear, and the pattern of developments is not lost amidst an excessive word count. But while much redundancy and excessive detail have been eliminated, so too has important transitional and contextualizing material. Every attempt has been made to provide as much continuity as possible, but there are still significant challenges to the reader in holding the elements of the larger narrative in mind, particularly since these analyses grow out of a previous five years of writing about the north-south civil war and tortuous peace negotiations that ended it, at least provisionally. These negotiations were very far from complete, or even certain, as Darfur emerged into international visibility. Inevitably, the connections between the conflict in Darfur and southern Sudan often figure prominently in analyses written during the first year and a half of the period represented here, and to a lesser extent in more recent analyses. No book has yet been written on the final chapter of the north-south war and last stages of the peace process, and I am left to refer readers to the several hundred analyses on the subject archived on my website, www.sudanreeves.org.

An inevitable feature of this compilation, from so many discrete analyses, is redundancy and repetition – of key statements, statistics, characterizations, historical facts, as well as the painfully familiar diplomatic and moral failures. But the terrible truth is that genocide, particularly as it unfolds in Darfur, is highly repetitive; it is not in any consistent sense "newsworthy"; there is a ghastly, finally numbing familiarity to the individual episodes of horror that are at the heart of what this books attempts to render, or at least suggest. If there are indeed "critical moments" in the Darfur genocide, there is for the most part only very routine cruelty, suffering, and destruction. And the world has become inured to this agony precisely because it is so routine. Readers will have to endure repetition because it cannot be "edited out": it is finally the essence of genocide as we must see it in Darfur.

Such repetition can also serve a corrective function. For self-exculpatory history writing has already begun in earnest as international actors seek to excuse themselves of responsibility for their inaction, diffidence, and cowardice in the face of almost four years of catastrophic human destruction – destruction that the world has always been able, if willing, to stop. Repetition in this context serves to emphasize the most basic realities of the Darfur genocide, the most inescapable truths that were nonetheless so consistently elided from deliberations and pronouncements at "critical moments." Repetition and redundancy may not be an antidote to the disingenuousness and expediency that have been so prominent in the world's response to Darfur, but they work to prevent at least some of the more convenient exercises in mendacity. This in itself seems sufficient justification.

At the same time, these pages inevitably reflect a growing understanding on the part of the author, an increasing awareness in particular of the complexity of issues of "race" and "ethnicity" in Darfur. Earlier analyses often refer to both these anthropological constructs, typically in conjunction with one another. "Racial" consciousness and self-consciousness have in fact been key elements of the Darfur conflict, particularly in the hateful racial supremacism on the part of the *Janjaweed*, and finally on the part of the ruling elite in Khartoum. "*Zurga*," "Nuba," "*abid*," are all words with racial and strongly derogatory meanings; *abid* in particular – a word long used to characterize southern Sudanese – means "slave" in Arabic, but also carries many connotations of the hateful English word "nigger." These words have very consistently been used, with conspicuous racial intent, by the *Janjaweed* in their attacks on African tribal populations.

But of course it is also true, as many insist, that all in Darfur are "Africans," and that perhaps the most important distinction is between "Arabs" and "non-Arabs." Indeed, it is largely impossible for non-Darfuris to distinguish on the basis of physiognomy between "Arabs" and "non-Arabs." Although there is considerable justification for this way of distinguishing between ethnicities in Darfur, it fails to capture the racial elements that underlie perceptions on the part of the *Janjaweed* and the Khartoum junta, and the increasing tendency by the targeted "non-Arab" groups to identify themselves as "African" in the face of a continuing racist onslaught. Moreover, characterization or definition by negation inevitably begs a number of questions; one has only to think of the radical ambiguity of a phrase such as "non-European" to see the limits of this means of speaking about the ethnic identity and self-perceptions of the Fur, Massaleit, Zaghawa, Birgid, Dajo, and other tribal groups – groups I've chosen to characterize as "African."

The analyses here have been edited, except in quotations, for consistency of transliteration from the Arabic; for a standard method of reference and citation, particularly of news wire reports; for clarity; and for purposes of providing necessary transitional language. The full, unedited texts of all analyses can be found in the *Archives* of my website.

WRITING ABOUT an ongoing and deepening crisis is difficult enough with the delays inherent in newspaper and news magazine publication, as I have discovered in my many formal publications on Sudan, extending back to early 1999 (a complete bibliography of these can also be found at www.sudanreeves.org). But the delays in writing, editing, and production of a book inevitably increase the likelihood that significant changes will overtake specific assessments and characterizations. Nonetheless, the catastrophic turn of events following the so-called "Darfur Peace Agreement," signed in Abuja, Nigeria on May 5, 2006, obliged some effort at historical analysis and synthesis of recent events. For the precipitous decline in security for humanitarians and civilians in Darfur that accelerated through fall and early winter 2006 created a compelling point of provisional conclusion for the present archival history. As of late December 2006, a ghastly "genocide by attrition" seems to have settled remorselessly over Darfur.

All too conspicuously, the international community has demonstrated no will to intervene, with or without Khartoum's consent. There were, in the very last week of December 2006, a few concessions by the National Islamic Front/National Congress Party on participation by personnel from the UN Department of Peacekeeping Operations in Darfur, but far from enough to change the overall security dynamic. Indeed, these concessions were designed to allow international actors of consequence to save face in accepting the continuation of the African Union (AU) as the primary security presence on the ground in Darfur. Although this is a force that is manifestly incapable of protecting either civilians or humanitarians in the region, Khartoum's refusal to allow any significant UN augmentation of the AU ensures a genocidal status quo. Several of my analyses provide overviews of AU weaknesses, and establish a clear consensus among military experts that this under-manned, poorly equipped, logistically overwhelmed force cannot halt violence or offer meaningful protection in a region that is the size of France, without significant infrastructure, and exceedingly remote from navigable bodies of water.

Despite these longstanding shortcomings, the African Union Mission in Sudan (AMIS) was given exclusive responsibilities for overseeing the disastrous Darfur Peace Agreement (DPA). The DPA had many weaknesses that made it unacceptable to the vast majority of Darfuris, both in the camps and in the diaspora. Inadequate compensation – the only installment to date amounts to less than $8 per conflict-affected person; weak political representation nationally; and a failure to allow for sufficient regional self-governance: all were quite clear even in an exceedingly long and complex peace agreement document that was not fully understood by the fractious rebel leaders who were negotiating on behalf of all Darfuris.

But what ensured the failure of the DPA was that it provided no meaningful guarantors for the various security arrangements of the agreement, only more responsibilities for an AU force that was already overwhelmed by the tasks it had taken on in Darfur. In seeking to create security throughout Darfur, the DPA stipulated a number of new tasks and mandates for the AU, as well as formation of a welter of commissions and committees. The DPA also set a time-line for creation of buffer zones, demilitarization, and most critically, disarmament of the *Janjaweed*. But ultimately, without guarantors much more robust than the AU, all the DPA security arrangements relied upon the good will of the Khartoum regime. Since the regime was and remains actively in violation of many of the key protocols that make up the Comprehensive Peace Agreement that ended the 1983 – 2005 north-south civil war, there was good reason to be suspicious of Khartoum's willingness to disarm what had proved its indispensable military asset in Darfur. Indeed, over the course of 17 years in power, the National Islamic Front/National Congress Party has never abided by any agreement with any Sudanese party.

The conspicuous failures of the DPA, hastily made into an ultimatum by the US and other last-minute negotiating partners in Abuja, ensured that the most representative rebel leader, Abdel Wahid al-Nur, would not sign. And even he had been viewed suspiciously by many of his own commanders, who anticipated a sell-out and thus split from Abdel Wahid well before the May 5 deadline that was arbitrarily imposed by negotiators. In the end, only Minni Minawi signed.

Minawi is a Zaghawa, and had surrounded himself almost exclusively with Zaghawa advisors; this ethnic parochialism had disastrous consequences for the DPA on the ground in Darfur. Minawi's decision to sign alone was certainly made under extreme duress; but his own calculation was weightier than any duress, and in retrospect was clearly misguided from the standpoint of not only his own interests, but those of the Zaghawa, and certainly those of the people of Darfur as a whole. Minawi has been almost completely abandoned politically in Khartoum, where he is nominally the fourth-ranking member of the Presidency in a notional "Government of National Unity." On the field in Darfur, his commanders have all abandoned him – some expediently siding with Khartoum, others becoming little more than opportunistic bandits. But there is also growing evidence that the majority of Minawi's SLA commanders have rejoined non-signatory rebel groups. This is of significance because it ensures that

Khartoum cannot achieve military victory in Darfur through a "divide and conquer" strategy of the sort it has so often used successfully in the past.

The international response to the failure of the Abuja agreement came belatedly in the form of UN Security Council Resolution 1706, passed on August 31, 2006. The resolution enjoyed Chapter VII authority of the UN Charter, which conferred enforcement responsibility. Resolution 1706 called for deployment of approximately 22,500 UN troops and civilian police. The UN Department of Peacekeeping Operations based this figure on an extensive assessment in July 2006. Such a force, if expeditiously deployed and provided with adequate resources and trained personnel, could significantly mitigate the genocidal destruction that is currently ongoing. And yet despite passage of the Resolution, and despite the UN's formal acceptance of a "responsibility to protect" civilians endangered by genocide, ethnic cleansing, and crimes against humanity (UN World Summit of September 2005), no force was deployed or even assembled.

For Khartoum – backed by China, Russia, and the Arab League, most notably by Egypt – adamantly rejected any deployment of a UN peace support operation in Darfur as infringing upon its national sovereignty, indeed constituting a form of "re-colonization" by the West. In responding to Khartoum's obdurate refusal to accept the force authorized by Resolution 1706, UN and Western officials faced a choice: non-consensual deployment or accepting whatever Khartoum decided to allow. Although morally and legally obligated to intervene to protect civilians being indiscriminately attacked by their own government, the UN and international community clearly had no intention of committing the resources – military and political – necessary for non-consensual deployment. Such deployment would certainly have been made enormously difficult by logistical challenges, as well as the realities of Darfur's size, remoteness, and arid climate.

In the end, the world allowed Khartoum to accept what elements it chose from a modified UN plan first proposed at AU headquarters in Addis Ababa on November 16, 2006. In late December, a face-saving arrangement had been worked out that would do nothing to change the fundamental security conditions in Darfur, but allowed outgoing UN Secretary-General Kofi Annan to declare that there would be a UN presence on the ground in Darfur. The US, which had postured shamelessly during the period subsequent to passage of Resolution 1706, was allowed to back away from its threatened "Plan B" – which turned out to be a thoroughly vacuous bluff of "coercive" actions. The Europeans, who had never felt domestic political pressure to respond to Darfur, merely shrugged.

As 2007 began, there was no reason to believe that humanitarian organizations would be able to survive the year amidst what had become intolerable security conditions; more than a dozen aid workers were killed in Darfur in 2006, nearly all of them after the Abuja peace agreement. At the same time, UN estimates for the number of conflict-affected civilians in the greater humanitarian theater had grown to 4.5 million – a population increasingly desperate after three years of largely failed harvests and the exhaustion of all food reserves. A significant withdrawal of humanitarian organizations and personnel had already begun, with a number of groups either withdrawing altogether, or suspending operations – or simply hunkering down in the major urban areas, unable to reach many of the almost 300 camps and concentrations of displaced and affected civilians.

The world simply watched as the critical but fragile humanitarian lifeline became increasingly frayed, with a total severing of assistance possible at any moment. I write in one of my last analyses, of December 23, 2006, about the most ominous threat consequent upon large-scale humanitarian evacuation: the bulldozing of camps that hold more than 2 million internally displaced persons, and forced "returns" of civilians to their villages. In fact, such "returns" would be in the vast majority of cases not to villages, but to their burned out remains, with no meaningful security. And the fields these people had held for countless generations were already claimed by others, and in many cases turned into pasturage for the cattle and camels of nomadic groups. An even more terrifying prospect, in the event of humanitarian withdrawal, is wholesale assault by *Janjaweed* forces on camps for displaced persons. The first such attack occurred in September of 2005; since then, these brutal attacks on defenseless civilians have become too common. In the absence of international witnesses, it becomes terrifyingly likely that the camps will become slaughterhouses.

IN A NOTORIOUSLY famous moment, Lieutenant-General Roméo Dallaire – UN force commander during the Rwandan genocide – declared that "Peux ce que veux. Allons'y" ("Where there's a will, there's a way. Let's go."). This was the conclusion of a crucial fax (January 11, 1994) to Kofi

Annan, then head of UN peacekeeping operations. Dallaire was urgently requesting permission from the UN to act in ways that might forestall the clearly looming bloodbath. There was no response from New York other than to tell Dallaire to sit tight. A little more than half a year later, following the explosion of violence that began on April 7, 1994 in the Rwandan capital of Kigali, more than 800,000 Tutsis and moderate Hutus had been slaughtered.

And yet a decade later, we were witnessing a ghastly reprise. For over three and a half years, the international community has demonstrated neither the "will" nor any interest in finding a meaningful "way" of halting genocide in another African country. Darfur has many times been referred to, with good reason, as "Rwanda in slow motion." What I believe is evident in the analyses of this volume is just how clearly and fully, at every step of this slow-motion horror, the international community has known what was occurring – and failed to act to confront the ultimate human crime. I fear that to read these accounts is to look into what Joseph Conrad called the "heart of an immense darkness." A light is nowhere to be seen.

Northampton, Massachusetts
January 21, 2007

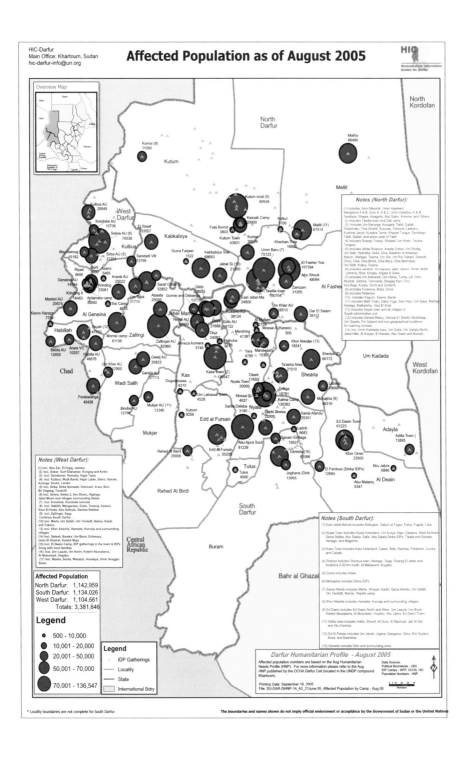

Affected Population as of August 2005

HIC-Darfur
Main Office: Khartoum, Sudan
hic-darfur-info@un.org

HIC
Humanitarian Information
Centre for Darfur

Overview Map

Notes (North Darfur):
(1) includes Umm Marahik, Umm Hajireed, Mangolouh A & B, Guio A, B & C, Umm Gafelbou A & B, Sarafaya, Shegra, Azagarfa, Abu Sakin, Komma, and Others
(2) includes Tawilla town and Deli camp
(3) Includes Um Barunga, Kungara, Tabit, Galab, Shakshaku, Tina Gharib, Susuwa, Tandona, Leskany, Kushina, Janub, Kunjara Tama, Khazan Tungur, Sendimgo, Tabit, Gallab, and areas west of Tabit
(4) includes Shangil Tobayi, Shadad, Um Khair, Teyiba, Tangara
(5) includes Abdel Shakour, Arada, Edour, Um Shidig, Um Sidir, Hashaba, Anka, Disa, Baashim & Amarayi, Bakium, Malagat, Teema, Um Rai, Um Rai Osbani, Delaielh Onyo, Disa, Disa Birdik, Disa Beiry, Disa Beirmaze, Um Sidir, Kulkul, Teema
(6) includes Jambob, Um layona, Jabir, Idurum, Amar Jedid, Lemena, Nina, Korgay, Argala & Gobe
(7) includes Um Maharerik, Um Horaz, Turba, Lilt, Orrin, Muzbat, Jukhora, Tamowrta, Shegeg Karo, Oro, Ana Bagi, Korbia, Orohi and Gorbere
(8) includes Furawiya, Bobs, Eima
(9) includes Mistanya
(10) includes Kagum, Kawra, Barde
(11) includes Malit Town, Daba Tuga, Saro Hayz, Um Ayaa, Martajl, Hanaga, Elelkarsha, Goz El Arab
(12) includes Sayah town and all villages at Sayah administrative unit
(13) includes Dennar Masry, Dannar El Sheikh Abdelbagi, Um Sayela, Por Saeed and non-geographical locations for roaming nomads
(14) incl. Umm Keddada town, Um Sidra, Um Gelala North, Jebel Hilla, Al Arayes, El Karada, Abu Gdam and Burush.

Notes (West Darfur):
(1) incl. Abu Zar, El Hujej, Jamma
(2) incl. Goker, Gurf Elahamar, Kongorg and Kirkir.
(3) incl. Gendermei, Romalla, Hajar Tama
(4) incl. Kulbus, Wadi Bardi, Hajar Laben, Betro, Hailate, Aoriaga, Kouta, Lembo
(5) incl. Sirba, Sirba Nomads, Dohoush, Arwa, Buri, Bir Degeeg, Tandulti
(6) incl. Seleia, Seleia 2, Aru Sharu, Higleigs, Jebel Moon and villages surrounding Seleia
(7) incl. Kondobe, Kondobe nomads
(8) incl. Habilla, Mangaressa, Gobe, Tewerg, Sawani, Nour El Huda, Abu Dahlyda, Gemiza Babikar
(9) incl. Zallingei, Saga
Continue South Darfur ...
(12) incl. Marla, Um Safati, Um Tendalti, Naima, Kasib and Tokoru.
(13) incl. Khor Abeche, Hamada, Kurunje and surrounding villages
(14) incl. Seleah, Bareka, Um Boim, Eshereya, Umm El Khairat, Kekebil Muju
(15) incl. El Neem Camp, IDP gatherings in the town & IDPs living with host families.
(16) incl. Um Laaute, Um Boim, Kelekil Abusalama, Al Muturwad, Ungabo
(17) incl. Mealia, Sunta, Wazazin, Assalaya, Umm Greggio, Selea.

Notes (South Darfur):
(1) East Jebel Marrah includes Kidbegeer, Sabon al Fagur, Feina, Fugoly, Liba
(2) Nyala Town includes Nyala hinterland, Um Kunja, Hijar, Dawana, Wadi Almirams, Sania Deliba, Abu Salwia, Safia, Abu Salela Dinka IDPs, Tiwala and Sonata, Henega, and Magerrine.
(3) Kass Town includes Kass hinterland, Dawis, Bido, Ramtas, Fidishork, Cucka, and Calyat.
(4) Shenyis includes Shereiye town, Neitega, Tegy, Sharag El Jebel and locations 0-20 km south, Al Matawarol, Angabo.
(5) Duma includes Adwa.
(6) Muhajeria includes Dinka IDPs
(7) Sania Alandu includes Marla, Khazan Gadid, Sania Afandu, Um Safati, Um Tendalti, Naima, Rejella camp.
(8) Khor Abeche includes Hamada, Kurunje and surrounding villages.
(9) Ed Daein includes Ed Daein North and West, Um Laauta, Um Boim, Kelekil Abusalama, Al Muturwad, Ungabo, Abu Jabra, Ed Daein Town
(11) Adilla town includes Adilla, Sharef, Al Gora, Al Mazroub, Jed Al Sid and Abu Karinka.
(12) Ed Al Fursan includes Um Janah, Jugma, Danganur, Ginui, Em Gozem, Buta, and Baterkha.
(13) Gereida includes Ditto and surrounding area.

Affected Population
North Darfur: 1,142,959
South Darfur: 1,134,026
West Darfur: 1,104,661
Totals: 3,381,646

Legend
- 500 - 10,000
- 10,001 - 20,000
- 20,001 - 50,000
- 50,001 - 70,000
- 70,001 - 136,547

Legend
- ∧ IDP Gatherings
- ⌒ Locality
- — State
- ▢ International Bdry

Darfur Humanitarian Profile - August 2005
Affected population numbers are based on the Aug Humanitarian Needs Profile (HNP). For more information please refer to the Aug HNP published by the OCHA Darfur Cell (located in the UNDP compound Khartoum).

Data Sources:
Political Boundaries - CBS
IDP Camps - WFP, OCHA, HIC
Population Numbers - HNP

Printing Date: September 18, 2005
File: SU-DAR-DHNP-14_A3_21June 05_Affected Population by Camp - Aug 05

The boundaries and names shown do not imply official endorsement or acceptance by the Government of Sudan or the United Nations

Chad - Sudan, Refugee and IDP population

Darfur IDP Gatherings Map

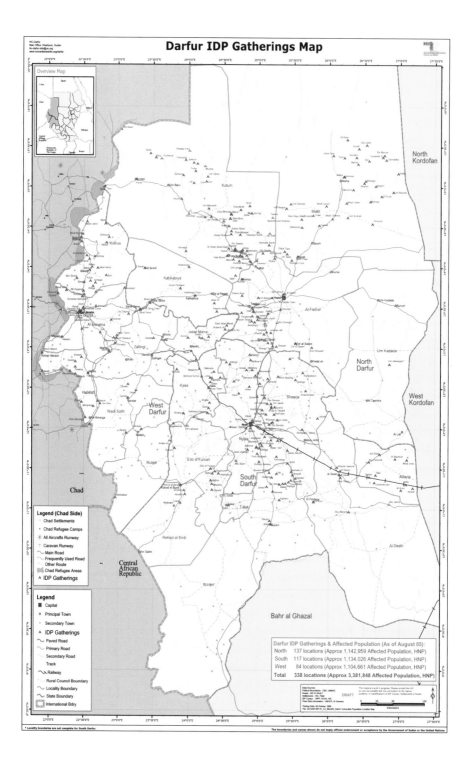

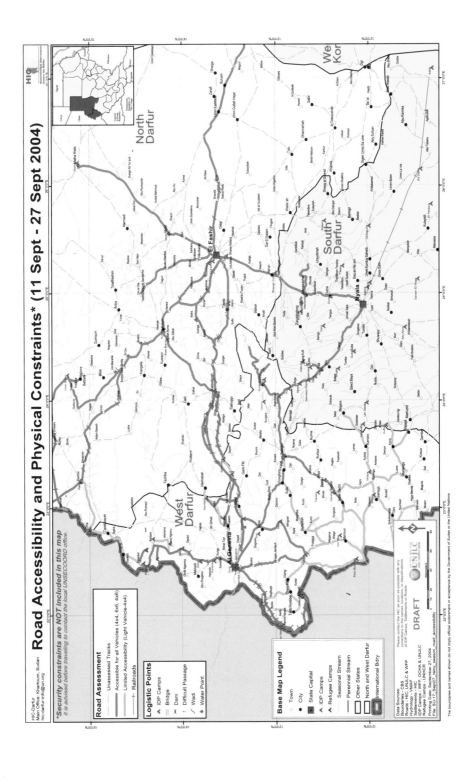

Road Accessibility and Physical Constraints* (11 Sept - 27 Sept 2004)

HIC-Darfur
Main Office, Khartoum, Sudan
hic-darfur-info@un.org

HIC

*Security constraints are NOT included in this map
It is advised before travelling to contact the local UNSECOORD office.

North Darfur

West Darfur

South Darfur

El Fashir

Nyala

Al Geneina

We

Kor

Road Assessment

— Unassessed Tracks
━ Accessible for all Vehicles (4x4, 6x6, 4x6)
━ Limited Accessibility (Light Vehicle-4x4)
━ Railroads

Logistic Points

▲ IDP Camps
⊟ Bridge
⊟ Dam
⊺ Difficult Passage
✛ Wadi
⬤ Water Point

Base Map Legend

○ Town
● City
▣ State Capital
▲ IDP Camps
▲ Refugee Camps
━ Seasonal Stream
━ Perennial Stream
▢ Other States
▢ North and West Darfur
▣ International Bdry

DRAFT

N

UNILC

Kilometers
0 10 20 40 60 80

Data Sources
Boundaries - CBS
Roads - HIC, UNJLC & WFP
Hydrology - VMAP
Settlements - HIC
IDP Camps - WFP, OCHA & UNJLC
Refugee Camps - UNHCR

Printing Date: September 27, 2004
File: SU-17_Sept27_rainy_season_road_accessibility

Please contact the HIC as soon as possible with any corrections to the names, locations, boundaries of IDP Camps, Settlements or Roads.

The boundaries and names shown do not imply official endorsement or acceptance by the Government of Sudan or the United Nations

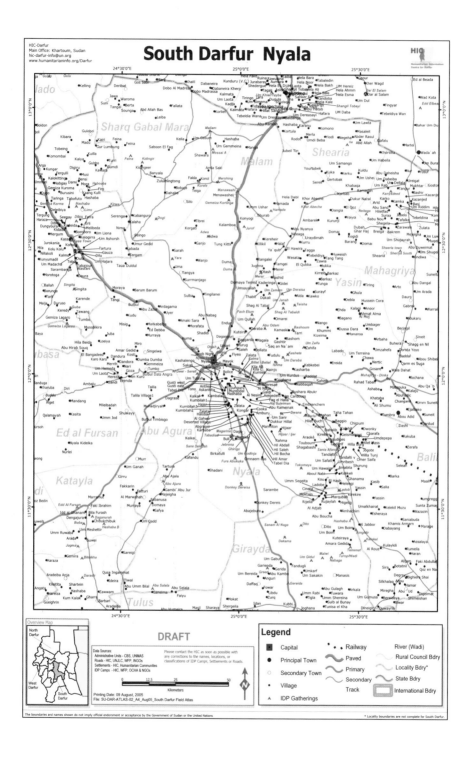

South Darfur Nyala

HIC-Darfur
Main Office: Khartoum, Sudan
hic-darfur-info@un.org
www.humanitarianinfo.org/Darfur

HIC

DRAFT

Data Sources:
Administrative Units - CBS, UNMAS
Roads - HIC, UNJLC, WFP, INGOs
Settlements - HIC, Humanitarian Communities
IDP Camps - HIC, WFP, OCHA & NGOs

Please contact the HIC as soon as possible with
any corrections to the names, locations, or
classifications of IDP Camps, Settlements or Roads.

Printing Date: 09 August, 2005
File: SU-DAR-ATLAS-02_A4_Aug05_South Darfur Field Atlas

Overview Map

North
Darfur

West
Darfur

South
Darfur

0   12.5   25   50
Kilometers

Legend

■ Capital
● Principal Town
○ Secondary Town
• Village
▲ IDP Gatherings

•••• Railway
∿ Paved
∿ Primary
∿ Secondary
∿ Track

River (Wadi)
Rural Council Bdry
Locality Bdry*
State Bdry
International Bdry

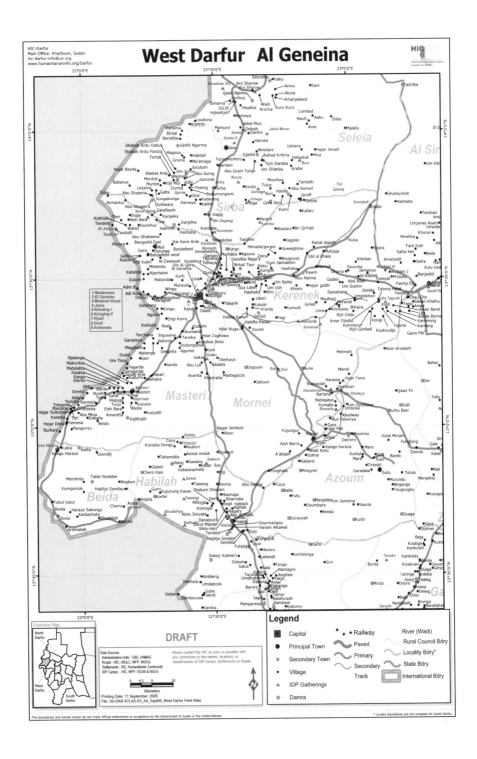

West Darfur Al Geneina

HIC-Darfur
Main Office: Khartoum, Sudan
hic-darfur-info@un.org
www.humanitarianinfo.org/Darfur

DRAFT

Data Sources:
Administrative Units - CBS, UNMAS
Roads - HIC, UNJLC, WFP, INGOs
Settlements - HIC, Humanitarian Community
IDP Camps - HIC, WFP, OCHA & NGOs

Please contact the HIC as soon as possible with
any corrections to the names, locations, or
classifications of IDP Camps, Settlements or Roads.

Printing Date: 11 September, 2005
File: SU-DAR-ATLAS-03_A4_Sept05_West Darfur Field Atlas

Overview Map

North Darfur

West Darfur

South Darfur

Kilometers
0   4.5   9   18

Legend

■ Capital	✦ Railway	River (Wadi)
● Principal Town	〜 Paved	Rural Council Bdry
● Secondary Town	〜 Primary	Locality Bdry*
• Village	〜 Secondary	State Bdry
▲ IDP Gatherings	Track	International Bdry
⊚ Damra		

1:Madarassa
2:El Geneina
3:Medinat Huzaz
4:Jams
5:Krinding I
6:Kringing II
7:Riyad
8:Dorti
9:Ardamata

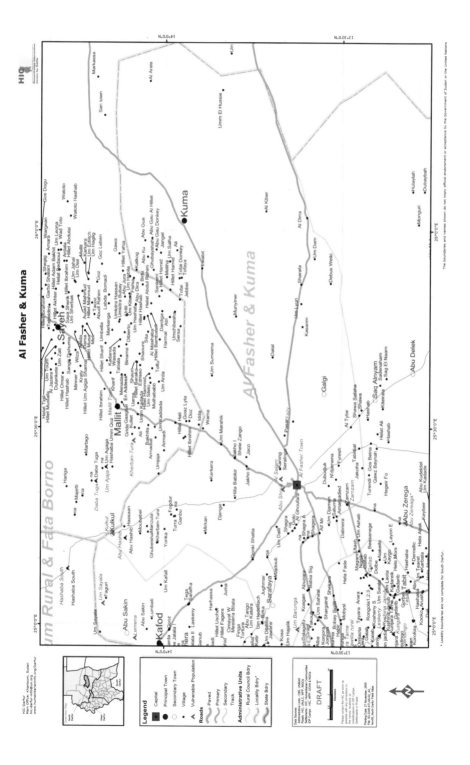

Al Fasher & Kuma

HIC

Legend

- ● Capital
- ● Principal Town
- ● Secondary Town
- ○ Village
- ▲ Vulnerable Population

Roads
- Paved
- Primary
- Secondary
- Track

Administrative Units
- Rural Council Bdry
- Locality Bdry*
- State Bdry

Data Sources:
Administrative Units : CBS, UNMAS
Roads : HIC, UNJLC, WFP, INGOs
Settlements : HIC, Humanitarian Communities
IDP Camps :

Please contact the HIC as soon as
possible with any corrections to
the names, locations or
classifications of IDP Camps,
Settlements or Roads

Printing Date: 27 November 2005
File: SUDAR-ATLAS-02_A4
North_South Field Atlas

HIC-Darfur
Main Office: Khartoum, Sudan
hic-darfur-info@un.org
www.humanitarianinfo.org/Darfur

DRAFT

Kilometres

2
—

SUDAN'S KILLING FIELDS MOVE WESTWARD

November 11, 2003 – Divided Conflicts

THE MASSIVE AND growing humanitarian crisis in Darfur Province in western Sudan is not typically seen in the context of peace negotiations between Khartoum's National Islamic Front (NIF) regime and the Sudan People's Liberation Movement/Army (SPLM/A), representing southern Sudan and the country's marginalized areas. And to be sure, it is important to note that the Sudan Liberation Movement/Army (SLM/A) in Darfur is not directly related to the forces struggling against Khartoum in the south and other marginalized areas. What both conflicts have in common, however, is the refusal to accept any longer the Islamic fascism that has ruled Sudan for the last fourteen years.

At the same time, it is critically important to understand all that lies implicit in Khartoum's present response to the human catastrophe in Darfur. We will then come much closer to seeing the nature of remaining obstacles in the peace process for the north-south conflict, and the challenges that will follow immediately upon any peace agreement. This is especially true if we consider very recent and ominous militia movements in Upper Nile Province of southern Sudan, as well as inflammatory statements by NIF President Omar al-Bashir on the key outstanding issue in negotiations, the status of the three contested areas of Abyei, the Nuba Mountains, and Southern Blue Nile.

With all this in mind it may not be so difficult to understand why local observers in Khartoum are reporting that the mosques in the city are generating a greatly heightened rhetoric directed against a peace agreement. Though such an agreement seems increasingly likely to be reached in Kenya, Khartoum still seems to be preparing for a possible strategic collapsing of the peace talks – or perhaps a full-scale reneging on any actual signed agreement. There is in any event a good deal in recent days that bears close scrutiny and is cause for deep concern.

Strikingly, the US charge d'affaires in Khartoum – presently the ranking US diplomat in Sudan – was prevented from traveling to Darfur two days ago. Deutsche Presse-Agentur (dpa) reports that the American Embassy in Sudan published a statement Sunday November 9, 2003,

> [E]xpressing regret that the US charge d'affaires in Sudan, Gerard Galluci, and other representatives of the Embassy and US AID [Agency for International Development] were prohibited from traveling to Nyala town in the South Darfur region of western Sudan. The statement said that Humanitarian Aid Commission (HAC), a government establishment regulating the work of local and international relief organizations cancelled the trip despite the Ministry of Foreign Affairs granting permission to travel.

This comes even as a number of reports from the UN are directly critical of the Khartoum regime for obstructing humanitarian access to Darfur. Agence France-Presse reported November 10, 2003,

> Sudan's government is hampering an adequate response to an escalating humanitarian crisis in the war-ravaged Darfur region by reneging on a pledge to process aid workers' travel permits speedily, the UN accused on Monday. "Some aid operations haven't been able to start. Aid workers who are ready to go (to Darfur) are getting stuck," because their permit applications have not been turned around within a promised 24-hour period, Ben Parker, the Nairobi-based

spokesperson for the UN's Humanitarian Co-ordinator in Sudan, Mukesh Kapila said.

A further statement made November 10, 2003 by the UN's Humanitarian Coordinator for Sudan noted,

> New regulations [from Khartoum] on travel permits that entered into force on 1 October 2003 have not been followed consistently. As a result, travel procedures remain slow and cumbersome and, in some cases, permission to visit affected areas is withheld.

The UN's Humanitarian Coordinator for Sudan continued by giving a sense of the vast dimensions of Darfur's crisis,

> The number of displaced people continues to increase thanks to the escalation of armed conflict in the region since February 2003. The estimated 500,000 to 600,000 newly displaced people live in North, South and West Darfur. 70,000 people have sought refuge in Chad, and one million others have been affected by the war.

The situation of many of these people is dire in the extreme: that the NIF regime should be manipulating humanitarian access for military advantage suggests all too clearly the manner of thinking of those who are presently negotiating with the SPLM/A in Kenya. The UN statement continues by giving a comparative sense of the disaster,

> The United Nations in Sudan warns that the situation in the Greater Darfur Region of western Sudan may emerge as the worst humanitarian crisis in the Sudan since 1998.

This reference is ominous in the extreme, as 1998 was the year of the terrible famine in Bahr el-Ghazal Province, when Khartoum's denial and manipulation of humanitarian access was the major factor in the death by starvation of perhaps 100,000 human beings. The unspeakable barbarism of denying and manipulating humanitarian aid for destructive purposes also tells far too much about the people representing the Khartoum regime in the north-south peace talks conducted under the auspices of the organization of East African countries known as the Intergovernmental Authority for Development (IGAD).

That a cease-fire agreement for Darfur has not resulted in a halting of attacks by Khartoum-backed Arab militias offers a clear warning about one of the central threats to any peace agreement between the SPLM/A and the NIF regime. For a number of highly reliable regional sources are reporting on new military activities by those Khartoum-backed militias based in the oil regions of Upper Nile. Humanitarian organizations have apparently been evacuated from Central Upper Nile because of the threat of militia activities – activities that may be related to efforts to secure more of the oil regions prior to the resumption of peace talks.

Khartoum appears to have adopted a policy of using its militia forces before more of them return to the SPLM/A, as was the case last week with the return of Lam Akol and the SPLM-"United." A number of other militia commanders are widely reported to be in active negotiations with the SPLM/A leadership about abandoning Khartoum as a possible peace agreement approaches. Sensing the military implications of such losses, Khartoum may be intent on using those militias that remain dependent upon them for food, military supplies, and logistics. Given the number of dangerous flash points in Upper Nile Province, this is a highly risky policy, and one that clearly threatens the overall peace process.

In light of such evident willingness to threaten the peace process, it is no surprise that a November 7, 2003 Deutsche Presse-Agentur dispatch reported that NIF President Omar al-Bashir declared to the paramilitary "Popular Defense Forces" that his regime would "never surrender the three areas [Abyei, Nuba Mountains, Southern Blue Nile] at the center of a territorial dispute." Speaking in El Obeid, Kordofan Province, according to an Agence France-Presse dispatch of November 9, 2003, al-Bashir was explicit about the Ngok Dinka enclave of Abyei, which was promised, but never granted, a self-determination referendum in the 1972 Addis Ababa peace accord,

"Abyei has never been part of Bahr al-Ghazal and will therefore remain part of Kordofan."

Al-Bashir in a November 7, 2003 Deutsche Presse-Agentur dispatch went on to declare of the notoriously brutal PDF that, "the Popular Defence Forces are the sole pillars and cornerstone of the government of national salvation revolution." For "government of national salvation revolution" we may quite accurately read "the Islamist project of the National Islamic Front" regime that al-Bashir heads. Such inflammatory talk may, of course, be mainly for domestic consumption; but it hardly makes more credible al-Bashir's declaration in a television interview with pan-Arab television network Al-Arabiya that peace talks could resume prior to the December 1, 2003 date presently scheduled, as Associated Press reported from Cairo, November 10, 2003.

In the same interview, al-Bashir also revealed an unwillingness to accept a peacekeeping force to bolster any Sudan peace agreement when he declared, as Associated Press reported on November 10, 2003,

> Concerning the joint armed forces, el-Bashir said he would accept foreign observers but that a peacekeeping force is not necessary now that the warring parties have signed cease-fire agreements and are working toward a peace deal.

This is, of course, yet another instance of spectacular disingenuousness on al-Bashir's part. His notion that because there might be a signed peace deal there is no need for a robust international peacekeeping force simply ignores the fact that Khartoum has been, for over a year, relentlessly and significantly in violation of the same "cease-fire agreements" that al-Bashir refers to, such as the "cessation of hostilities agreement" of October 15, 2002 and the February 4, 2003 "addendum" to the October 15 agreement. More consequentially, al-Bashir ignores the fact that Khartoum has violated or reneged on every single agreement it has ever made with any Sudanese party. A peace agreement is meaningful only if there are credible and fully adequate international guarantees – and guarantors.

The same refusal to accept the essential role of the international community is evident in Khartoum's rejection of observers in the Darfur peace talks, or in Darfur itself. The UN Daily Press Review for Sudan on October 30, 2003 included a dispatch from Khartoum's *Al-Ayam* newspaper, which reported NIF Foreign Minister Mustafa Ismail as saying that "the sending of international monitors to Darfur is ruled out because this will be an internationalisation of the problem," and further that "there shall be no such [international monitoring] arrangement and Darfur is not like the South so that people can talk about monitoring." This arrogant denial of a role for the international community comes even as it becomes daily more evident that Khartoum is unable to bring peace or to provide anything like adequate access or protections for humanitarian relief to Darfur. The need for a larger international role in the Darfur crisis could not be clearer.

How can Khartoum's callous attitudes and actions be the basis for an effective transition to peace in southern Sudan, should an agreement be reached? On November 11, 2003, the UN Integrated Regional Information Networks (IRIN) released *SUDAN: Special Report on the Impact of a Future Peace Agreement on Refugees and IDPs.* It is an analysis of the problems associated with a post-war Sudan, concentrating on the immense challenges in southern Sudan that will be occasioned by returning refugees and Internally Displaced Persons (IDPs). Behavior by Khartoum such as we see in Darfur ensures that these people will be part of a massive human catastrophe.

IRIN's *Report* treats not only the impact of a peace agreement on refugees and IDPs, but the likely upsurge in HIV/AIDS and the particular predicament of women returning to southern Sudan. It is blunt in its largest generalization,

> The only certainty is that if people do move quickly, they will experience tremendous hardship as they walk for days across a country the size of Kenya, Tanzania, Uganda, Burundi and Rwanda combined. With practically no roads, health care, sanitation facilities or infrastructure of any kind to welcome them, they will be vulnerable to hunger and outbreaks of disease both en route and when they arrive. Keeping their deaths to a minimum is one of the key challenges facing the international community.

Nothing will be cheap, given the immense numbers involved. Though the IRIN *Report* highlights the uncertainty about numbers of IDPs, and their intentions following a peace agreement, there is clear consensus that a huge number will move soon after a peace agreement, including perhaps two thirds of the estimated 2 million people living in squalid camps and slums around Khartoum alone.

These people simply must have assistance in moving home across this vast and difficult land. One effective strategy has been recommended by Stephen Houston, a senior IDP adviser in the office of the UN humanitarian coordinator in Khartoum and is outlined in IRIN's *Report*,

> The possibility of establishing "way-stations" along key roads and the Nile is being discussed to provide food and medical care for them, and as the only means of registering who is moving where, Houston told IRIN. But the current thinking is that agencies and NGOs should improve conditions in the IDPs' home areas – such as schools and health care – for everyone in the community, instead of singling them out for special treatment or assistance.

But this will require substantial resources, of a sort that have not yet begun to be marshaled by the US or its European allies and Canada. Indeed, peace itself is clearly at risk not only from the military threat posed by the remaining Khartoum-backed militias, but from the competition for what will be, at least initially, highly limited resources, as the IRIN *Report* notes,

> Conflict with host communities which will see the refugees being assisted by the international community while they are not, coupled with increased competition for water, land, firewood, and food in certain areas, as well as the economic shocks of mass influxes of people into areas, are further potential sore points.

This situation holds all the potential for renewed fighting; and if such fighting may have a character different from the war of the last 20, the destructiveness of such potential conflicts should not be underestimated. Yet again, only substantial resources in the near term can avert what may quickly grow into a spreading human catastrophe.

Other problems loom very large as well. IRIN's *Report* notes at one point that,

Rates of HIV infection [in Sudan], currently estimated by UNAIDS at 2.6 percent country-wide, are expected to increase dramatically with the return of the refugees from neighbouring countries with much higher rates.

The experience of too many other African countries makes the nature of this threat alarming in the extreme. Prophylactic, medical, and educational measures now will save lives, perhaps millions of lives, and resources in the longer term; but there must be a substantial commitment of funds in the near term if this terrible pandemic is not to extend into southern Sudan and other parts of the country.

IRIN's *Report* also highlights in its third section the particular problems and vulnerabilities of women returning to southern Sudan. The issues are many, but one in particular looms especially large,

What will happen when tens of thousands of widows descend into this environment to reclaim land and cattle may become one of the country's future tragedies, [analysts] note. Many will have to choose between being "inherited" by their husband's clan – land is owned communally – or start a losing battle to regain their former wealth through the village courts.

May we reasonably expect that a Khartoum regime that has behaved so brutally in its conduct of the war over so many years will be adequately responsive to the human needs that IRIN outlines for a post-war Sudan? Does Darfur give us any hope that Khartoum has changed its attitudes toward humanitarian relief? Toward the role of the international community in protecting all the people of Sudan? Toward the obligations entailed in signed agreements?

The answers to all these questions are painfully obvious, and should put the international community on notice that the window of opportunity for making of any "peace agreement" for southern Sudan a truly just and sustainable peace will be exceedingly small. Despite Khartoum's reluctance to see peacekeepers deployed in the wake of an agreement, there must be immediate, urgent, detailed planning for a robust, fully staffed and fully equipped force, with an appropriate mandate, whether it be peacekeeping or, under Chapter VII authority per the UN Charter, peace-enforcing. There must also be a full and ready commitment of adequate resources for the various acute needs that IRIN has so authoritatively established in today's special report. In the short term these will be costly; in the long term, these same needs will be much, much more costly – in lives and resources.

Planning for peace, including funding commitments, is already far behind schedule on all fronts, should an agreement be reached by the target date of January 1, 2004. To be sure, Khartoum may yet collapse the peace talks on the remaining issues, especially the status of the three contested areas – which, significantly, all have strategic bearing on future oil development, as well as their own acute humanitarian needs. But the need for planning cannot be held hostage to this possibility: the assumption must be [1] that a peace agreement will be signed and [2] that its meaningfulness will depend almost entirely on the immediate and comprehensive response of the international community.

Darfur makes all too clear the logic of this latter claim.

November 24, 2003 – Ceasefire in the South – Darfur's Insurrection Pushes Khartoum to Civilian Destruction

Largely invisibly, but with remorseless intensity, the war and attendant humanitarian crisis in Darfur continue to expand. Human destruction and displacement have accelerated at an alarming rate, with many thousands dead or dying, and well over half a million displaced. The remoteness of this large region in Sudan, the most westerly province in northern Sudan, ensures that the war – as well as the growing death, displacement, and suffering – goes almost completely unobserved. There have been virtually no first-hand accounts by journalists, and the observations by humanitarian organizations are necessarily scattered and only secondarily part of their mandate. Moreover, frank public reporting is also extremely dangerous for such highly vulnerable organizations.

Even so, fragmentary accounts from humanitarian organizations, the flood of confirming second-hand accounts from within the province, evidence from those displaced from Darfur westward into Chad, and regional and international sources that have managed to see something of the situation in Darfur first-hand – all paint the grimmest picture of a part of Sudan that is now bearing the brunt of Khartoum's tyranny. The National Islamic Front regime has been able to concentrate its military power in Darfur while it enjoys the benefits of what has become a general ceasefire in southern Sudan. Indeed, a growing number of analysts and exceedingly well-placed observers are now convinced that Khartoum has gone as far as it has toward a peace agreement with the south only because of the military pressure exerted by the uprising in Darfur.

If this is so, it augurs very poorly for the long-term viability of a peace agreement between Khartoum and southern Sudan, as well as the marginalized areas allied with the south. For should the Darfur insurrection be put down, or some sort of expedient political agreement be reached, Khartoum will no longer face military pressure in the west, and may very well turn its attention again to the south. The massive human rights abuses that presently define Khartoum's war in Darfur will resume their terrible form in the south, especially the oil regions of Upper Nile Province. International humanitarian access, presently so severely constrained in Darfur, will also very likely wither in southern Sudan if war resumes there.

There are, however, two forces militating again such renewed military aggression by Khartoum in the south – two ways in which we can imagine that a peace agreement in the near term may have a chance to take hold, no matter what Khartoum's disposition to renege.

The first is the potency of the Darfur insurrection itself, and the deepening alienation of those peoples in Darfur who have suffered most at the hands of Khartoum and its Arab militia allies. The Fur, Massaleit, and Zaghawa – non-Arab or "African" tribal groups – have found that the fact of their being Muslim offers no protection against the Islamist zeal of Khartoum. As Douglas Johnson observes on page 140 in his recent book on Sudan's war, *The Root Causes of Sudan's Civil Wars,*

> The army-NIF takeover further enhanced the power of [the Arab militias in Darfur] when the Popular Defence Forces Act officially recognized them as paramilitary groups at the end of 1989 [the NIF came to power by military coup on June 30, 1989]. As the war in Chad spilled into Darfur, it sharpened the divide between "Arabs" and "Blacks" [Zuruq, a derogatory term], with the Sudanese Islamist parties now equating Islam with Arabism.

This "equating of Islam with Arabism" tells us far too much about the hateful animus at the heart of Khartoum's aggression in Darfur – and the nature of the oppression that will simply no longer be tolerated by the African peoples in this region, who find that racial and religious identity have merged in Khartoum's vicious ideology, and that this excludes them from the category of real human beings.

Johnson continues his analysis of recent history in Darfur on page 140 by noting that,

> At present the government's reassertion of its authority in Darfur has focused on strengthening the military and establishing direct control, with governors being appointed from outside the region.

As a result of these policies, key issues of equity in land disputes remain unresolved, even as Khartoum's heavy-handed rule runs counter to traditional forms of local and regional governance in this part of Sudan. Hence the inevitable emergence early this year of an insurrection that has as its goal the ending of discrimination, tyranny, and loss of political and cultural power.

To date, the Sudan Liberation Army/Movement in Darfur has proved a formidable military foe, winning the overwhelming number of direct confrontations with Khartoum's regular army forces. But Khartoum has responded by loosing its Arab militia allies on the civilian populations of Darfur, generating in the last six months over half a million displaced persons and over 70,000 desperate refugees who have been driven into Chad. It is nothing if not a ghastly reprise of how Khartoum has conducted its counter-insurgency campaigns in southern Sudan, the Nuba Mountains, and Southern Blue Nile for many years.

But as successful as Khartoum has been in disrupting and destroying civilian lives and livelihood in Darfur, there is little evidence that any progress is being in military terms. Having earlier in the year forgone the possibility of a political settlement with the peoples of Darfur, Khartoum now finds itself locked in a war that it cannot win soon in outright military terms, and this makes the resumption of war in the south less likely. Moreover, the military and political opposition against Khartoum has partly fractured, and the Justice and Equality Movement (JEM) has become an uneasy ally of the SLA/M, even as it controls significant swaths of northern and western Darfur. A number of SLA/M members felt that the September 2003 cease-fire agreement between their movement and Khartoum was a betrayal and have consequently joined cause with the more strident JEM.

All of this is further complicated by highly intricate local politics in Darfur, and some significant national political alliances. Thus it is of note that on November 22, 2003, as reported in an Agence France-Press November 23, 2003 dispatch, powerful NIF First Vice President Ali Osman Taha excoriated his Islamicist mentor Hassan al-Turabi for "fanning sedition in Darfur." Taha declared that Turabi's "Popular Congress [Party] has to reconsider its policy and the activities of its elements in Darfur, otherwise it will be eliminated from the political arena." We catch another distinctive glimpse of the ongoing character of Khartoum politics in this ironic vignette.

What are the moral obligations of the international community in light of the vast and accelerating human disaster in Darfur? It is first of all to recognize that the source of this disaster is again the NIF regime in Khartoum. If we don't have a sufficiently detailed understanding of the range and frequency of Khartoum-sponsored atrocities and war crimes in Darfur, we have only to recall what the regime has done in the south and the Nuba Mountains.

Genocide is the only fully adequate term for the relentless, deliberate destruction of non-Islamized and non-Arabized peoples in the south and marginalized areas. This has included engineered famine and the highly consequential obstruction of humanitarian relief to desperate populations; the intentional bombing of hospitals, schools, churches, relief operations; scorched-earth warfare in the oil regions; and countless atrocities directed at the viability of southern and Nuban civil society, as well as their agricultural economies.

It is only reasonable to assume that the regime so clearly responsible for such conduct of war is behaving in the same fashion in Darfur. Indeed, on November 22, 2003, Reuters reported a recent bombing attack that was chillingly similar to the many hundreds of such bombings that have been authoritatively confirmed in southern Sudan for years. This bombing attack also constitutes yet another violation by Khartoum of the cease-fire agreement the regime signed in early September,

Rebels in western Sudan accused the government on Saturday of violating a truce with air strikes and militia raids that killed 30 people, mostly civilians. The government said it knew nothing of the attacks in the arid Darfur area, where the rebels of the Sudan Liberation Movement/Army (SLM/A) emerged as a fighting force in February, saying Khartoum had marginalised the impoverished region.

"It's been very bad. Attacks by government militias and the air raid have killed 30 people and lots of livestock," SLM/A Secretary-General Minni Arcua Minnawi told Reuters by phone from western Sudan. "They used an Antonov airplane to bomb civilians areas today (Saturday)."

BBC correspondent Andrew Harding reported on November 13, 2003 from Khartoum on the inevitable conclusion to be drawn from the nature of Khartoum's war against the African peoples of Darfur,

> Diplomats have described the fighting in Darfur as "ethnic cleansing" with Arab militias, possibly backed by the government, destroying entire villages.

Of course all available evidence indicates that Khartoum's backing of the Arab militias is more than a possibility. It is the essential feature of these relentless assaults on the Fur, Massaleit, and Zaghawa civilians who are perceived by Khartoum as providing the essential support for SLA/M military efforts. Again, this is precisely the military thinking that has governed Khartoum's conduct of war in the south for many years, conduct that has been authoritatively chronicled by many human rights groups and investigations for over a decade.

In yet another parallel between Khartoum's war against the south and its present war against the people of Darfur, the manipulation of humanitarian aid has become a key weapon. Agence France-Presse reported on November 14, 2003, in "Alarming Food Crisis in Western Sudan,"

> International relief agencies are sounding the alarm about a looming food crisis in western Sudan as they report a growing number of people fleeing militias burning their villages and farmland.

But even as this alarming food crisis grows more urgent, Khartoum has refused to accept food aid from the US Agency for International Development (USAID) on completely spurious grounds. Claiming that US sorghum and wheat are genetically modified, the Khartoum regime denied entrance at Port Sudan to a critical food shipment. But as Khartoum well knows, the US does not export or even grow genetically modified sorghum or wheat. Some strains of other grains have been genetically modified – but not these two key staples. Extraordinarily, Kamal al Sadig reported this denied entry of food into Port Sudan in *Al-Ayam* Issue No. 7825, November 16, 2003,

> In a new development on the USAID confined food crisis, the Ministry of Agriculture has reaffirmed refusal to allow entrance of the food into the country and distributing it, claiming that the food is genetically modified. The new excuse was announced yesterday in a meeting held for all concerned bodies

It is this same *Al-Ayam* newspaper that was recently suspended by the regime for posing a "security threat to the state." And we may be sure that speaking truth in Khartoum is indeed a threat to the present Islamic fascism.

But the grim parallels between the denial of humanitarian aid to Darfur and to southern Sudan are all too clear and have begun to be articulated – despite Khartoum's propaganda. A November 14, 2003 Agence France-Presse dispatch cites a senior aid official,

> One relief official said the Darfur region suffers from the same factors that produced the famine in the Bahr al-Ghazal region in 1998: limited access for relief groups, marauding militiamen, and entrenched poverty. "The parallels are evocative," the official said on condition of anonymity.

Perhaps as many as 100,000 people starved to death in the terrible Bahr el-Ghazal famine of 1998 – and nothing was more consequential than Khartoum's precipitous cutoff of humanitarian aid at the height of the crisis.

In a final and particularly ominous parallel with Khartoum's war against the south, the regime has refused to allow for any "internationalization" of the crisis in Darfur. This means no international observers have been permitted at the peace negotiations in Chad or on the ground in Darfur – even as there is no adequate international humanitarian access. On this latter score in particular, we are morally obliged to face squarely the fact that in present circumstances, Khartoum's claim to sovereignty will inevitably entail thousands of innocent people dying from starvation and from the illnesses that become so threatening to displaced persons in the harsh environments of Darfur.

UN humanitarian offices have already spoken bluntly about the need for more access, and for their efforts received a furious denial from Khartoum. But of course the UN has no motive to distort the realities of Darfur, while Khartoum has every reason to do so. It is with this in mind that we should recall the recent extraordinarily frank comments from UN spokesmen in an Agence France-Presse dispatch of November 10, 2003,

> Sudan's government is hampering an adequate response to an escalating humanitarian crisis in the war-ravaged Darfur region by reneging on a pledge to process aid workers' travel permits speedily, the UN accused on Monday. "Some aid operations haven't been able to start. Aid workers who are ready to go (to Darfur) are getting stuck," because their permit applications have not been turned around within a promised 24-hour period, Ben Parker, the Nairobi-based spokesperson for the UN's Humanitarian Co-ordinator in Sudan, Mukesh Kapila said.

The UN Humanitarian Coordinator for Sudan on November 10, 2003 noted in a statement from Nairobi/Khartoum,

> New regulations [from Khartoum] on travel permits that entered into force on 1 October 2003 have not been followed consistently. As a result, travel procedures remain slow and cumbersome and, in some cases, permission to visit affected areas is withheld.

But if continued military resistance in Darfur is, perversely, one means by which the chances for peace increase for southern Sudan, what is the second way? How else might a peace agreement for southern Sudan be sustainable, presuming that a just settlement is reached, and that the difficult outstanding issues are resolved?

This second way for securing a real peace in southern Sudan would derive from the willingness of the international community to provide truly adequate resources for emergency transitional aid following a negotiated agreement, and the resources for a peace support operation that gives peace a real chance to take hold in the ravaged regions of southern Sudan and the marginalized areas. Tragically, the evidence grows daily that neither emergency transitional aid nor peacekeeping will be either timely or sufficiently funded. The international community is poised to betray Sudan yet again, and at its moment of greatest hope and need.

The US administration in particular is guilty of an unforgivable reneging. Then Assistant Secretary of State for Africa Walter Kansteiner promised, in Congressional testimony of May 13, 2003, that "we stand ready to support reconstruction and development in post-war Sudan." In speaking of the need for the Khartoum regime and the opposition Sudan People's Liberation Movement to reach peace under presently auspicious circumstances, Kansteiner declared further that, "both sides know that there will be a large peace dividend for reconstruction and development if, but only if, there is peace."

The budgetary realities of the Bush administration $87 billion supplemental foreign operations bill make clear that all this really meant was $20 million for "famine assistance" in Sudan. This is an amount so absurdly disproportionate to the needs that will be occasioned by peace that the real nature of the Administration's commitment to Sudan has been called deeply into question. Further supplemental funding for Sudan now seems impossible until the next fiscal year, so the presently appropriated amount stands as the "large peace dividend" promised by the Bush administration.

If the marginalized and tyrannized peoples of Darfur see this betrayal, we may at least be sure that they will understand that their survival depends not on the international community, but their own resilience and fighting prowess. It is a grim prospect, but one that the international betrayal of southern Sudan – in which the US has all too many partners – makes inevitable.

December 12, 2003 – War, Humanitarian Access, and "Ethnic Cleansing"

A range of international diplomats are now speaking of the vast human destruction and displacement in Darfur Province of western Sudan as "ethnic cleansing." UN officials are also speaking of the crisis in Darfur within the context of allegations of "ethnic cleansing." Reports from early December 2003 – from the UN News Centre, IRIN, the International Crisis Group, Deutsche Presse-Agentur, and the BBC – have put this ominous term squarely at the center of discussion concerning Darfur. The increasingly desperate accounts of an accelerating human catastrophe in this remote region of Sudan are consequently taking on a more urgent moral character.

Certainly the emphatic findings by the UN, as well as humanitarian and human rights organizations, create a sense of human scale in which moral clarity is imperative. As many as 700,000 people have been displaced over the last nine months; the UN speaks of a war-affected population of as many 1 million people; the humanitarian organization Save the Children has reported, December 10, 2003, on rapidly rising malnutrition rates. Senior UN officials have also very recently highlighted Khartoum's deliberate obstruction of humanitarian access to these desperate populations.

We had best be certain that we are using the right terms to describe what is happening.

The General Assembly of the United Nations passed Resolution 96 (I), the Convention on the Prevention and Punishment of the Crime of Genocide, on December 9, 1948. The Convention defines genocide as follows.

> In the present Convention, genocide means any of the following acts committed with intent to destroy, in whole or in part, a national, ethnical, racial or religious group, as such:
>
> (a) Killing members of the group;
> (b) Causing serious bodily or mental harm to members of the group;
> (c) Deliberately inflicting on the group conditions of life calculated to bring about its physical destruction in whole or in part;
> (d) Imposing measures intended to prevent births within the group;
> (e) Forcibly transferring children of the group to another group.

Here it is critical to realize that all evidence indicates that people being targeted by Khartoum's Arab militia proxies, the *Janjaweed*, are overwhelming the ethnically African tribal groups of the Fur, Massaleit, and Zaghawa. These sedentary agriculturalists are perceived by Khartoum as the base of support for the two insurgency movements in Darfur, the Sudan Liberation Army/Movement and the Justice and Equality Movement. They are being displaced and destroyed accordingly. It no longer matters where the noncombatant populations are located, or whether there really is an insurgency military presence in the areas being attacked. The African peoples of Darfur are being attacked, displaced, and denied humanitarian access, because of who they are – "as such." This latter phrase is of course central to the definition of genocide in the 1948 Convention.

That the conflict in Darfur is driven in such fundamental fashion by Khartoum's racial and ethnic animus should put the recurrently euphemizing term "ethnic cleansing" once more under fierce scrutiny. We should first recall that the Nazis referred to ethnic extermination as the "cleansing" or *Säuberung* of Jews from German society and culture. In turn, the advent of the phrase "ethnic cleansing" during the Balkan conflicts produced a UN definition, one whose history has recently been recounted by Samantha Power in her Pulitzer Prize-winning study, *"A Problem from Hell": America and the Age of Genocide*, p. 483,

> In February 1993 the [UN] commission's five lawyers presented an interim report to the UN secretary-general in which they defined "ethnic cleansing," the term that was then being used as a kind of euphemistic halfway house between crimes against humanity and genocide.

Among the elements of this definition of "ethnic cleansing" – efforts to produce ethnically homogenous regions – were,

> murder, torture, rape, sexual assault, forcible removal, displacement ... of civilians, deliberate military attacks or threats of attacks on civilians and civilian areas, and wanton destruction of property.

Significantly, according to Power, the UN commission of lawyers concluded that such actions "might well be considered genocide under the [1948 UN Genocide Convention]."

And these are precisely the actions that are being reported with ever greater insistence and authority from Darfur – actions whose motives are unambiguous in the minds of the African peoples under relentless assault. IRIN reported December 11, 2003 from el-Geneina, Darfur,

> "I believe this is an elimination of the black race," one tribal leader told IRIN.

IRIN amplifies this point, citing a conversation with an indigenous source in el-Geneina, West Darfur,

> "The fact is the government is arming some tribes, just Arabs, they go and kill, take the belongings and rape the women, the militias have been given access to good arms, they are better than the army's."

The International Crisis Group, in a December 10, 2003 press release and a December 11, 2003 Report, *Sudan: Towards an Incomplete Peace*, notes that in response to the insurgency by the SLA and the JEM, and after a signed cease-fire agreement, Khartoum has stepped up its assaults on the Fur, Zaghawa, and Massaleit peoples,

> The government of Sudan has mobilised and armed Arab militias (*Janjaweed*), whose salary comes directly from booty captured in raids on villages, to terrorise the populace of Darfur.
>
> Government-supported militias deliberately target civilians from the Fur, Zaghawa, and Massalit groups, who are viewed as "Africans" in Darfur and form the bulk of the SLA and JEM ethnic base. . . . The latest attacks [by the government-supported Arab militias] occurred deep inside the Fur tribal domain, against unprotected villages with no apparent link to the rebels other than their ethnic profile.

Amnesty International in its November 27, 2003 Report, has found that there is "compelling evidence" the Khartoum regime "is largely responsible for the human rights and humanitarian crisis in Darfur in the western Sudan." And Amnesty International anticipated UN and diplomatic comments by noting ominously, "the situation in Darfur is at risk of rapidly degenerating into a full-scale civil war where *ethnicity is manipulated* [emphasis added].

To be sure, there seems no journalistic or diplomatic will to use the word genocide. And as was the case in Bosnia, "ethnic cleansing" seems suitably euphemistic. Deutsche Presse-Agentur on December 10, 2003 reported,

> Darfur and other parts of western Sudan in recent months have been the scene of severe unrest. The violence, which diplomats have described as "ethnic cleansing," has resulted in the displacement of hundreds of thousands of people, according to the United Nations High Commissioner for Refugees.

The BBC on December 11, 2003 also reported,

> Diplomats have described the fighting in Darfur as "ethnic cleansing" with Arab militias, possibly backed by the government, destroying entire villages inhabited by dark-skinned people who speak African languages.

Significantly, the UN seems finally to have found its voice on Darfur, and if it is very unlikely to feel itself in a position to speak directly of either ethnic cleansing or genocide, some UN officials' comments have clear implications in any assessment of Khartoum's actions in Darfur. Mukesh Kapila, the UN's Humanitarian Coordinator in Sudan, is quoted by IRIN in its December 11, 2003 dispatch,

> "One must say there is a prima facie case that some of the denials of access may well be related to the discomfort of the parties concerned to allow international witnesses."

The implication here is unmistakable: the denial of humanitarian access is not only being used as a weapon of war – as it has by the Khartoum regime in southern Sudan for many years – but as a means of ensuring that there are no "international witnesses" to genocide. The IRIN December 11, 2003 report went on to note that "areas held by the Sudan Liberation Movement/ Army (SLM/A) rebel group have not received medical aid for months and only limited food supplies."

Kapila commented further, "The reports, allegations of human rights violations are too persistent, too systematic, too repetitive from different sources to not be given credibility."

The key word here is "systematic," and it picks up on an assessment offered December 8, 2003 by Ambassador Tom Vraalsen, the UN Secretary-General's Special Envoy for Humanitarian Affairs for Sudan, in his Note to the Emergency Relief Coordinator Sudan, *Humanitarian Crisis in Darfur*,

> Delivery of humanitarian assistance to populations in need is hampered mostly by *systematically denied access* [emphasized in text]. While [Khartoum's] authorities claim unimpeded access, they greatly restrict access to the areas under their control, while imposing blanket denial to all rebel-held areas.

Vraalsen observes that while the Khartoum regime has "presented the security situation [in Darfur] as steadily improving," the actual situation on the ground,

> sharply contrasted with first-hand reports that I received from tribal leaders and humanitarian actors on the ground. They reported that [Khartoum-backed Arab] militias were launching systematic raids against civilian populations. These attacks included burning and looting of villages, large-scale killings, abductions, and other severe violations of human rights. Humanitarian workers have also been targeted, with staff being abducted and relief trucks looted.

Here it is important to emphasize how very closely the definition of "ethnic cleansing" established during the Balkan conflicts comports with the language Vraalsen is using. For in Darfur, what "system" can there be behind military raids if it is not a "system" based on race and ethnicity, especially when so many of these raids occur well away from any insurgent military opposition forces? The Arab militias are, "systematically," attacking non-Arab populations – the Fur, Massaleit, and Zaghawa. "Systematic" in this context could hardly suggest a more ominous synonym for the linch-pin phrase of the genocide convention, " ... as such."

What are officials of the Khartoum regime saying about all this? The disingenuousness is characteristic, which is to say palpable. The regime has repeatedly declared that access to Darfur is "unimpeded" or impeded only by "security risks." But on the basis of a first-hand assessment, Special Envoy Vraalsen found that while in September 2003 humanitarian needs were being partially met, at "present [December 2003], humanitarian operations have practically come to a standstill" in Darfur. And citing denials of humanitarian access, United Nations Emergency Relief Coordinator Jan Egeland declared in a UN News Centre report on December 5, 2003 that "the humanitarian situation in Darfur has quickly become one of the worst in the world."

At the same time, acting governor in Nyala, Adam Idris Al Silaik told IRIN in its December 11, 2003 dispatch, that "it was 'too difficult' to send aid to rebel-held areas, . . . but he added that the situation in southern Darfur was calm and under control.' " And in an egregious and shockingly arrogant bit of mendacity, Dr. Sula Feldeen, Khartoum's national humanitarian aid commissioner, told IRIN in its December 11, 2003 dispatch that the marauding, nomadic Arab militias, the *Janjaweed*, responsible for so much of the humanitarian crisis, were "defending their property." Whereas IRIN notes "corroborating sources" that have "accused Khartoum of backing the militias," Dr. Feldeen and his National Islamic Front colleagues simply deny the charges in the Report.

But it is the NIF leadership that has, predictably, told the greatest lie about Darfur; in a December 6, 2003 Associated Press report,

> [NIF President Omar] al-Bashir declared that] all indications show
> that the war in the south, and *in all other areas* [emphasis added], has
> come to an end. What remains is only some final retouches for an
> agreement on a lasting, just and comprehensive peace.

But of course as soon as we turn from the gross prevarication of the NIF to the ugly and all too tangible truths on the ground in Darfur, we see just why there is a need for such lies. Humanitarian assessments have consistently, relentlessly, invariably reported a worsening human catastrophe deriving directly from intense counter-insurgency war and the attendant insecurity for humanitarian actors, as well as the outright obstruction by Khartoum of relief efforts. The humanitarian organization Save the Children, on December 10, 2003, issued a *Sudan Emergency Statement,*

> Parts of western Sudan are experiencing what has been called the worst humanitarian crisis in Sudan since Bahr el-Ghazal in 1998. Current overall malnutrition levels are reported to be alarmingly high with Global Acute Malnutrition rates reaching 25% in some of the affected areas of Darfur, Western Sudan, which are accessible to relief workers. The precarious nutritional situation of children and their families could dramatically deteriorate should a disease break out, or should they be displaced further as a result of the on-going conflict.

The grim reality of the overall situation is captured all too well by a local African tribal leader who told IRIN in their December 12, 2003 Report, "Now they [Khartoum, and its proxy Arab militias] are fighting with bullets, but the time will come when starvation will set in." IRIN's Report continues, in noting another extremely ominous development, that in Darfur,

> local farmers are unable to leave their homes to harvest or to go to local villages to trade for fear of being shot. Commercial traffic in western Darfur has all but stopped, and food prices have increased dramatically from 1,800 Sudanese dinar to 7,000 for a bag of millet.

This bears all the hallmarks of a major famine in the making; perhaps many tens of thousands of people will starve to death, as they did in Sudan's southern province of Bahr el-Ghazal in 1998. One senior humanitarian aid worker, who recently traveled to Darfur, has told the author that the similarities between Darfur today and Bahr el-Ghazal in 1998 are indeed all too clear.

These realities must be declared and addressed. Whether or not we choose to use the euphemistic language of ethnic cleansing, the nature of Khartoum's ethnically-driven war in Darfur, conducted by means of Arab

militia proxies, must be fully rendered. And if it does so honestly, the international community will come up against the inescapable need to take full
control of humanitarian access to Darfur. Khartoum's claim of "national
sovereignty" cannot again be, as it has so often been in southern Sudan, an
impediment to full access for emergency medical and food aid. Whatever
cross-border efforts are required must be undertaken if Khartoum continues to obstruct critical humanitarian access. The intolerable alternative is to
watch the African peoples of Darfur suffer and die in large numbers in the
very near future – this as a result of deliberate policies emanating from
Khartoum.

In terms of the larger Sudanese context, the International Crisis Groups's
John Prendergast has crystallized the issue forcefully in the organization's
December 10, 2003 Press Report,

> The international community has thus far failed to respond appropri-
> ately to these developments [in Darfur], in part because the attention
> of the world remains focused squarely on the [north-south] IGAD
> peace process. . . . The government of Sudan is being feted by the
> international community for its transition to peacemaker through the
> IGAD process, while it continues to carry out a bloody campaign by
> proxy against the people of Darfur. The end of one tragic civil war in
> Sudan should not be allowed to be a catalyst for a new one.

But the suggestion by the International Crisis Group (ICG) that a peace
process for Darfur be "coordinated" with the north-south IGAD peace
process, now in its final round at Naivasha, Kenya, is belated and impracticable. Moreover, it is critically important that Khartoum not be allowed to
drag out the Naivasha talks any further. To be sure, there should be no arti-
ficial deadline, nothing that produces a document that is unjust because of
haste. But we have seen multiple declared deadlines come and go since April
2003 and there is still the possibility that if a deal is not consummated in the
very near future, with all significant details negotiated, we may see an
unraveling of the whole process. Khartoum must face the reality of a completed negotiated agreement, one that stipulates clearly the regime's obligations per the terms of the final document. The international community
must use the occasion of this diplomatic consummation to put in motion,

albeit belatedly, the essential peacekeeping efforts and emergency transitional humanitarian relief.

In any event, it is clear that Darfur is not on the agenda at Naivasha, nor will it be. Acting US Assistant Secretary of State for Africa Affairs Charles Snyder declared, according to an Agence France-Presse December 11, 2003 report from Naivasha, that an agreement was imminent in the IGAD negotiations,

> [Snyder] said some specifics – notably a "detail or two" on a ceasefire and a "dollar or two" in terms of a wealth-sharing deal – might have to be left for experts to conclude in January, but that "the essence of the deal could easily be done provided they don't surprise us with some new agenda item."

Of course Darfur would be precisely such a "new agenda item," and we may be sure that Khartoum would adamantly and uncompromisingly oppose any discussion of Darfur at Naivasha. Indeed, Khartoum has already made fully explicit its desire that there be no "internationalizing" of the Darfur crisis, either in the form of international observers on the ground or in the peace talks, which are presently being nominally hosted under the extremely weak auspices of the government of Chad and President Idriss Déby.

But ICG is certainly right that if peace does not come to Darfur, this will inevitably threaten any peace negotiated between Khartoum and the SPLM/A. Certainly peace for Sudan cannot come if Khartoum is given a "peace agreement" that allows for it to crush an insurgency in the west, one growing out of the long-standing and compelling grievances of the marginalized African peoples of Darfur. And if Khartoum is unwilling to make a just peace with the people of Darfur, we may wonder how great is its commitment to a just peace for the people of southern Sudan. Is the peace agreement now being concluded simply a means of buying time, an attempt by Khartoum to ensure that its military needn't be stretched to fight on two major fronts at once?

However we answer this question – and Khartoum continues to provide evidence supporting the most pessimistic conclusion – the international community must respond immediately to the unfolding human catastrophe in Darfur. The terrible realities of human suffering and death must be spoken of honestly – and the humanitarian response, in turn, cannot be constrained by Khartoum's willingness to use the denial of food and medical aid as a weapon of war. The international community is obliged to secure in the very near term, by whatever means are necessary, unimpeded humanitarian access.

Who will say as much? What moral justification is there for saying less?

December 17, 2003 – "Ethnic Cleansing" – US State Department Statement on Crisis in Darfur (December 16, 2003) – Silence

Though expressing "deep concern" and offering at least a glimpse of the catastrophe unfolding in Darfur province in western Sudan, the December 16, 2003 statement by the US State Department's Richard Boucher does not address key issues in the Darfur crisis. It is compromised in particular by a failure to speak of the non-Arab or African ethnic makeup of those civilian noncombatants that have been continuously subjected to brutal assault by Arab militias backed by Khartoum's National Islamic Front. The same failure obscures the racial and ethnic motives behind Khartoum's denial of critical humanitarian access. Moreover, in calling upon the parties in the conflict to "engage in substantive dialogue on ending the hostilities in Darfur," the State Department does nothing to indicate the very different moral equities of those involved in the conflict.

To be sure, the State Department statement highlights the fact that Khartoum has armed militia groups, and also declares, "the United States calls on the Government of Sudan to take concrete steps to control the militia groups it has armed." Moreover, simply by clearly calling attention to the heretofore vast but invisible crisis in Darfur, the State Department has put Khartoum on notice that its brutal war by militia proxy is recognized for what it is. Others in the international community will be encouraged to follow the US lead in saying what has long been evident.

But the US has failed to do more than "call on the parties to agree to an observable humanitarian cease-fire" and "deplore the parties' lack of engagement to end hostilities." These words might have been appropriate two or three months ago, but are woefully inadequate to the situation at hand. Tellingly, there is no clear plan for internationalizing the response to the crisis in Darfur, either diplomatically or through humanitarian intervention if necessary.

Indeed, in an ironically appropriate development, the very day that the State Department finally found its voice on Darfur, the Associated Press reported, December 17, 2003, that the tenuous peace talks between Khartoum's NIF regime and the insurgency groups in Darfur had collapsed completely. To be sure, such a collapse was inevitable, given Khartoum's intransigent and brutal military ambitions in Darfur, and the exceedingly weak auspices for negotiations provided by the government of Chad. But this basic fact should not have been skirted in the State Department's speaking of "substantive dialogue" as a means of "ending the hostilities." What is needed is not a vague hortatory statement about a woefully inadequate negotiating forum, but a clear commitment to a robust international presence in peace talks and an international observer presence on the ground in Darfur. Even more urgently, the US must respond effectively to what is an extremely serious and rapidly deteriorating humanitarian situation in Darfur, animated by what observers are increasingly characterizing – implicitly and explicitly – as ethnic cleansing.

There is a perverse and perhaps expedient unwillingness on the part of the State Department to characterize or even name the parties in the Darfur conflict. Nowhere do we catch even a glimpse of the ethnic and racial realities that virtually all observers are now highlighting in accounts of the fighting, civilian destruction, and Khartoum's denials of humanitarian access.

The State Department speaks of Khartoum needing to "take concrete steps to control the militia groups it has armed." But nowhere does it indicate the fact that these militia groups are nomadic Arab fighters, the *Janjaweed*, whose terrible predations are directed against the non-Arab or African sedentary agriculturalists of the Darfur regions. The SLA/M and the JEM – uneasy allies, divided primarily by virtue of the former's commitment to a secular Sudan – are for the State Department simply "indigenous opposition groups."

Why does this matter so much? Why is such absence of characterization of the parties so telling? It is because such a neutral description frees the State Department from any need to respond to the increasingly compelling evidence that the conflict in Darfur is characterized by ethnic cleansing –

with military assaults directed systematically against the African populations of Darfur, and with humanitarian access denials also systematically
directed at the African populations. Of course once freed from any need to
take account of these ethnic and racial realities, the US State Department
has much less need to speak to the issue of whether or not a humanitarian
intervention is required in the presently rapidly deteriorating situation.

For such an intervention, which entails a refusal to recognize Khartoum's
claim of "national sovereignty" in Darfur, appropriately requires a very high
threshold. But presumably ethnic cleansing, directed against hundreds of
thousands of people already displaced and at growing risk, would clearly
reach such a threshold, even in the minds at the State Department. Of
course there must be evidence for such ethnic cleansing, and the State
Department may simply be maintaining a reasonable agnosticism in the
matter. But is such agnosticism indeed reasonable or justified? Does the
transparent urgency of the situation permit a leisurely process of evidentiary assessment?

Nonetheless, the US State Department does report that "more than
600,000 civilians have been internally displaced," and that "75,000 refugees
have fled into neighboring Chad," and that thousands of unarmed civilians
have been killed or prevented from planting or harvesting crops. The statement even notes that "humanitarian access continues to be inhibited by
ongoing insecurity and the Government of Sudan's denial of travel permits
to humanitarian workers."

What further evidence of ethnic cleansing is necessary? What basis for
agnosticism, given readily apparent realities. Must we wait until there is yet
more evidence before mounting a humanitarian intervention in Darfur?
Given the human stakes in this crisis, is such a higher evidentiary threshold morally justifiable? The history of "ethnic cleansing" and genocide in
the last century is filled with examples of precisely such belatedness, such
refusal to act on partial information, even when it has all pointed toward
one conclusion. The same is true in Darfur today, despite the State Department's evident agnosticism. History already has shown the terrible costs of
such agnosticism in too many instances. It will almost certainly reveal, and
in the very near term, the ghastly consequences of this present excessive
diffidence.

December 30, 2003 – "Ethnic Cleansing" in Darfur Prevents Any Sustainable Peace Agreement

Peace talks in Naivasha, Kenya between Khartoum's National Islamic Front regime and the Sudan People's Liberation Army/Movement are now addressing the last major issue outstanding, the status of the three marginalized areas of Abyei, the Nuba Mountains, and Southern Blue Nile. The indigenous peoples of these regions along the historic north-south border identify themselves as "African" and have long been allied militarily, politically, and culturally with southern Sudan. The Khartoum regime has responded accordingly, and as a result the argument for genocide in Sudan can be made nowhere more compellingly than in the context of the Nuba Mountains, the largest of the three areas, where the civilian population endured years of an immensely destructive humanitarian aid embargo and relentless, deliberate destruction by Khartoum's military forces.

Despite the importance of the issues involved in resolving the status of these three areas in a truly just fashion, there is intense international pressure, especially from the United States, to see a peace agreement signed within the next week, a time frame publicly reiterated December 29, 2003 by NIF President Omar al-Bashir in a Reuters dispatch. But this last issue in the Naivasha negotiations is in many ways the most difficult, even as it is fraught with immense implications for the rest of Sudan and the other marginalized regions. Nowhere is this truer than in Darfur Province, in the far west of Sudan.

In recent weeks there have been a series of extremely ominous statements from senior UN officials about the impending human catastrophe in Darfur. In addition to Jan Egeland, UN Under-Secretary for Humanitarian Affairs, declaring that the humanitarian crisis in Darfur is probably the "worst in the world today," UN officials have put in place all the evidence necessary for us to draw the inevitable conclusion: destruction of the African peoples in Darfur – through deliberate attacks on civilian noncombatants by Khartoum-backed Arab militias, the *Janjaweed*, and by means of deliberate denial of urgently needed humanitarian relief – amounts to "ethnic cleansing."

Indeed, the UN Humanitarian Coordinator for Sudan, Mukesh Kapila, explicitly used this very phrase explicitly in a BBC/Public Radio International, December 18, 2003 radio interview for "The World." Although Kapila was making the point that the many reports of "ethnic cleansing" cannot presently be confirmed because of Khartoum's denials of humanitarian relief and international observers, other UN officials and Sudan analysts have been explicit in speaking of the systematic denial of humanitarian relief, as well as the *"systematic"* nature of militia attacks on noncombatant civilians, the word twice highlighted in a memorandum by Tom Vraalsen, the UN Secretary-General's Special Envoy for Humanitarian Affairs for Sudan, in a December 8, 2003 confidential memorandum to Kapila. Such a "system" in Darfur is nothing less than the organized destruction of the sedentary African agriculturalists – the Fur, the Massaleit, the Zaghawa, and other non-Arab tribal groups.

It is thus both deeply appropriate and timely that in January 2004, the Committee on Conscience of the United States Holocaust Memorial Museum will declare in a newsletter that Darfur has given new urgency to the Committee's longstanding "genocide warning" for Sudan, heretofore focused appropriately on southern Sudan and the Nuba Mountains. This continues the vigilance that has characterized the Committee on Conscience since it first issued a "genocide warning" for Sudan in its October 2000 *Report on Sudan: "Genocide Warning."* At that time, the Committee on Conscience indicated that its "warning was based on the following actions of the military government of Sudan,"

- a divide-to-destroy strategy of pitting ethnic groups against each other, with enormous loss of civilian life;
- the use of mass starvation as a weapon of destruction;
- toleration of the enslavement of women and children by government-allied militias;
- the incessant bombing of hospitals, clinics, schools and other civilian and humanitarian targets;
- disruption and destabilization of the communities of those who flee the war zones to other parts of Sudan; and
- widespread persecution on account of race, ethnicity and religion.

The Committee on Conscience concluded that, "taken individually, each of these actions is a disaster for the victims. Taken together, they threaten the physical destruction of entire groups."

Because so many of the tactics instanced in the *"Genocide Warning"* are now variously in evidence in Darfur, it is appropriate that the forthcoming Committee on Conscience newsletter highlight again the realities that have so relentlessly defined the military strategy of the Khartoum regime, as well as make fully explicit the relevance of this unprecedented "genocide warning" for the crisis in Darfur.

Certainly issues of race and ethnicity in the conflict in Darfur have been highlighted in a number of quarters over the last month. According to the BBC on December 11, 2003 and Deutsche Presse-Agentur on December 10, 2003, diplomats are now speaking explicitly of "ethnic cleansing" in Darfur. The International Crisis Group (ICG) declares in its December 11, 2003 report, *Sudan: Towards an Incomplete Peace*, that Khartoum-backed Arab militias are attacking "unprotected villages with no apparent link to the rebels other than their ethnic profile." Amnesty International warned in its November 27, 2003 Press Release *Sudan: Humanitarian Crisis in Darfur Caused by Sudan Government's Failures* that "the situation in Darfur is at risk of rapidly degenerating into a full-scale civil war where ethnicity is manipulated."

And while there are the very few voices from Darfur that have managed to find their way into the larger world, IRIN reported from el-Geneina, Darfur on December 11, 2003,

"I believe this is an elimination of the black race," one tribal leader told IRIN.

It is intolerable that the international community continues to allow what all evidence suggests is genocide. For surely if we are honest with ourselves we will accept that the term "ethnic cleansing" is no more than a dangerous euphemism for genocide, a way to make the ultimate crime somehow less awful. As Samantha Power has cogently observed on page 483 of *"A Problem from Hell": America and the Age of Genocide*, the phrase "ethnic cleansing" gained currency in the early 1990s as a way of speaking about the atrocities in the Balkans – "as a kind of euphemistic halfway house between crimes against humanity and genocide." But linguistic half-measures are not enough when the question is whether an "ethnical [or] racial group" is being destroyed "in whole or in part" – "as such," to use the key phrase from the 1948 UN Convention on the Prevention and Punishment of the Crime of Genocide.

The present realities in Darfur must urgently be rendered for the world to see and understand – fully, honestly, and on the basis of much greater information than is presently available. In turn, these realities must guide a humanitarian effort that will not allow Khartoum's claim of "national sovereignty" to trump the desperate plight of hundreds of thousands of innocent civilians caught up in a maelstrom of destruction and displacement. That no such efforts are presently being undertaken – Ambassador Vraalsen declared on December 8, 2003 that humanitarian operations in Darfur have "practically come to a standstill" – is of the gravest concern.

Indeed, the logic of the situation is so compelling that one can only surmise that the failure of the international community even to speak of the possibility of a humanitarian intervention in Darfur derives from some morally appalling failure of nerve, and an unwillingness to roil the diplomatic waters with a peace agreement so close between Khartoum and the SPLM/A. But this latter concern represents exactly the wrong way to view both Darfur and its relation to the last major issue outstanding in the present peace negotiations between Khartoum and the south, viz. the status of the three contested areas of Abyei, the Nuba Mountains, and Southern Blue Nile. Unless the international community shows its concern for the various marginalized peoples of Sudan, peace will be only very partial and ultimately unsustainable.

In fact, we may be sure that the long-aggrieved and marginalized people of Darfur, as well as such other marginalized populations as the Beja in the east of Sudan, are watching closely the fate of the three contested areas along the historic north-south border. These people have also suffered, at the hands of Khartoum's tyranny, terrible brutality, discrimination, and lack of representation as well as a share of the national wealth. If the peace talks in Naivasha do not produce justice for the people of Abyei, the Nuba Mountains, and Southern Blue Nile, it is extremely unlikely that Sudan's other marginalized people will see in diplomacy a means to secure basic rights and representation or an end to repression. The invitation to armed insurrection is likely to be irresistible. Indeed, this is precisely what we are seeing in Darfur presently, and armed resistance will almost certainly intensify if diplomacy at Naivasha fails to offer justice to these three key areas of Sudan.

At the same time, if Khartoum sees that the international community is willing to respond expediently to the massive humanitarian crisis in Darfur, if the world is unwilling to challenge Khartoum despite clear evidence that the denial of humanitarian aid is "systematically" based on race and ethnicity, then the regime may conclude that it need only remain obdurate in Naivasha and the status of the three contested areas will be decided on its terms.

Again, there is immense pressure to get a peace agreement signed. On December 30, 2003 US Secretary of State Colin Powell called both National Islamic Front (NIF) President al-Bashir as well as First Vice President Ali Osman Taha, chief NIF negotiator in Naivasha, and John Garang, Chairman of the SPLM/A. There have been previous such calls from both Powell and President Bush, giving peace in Sudan an extraordinary foreign policy profile for this administration.

But while pressure alone may produce a peace signing, it will not produce a just peace, and only a just peace can be meaningful. The US, Norway, and the UK – the so-called "troika – as well as the East African Intergovernmental Authority for Development (IGAD) countries, most notably Kenya, should all be looking comprehensively at Sudan's problems if the goal is to secure a just peace. If it is too late to incorporate Darfur formally into the Naivasha negotiations, it is certainly not too late to demonstrate a concern for the fate of the people of the three contested areas. This in turn will be a powerful signal to the people of Darfur that they may also be the beneficiaries of focused international concern.

At the moment, it is all too reasonable for the people of Darfur – and other marginalized regions in Sudan – to conclude that the international vision of peace for Sudan is focused only on Khartoum and the south. Such myopia may indeed produce a peace agreement, but it will not produce peace in Sudan.

March 26, 2004 State-Sanctioned Ethnic Cleansing

Mukesh Kapila, UN Humanitarian Coordinator for Sudan, courageously and remarkably forthrightly, as reported in a March 26, 2004 Reuters dispatch from Khartoum, has said that those responsible for the immense, deliberate, ethnically-motivated human destruction in Darfur must be held accountable,

> I see no reason why the international community should not consider some sort of international court or mechanism to bring to trial the individuals who are masterminding and committing the war crimes [in Darfur].

Indeed, Kapila continued and declared such tribunals an international obligation,

> War crimes tribunals must be held to try those responsible for raping, looting and killing in African villages in Sudan's western Darfur region, a senior UN official said, accusing the state of complicity. "There are no secrets," UN Humanitarian Coordinator for Sudan Mukesh Kapila said. "The individuals who are doing this are known. We have their names. The individuals who are involved occupy senior positions [in the government of Sudan]."
> [Kapila] said the violence, which he described as "ethnic cleansing," was mostly carried out by Arab militias known as *Janjaweed* who were supported by government forces. "Under those circumstances one can only conclude that it is state-sanctioned."

Kapila's statements were at least in part a response to the Khartoum regime's characterization of his previous remarks concerning Darfur as "a heap of lies," as his words were reported by the BBC on March 21, 2004. In these remarks, reported also in an IRIN, March 22, 2004 dispatch, Kapila likened the deliberate human destruction in the region to what occurred ten years ago in Rwanda, "the only difference between Rwanda and Darfur now is the numbers involved." "[The slaughter in Darfur] is more than just a conflict, it is an organised attempt to do away with a group of people."

Kapila was even more forceful in a March 19, 2003 BBC dispatch,

"I was present in Rwanda at the time of the genocide, and I've seen many other situations around the world and I am totally shocked at what is going on in Darfur. . . . This is ethnic cleansing, this is the world's greatest humanitarian crisis, and I don't know why the world isn't doing more about it."

And things are getting worse, despite the claims by Khartoum in early February 2004 to have brought the situation in Darfur under "total military control." Kapila countered in an IRIN March 22, 2004 dispatch,

The pattern of organised attacks on civilians and villages, abductions, killings and organised rapes by militias was getting worse by the day, [Kapila] said, and could deteriorate even further. "One can see how the situation might develop without prompt [action] . . . all the warning signs are there."

Kapila's sense of a deteriorating situation echoes recent statements by Amnesty International in a March 15, 2004 London Press Release,

"the government of Sudan has made no progress to ensure the protection of civilians caught up in the conflict in Darfur" Amnesty International said today. "This is not a situation where the central government has lost control. Men, women and children are being killed and villages are burnt and looted because the central government is allowing militias aligned to it to pursue what amounts to a strategy of forced displacement through the destruction of homes and livelihood of the farming populations of the region," Amnesty International said.

International concern over the human catastrophe in Darfur has belatedly increased, and in recent days yet more prominent voices have weighed in. Of particular note, eight UN human rights fact-finding experts have issued a statement in a March 29, 2004 New York UN News Service dispatch saying they are "gravely concerned" by the reports of ethnic cleansing and widespread human rights abuses occurring in the Darfur region of western Sudan. The experts, mostly special rapporteurs who have been charged by the UN with monitoring issues such as torture, extrajudicial executions, and the right to food, declared that they have informed the Khartoum regime about their concerns,

> In their statement, the experts said they were alarmed after the UN coordinator in Sudan, Mukesh Kapila, told the media that an ethnic cleansing campaign was taking place that was comparable in character, if not scale, to the Rwanda genocide of 1994. The experts pointed to reports that militias such as the *Janjaweed*, the Muraheleen and the Popular Defence Forces, encouraged by the Sudanese Government, are trying to forcibly remove the non-Arab segment of the local population.

This statement was issued the same day as a March 26, 2004 report entitled *A Briefing Paper on the Darfur Crisis: Ethnic Cleansing*. The *Briefing Paper* was "prepared by a group of concerned humanitarian workers in Darfur who requested the UN Resident and Humanitarian Coordinator to bring their concerns to the attention of the international community." Some of the findings of *A Briefing Paper on the Darfur Crisis* include,

> In order to increase its capacity to fight Sudan Liberation Army, the Government of Sudan has called for the support of a proxy force constituted by ethnic Arab fighters, the *Janjaweed*. Though the intention of Government of Sudan may initially not have been to target civilians, but potential SLA fighters, it is clear that today all Fur and Zaghawas villagers or town residents are systematically targeted. It seems to have become a military logic of Government of Sudan that the only way to defeat SLA is to remove the entire support

base (villages where to hide, and villagers who could provide SLA cover and food).

Ethnic cleansing is characterized by a deliberate policy executed through clear command-and-control arrangements by which a group, based on its race, origin or religion, is forcibly removed from an area. The pattern witnessed in the Darfur region to forcibly remove non-Arab tribes (mainly Fur, Zaghawas, Messalites and Birgit) from their villages is consistent in all areas.

[Arab nomads who have joined the *Janjaweed*] make it clear that the Government of Sudan has now given them a mandate to make these areas "Zurga free" (Zurga is a derogatory term for Black) and that they represent the Government of Sudan in the area. Violence is systematically reported, people killed (especially males), goods including cattle looted, and houses burned. If people do not move immediately, a second more deadly attack is launched, and civilians are left with no option but to move away to the nearest "safe haven," which is usually also attacked within the next few days.

What more can the international community require, short of a full investigation on the ground in Darfur – something the Khartoum regime adamantly refuses to permit? Indeed, as several UN officials have suggested, including Dr. Kapila, Khartoum's denial of humanitarian access constitutes prima facie evidence that the regime wishes to conceal something. The total ban on news reporters, the highly restrictive control of travel permits for humanitarian aid workers, and the refusal to allow human rights monitors in any form – all must contribute to the conclusion that Khartoum has a great deal to fear from any thorough investigation or full reckoning of the terrible consequences of months of concerted, systematic, purposeful human destruction, whether we call it "ethnic cleansing" or genocide.

The need to prepare for an international humanitarian intervention is clear. The alternative to present intervention will be impotent hand-wringing later, once the scale of the catastrophe becomes fully known. But at the very least the international community must signal to Khartoum, both its political and military leadership, and to those controlling the *Janjaweed* militia, that there will be a day of reckoning. The tribunals Mukesh Kapila has declared so obviously necessary – "I see no reason why the international community should not consider some sort of international court or mechanism to bring to trial the individuals who are masterminding and committing the war crimes" – must become a reality.

Such tribunals must not be negotiated away under any circumstances in the Naivasha peace talks, where Khartoum so obviously hopes to receive, as part of a final agreement, an amnesty for its years of atrocities in southern Sudan, the Nuba Mountains, Southern Blue Nile, and Abyei. Darfur now has its own immense moral equities, and the world must ensure that these are weighed judiciously in an international tribunal.

Whether the term is "ethnic cleansing" or genocide, the terrible crimes occurring in Darfur must not be ignored. The cries of the dead and dying demand justice, and future génocidaires are listening closely, noting carefully any and all failures of international resolve.

March 31, 2004 – the N'Djamena, Chad Peace Talks – Khartoum's Contempt

The National Islamic Front (NIF) regime's profound contempt and ongoing disregard for both international humanitarian assessments and international diplomatic efforts to bring peace and justice to Sudan were fully in evidence during the March 30, 2004 start of the N'djamena, Chad peace talks. The NIF, as reported in a March 30, 2004 Agence France-Presse dispatch,

accus[ed] UN experts of lying with reports of "systematic" human rights abuses in Sudan's western Darfur region. Foreign Minister Mustafa Ismail told reporters "some UN officials do not keep to the truth when speaking about the situation in Sudan to the extent at which we can label some of their statements as lies and acts of deception."

[Ismail] was reacting to a statement issued by eight experts of the UN Commission on Human Rights, expressing their grave concern "at the scale of reported human rights abuses and at the humanitarian crisis unfolding in Darfur."

The eight distinguished UN special rapporteurs accused of lying include the Special Rapporteur on torture, Theo van Boven; the Special Rapporteur on violence against women, Yakin Ertürk; the Special Rapporteur on racism, Doudou Diène; the Special Rapporteur on the right to health, Paul Hunt; the Special Rapporteur on extrajudicial, summary or arbitrary executions, Asma Jahangir; the Special Rapporteur on the sale of children, child prostitution and child pornography, Juan Miguel Petit; the Special Rapporteur on the right to food, Jean Ziegler; and the Secretary-General's representative on internally displaced persons, Francis Deng.

In a similar vein, the NIF delegation refused to "take part in the opening ceremony" of peace talks in N'Djamena, the capital of Chad – peace talks that have gained some credibility with a meaningful international presence – precisely because it objected to the presence of international observers. Sudan's Secretary of State for Foreign Affairs, Tidjani al-Fidail, told Agence France-Presse in N'Djamena, "Apparently there are others who are trying to play at being observers, which was not planned." Reuters on March 30, 2004 also reported that, "the Sudanese government on Tuesday boycotted the opening session of peace talks in Chad with western rebels in protest at the presence of international observers."

Agence France-Presse reported on March 30, 2004 that the "observers" Khartoum found so objectionable – those seeking to end a war that has produced what many are describing as the world's greatest humanitarian crisis – included "representatives of the European Union, the United States, and the Henri Dunant Centre for Humanitarian Dialogue, a Geneva-based organisation which aids peace talks. [They] were in N'djamena as 'facilitators' at the talks."

Associated Press reported on March 31, 2004 from N'Djamena that Ahmad Allam-mi, an adviser to Chad's President Idriss Déby, said,

> the Sudanese government refused to attend to the ceremony because it did not want the conflict in Darfur "internationalized." The talks are being mediated by the Chadian government and the African Union, while, European Union, and French officials will have observer status.

No doubt Allam-mi speaks correctly when declaring that Khartoum does not wish to "internationalize" the conflict, has no wish to see international observers in Darfur, and certainly has no wish to see real international mediation in a process for which Chad and an uninspired AU provide hopelessly inadequate auspices and diplomatic resources.

United Press International underscored the NIF's attitude toward international monitoring of human rights in Sudan in a dispatch from Khartoum on March 30, 2004,

> Sudanese President Omar el-Bashir Tuesday rejected a draft proposal by the European Union requesting international monitoring of human rights in Sudan. El-Bashir was quoted by his foreign minister Mustafa Ismail as saying "he opposed placing Sudan under international supervision to verify the state of human rights" in the country torn by decades of civil war. . . . The EU is planning to submit the draft proposal to the UN Commission for Human Rights, which is meeting in Geneva.

It should be noted that the European Union proposal is merely to provide technical assistance to Sudan for the monitoring of human rights. This is a so-called Item 19 resolution, as opposed to the much more robust Item 9 resolution that was not renewed last year; only this latter monitoring regime would oblige the appointment of a UN special rapporteur for human rights. Support for an Item 19 resolution is already a painful abandonment of responsibility on the part of the EU; but the Europeans have been encouraged by African nations that have made clear they oppose any UN resolution that imposes human rights monitoring that is not entirely voluntary. A more absurd and destructive attitude is difficult to imagine, and the UN Commission on Human Rights, meeting in Geneva, has almost fully succeeded in making itself irrelevant to the real cause of human rights.

Khartoum continues to restrict in severe and highly consequential fashion humanitarian access to the Darfur region of western Sudan. The NIF regime still refuses to grant travel permits to humanitarian organizations for no reason, still refuses to accept the presence of international monitors, and still refuses access to humanitarian assessment teams. This continuing denial of humanitarian access, assessment, and human rights monitoring comes even as UN agencies emphatically declared in a March 30, 2004 UN News Centre dispatch,

> The already dire humanitarian situation in the Darfur region of western Sudan has worsened, United Nations agencies said today, with thousands of internally displaced people now facing water shortages and outbreaks of communicable diseases such as measles. In an update issued today, the UN Office for the Coordination of Humanitarian Affairs (OCHA) said attacks against civilians are reported to be occurring daily and across the whole of the region.... The UN agencies said the attacks have forced internally displaced people to congregate in larger or more urban areas, increasing the chance of disease outbreaks and using up scarce water supplies.

But even as the UN and various humanitarian and human rights organizations are declaring that, "the humanitarian situation in Darfur has worsened," Khartoum cynically asserts the opposite in a March 31, 2004 IRIN dispatch,

> Officials at the Sudanese Embassy in Nairobi told IRIN on Wednesday that they had no information about the continuing attacks. On the contrary, they said, the situation in Darfur region was "actually improving."

This vicious mendacity, this assertion that the situation in Darfur is "actually improving," distills perfectly Khartoum's contempt for the international community and for the integrity of the UN and its humanitarian officials, and reveals ultimately the regime's complete contempt for the African peoples of Darfur.

For the catastrophe in Darfur is clearly accelerating. This is unmistakable, as all credible evidence indicates, and assertions to the contrary derive from the worst of motives and ultimately from ethnically-animated hatred. A terrible vignette of this hatred was provided in a March 30, 2004 email to the author from Eltigani Ateem Seisi, former governor of Darfur, now living in exile in Great Britain. A humanitarian official has independently confirmed Eltigani's account. Eltigani urgently declared,

I am writing again to highlight the plight of those who have been trapped in the Kailake [also Kailek] area to the south of Kass [South Darfur]. I have just been speaking to some of those who managed to escape from the Kailake concentration camp where about 5400 people are surrounded by the *Janjaweed* militia. The people have been deprived of food and water for almost four weeks. People are now dying every day. There is an outbreak of Cholera, which kills on average 17 people/day.

The Kailake experience is now repeated in Korele area to the East of Zalingi [Western Darfur] where 17 villages have been torched on Sunday. The villagers have also been surrounded by the militia. Government troops demanded 5 million [Sudanese pounds] from the villagers to protect them from the *Janjaweed*, but as soon as the money was paid the troops left the area and the villagers are now being abused by the *Janjaweed*. Witnesses I talked to today reported the following,

1. The *Janjaweed* are summarily executing the villagers. 2. Mass rape of women. 3. Mass rape of children as young as 7 years. 4. Tying the innocent villagers from their legs and dragging them by camels. 5. Denying the villagers access to food and water, a carbon copy of the . . . Kailake tragedy.

Such accounts – and the scores of others accumulated by Amnesty International, Doctors Without Borders, the International Crisis Group, and increasingly by intrepid journalists – despite their ghastliness, give only a partial sense of the whelming human destruction. For the full realities of food shortages, agricultural disruption, and the consequences of Khartoum's denial of humanitarian access are only now coming fully into focus. For example, Roger Winter of the US Agency for International Development reports from the region in a March 24, 2004 Reuters dispatch,

[Winter] told reporters food shortages were inevitable because so many people had left their land, been robbed or had no seeds left. "We believe the conflict there is so severe that a substantial number of people are going to be affected by severe food shortages. Even if there was a ceasefire arranged at this meeting in Chad, still a large number of people would die."

The absence of a resumption of adequate food production in the near future has recently been highlighted by the UN's World Food Program in a March 25, 2004 IRIN dispatch,

> With no signs of an improvement in the conflict, the next planting season in April/May [2004] may also be "very limited," [Laura] Melo [of the UN World Food Program] warned. This would have a major impact on food availability and leave people dependent on food aid for another year, she said. "A widespread humanitarian disaster looms for the population of Darfur unless large-scale humanitarian assistance is rapidly made possible," commented a humanitarian source working in the region.

And on top of this, Khartoum's Arab militia allies are badly disrupting such humanitarian aid as can reach the people of Darfur, as reported in a February 27, 2004 UN News dispatch from New York,

> . . . Internally displaced people in western Sudan's strife-torn Darfur region are reporting that aid given to them by United Nations agencies and non-governmental organizations (NGOs) is being stolen by armed militia. The UN's World Food Programme (WFP) is considering feeding recipients directly instead of giving them rations that could be stolen, the Office for the Coordination of Humanitarian Affairs (OCHA) said today. The inhabitants of one Darfur village are so fearful of militia attacks that they have asked UN staff not to distribute aid to them in case they become a target.

It remains the case that urgent planning for cross-border humanitarian intervention must begin immediately. The alternative is acquiescence in ongoing genocidal destruction, in which more than 1,000 people are dying every week.

Continuing violence in Upper Nile Province, southern Sudan

Khartoum's actions over the last several months in Upper Nile Province, including the deliberate arming and inciting of militia groups, threaten to re-ignite war in the south, even as talks struggle toward closure in Naivasha, Kenya. The situation is complex, and obscured by the security risks that steadily increase and prevent humanitarian presence in many areas, but the basic facts are clear.

In the area of Upper Nile known as the Shilluk Kingdom – the Shilluk, like the Dinka and Nuer, are part of the Nilotic tribal group – government military activity has been steadily increasing, along with that of its militia proxies. This has produced many hundreds of civilian casualties and has displaced tens of thousands. Moreover, many more tens of thousands of needy civilians are now beyond the reach of humanitarian assistance because of compromised security. The destructive and destabilizing effects of Khartoum-sponsored militia attacks are, of course, long-familiar features of war in the south, even as they are now being given brutal and widespread reprise in Darfur.

One key event in generating this present round of violence in the south was the defection of commander Lam Akol back to the SPLA. Lam Achol, a Shilluk, defected from the Sudan People's Liberation Movement/Army (SPLM/A) in 1991 and returned in October 2003, though not with all his followers. Khartoum has deliberately incited those remnants of Lam Achol's militia organization in the region, as the regime has done with other such militia organizations – in effect paying the militias to wreak havoc among the civilian populations, especially in the Shilluk Kingdom. The scale is suggested by a humanitarian source working in southern Sudan, who indicates today that at least 13,000 Internally Displaced Persons have arrived in the Upper Nile town of Malakal since January, fleeing constant fighting and attacks on civilian targets by Khartoum-backed militia.

Authoritative reports coming from several sources in the region yesterday make clear that a major new militia offensive is just underway. One report indicated that the son of the Shilluk king has been killed in this offensive. These military activities, conducted by Khartoum directly and by means of militia proxy, are clear violations of the "Cessation of Hostilities Agreement, the Memorandum of Understanding Between the Government of the Sudan and the SPLM/A on Resumption of Negotiations on Peace in Sudan," signed on October 15, 2002 under the auspices of the Intergovernmental Authority for Development (IGAD) in Nairobi. This agreement specifies that the parties undertake to, maintain a period of tranquility during the negotiations by ceasing hostilities in all areas of the Sudan and ensuring a military stand-down for their own forces, including allied forces and affiliated militias.

The agreement also specifies that the parties will "retain current military positions," "cease supplying all areas with weapons and ammunition," and "refrain from any acts of violence or other abuse on the civilian population." These various commitments are all being violated in egregious fashion by Khartoum and its militia allies. The regime is evidently convinced that between negotiations in Naivasha and the catastrophe in Darfur, the international community will simply look away from this clear abrogation of a signed agreement. And such conviction is all too well justified by past inaction in enforcing the October 2002 agreement. Such violations also augur extremely poorly for Khartoum's observance of the terms of the Agreement on Security Arrangements, signed by the regime on September 25, 2003.

Though there has been only very limited international reporting on this particular instance of Khartoum's contemptuous violation of a signed agreement, we should note carefully the information available. Deutsche Presse-Agentur reported on March 14, 2004,

A government source, who requested anonymity, told Deutsche Presse-Agentur that initial figures showed scores of civilians had been killed in pro-government militia attacks on villages close to Malakal town, provincial capital of the Upper Nile region. In the attack the headquarters of Shilluk Community King Alak was badly damaged, homes set ablaze and cows looted. The attackers also raped women, the source added. Militias have renewed attacks on Obai, Pakang, Dot, Oweci and the Panyikango areas in the Shilluk Kingdom in the Upper Nile region.

IRIN from Nairobi reported on March 19, 2004,

Clashes involving a number of government-backed militias and government forces in the Shilluk Kingdom region of southern Sudan are resulting in an increasing number of deaths and displacements. On 11 March, militias and government forces from Malakal attacked villages west of Awajwok including Alaki, the village of the Shilluk king, according to the Fashoda Relief and Rehabilitation Association (FRRA). The FRRA is the humanitarian wing of [Lam Achol's] Sudan People's Liberation Movement-United (SPLM/U), which realigned with the SPLM/Army (SPLM/A) in October 2003.

In Alaki, houses were set on fire and cattle driven away by attacking forces, Gabriel Otor Marko, the FRRA executive director, said on Thursday. The militias were reinforced by government forces in gunboats on the River Nile, who then attacked Nyilwak, where they dispersed a large civilian population. "An unknown number of people were killed or wounded, houses set on fire and properties looted," he said. On 10 March militias had also attacked the village of Adodo, displacing its civilians.

These reports, though confirmed by numerous highly authoritative accounts from the region, including from Western Upper Nile, seem of no consequence to the US-sponsored Civilian Protection Monitoring Team (CPMT) or the Verification and Monitoring Team (VMT), based in southern Sudan and charged with investigating both attacks against civilians and violations of the Cessation of Hostilities agreement. Indeed, the VMT is a revealingly useless entity, one that has – at considerable expense – done absolutely nothing of note since its notional creation in February 2003 in response to Khartoum's serial violations of the October 2002 agreement. The silence and uselessness of both the CPMT and VMT, over many months, and most strikingly in the present moment, make clear that they are governed most essentially by political expediency.

But if Khartoum's actions of the past few days are rationally assessed by the international community, it should be clear that the price of expediency, whatever apparent short-term gain, will always be to retard real progress toward peace and justice in Sudan. The Khartoum regime is cynical, it is evil, it is governed by a ruthless survivalism – and it will not make a just peace, in the South or in Darfur, unless compelled to by the most relentless international pressure. Though there has been a welcome increase in the volume of outrage over the atrocities and humanitarian crisis in Darfur, this hasn't translated into meaningful responses. If present talks in Chad fail – and the opening day could hardly have been less auspicious – there will simply be no option at the ready.

And in Naivasha, Kenya, Khartoum continues to survey the lack of international will and has concluded that even if compelled by circumstances to sign a peace agreement, there will never be sufficiently sustained international commitment to make this agreement the basis for a just and lasting peace. Again, such a conclusion on Khartoum's part has far too much justification in recent and more distant history.

The days in which to consummate peace in Naivasha and avert total catastrophe in Darfur are dwindling. When they expire, what will the international community be prepared to do? To ask the question is to see too much of an answer.

May 3, 2004 – Khartoum Expands Its Genocidal War into Chad, Threatening Relief Efforts

Reports continue to stream in from the Chad-Darfur border, and from within Darfur itself, making clear that the nominal cease-fire agreement concluded on April 8, 2004 exists chiefly as an example of yet another worthless piece of paper bearing the signature of the Khartoum regime. Amnesty International, in an April 30, 2004 Public Statement, reported that "on 28 April [2004] Sudanese planes bombed Kolbus village in Chad and the Janjawid attacked refugees and Chadian civilians across the border." The US State Department reported aerial attacks in Darfur by Khartoum the first day of the cease-fire, April 12, 2004.

The BBC reported on April 30, 2004 particularly serious instances of Khartoum's escalation of the conflict into neighboring Chad, where 120,000-130,000 refugees have fled Khartoum's violence against the African civilian populations in Darfur,

> Chadian troops have deployed on their border after a clash with
> Sudan forces. A Chadian government spokesman said the troops
> would protect local civilians and refugees from the Darfur region of
> Sudan who are sheltering in the area. The clash is the first to involve
> army troops since Sudanese civilians began fleeing into Chad a year

ago. The incident occurred after Arab militia staged a cross-border raid in Chad. Chad troops pursued them until they encountered Sudanese forces.

Chadian official Allami Ahmat, who helped to negotiate a cease-fire in the conflict in the western Sudanese region of Darfur earlier this month, said the incident was proof that the *Janjaweed* militia had not been disarmed as promised by the Sudanese government delegation at the peace talks. "[T]his situation is all the more unacceptable because the Sudanese army tolerates and offers land and air backup to the *Janjaweed* militias," he said. The UN has accused Sudan of backing Arab militias in a campaign of "ethnic cleansing" against black residents in Darfur.

But in addition to the continuously reported cross-border raids by the *Janjaweed*, attacking fleeing civilians and refugees, there are now extremely credible reports from the ground in Chad indicating that Khartoum is preparing for much greater military incursions. Indeed, within the humanitarian community on the ground in Chad there are increasing concerns about the larger implications of escalating military tensions along the Chad-Darfur border. The growing number and seriousness of these military incursions into Chad, by both Khartoum's regular forces and its *Janjaweed* militia allies, not only threaten refugees but also put threaten humanitarian aid personnel at risk. We must bear in mind that the area east of Abéché, which is 90 miles from the Chad-Darfur border, is quite remote, and that it will be very difficult to control and patrol this part of the country if Khartoum decides to make international humanitarian presence untenable by creating excessive levels of insecurity.

And this appears to be precisely the goal. A humanitarian official in Chad has reported to the author a conversation in which a Khartoum official was heard declaring that, "Abéché will not be made into another Lokichokio." This strongly suggests that Khartoum has decided that Abéché will not serve as a humanitarian staging area, as Lokichokio in northwest Kenya now is for southern Sudan, through the UN's Operation Lifeline Sudan. Khartoum's counter-insurgency strategy of destroying the civilian base of support for the SLM/A and JEM requires that there be no viable base for humanitarian operations near the border area.

Khartoum's long history of obstructing humanitarian aid in southern Sudan and the Nuba Mountains, and its present "systematic denial" of humanitarian aid within Darfur, an assessment of senior UN officials, make all too clear the likelihood of a policy of humanitarian interference in Chad. Indeed, there is increasingly persuasive evidence that such interference is rapidly moving further and further into Chad toward Abéché, and that Khartoum is prepared to carry out military operations well within Chadian territory. Evidence also suggests that it is highly likely that covert military intelligence operations are now underway.

This should hardly be surprising given the impunity with which Khartoum is violating the presently unmonitored cease-fire agreement. Amnesty International's April 30, 2004 Public Statement reported,

> Attacks on villages continue; indiscriminate and deliberate killings of civilians continue; looting continues and rapes continue. Most detainees imprisoned because of the conflict have not been released. The African Union monitors designated to investigate every ceasefire violation are not yet in place.
>
> This is not an unavoidable ethnic conflict. It is a tragedy deliberately created by the government's support for the Janjawid and fuelled by total impunity for grave violations of human rights.

Because Khartoum enjoys impunity in its continuing violations of the cease-fire agreement – moderating its genocidal campaign with what can only be described as tactical curtailments of certain military actions – there is no chance whatsoever that civilians remaining in Darfur will be able to take advantage of the little time left before present seasonal planting must be completed. And the UN acknowledges as much. Rather, instead of returning to their lands, the African peoples of Darfur continue to stream into Chad, unwilling to confront the relentless menace of Khartoum and its *Janjaweed* allies. The UN News Centre on April 27, 2004 reported from Bahai, site of the northernmost of the UN refugee camps in Chad that,

> 200 to 300 Sudanese refugees have been crossing weekly from the Darfur region into Chad since the beginning of April, an agency spokesman said today. The UN High Commission for Refugees

(UNHCR) spokesman, Ron Redmond, said in Geneva that new refugees in the town of Bahai, joining the 7,000 already registered there, told the team that they fled after Sudanese militia members attacked them on 2 April, looting and burning their homes.

IRIN reported on May 3, 2004,

> More refugees continue to arrive at Tolom daily [the north-central sector of the UN refugee camps]. "Everyday new people are coming on foot, on donkeys, in convoys," Alfred Demotibaye the Tolom camp manager, who works for the Chadian branch of Caritas, told IRIN.

The response of the international community, both to the humanitarian crisis and to the genocidal ambitions that have created this crisis, remains disgracefully inadequate. Instead of speaking with urgency and focus about the nature of the humanitarian intervention that is so clearly required, both the UN and the Western democracies continue to speak as if there is still time to avert catastrophe. To be sure, their pronouncements contain partial truths, as this May 1, 2004 UN News Service report from New York suggests,

> The United Nations warned today that the crisis in Darfur, western Sudan, will worsen dramatically unless security there is immediately improved and humanitarian agencies have better access to those in need.

But this does not tell the full and more consequential story. For even with immediately improved security, and there is not a shred of evidence that this is in prospect, the crisis will worsen dramatically. The UN and the rest of the international community have simply waited too long. With the onset of seasonal rains, there is no way that adequate supplies, especially of food, can be pre-positioned. This can occur now only with robust humanitarian intervention. A more appropriate sense of urgency is captured in the April 28, 2004 press release from Doctors Without Borders/ Médecins Sans Frontières (MSF), presently operating heroically, under extremely difficult circumstances, in the West Darfur areas of Zalinge, Mornay, Kerenik, Garsila, Um Kherr, Bindisi, Mukjar, Deleig, and Nyertiti,

> Without an urgent response and the massive and immediate pre-positioning of food, medicines and shelters, the threat to the survival of hundreds of thousands of displaced persons will increase when the rainy season begins in May and roads become impassable, further hindering the delivery of assistance. Urgent action is required.

Seasonal rains are beginning, and there is nothing remotely approaching what will be required to feed the more than 1 million food-dependent civilians in Chad and Darfur for a year or more. With characteristically blunt honesty, MSF declared in its April 28, 2004 Press Release,

> Despite announcements of forthcoming aid, assistance is utterly inadequate. Mobilization of aid efforts is slow and the few organizations operating in Darfur cannot meet the full range of needs.

Most of the world continues to speak as though this crisis can be managed with present plans, with prospective supplies, and with the transport scheme presently in use. But this is simply not the case. The road between the Chadian capital of N'Djamena and Abéché will soon be cut by the rains and the subsequently flooded wadis, as will the road from Abéché to the Darfur-Chad border. And those transport vehicles that might be able to make the journey from Abéché to the border region, over the next few weeks and during the next dry season, are now clearly threatened by the growing insecurity deliberately being engineered by Khartoum. The crisis in Darfur itself is just as difficult and much greater in scale. Here alternate transportation routes must be found and transport capacity increased – and time is of the essence. MSF's blunt assessment continues,

> The Health of Hundreds of Thousands of Displaced People Worsens Dramatically [press release headline]
> Because of the lack of appropriate, urgently needed aid, the health of displaced people in Sudan's Darfur region – particularly children

– is radically worsening. MSF teams also see a drastic decline in people's nutritional status, particularly among children.

People in the region are completely dependent on aid to survive.

The food pipeline is drying up, with up to one million people trapped with no protection, little assistance, and little food or shelter.

A region terrorized by uncontrolled marauding militia forces, with no harvest in sight for next fall, with road access on the verge of being severed, facing Khartoum's "systematic denial" of humanitarian aid, and without any adequate pre-positioning of food, Darfur is poised for utter, cataclysmic disaster. Figures from the US Agency for International Development's (USAID) December 2003 Report and Chart, *Projected Mortality Rates in Darfur, Sudan 2004-2005*, suggest that hundreds of thousands may die from famine and disease over the next year; at the peak of the projected famine perhaps 2,500 people will be dying every day.

There is only one question that honesty and any real concern for the people of Darfur can permit. Are we prepared to allow the brutal and unrepresentative National Islamic Front regime to assert national sovereignty and thereby ensure the deaths of hundreds of thousands? Or is the international community prepared to ignore this absurd claim of sovereignty by Khartoum's génocidaires and work urgently, insistently, and resourcefully to diminish as much as possible the already inevitable catastrophe in Darfur?

Kenneth Roth, Executive Director, and Joanna Weschler, UN Advocacy Director, Human Rights Watch, in a powerful April 28, 2004 letter to the UN Security Council, recall the words of UN Secretary-General Kofi Annan,

In his April 7 [2004] speech to the Commission on Human Rights, coinciding with the tenth anniversary of the onset of the genocide in Rwanda, Secretary-General Kofi Annan warned that "the risk of genocide remains frighteningly real" in Darfur. "It is vital that international humanitarian workers and human rights experts be given full access to the region, and to the victims, without further delay. If that is denied, the international community must be prepared to take swift and appropriate action. By action in such situations, I mean a continuum of steps which may include military action."

But we have heard no more from Kofi Annan, certainly nothing of this "continuum of steps" – or even what the first step must be. Mr. Annan has said nothing recently that speaks to the terrifying urgency of the crisis; rather he has retreated into banal comments, bland expressions of concern, and meaningless "urgings." But silence, inconsequential pronouncements, and continued inaction change nothing on the ground in Darfur. The world's greatest humanitarian crisis, growing directly out of Khartoum's genocidal conduct of war, continues to gather pace. Will the international community intervene to save hundreds of thousands of African lives at the most acute risk?

This is the question. No one is asking it aloud.

May 5, 2004 – Living Conditions Leading to Death – Khartoum Commits to the Ultimate Crime

Disturbingly expedient skepticism about genocide in Darfur has begun to emerge in some quarters, even as evidence for this ultimate crime increases daily. Indeed, all available evidence – from both human rights and humanitarian organizations – clearly points to a policy by Khartoum and its *Janjaweed* militia allies of "deliberately inflicting on the African groups of Darfur conditions of life calculated to bring about their physical destruction."

The evidence in aggregate is simply overwhelming, both in authority and unanimity: the UN speaks of "ethnic cleansing" and "crimes against humanity;" the US government now also speaks of "ethnic cleansing"; Human Rights Watch speaks of "ethnic-based murder"; Amnesty International has continually highlighted the racial/ethnic animus in the human destruction and displacement; so too has the International Crisis Group.

On May 5, 2004, a confidential source brought to light an utterly extraordinary document dated April 24, 2004, *United Nations Inter-Agency Fact Finding and Rapid Assessment Mission: Kailek Town, South Darfur*. The mission team consisted of technical staff from UNICEF, WHO (World Health Organization), FAO (Food and Agriculture Organization) and OCHA (Office for the Coordination of Humanitarian Affairs) (lead). The team investigated conditions in the already infamous Kailek concentration camp south of Kass in South Darfur. The unambiguous reality of genocide in Darfur was made very clear. The UN inter-agency team declared,

We are sure that the team would have learned more about the crimes committed against civilians in the region had it been granted wider access to the areas of conflict. The stories that we have received from the survivors of the acts of mass murder are very painful for us and they remind us of the brutalities of the Rwanda genocide.

The Team further found that "the circumstances of the internally displaced persons in Kailek [must] be described as imprisonment."

The Team also noted that,

> with a under five child mortality rate of 8-9 children per day due to malnutrition, and with the Government of Sudan security representatives permanently located in the town without having reported this phenomena to the UN, despite it having taken place for several weeks, [this] also indicates a local policy of forced starvation.

In addition to a "policy of forced starvation," the Team found that,

> the numerous testimonies collected by the team, substantiated by the actual observations on the ground, particularly the longstanding prevention of access to food, [amounts] to *a strategy of systematic and deliberate starvation being enforced by the Government of Sudan and its security forces on the ground* [emphasis added].

The Team further found that,

> the Government of Sudan has deliberately deceived the United Nations by repeatedly refuting claims to the seriousness of the situation in Kailek as well as having actively resisted the need for intervention by preventing the UN access to the area.

And the Team also found that,

> despite having been directly informed of the grave findings made by the UN mission in Kailek, the Government of Sudan continues to stall any concrete actions related to this urgent relocation.

This is genocide. Let those who would deny explain why it is not.

These are not second-hand reports or "allegations." These are first-hand observations by experienced experts in humanitarian affairs, working for various agencies of the United Nations. We must hear, then, with the utmost seriousness their terrifying words, "The stories that we have received from the survivors of the acts of mass murder are very painful for us and they remind us of the brutalities of the Rwanda genocide."

This full and fully professional account should incinerate all agnosticism about what is happening in Darfur, and all doubt about whether this is genocide. For we know that Kailek is but one of many concentration camps. Kailek fortuitously gained a profile by virtue of a truly courageous first-hand account, forwarded to the author in a March 30, 2004 email from Eltigani Ateem Seisi, a former governor of Darfur.

But Kailek is only one place; there are many, many such places – far too many.

For just this reason, Khartoum has begun a concerted campaign to obscure both the scale of destruction in Darfur and the regime's own responsibility for genocide. As part of this grotesque public relations effort, we have NIF Foreign Minister Mustafa Ismail declaring in an April 28, 2004 Voice of America report,

> "I would like to assure you that all those who have been killed in Darfur from the militia, from the rebels, from the government soldiers, from civilians who've been caught in fighting – it will not reach one thousand,"

NIF regime officials spoke of the situation in Darfur as "improving" in a March 31, 2004 IRIN report,

> Officials at the Sudanese Embassy in Nairobi told IRIN on Wednesday that they had no information about the continuing attacks. On the contrary, they said, the situation in Darfur region was "actually improving."

So we must choose – between this vicious mendacity and the assessment of the Nobel Peace Prize-winning medical humanitarian organization Doctors

Without Borders/Médecins Sans Frontières, which stated in an April 28, 2004 New York Press Release,

> Because of the lack of appropriate, urgently needed aid, the health of displaced people in Sudan's Darfur region – particularly children – is radically worsening.

History of course dictates that we must expect mendacity, obfuscation, deceit, and bad faith from Khartoum. These are the regime's primary weapons, both in the present campaign to destroy resistance in Darfur and in waging war on various peoples of Sudan over the entire 15 years of its tyrannical existence. But what is disturbing is the growing evidence of wider complicity in Khartoum's lies, and the consequent refusal to acknowledge genocide.

Some, both in the UN and in the world of nongovernmental organizations, are reluctant to offend this brutal regime, and thus they expediently acquiesce before its lies. The effort is either to improve humanitarian access or to avoid political confrontation with a regime that continues to enjoy strong support from both the Arab League and the Organization of the Islamic Conference. But either way, such expediency is a deal with génocidaires.

We caught a glimpse of this disgraceful expediency in the recent annual meeting in Geneva of the UN Commission on Human Rights. As a powerful and insightful April 26, 2004 *Washington Post* editorial emphasized, this particular travesty,

> will stand out for another reason as well: Perhaps for the first time, the commission has suppressed one of its own reports. The report, written by a team of UN human rights investigators, was based on interviews with Sudanese refugees who had escaped across the border from Darfur, into Chad. Leaked versions of the report show that the authors did not mince words. They write of Khartoum's "reign of terror" in Darfur and speak of rape, torture, and arson. But just before the report was due to be released and discussed in Geneva, Sudan suddenly announced that it would allow the team into the country. The acting high commissioner on human rights, Bertrand

Ramcharan, immediately agreed to suspend publication of the report, which he (and official UN Web sites) have said contains only "allegations" of human rights abuse.

But of course the suppressed report, *Report of the Office of the High Commission for Human Rights Mission to Chad, April 5-15, 2004*, contains far more than "allegations." For example, Paragraph 13 finds that in some places 80% of the refugee population in Chad were women or children; this was no "allegation," but rather the chilling context in which the report in Paragraph 19 also found "frequent reports of killings [with] men, and even boys, particular targets."

Nor, for example, was it an "allegation" that meningitis "above the epidemic threshold" had been found in the terribly overcrowded camp in Tine, Chad where refugees had been driven by the attacks of Khartoum's regular and *Janjaweed* militia forces.

To be sure, the team members were not eyewitnesses to mass murder, to the bombings and aerial attacks, the burning and destruction of many hundreds of villages; they did not see the rapes, the torture, the theft of cattle, and the systematic destruction of water wells and agricultural resources.

But they did find, not "allege," "there was a remarkable consistency in the witness testimony received" (Paragraph 15). The team found, not "alleged," that reports on aerial attacks and ground attacks had an "invariable" quality (Paragraph 17). The team found, not "alleged," that "refugees interviewed invariably described the *Janjaweed* as being exclusively 'Arab,' as opposed to 'black' or 'African'" (Paragraph 21). The team also found, not "alleged," that "all reports indicated that such bombardments [by Khartoum's military aircraft] indicated that such bombardments are indiscriminate," and that "it is clear that these attacks fail to distinguish between civilians and combatants and are disproportionate in nature" (Paragraph 32).

These are findings; UN acting High Commissioner on Human Rights Bertrand Ramcharan describes them only disingenuously as mere "allegations."

The same UN human rights investigating team has now returned from its brief assessment inside Darfur. It has tersely suggested that its findings in the previous report had been confirmed. But notably the UN team did not brief humanitarian organizations on exiting Darfur, a disturbing sign that the results will be politically tailored. Even more disturbing are the highly authoritative reports from within Darfur that the team was denied access to many of the places where investigation was most obviously warranted. Instead, the team traveled only to the areas of the larger towns, where people are fully under the control of an ever-watchful Khartoum military intelligence and clearly can speak only at exceedingly great risk.

Representatives of the Massaleit Community in Exile reported in a dispatch dated May 5, 2004, and confirmed by Darfurians in exile with contacts inside Darfur, that,

> the team visited only Al Fashir, Geneina and a few other areas; but not places containing mass graves such as Koca, Kodomi, Gondorong Menmery, Berty, Jabel, Hashaba, Wadanala, Sanidada, Gergira, Sera-omra, Habeela-Kjengessy, Omtandelti, Omderebirro, Salaa, Beida Kaino, Tulos, Solu, Morny, Habeela-Kanari, Mejmejy, Mully, Tory, Damkoro, Gokar, Habeela-Beida, Jabbon and others.

Perhaps most scandalously, the UN team interviewed a survivor of a previously reported mass execution, was given the precise coordinates for the mass execution – and yet did not travel to this location to confirm the atrocity. The author spoke with the survivor via translator in Nyala, South Darfur, and is completely confident on the basis of extensive subsequent communications that the UN team was provided with his location, and was able to interview him at great length. Still the team did not go to the site of the massacre this survivor reported in the Wadi Saleh area of West Darfur.

Though the UN team has not yet spoken to the issue of whether or not it was given "unimpeded access" in Darfur, a disingenuous answer seems all too likely, given the increasingly political nature of the UN response to Khartoum's obvious campaign of intimidation: "if you tell the truth about what you know of Darfur, then we will deny you access for humanitarian aid." A more vicious form of blackmail can hardly be imagined, and yet it is succeeding.

So how will the denial of access to the UN human rights team be explained? Because Khartoum preemptively denied access to the area of this atrocity as the team was entering Darfur, and to those areas specified in the dispatch from the Representatives of the Massaleit Community in Exile, the

UN team never formally requested access. Thus the team will say it was never actually denied access. What it will not say, but what is critically true, is that it knew such a request for access would be denied, and for that reason did not make the request.

This is the very embodiment of disingenuousness.

For the moment we have only the statement of UN human rights spokesman Jose Diaz in Geneva in a May 4, 2004 Agence France-Presse dispatch,

> "Following this latest mission, the [UN human rights investigating] team confirmed the assessment it made after its visit to refugee camps in Chad from 5 to 14 April."

The assessment referred to is suggested only very partially by the excerpts above. But what is essential in this assessment is its conclusion, found in Paragraph 54,

> The [UN human rights investigative] mission was able to identify disturbing patterns of massive human rights violations in Darfur, many of which may constitute war crimes and/or crimes against humanity.

Any subsequent conclusions, based solely on interviews with witnesses speaking without the freedom enjoyed by refugees in Chad – evidently all the people the UN team interviewed – should fully incorporate these previous findings. If the new report ends up expediently "editing" previous findings, or exculpating Khartoum and its *Janjaweed* militia allies on the basis of such interviews, the corruption of the investigative process will be palpable, even as the motives for such corruption will be deeply disturbing.

But there is additional evidence of a policy of expediency, disingenuousness, and a patent desire to appease Khartoum's international sensibilities, now thoroughly offended by the growing attention Darfur has at last garnered. For example, the recently concluded UN humanitarian assessment mission, which is entirely different from the UN human rights assessment mission, has also now recently returned from Darfur. James Morris, Executive Director of the UN World Food Program, led this team. In a

May 4, 2004 question and answer session in London, the following exchange occurred:

> QUESTION: I'm somewhat puzzled that you say the ceasefire is holding, when there are still reports of attacks and fighting?

> JAMES MORRIS: Well, the *Janjaweed* is not party to the ceasefire agreement. The ceasefire is between the rebels in the south and the government, and that's a big piece of the problem, that they're not bound by the same agreement.

> QUESTION: I'm interested to know what the government people accompanying you told you about why the villages were burnt out. Did you meet any militia? And did you see any sign that the government is controlling the militias?

> JAMES MORRIS: We were there for just a short period of time. We had extensive conversations about the protection and the security issue. Ultimately, the responsibility for the people at risk, is the responsibility of the Government of Sudan. All the UN community or the NGO community can do is to help, and to respond to humanitarian issues.

But Morris is simply in error here, and suspiciously in error. For one of the clauses of the April 8, 2004 cease-fire agreement required that Khartoum's regular military forces disarm the *Janjaweed* militias. To declare baldly that "the *Janjaweed* is not party to the cease-fire" is deeply misleading. They are bound because Khartoum nominally bound itself to disarm and control the *Janjaweed*. Of course we should not be surprised that the National Islamic Front regime has violated this agreement – as it has every other agreement it has ever signed.

But it is suspiciously inaccurate to suggest as a problem in the cease-fire agreement that the central issue of the *Janjaweed* has been left unaddressed. Since so much of the physical insecurity that is fueling the genocide in Darfur derives from the continuing and unconstrained predations of the *Janjaweed*, in concert with Khartoum's regular forces, Morris is either culpably ignorant – or trying, for expedient reasons, to mitigate the significance of Khartoum's violation of the terms of the cease-fire agreement.

Morris' puzzling reference to the "rebels in the south" suggests a possible conflation of the April 8, 2004 cease-fire, N'Djamena, Chad and the October 15, 2002 cessation of offensive hostilities agreement, Nairobi, Kenya between Khartoum and the southern SPLM/A.

Morris was asked the appropriate follow-up question, "And did you see any sign that the government is controlling the militias?" His conspicuous failure to answer the question directly was deeply telling, and clearly suggestive of the "political" considerations that Khartoum's present campaign has managed to intrude upon UN thinking and pronouncements. This is despicable disingenuousness.

For a true account of the relationship between the *Janjaweed* and Khartoum's regular forces, we must turn to another UN investigative team and its confidential assessment of one of the most notorious concentration camps, at Kailek. It is here that Khartoum's genocidal ambitions are most conspicuously on display, albeit in only one ghastly example. But Kailek is not an isolated instance; it is what all accounts from Darfur suggest is the case in areas throughout the region, especially South Darfur and West Darfur. This extensive excerpt comes from the conclusion of the single most revealing account of realities in Darfur to have emerged in recent months, *United Nations Inter-Agency Fact Finding and Rapid Assessment Mission: Kailek Town, South Darfur. April 24, 2004,*

> The team members, all of whom are experienced experts in humanitarian affairs, were visibly shaken by the humanitarian state and conditions in which we found the caseload of Internally Displaced Persons (IDPs) in Kailek.
>
> The clear presence of the Jenjaweed, and the inability to distinguish between them and the Government of Sudan police officers when carrying out their "duties" in town call for the circumstances of the IDPs in Kailek to be described as imprisonment. With a under five child mortality rate of 8 - 9 children per day due to malnutrition, and with the Government of Sudan security representatives permanently located in the town without having reported this phenomena to the UN despite it having taken place for several weeks also indicate a local policy of forced starvation.

In addition to this, the UN team wishes to raise its concern regarding the following:

The numerous testimonies collected by the team, substantiated by the actual observations on the ground, particularly the longstanding prevention of access to food, alludes to a strategy of systematic and deliberate starvation being enforced by the Government of Sudan and its security forces on the ground.

Information and findings obtained from Kailek IDPs in Kass and Kalma, as well a CARE International assessment report from early April 2004, all contain information which confirms the findings in the present report, [which] have been persistently refuted by the Government of Sudan when presented by the UN Nyala team for clarification.

Following the CARE report, the UN continued to press the Government of Sudan for clearance to visit Kailek town and to follow up on the findings from the CARE report but to no avail. UNSECO-ORD was only allowed access on 17 April after having been "advised" not to visit the area after the ceasefire, while the Government of Sudan has consistently informed that there were no problems of security and assistance in Kailek and that the IDPs in the location were free to go.

Therefore, in light of this, a first conclusion by the mission team is that the Government of Sudan has deliberately deceived the United Nations by repeatedly refuting claims to the seriousness of the situation in Kailek as well as having actively resisted the need for intervention by preventing the UN access to the area. The fact that Government of Sudan's own security forces have monitored the deteriorating humanitarian situation in Kailek due to their constant presence on the ground only helps to underscore this fact.

[D]espite having been directly informed of the grave findings made by the UN mission in Kailek, the Government of Sudan continues to stall any concrete actions related to this urgent relocation. Thus, the UN continues to await confirmation that the rapid relocation of the IDPs will commence.

It is a grave concern to the United Nations team in Nyala that Kailek is but one of several locations where civilians are living under similar conditions without having been able to communicate their ordeal to the humanitarian community.

Will we hear the voices of Kailek? The starving, brutalized occupants of this concentration camp are crying out with a terrified urgency no less than that which filled the voices of those who cried in vain from Dachau, Treblinka, Auschwitz.

Expediency here is a crime against humanity.

May 11, 2004 – African Auschwitz: The Concentration Camps of Darfur – Acquiescing before Genocide

There are no trains leading to the death camps of Darfur. Transportation takes the form of militarily coerced displacement, forcing the African tribal peoples of Darfur – bereft of all resources – to trek over a harsh and unforgiving landscape. We have no idea how many have perished on these journeys of terror because the National Islamic Front regime in Khartoum has worked to restrict all news access and continues to impede humanitarian access to all but a few areas. But we can be sure that the number is measured in the tens of thousands.

There are no crematoria in the Darfur camps. Blistering heat, rapid decomposition, and scavenging animals have disposed of most of the bodies to date, and Khartoum's military transport assets are now removing many more bodies from the sites of better reported atrocities and mass executions, dumping them in remote locations. Still, when the death rate soars, when engineered famine begins to accelerate beyond control later this fall, the bodies will simply decompose where they fall. The piles of corpses, presently missing from the picture of genocide that is apparently required for UN or international action, will be increasingly in evidence.

Khartoum and its Arab militia allies, the *Janjaweed*, their genocidal task completed, will then abandon the camps. Survivors, the few who manage to fashion a means of existence over these cruel months, will have no land to which to return. Their livelihoods and culture will have been destroyed. Present skeptics about whether there is genocide in Darfur will no doubt retreat into variously disingenuous professions of ignorance such as "we didn't know that conditions were so bad," or "we didn't have the pictures," or most disgracefully, asking "how could we have known that this would happen?"

But there is no ambiguity in Darfur. There is no lack of unassailable evidence or authority in previously conducted human rights investigations, especially by Amnesty International and Human Rights Watch. Even the recently released UN report on the human rights catastrophe in Darfur, hedged and trimmed by the political realities of the UN in New York, makes fully clear the immense human suffering and destruction deriving from Khartoum's genocidal ambitions.

Within this widespread, deliberate, and systematic assault on the African civilian populations of Darfur a new holocaust is burning. Genocide has begun again, threatening the Fur, the Massaleit, the Zaghawa, and other African peoples – "as such."

Khartoum's strategy of massive civilian displacement has been in place for over a year, generating a highly vulnerable displaced population of over 1 million Darfuri people, overwhelmingly from the African tribal groups of the region. This is the population that continues to fill badly overcrowded camps, in conditions that are presently appalling and rapidly deteriorating. These camps are already ghastly arenas of catastrophic child mortality, acute malnutrition and water shortages, surging disease rates, even as entire inmate populations face rape, torture, and murder on a daily basis. It will soon become much worse.

There are no sanitary provisions in the camps. As a consequence, disease – especially the water-borne diseases that proliferate with the seasonal rains – looms as the source of many tens of thousands of casualties in the very near future. Outbreaks of cholera have been reported, and meningitis above the "epidemic" threshold has been reported in at least one camp for the displaced in Chad. Cholera, while eminently treatable with proper medical intervention, is likely to spread uncontrollably soon, taking huge numbers of casualties. Measles, frequently fatal among weakened child populations, has been reported in a number of locations. The already catastrophic child mortality rates will soon spiral out of control.

But, perversely, the camps continue to beckon as "safe havens" from the military threat of Khartoum and its *Janjaweed* militia allies; unconstrained and ongoing savagery has turned the lands of the Fur, the Massaleit, the

Zaghawa, and others into killing fields. Terror beyond description has left these agriculturally productive civilians no choice but to flee toward camps located throughout Darfur and even into Chad. In turn, the camps in Darfur are too often controlled by Khartoum's regular military and intelligence forces, and even by the *Janjaweed*. Even Chad is not a sanctuary as cross-border raids by the *Janjaweed* against refugee camps and Chadian villages are being reported by international news services and humanitarian organizations on an ongoing basis.

Once in the camps, the displaced Darfuris become inmates, restrained by force, by the surrounding presence of menacing *Janjaweed* forces, and by a desperate hope for the food and security that no longer exist in their homelands. This hope seems no more warranted than that offered to European Jews in the form of Nazi promises of work and survival to "the East." In the main, there is no escape from the camps, even when it becomes clear that the most likely fate they offer is extermination through disease, starvation, and murder.

The camps, to be sure, vary considerably – depending largely on whether or not there is an international humanitarian presence. But food is rapidly running out throughout Darfur, and there are not nearly enough pre-positioned stocks for the coming months. The very *Janjaweed* militias that have done most to disrupt food production in Darfur will commandeer, as they already have on a number of occasions, future humanitarian deliveries. UN maps of the increasingly numerous and overcrowded camps make clear that humanitarian access and presence is already extremely limited. When the food does run out, this will precipitate a radically new and extraordinarily dangerous humanitarian crisis for which there is no contemplated response.

For the present, we may be sure that all too many of the camps are like the Kailek concentration camp south of Kass in South Darfur, definitively assessed by a UN inter-agency team in their Report, *United Nations Inter-Agency Fact Finding and Rapid Assessment Mission: Kailek Town, South Darfur*. It is important to note that this team is not the UN human rights investigative team whose report on Darfur was suppressed at the annual Geneva meeting of the UN Commission on Human Rights.

Most strikingly, the UN inter-agency team made clear that the realities of the Kailek concentration camp justify an explicit comparison between

Darfur and Rwanda. Their report thus joins a growing chorus of human rights and humanitarian professionals who find the Rwandan genocide the only appropriate point of historical reference.

Mukesh Kapila, former UN humanitarian coordinator for Sudan, declared in the closing days of his tenure in a March 22, 2004 UN IRIN release that "the only difference between Rwanda and Darfur now is the number" of casualties, and that Darfur was not simply a conflict but an "organized attempt to do away" with ethnically defined groups of people. Kapila was in Rwanda at the time of the genocide in 1994.

Samantha Power, author of "A Problem from Hell": America and the Age of Genocide, expressed at a recent Congressional hearing on Rwanda her fear that, "in ten years we'll be sitting on a similar panel," talking about Darfur instead of Rwanda.

John Prendergast of the International Crisis Group testified before the US House Committee on International Relations on May 6, 2004 that Darfur had become "Rwanda in slow motion," this in his presentation Ethnic Cleansing in Darfur: A New Front Opens in Sudan's Bloody War.

Human Rights Watch, in the introduction to its May 6, 2004 Darfur Destroyed: Ethnic Cleansing by Government and Militia Forces in Western Sudan – its compelling new report on Darfur, based on extensive research in both Darfur and Chad – declares,

Ten years after the Rwandan genocide and despite years of soul-searching, the response of the international community to the events in Sudan has been nothing short of shameful.

What did the UN team find in Kailek? It is important to note first the team's keen awareness that it caught only a glimpse of the horrors of the camps: "We are sure that the team would have learned more about the crimes committed against civilians in the region had it been granted wider access to the areas of conflict. The stories that we have received from the survivors of the acts of mass murder are very painful for us and they remind us of the brutalities of the Rwanda genocide."

Kailek may have gained sufficient profile to force a UN investigation, but there are now dozens of camps completely beyond reach, beyond scrutiny, and in all likelihood beyond hope. The total population has pushed well over 1 million, as more and more of the displaced see no option but to enter the camps.

In aggregate, these concentration camps in Darfur have become an African Auschwitz. Their purpose is human destruction. Those being destroyed have been displaced and concentrated in these camps because of who they are, because of their racial/ethnic identity as Fur, Massaleit, Zaghawa, and members of other African tribal groups.

The specific findings at Kailek thus demand the closest possible attention, as access to other camps will now likely be even more severely restricted. Khartoum's obstructionism is highlighted at several points in the UN team's report. We are morally obliged to infer from these limited data larger conclusions about the camps throughout Darfur. Moreover, numerous reports emerging on a daily basis from Darfuri sources, including the original source reporting on conditions in Kailek, make clear that this particular camp is distinctive only by virtue of having come under scrutiny.

New evidence of Khartoum's efforts to silence witnesses to the realities of Darfur comes from the Sudan Organization Against Torture (SOAT). SOAT reports in a May 10, 2004 Press Release that a number of people from the Fur tribe were arrested for meeting with the International Committee of the Red Cross on May 9, 2004 in order to report on human rights abuses, graves containing bodies from mass executions, and conditions in the camps of Darfur. The men are all being held incommunicado in the regime's Kabkabia security offices.

But tragically, the most painfully telling feature of the Auschwitz analogy is the international response to the crisis, and the increasingly contrived refusal to accept or assign responsibility for what is occurring in Darfur. Nowhere is this rapidly compounding moral failure clearer than at the United Nations. Here, Bertrand Ramcharan, acting UN High Commissioner for Human Rights, offers a signal example of such failure. In presenting a UN human rights report on Darfur, Ramcharan declared in an Associated Press May 8, 2004 dispatch, "first, there is a reign of terror in this areas; second, there is a scorched-earth policy; third, there is repeated war crimes and crimes against humanity; and fourth, this is taking place before our very eyes."

But while declaring further that the Khartoum regime "clearly has supported the militias, organized the militias, and this is taking place with the knowledge and support, and the active complicity of the [Khartoum] government," Ramcharan concluded with a piece of semantic incoherence when he was asked if the government of the Sudan was responsible for the atrocities,

"I condemn the government of Sudan and I do not think it was responsible."

Out of such diplomatic failure of nerve and dishonesty, genocides are fashioned.

For the destruction of Darfur is not spontaneously occurring. Nor is it mere collateral damage, as Khartoum's ambassador to the UN, Fatih Erwa, declared in his contemptuous response to the findings in the UN report, as reported by Reuters in a May 7, 2004 dispatch. On the contrary, Khartoum's campaign of displacement and its system of concentration camps amount to deliberate, systematic, widespread human destruction animated by racial/ethnic hatred. It can be halted only if the génocidaires in Khartoum, who have so far enjoyed immunity from any meaningful international sanctions, are held accountable, and presented with an ultimatum concerning the imminent prospect of humanitarian intervention.

All too predictably, the UN Security Council – though fully briefed by Ramcharan and by the UN humanitarian assessment team recently back from Darfur – declined on May 8, 2004 to condemn Khartoum, let alone begin the urgent task of planning for an international humanitarian intervention. The long slide toward utter catastrophe in Darfur continues to accelerate.

For humanitarian intervention, so conspicuously unmentioned by the Security Council, is now all that can save hundreds of thousands of Darfur civilians. Plans for such intervention must confront squarely and honestly the present realities in Darfur if there is to be any chance for real success. Comments like those by Ramcharan, silence on the part of the UN Security Council, and suggestions from various quarters that the humanitarian crisis is somehow still manageable – all make the task of a meaningful response more difficult.

The first truth that must be acknowledged is that this catastrophe can no longer be averted, only mitigated. As many as fifty thousand or more may have died already; more than twice that number will surely die in the next few months. The world simply must not learn to live with a moral or geopolitical calculus in which the deaths of well over 100,000 Africans are acceptable, or count as anything but a profound international failure.

Secondly, the greatest challenge over the next eighteen months will be providing food for a population that has now missed the 2004 planting season that might have produced a critically important fall harvest. This planting season has been missed because there is no security from *Janjaweed* predations, even as most of those who have been displaced from their lands are desperate to return. Without the fall harvest, and with their own food reserves already exhausted, the people of Darfur will require humanitarian food assistance for more than a year. The affected population is well over 1 million. 1.2 million is the most recent figure from the USAID for the war-affected population, and this number continues to grow steadily.

The only way in which food in sufficient quantity can be supplied for a population this large and dependent, over an extended period of time, is by overland transport. Airlifting such quantities of food for so many people is simply not practicable over the longer term. Since the road arteries in Darfur and eastern Chad will shortly be fully severed by the seasonal rains, the most logistically suitable means of transport is Sudan's rail line from Port Sudan through El Obeid, terminating in Nyala, South Darfur. The challenges of such food transport by rail are very considerable. Implementation will almost certainly entail an infringement upon Khartoum's inevitable claim of "national sovereignty."

But this only serves to put the real issue in the starkest possible form. Is the international community prepared to allow Khartoum's génocidaires to obstruct food aid to over 1 million people? Is the international community prepared to accept the hundreds of thousands of casualties that will follow from such obstruction? Roger Winter, Assistant Administrator at the USAID, testified before the full House International Relations Committee on May 6, 2004 that the number of dead would be between 300,000 and 400,000 if humanitarian access and security in Darfur did not increase dramatically. Is this a number that we may in any way countenance? Can we do so without giving full meaning to Prendergast's terrible phrase: Darfur "is Rwanda in slow motion"?

Acquiescing in Khartoum's claim of "national sovereignty," given the inevitable consequences, is morally indistinguishable from the international refusal to intervene in Rwanda during the 100 days of slaughter in the spring of 1994. The international community either does what is necessary to provide food and security on the ground in Darfur – especially in liberating the death camps and protecting humanitarian workers and assets – or we will indeed be holding meaningless hearings on Darfur ten years from now.

To be sure, some in the UN and the international community are desperate not to confront Khartoum, given the regime's continued support from the Arab League and the Organization of the Islamic Conference. And some are dignifying their refusal to act by virtue of a contrived agnosticism. Dismayingly persuasive accounts of high-level expressions of doubt within the UN and some nongovernmental organizations about the scale of Darfur's catastrophe are emerging. Human rights organizations are being accused of rushing to conclusions, generalizing from insufficient and doubtful data. Again the cynically skeptical query, "where are the piles of dead bodies?"

The question is posed with what seems an astonishingly willful ignorance of both the terms of the 1948 UN Convention on the Prevention and Punishment of the Crime of Genocide, as well as the statistical data that are now available. It certainly takes no cognizance of a key element of the definition of genocide found in the 1948 Genocide Convention, Article 2, Clause C,

> Deliberately inflicting on the group conditions of life calculated to bring about its physical destruction in whole or in part.

Perhaps because this language – so clearly characterizing Khartoum's actions in Darfur – does not require "piles of dead bodies" to justify a finding of genocide, there has been a corresponding skepticism about the projected morality rates for Darfur, particularly in USAID's chart, *Projected Mortality Rates in Darfur, Sudan 2004-2005.*

The data for these projections were the basis for much of USAID Assistant Administrator Roger Winter's recent Congressional testimony. Despite the authority of these data, they seem to have become a focus for doubt, if not scorn. Such doubt and scorn are perversely misplaced.

The epidemiological data in the USAID chart for Darfur draw fully on data from famines in Ethiopia and in Bahr el-Ghazal Province in southern Sudan in 1998. USAID's superb epidemiological experts for this particular report have drawn on the most current data available from Darfur. The authority of the data and methods easily withstands the expedient carping of those evidently intent on downplaying the largest implications of Darfur's catastrophe. The realities in Darfur are in fact so shocking, so clearly bespeak genocide, that we must surmise that there are some who simply wish to avoid the difficult decisions about humanitarian intervention in Darfur, decisions forced by these uncomfortable truths.

But whatever the urges of expediency, we cannot wish away Assistant Administrator Winter's figure for deaths from the impending famine and epidemics – 300,000 to 400,000 without dramatically improved humanitarian access and security. Yet such improvements in access and security are nowhere in sight; nor is there any honest discussion of the means necessary to provide them. All that is apparent is a shameful willingness to continue with present efforts, wholly inadequate, despite a clearly imminent cataclysm.

For those cynical skeptics determined to see the "piles of dead bodies," the wait will not be long. To be sure, they will not be the images familiar from Auschwitz or Rwanda. They will have their own terrible singularity. As Samantha Power has recently reminded us, no two genocides are alike.

June 1, 2004 – Acquiescing Before Unambiguous Genocide in Darfur: The United Nations, Europe, Canada, the Arab League, the African Union

Continued expressions of doubt about the reality of genocide in Darfur are now little more than ignorance, factitious maneuvers of moral self-defense, or a desperate desire not to honor the obligations for international action that are part of Article 1 of the 1948 UN Convention on the Prevention and Punishment of the Crime of Genocide,

> The Contracting Parties confirm that genocide, whether committed in time of peace or in time of war, is a crime under international law which they undertake to prevent and to punish.

The intention of the National Islamic Front regime in Khartoum to destroy the African peoples of Darfur – "as such," in the key phrase of the UN Genocide Convention – can no longer be doubted, nor can the catastrophic consequences of this animating intention be denied by anyone who will only look at the overwhelming body of evidence now clearly before us. In addition to very substantial regional investigations by Amnesty International, Human Rights Watch, and various UN teams, there is now virtually daily confirming evidence coming in the form of news dispatches from Darfur. And there is remarkable, and chilling, congruence and similarity between all these accounts.

What scores of dispatches and reports reveal is unambiguous evidence of genocide. Indeed, we can do no better by way of summarizing the intent and effects of Khartoum's regular military and the *Janjaweed*, its Arab militia proxies, than to recall Article 2, Clause C of the Genocide Convention,

> Deliberately inflicting on the group conditions of life calculated to bring about its physical destruction in whole or in part.

In the case of Darfur, the African tribal groups of the region have had their foodstocks destroyed, their cattle looted, their villages burned, their wells dynamited, bulldozed, or poisoned, their seeds and agricultural implements destroyed. Women and girls are gang-raped and branded, often before their families. Men and boys are rounded up for mass executions. Moreover, Khartoum has "systematically" – this characterization is that of senior UN officials – denied humanitarian access to these terribly distressed peoples.

Those who survive are forced to flee into the desert to escape further attacks by the *Janjaweed* and Khartoum's regular military forces – or vainly to seek refuge in camps such as Kailek in southern Darfur, where a UN inter-agency investigative team found in their April 24, 2004 report, *United Nations Inter-Agency Fact Finding and Rapid Assessment Mission: Kailek Town, South Darfur,* a strategy of systematic and deliberate starvation, a policy of imprisonment, a policy of forced starvation, an unreported cata-strophic child mortality rate of 8-9 per day, and the continued obstruction of humanitarian aid for this critically distressed, forcibly confined popula-tion. This assessment led these professional humanitarian aid workers to make explicit comparison to the Rwandan genocide.

Can there be a shred of intellectually respectable doubt that such actions do not have as their intention "deliberately inflicting on these groups con-ditions of life calculated to bring about their physical destruction in whole or in part"? We should bear in mind here that the targeted African tribal groups include – in addition to the Fur, Massaleit, and Zaghawa – a number of other African groups. The UK Minority Rights Group rightly reminds us in their May 19, 2004 report that this list includes the Kietinga, the Dajo, the Medoob, also known as Midob and Midop, and the Tunjur. These groups are also "victims of the current atrocities."

Some perhaps demand even more explicit evidence of genocidal "inten-tion" than Darfur so abundantly offers. Such a perverse evidentiary stan-dard substitutes an impossible legal requirement for common sense. In dealing with questions of "intention" to commit genocide in Darfur, we are hardly confronted with any complex legal issues, or philosophical questions about states of mind. For the purposes of moral judgment and political action, we must do what we always do when there are no explicit declara-tions of intent – no text, for example, in which Khartoum makes explicit its plans for a "final solution" to its "African problem" in Darfur. We infer intent from actions; the more actions, the more evidence of intent. The more relentlessly and exclusively the African tribal groups in Darfur are tar-geted for destruction, the more reasonable the inference that this destruc-tion is intended to destroy them – "as such."

We have enough such evidence; we have more than enough.

Why should it be necessary to belabor the issue of whether or not the destruction of the African peoples of Darfur is genocide? Why shouldn't it be enough that senior UN officials, the US State Department and Agency for International Development, Human Rights Watch, and many, many others have found that what is occurring in Darfur is "ethnic cleansing"? Why shouldn't it be enough that the International Crisis Group has found, in its May 16, 2004 Report, *End the slaughter and starvation in western Sudan*, that as a result of ethnic cleansing, in the best-case scenario, "only" 100,000 people are expected to die in Darfur from disease and malnutrition in the coming months; sadly, there is little reason for even this desperate optimism

Why shouldn't it be enough that recently updated data from the UN on the number of "war-affected," along with data on morality rates from the USAID, suggest that as many as 500,000 people will be die from engineered famine and epidemics in the coming months? For what none can possibly deny is that the impending cataclysm of human destruction is no natural disaster, but derives directly from the way in which Khartoum has chosen to wage war against the insurgency in Darfur, viz. destroying the entire civilian base that might provide support for the insurgency forces.

Why isn't all this enough, even without a finding of genocide?

The answer lies in the shameful acquiescence within the international community that is now all too evident. Darfur, so long as it doesn't reach the perverse gold standard of genocide, does not oblige the contracting parties of the 1948 UN Genocide Convention to "undertake to prevent and to punish" genocide. Since the contracting parties include the US, Canada, the countries of the European Union, and most countries in the Arab League and the African Union, none of these is obliged to act under the Genocide Convention. Rather, they can continue to speak of Darfur as if it were a purely humanitarian crisis, rather than a massive reflection of the consequences of genocidal warfare. Or if shame obliges some response, Khartoum will be subject to a further parade of comments "deploring," "urging," "condemning," "requesting" and "calling on."

Of course none of this hortatory blather matters now. Moreover, such moral self-congratulation only encourages expediency and disingenuousness of a sort embodied in Alan Goulty, Britain's Special Envoy for Sudan. Goulty is one of those most responsible for muting international criticism of the Darfur catastrophe in the interests of getting a deal done in Naivasha between Khartoum and the SPLM/A. This expedient diplomatic strategy of course backfired, disastrously, giving Khartoum powerful incentive to delay for months a final conclusion to an agreement with the south. For as long as Khartoum was able to make it appear that a deal in Naivasha was imminent, the regime felt confident that it could continue its genocidal campaign in Darfur without any robust international criticism from the UK or the US. This accounts for a shamefully great deal of international belated-ness in responding to Darfur.

But Goulty even now is determined to accommodate Khartoum's géno-cidaires rather than move aggressively to save the hundreds of thousands of lives at risk. *The Telegraph* (UK) reported May 31, 2004 that Goulty is dis-missing efforts to impose targeted sanctions against Khartoum's leadership as "dithering," but he casts his reasoning in bizarrely incongruous terms,

> "In the long term, threats of sanctions don't seem likely to produce immediate action and immediate action is what we need."

"Immediate action" is indeed what is needed, but that hardly means that the present, credible threat of targeted UN sanctions against senior National Islamic Front leaders directed at overseas travel and overseas assets would not have at least modest immediate effects. Goulty here is either not think-ing or has become too careless in his expediency.

Even more disturbing is Goulty's dismissal of humanitarian interven-tion to ensure the delivery of humanitarian supplies to Darfur and the creation of safe havens for the more than 1 million internally displaced persons presently at extremely acute risk. Goulty declared in *The Telegraph*, May 31, 2004,

> "[Humanitarian intervention] would be very expensive, fraught with difficulties and hard to set up in a hurry."

Yes, humanitarian intervention to save hundreds of thousands of lives would be "very expensive, fraught with difficulties and hard to set up in a hurry," as has been repeatedly stressed in all calls for humanitarian inter-vention. But is the difficulty of such intervention reason enough for not attempting what alone will provide the food, medical supplies, and security necessary to save hundred of thousands of lives from genocidal destruc-tion? What moral universe does Mr. Goulty inhabit that such difficulties become insuperable obstacles?

And to be sure, intervention will be very expensive, though likely no more expensive than piece-meal efforts to provide humanitarian aid for so many people over such a large area for over a year without efficient access.

How much are African lives worth, Mr. Goulty? Perhaps a budget, or moral calculus of "dollars per life," can be provided so that the world knows how much is too much for people who have the misfortune of being the victims of genocide in Africa.

And yes, such a humanitarian intervention will be very difficult to set up in a hurry – the more so because of callous comments such as those by Mr. Goulty.

If we wish to understand the importance of declaring the realities of Darfur by their appropriate name – genocide – we can do no better than to examine closely what lies behind Mr. Goulty's refusal to work for or support humanitarian intervention, or threaten sanctions against the génocidaires in Khartoum.

But temporizing by Goulty and his ilk within the international community can do nothing to halt the relentless movement of the seasonal rains toward Darfur and the Chad-Darfur border, or to halt the continuing brutal predations of the *Janjaweed*, or to obscure Khartoum's recent aerial attacks against villagers in flagrant violation of the terms of the April 8, 2004 cease-fire, or to retard spiking mortality rates in the concentration camps, or to improve humanitarian access in Darfur, which Khartoum is now restricting by new means. Darfur's catastrophe continues to accelerate, and an abyss of human suffering and destruction opens ever more widely, despite all efforts to temporize.

Of extremely urgent concern is the impending loss of road corridors in Darfur and Chad because of the rains that have now begun. The consequences of this seasonal development are captured in the May 28, 2004 UN News Centre dispatch, "Rains in Chad interrupt refugee transfers from Darfur, Sudan, UN agency says,"

The United Nations refugee agency got the first indication of how the rainy season could block the transfer of thousands of Sudanese refugees from the insecure Chadian border when two of its teams had to stop driving their vehicles for safety's sake after downpours lasting less than an hour. Heavy rain fell for just 45 minutes yesterday in the Abeche area of eastern Chad and one UNHCR team had to stop travelling on one side of a seasonally dry riverbed, or "wadi," because of the sudden rushing waters. The team was soon joined by other UNHCR staff members, returning to Abeche from Farchana camp, who walked from the other side of the wadi after abandoning their vehicle to avoid having it sink into mud and water. "This signals the sort of challenges we're going to face as the rainy season sets in," said UNHCR spokeswoman Jennifer Pagonis at a news briefing in Geneva.

The dispatch continued by noting "the situation is especially urgent as the cross-border attacks [by Khartoum's *Janjaweed* militia] have continued, UNHCR [UN High Commission for Refugees] said."

The Guardian (UK) also reported June 1, 2004 on the threat posed by the seasonal rains that have now arrived and are slowly encompassing more of the regions affected by war in Darfur and Chad,

> An ominous blue bubble on an aid agency map, for a remote con-
> flict in an even remoter part of Africa, could mean mass starvation
> before June is out. The map, published on the web by the Famine
> Early Warning System Network, shows the "rain timeline" for the
> seasonal monsoon now moving northwards into eastern Chad and
> the Darfur region of western Sudan. Day by day more territory now
> suffering from hot winds and blowing dust will bear the even
> heavier burden of rainstorms which turn roads into swamps and
> wadis into torrents.

As overland corridors in Chad and Darfur are severed by these rains, the necessity of finding alternative land routes becomes ever more urgent. For there is not nearly enough food, or medical supplies, pre-positioned for distribution by the humanitarian personnel that Khartoum is only now gradually and partially allowing into the region. These aid workers will arrive and almost immediately begin overseeing what *The Guardian* correctly reports as the high likelihood that there will be "mass starvation before June is out."

Moreover, since there has been no spring planting, and thus no fall harvest, famine affecting a huge percentage of Darfur's total population will continue into 2005. This catastrophe, so clearly and remorselessly advancing, can be mitigated only by the most robust and urgent humanitarian intervention – one that in the next few weeks would internationalize the rail line running from Port Sudan through Khartoum and El Obeid and on to Nyala, South Darfur, which is strategically located for distribution to many key areas.

Security for the more than 1 million internally displaced persons, many in highly threatened concentration camps, must also be a key part of any humanitarian intervention. For even as Khartoum's "systematic" denial of humanitarian access has done so much to prevent food and medicine from reaching the displaced African populations of Darfur, the regime continues to give free rein to its *Janjaweed* militias in attacking these same populations – producing yet greater displacement and subsequent swelling of camp populations. IRIN reported on June 1, 2004 that,

[The US Agency for International Development] said that armed Janjawid militia were continuing to attack civilians in all three states of Darfur and that killings, rapes, beatings, looting and burning of homes were still being reported. In Northern Darfur State, attacks on villages had only decreased because "a significant number" of villages had already been destroyed, while attacks on camps for internally displaced persons were continuing.

Khartoum is also continuing with its aerial attacks on civilian targets. One such attack was widely reported several days ago by various wire services, with additional details of the attack from Eltigani Ateem Seisi, former governor of Darfur. Reuters reported on May 28, 2004,

The witnesses [from a village in West Sudan] told Reuters by mobile and satellite telephone from the area that an Antonov plane and helicopters bombed the village of Tabit, about 25 miles southwest of al-Fashir, the capital of Northern Darfur state. . . . "There were two helicopters and one Antonov and they started bombarding the market," said one witness, asking not to be identified.

Agence France-Presse provided additional detail on May 28, 2004,

Government air strikes on a market near Al-Fasher, capital of west Sudan's war-torn North Darfur State, left 20 people dead and 17 wounded. An Antonov jet and two helicopter gunships were used in Friday's attack on the market in the town of Tabet, said Muhammad Mersal, who heads the office of SLM secretary general Mani Minaoui, in a telephone call from Darfur.

Eltigani Ateem Seisi in his May 29, 2004 e-mail to the author has provided yet further information on the basis of contacts on the ground in Darfur, indicating that "22 villagers were killed in the market place" as they prepared for Friday evening prayers. The names of many of the civilians killed in the attack were also provided.

Humanitarian access continues to be impeded in highly consequential ways, despite Khartoum's promise of a week ago to expedite visas for humanitarian personnel. Though partially fulfilling this particular pledge, and though the UN is obviously trying to encourage Khartoum to provide more access by celebrating very limited achievements, a June 1, 2004 IRIN dispatch makes clear that Khartoum has simply resorted to other means in restricting humanitarian access and the delivery of food and medicine to those most critically in need. A good example of the regime's ongoing intent to deny humanitarian supplies to the population is the contrivance of various bureaucratic obstacles,

> The advocacy group Refugees International (RI) said last week that "Khartoum was continuing to place obstacles" in the way of agencies seeking to respond to the Darfur crisis by requiring relief supplies to be transported on Sudanese trucks and distributed by Sudanese agencies.
>
> [This obstruction occurs even as Doctors Without Borders/ Médecins Sans Frontières] warned last month that the entire population of Darfur, numbering several million, was "teetering on the verge of mass starvation" as a direct result of the conflict.
>
> A further problem was Khartoum's insistence that all medical supplies being shipped into Sudan needed to be tested before they were used, Refugees International added.

Nothing could better indicate Khartoum's unfathomable callousness than the "insistence that all medical supplies being shipped into Sudan needed to be tested before they were used." Children are dying in numbers that constitute "catastrophic mortality rates," according to MSF, and dying often from lack of medical supplies, including inoculations, antibiotics, and surgical kits and supplies. This is the context in which Khartoum is insisting that all medical supplies be tested, with delays of unforgivable length.

IRIN's June 1, 2004 report continues,

> A more serious impediment to the delivery of aid was the reported "requirement" by Khartoum that agencies only use local NGOs to deliver aid, he told IRIN. The new policy had "hampered effective distribution of assistance, including food," the UN reported last week, stating that the existing local NGOs were limited in number and lacked the necessary capacity.

Khartoum is of course well aware that its insistence on local NGOs will adversely affect efficient food delivery; indeed, this is precisely the point. The tactful words of the UN obscure how this deliberate inefficiency is, in effect, the continuation of genocide by other means.

IRIN's June 1, 2004 report also gives a synopsis of a May 2004 USAID Assessment,

> The US Agency for International Development (USAID) reported last week that Khartoum was "interfering" in humanitarian aid efforts. Government officials had questioned relief workers on their reporting of human rights abuses, told agencies not to carry out protection activities, and threatened to expel organisations failing to comply with restrictions. Khartoum also required 72-hour advance notification for passengers travelling on UN flights to Darfur, which was "an impediment to the rapid deployment of emergency staff and equipment," USAID added.

All this is in addition to the continued denial of access to some aid workers from the UN Office for the Coordination of Humanitarian Affairs. IRIN's

June 1, 2004 report recalls the deliberate "[delaying of] some relief assistance, equipment and vehicles essential to the delivery of aid," and the requirement that all "staff already in Darfur still had to give the local humanitarian aid commissioners 24-hour notice when they were travelling outside the three main towns of Nyala, Al-Junaynah and Al-Fashir." This latter policy ensures that there is no real independence of movement, even as it is part of Khartoum's larger policy – still in effect – of denying all humanitarian access to the very large areas of rural Darfur controlled by the insurgency groups, the SLM/A and JEM.

What is the international response to genocide in Darfur? What means are being contemplated to provide humanitarian assistance that can truly respond to the needs of the 2 million the UN now estimates are "war-affected" and at acute risk? What is the world prepared to do to save hundreds of thousands of lives at risk because of another African genocide?

The UN Security Council has registered its "grave concern."

The African Union will be deploying all of 10 cease-fire monitors to Darfur Wednesday June 2, 2004, with vague possibilities of expansion. Darfur is an area roughly the size of France, and the cease-fire nominally to be monitored has largely collapsed.

Germany and France seem to be doing their best to offer nothing more than unctuous hand-wringing, and are finding plenty of company in the EU.

Canada continues to mouth the platitudes of "soft power," which for Darfur amounts to little more than vague moral drooling.

The UK as represented by Alan Goulty is committed to a "quiet diplomacy" with Khartoum's génocidaires that will certainly work to convince the regime that it has nothing to fear from continuing its violent and intransigent ways.

The US, for all its commitment to Sudan, has yet to determine upon a well-articulated course of fully adequate humanitarian response – and has yet to explain why such a response will not inevitably entail humanitarian intervention.

And the Arab League seemed content in its recent Tunis summit to do nothing meaningful to stop the slaughter of Muslims in Darfur, though there has been some belated public recognition that something quite terrible is happening in the western part of Arab-League member Sudan.

But the rains have arrived; the aggregate mortality rates from camps and a compilation of statistics from various humanitarian assessments suggest that the weekly civilian death toll is well above 2,000 human beings, primarily children. There is not nearly enough food or medicine in place or moving along a corridor that will remain open once the rains begin in earnest. And the grim mortality projections from the US Agency for International Development make clear that hundreds of thousands will die if more is not done in the very near future.

If we wish to quantify the "slow-motion" Darfur genocide of 2003-2005, we may at present either look back to the 40,000 to 60,000 who have already died – or ahead to the 300,000 to 500,000 who will die without humanitarian intervention. There can be no forgiveness for the acquiescence that has already seen tens of thousands die. There can be no moral comprehension of the refusal to act when hundreds of thousands may yet be saved. In the end, it appears that the only lesson of the grim 10th anniversary of the Rwandan genocide is that the world has learned no lesson about genocide in Africa.

June 16, 2004 –Unmistakable Evidence of Genocidal Intent – The Issue in a Legal Context

For a long time, Khartoum has deliberately denied, impeded, and made excessively difficult humanitarian access to the war-affected African peoples of Darfur. Tom Vraalsen, UN special envoy for humanitarian affairs in Sudan, declared on December 8, 2003 in a Note to the Emergency Relief Coordinator, *Sudan: Humanitarian Crisis in Darfur*, that the denial of aid to these peoples was "systematic," ultimately based on race/ethnicity. For, as was the case then and now, the war-affected peoples of Darfur most in need of humanitarian assistance are overwhelmingly the African tribal groups, primarily the Fur, the Massaleit, and the Zaghawa. These are the people who have been and will be destroyed by Khartoum's past and continuing denial of humanitarian access.

The deliberate obstruction of humanitarian aid offers clear and unambiguous evidence of intent to destroy these peoples "as such." It is yet another aspect of Khartoum's wider effort to "deliberately inflict on the [African groups] conditions of life calculated to bring about [their] physical destruction in whole or in part" under the definition for genocide framed by the 1948 UN Convention on the Prevention and Punishment of the Crime of Genocide, Article 2, Clause C.

Certainly the world knows full well that it is Darfur's African tribal groups that have been displaced or turned into refugees by Khartoum's military and Arab militia allies, the *Janjaweed*. This is what has prompted the so far diffident characterizations of realities in Darfur as "ethnic cleansing." But the world should also know full well that hundreds of thousands of people from these African tribal groups have been forced into concentration camps – the majority without humanitarian access – where there are continuous executions, and where extermination grows directly out of living conditions deliberately made intolerable.

It is the African peoples of Darfur that make up the overwhelming majority of the 2.2 million people now defined as "war-affected" by the UN, the US, and the European Union. And it is this "war-affected" population that is critically dependent upon the very humanitarian aid so relentlessly and resourcefully obstructed by Khartoum. Given the numbers of people at risk, we must speak in terms of a "very substantial part" of the African tribal populations of Darfur, whose destruction holds clear potential for a "highly significant impact on the populations as a whole." In short, given the racial/ethnic character of the populations most acutely in need of humanitarian aid, the denial and obstruction of such aid is clear evidence of genocidal intent.

Now that the Bush administration has committed itself to make a legal determination of whether the actions of the Khartoum regime and the *Janjaweed* rise to the level of genocide in Darfur, it will be useful to keep in mind some of the legal standards that have been established over the past decade. Further, an especially significant review of the crime of genocide, and the nature of the "intent" essential to any finding of genocide, has recently been undertaken by the Appeals Chamber of the International Tribunal for violations of international law in the former Yugoslavia. The case, involving a review of "Prosecutor v. Radislav Krstic," Case No. IT-98-33-T, speaks directly to various questions that bear on any finding of genocide in Darfur, and the question of whether the "intent" of Khartoum and its *Janjaweed* allies is genocidal.

At all points, the case review strongly supports a finding, *mutatis mutandis*, of genocide in Darfur. In particular, the deliberate, systematic denial of humanitarian access to the African populations of Darfur conforms to various stipulations and precedents cited by the Appeals Chamber.

We should recall here that the UN, the US, Human Rights Watch, the International Crisis Group, and many other authoritative sources are already using the term "ethnic cleansing" to describe realities in Darfur, this in order to highlight the racial/ethnic animus in the vast human destruction and displacement. It is in this context that we must ask about genocide and the meaning of the fully compelling evidence that Khartoum continues to obstruct, in clearly intentional fashion, humanitarian access to the African populations of Darfur. Khartoum's obstructionism has of course been condemned, but predictably without any apparent effect, as a June 14, 2004 Voice of America report illustrates,

> Deputy US Ambassador James Cunningham complained to the Security Council Monday that the Khartoum government is continuing to hamper the efforts to get humanitarian aid and workers to Darfur. "Unfortunately, the government continues to deny release of vehicles needed by humanitarian relief agencies," he said. "It has also in some cases denied release of radio equipment needed for workers to securely deploy to remote areas to deliver aid. In addition, the government has also delayed food shipments from Port of Sudan, potentially to the point of making the food useless."

The Associated Press noted in a June 15, 2004 dispatch,

> UN humanitarian chief Jan Egeland criticized the Sudanese government Monday for blocking aid workers, food and equipment from reaching the Darfur region, where 2 million people desperately need humanitarian aid. Calling Darfur the worst humanitarian crisis in the world today, Egeland told the UN Security Council that relief agencies are trying to get food, water, sanitation equipment and tents to the western Sudanese region before the rainy season. "We've been working for many, many weeks in a race against the clock, and we see that the government which should do its utmost to help us is still not helping," he said. "Some ministers are helping us, but some of their subordinates are sabotaging us." . . .

Egeland said UN international staff were now able to travel to Darfur, but other aid groups still faced visa problems. He also said red tape has prevented ships carrying food and equipment for Darfur from unloading for weeks. . . . . "Nowhere else in the world are so many lives at stake as in Darfur at the moment," [Egeland] said.

Reuters in a June 14, 2004 disptach continued,

Sudan is blocking aid groups from getting food and medicine to hundreds of thousands of people in its western Darfur region, despite promises to the contrary, a senior UN official said on Monday. . . . Groups, such as Médecins Sans Frontières (Doctors Without Borders), are experiencing undue delays in getting visas, bringing in equipment, medicine and food. For example, [UN humanitarian chief Jan Egeland] said, radios needed for emergency communications were stripped from vehicles because Sudanese authorities believed they were a security liability. "If they have no radio, they cannot go into Darfur," he said. "They see this as a security risk for the government. We see it as a security necessity for us."

"People are dying because we were denied access for so long, and people will be dying because we are not able to get through," Egeland said. . . . Egeland said a cease-fire in Darfur was sporadic. "We are still seeing grown men attacking defenseless woman and children with their automatic rifles," he said. Doctors Without Borders said late in May it had 50 pending requests for visas and had medical supplies impounded when they arrived by sea and not by emergency air transport.

Carol Bellamy, head of UNICEF, said in a June 16, 2004 IRIN dispatch,

"It is clear to me that a worsening crisis is upon us," [Carol Bellamy] said following a visit to Darfur. "The number of displaced people . . . continues to grow." . . . The images of burnt-out villages and markets on the road from al-Junaynah, the capital of Western Darfur, southward to Sisi were stark in her mind, she said, and they were repeated hundreds of times across Darfur.

[Bellamy said] there were not enough NGOs in Darfur to provide aid. "I seldom recall coming to a place with this expansion of internally displaced people, to see so little going on. There are almost no NGOs," she stated. "I understand it's not their fault – it's hard to get in. We in the UN have to work with NGOs, so the limited number of partners is a real problem for us."

A US Senate Foreign Relations Committee hearing of June 15, 2004 heard testimony from senior Bush administration officials and Sudan specialists, as this same-day Voice of America broadcast reported,

John Prendergast [of the International Crisis Group] says the Sudanese government is now using starvation and disease as weapons of war, blocking humanitarian relief from getting to those in need. Bush administration officials agree. "Have they been denying access to those who could go there to help the civil population or to see and report on what was going on? Yes, they do deny access," said Roger Winter, assistant administrator for the Democracy, Conflict and Humanitarian Assistance Bureau at the US Agency for International Development. "There has been very restricted access."

A June 15, 2004 Agence France-Presse dispatch also reported that the US State Department spoke out on Darfur's obstructionism,

"We're deeply concerned that, despite assurances from the government of Sudan that they are providing the humanitarian access, that there is, in fact, still considerable blockages to getting aid to the people in need," State Department spokesman Richard Boucher said. He said Khartoum continued to deny the release of vehicles needed to transport food and other assistance to Darfur, was refusing in some cases to release communications equipment needed by relief workers to coordinate their work and delayed the distribution of foreign food which has been sent by ship to Port Sudan. In addition, Mr. Boucher accused Sudanese authorities of continuing "to harass or delay humanitarian workers seeking to administer to the needy."

Khartoum's official views were offered by NIF Vice President Ali Osman Taha during a trip to Egypt, as Agence France-Press reported in the same dispatch,

> [Taha] accused the international media of deliberately magnifying the scale of the humanitarian problem in the region. He also claimed that the conflict was fabricated by the West.

In aggregate, these assessments from UN officials, humanitarian aid officials, Sudan specialists, and US government officials make clear a policy on Khartoum's part that continues what Ambassador Vraalsen described half a year ago as the "systematic" denial of humanitarian access. Six months after this UN assessment, access continues to be "systematically" manipulated, impeded and obstructed.

This represents an unconscionable moral and political failure on the part of the international community, a refusal to respond to what has clearly been genocide in the making. Khartoum for its part, sensing that it will pay no real price for obstructionism, has merely varied its methods of obstruction. The urgency of the demands for access we now hear from various international actors is months overdue – and this terrible belatedness has ensured that hundreds of thousands of people from the African populations of Darfur will die. They will die because their deaths are clearly what Khartoum intends.

This is genocide. Indeed, it is so clearly genocide that one must search for reasons to explain why any other characterization is offered.

The most conspicuous reason is that to characterize the present realities in Darfur as genocide forces an inevitable question. Why wasn't this characterization appropriate last month? Or several months ago? For the evidence has not changed in character. The numbers are of course increasing, indeed dramatically, but not in ways that somehow cross a particular categorical threshold. Nor are there new or different actions by Khartoum and its militia allies, or new evidence about Khartoum's intentions in committing or supporting these actions. Perversely, failure to have characterized Darfur as genocide in the past seems to make it more difficult to reach this determination in the present.

To be sure, there is evidence of considerable ignorance, willful or otherwise, about the meaning of genocide. UN Undersecretary for Humanitarian Affairs Jan Egeland offers an ironic example in a June 15, 2004 Associated Press dispatch,

> The conflict in the Darfur region of western Sudan is the worst in the world today and a result of "ethnic cleansing," [Egeland] said, "I think it's not genocide yet, and we can prevent it from becoming one."

But what can this possibly mean? What can be done to "prevent" Darfur from "becoming a genocide"? Is there some numerical threshold that Egeland feels must be crossed before genocide is reached? Are the staggering numbers that prompted Egeland to declare in December 2003 that "Darfur is probably the world's worst humanitarian crisis" not great enough? How many hundreds of thousands, killed or destined to be killed from deliberate actions, are required for a finding of genocide?

Are 2.2 million "war-affected" people not enough, even when the evidence is clear that they are at acute risk precisely because Khartoum has "deliberately inflicted on [these African groups] conditions of life calculated to bring about [their] physical destruction in whole or in part"? What of Amnesty International's prediction that "there are 350,000 people who are most likely to die in this period [the rainy season]"? Is this figure too low? And what of the MSF declaration that "the whole population [of Darfur] is teetering on the verge of mass starvation"? Or the grim assessment of the consequences of continued aid denial from the USAID, reported on June 3, 2004 by Agence France-Presse,

> "We estimate right now if we get relief in, we'll lose a third of a million people, and if we don't the death rates could be dramatically higher, approaching a million people," said US Agency for International Development (USAID) chief Andrew Natsios after a high-level UN aid meeting [in Geneva].

Are these numbers not more than enough to cross any conceivably required threshold for a determination of genocide in the context of Darfur?

Or is there some further evolution of "intent" on the part of the Khartoum regime that Egeland and others expect to see so that the "intent requirement" of the 1948 UN Genocide Convention is more fully met? What could "prevent" the racially/ethnically animated human destruction we now see in Darfur from becoming, or in fact being, genocide? What difference does Egeland mean to imply by distinguishing between "ethnic cleansing" and "genocide"?

We should bear in mind here that the UN General Assembly, when initially deploying the phrase "ethnic cleansing" in 1991, in the context of the Balkan conflicts, made clear that the phrase referred to a "form of genocide." A review of the term by UN lawyers in 1993, again in the context of the Balkans, found that "ethnic cleansing" "might well be considered genocide under the [genocide] convention" as Samantha Power notes in *"A Problem from Hell": America and the Age of Genocide,* page 483.

But the most substantial guidance comes from the Appeals Chamber of the International Tribunal for violations of international law in the former Yugoslavia, review of "Prosecutor v. Radislav Krstic," Case No. IT-98-33-T. Radislav Krstic was charged in connection with his role in the slaughter of 7,000 to 8,000 Bosnian Muslim men in the UN "safe area" of Srebrenica in July 1995, as well as the movement of Bosnian women, children, and elderly from the Srebrenica enclave. The Appeals Chamber speaks comprehensively to the issues of both "quantity" and "intent" in a determination of genocide. Attention to this articulate, intelligent, and deeply historically informed review should clear away some of the fuzzy and disinguous thinking about genocide that has begun to proliferate. Salient paragraphs from this document are identified and discussed below.

From an international legal perspective, how many people among the African populations of Darfur must be destroyed or confront "conditions of life calculated to bring about [their] physical destruction in whole or in part" in order to justify a determination of genocide?

The Appeals Chamber review notes that, "It is well established that where a conviction for genocide relies on the intent to destroy a protected group [i.e., "national, ethnical, racial or religious" group] 'in part,' the part must be a substantial part of that group. . . . The part targeted must be significant enough to have an impact on the group as a whole" (Paragraph 8).

In paragraph 10, citing Raphael Lemkin, who coined the term "genocide" and who was instrumental in drafting the UN Genocide Convention of 1948, the Appeals Chamber notes, " 'the destruction in part must be of a substantial nature so as to affect the entirety.' "

If we survey the situation in Darfur, with a total pre-war population of approximately 6.5 million, with an African majority but with large Arab tribal populations, it is clear that the 1.3 million persons – overwhelmingly African – internally displaced or displaced into Chad are a "substantial" part of the population. A fortiori, the figure of 2.2 million "war-affected" people, with the vast majority at acute risk because of Khartoum's deliberate impeding and obstructing of humanitarian access, also meets the criterion of "a substantial part of the [African tribal] groups," with a clear threat of "having an impact on these groups as a whole."

The Appeals Chamber review also notes in Paragraph 13,

> The historical examples of genocide also suggest that the area of the perpetrators' activity and control, as well as the possible extent of their reach, should be considered. Nazi Germany may have intended only to eliminate Jews within Europe alone; that ambition probably did not extend, even at the height of its power, to an undertaking of that enterprise on a global scale. Similarly, the perpetrators of genocide in Rwanda did not seriously contemplate the elimination of the Tutsi population beyond the country's borders. . . . The intent to destroy formed by a perpetrator of the genocide will always be limited by the opportunity presented to him.

This is a particularly important consideration, given the means available to Khartoum. Obliged, at least in part, to refrain from using its military air power by virtue of the April 8, 2004 cease-fire; constrained, in part, by the cease-fire and international attention to be more circumspect in its genocidal ambitions, Khartoum is presently "limited by the opportunity presented to [the regime]" to obstruct humanitarian access and to refuse to rein in the primary instrument of direct civilian destruction, the *Janjaweed* militia.

It is impossible to avoid the conclusion that Khartoum's actions – "systematically" obstructing humanitarian aid – deliberately threaten a "substantial part" of the African groups, that this will "have an impact on these groups as a whole," and that the extent of genocidal activity by Khartoum is constrained in significant ways by limitations on the "opportunities presented."

The Appeals Chamber review noted a number of issues bearing on a determination of "intent" to commit genocide in Paragraph 32. This is perhaps the central issue in any debate about genocide in Darfur. A particularly important finding is that while genocidal intent "must be supported by the factual matrix,"

> the offense of genocide does not require proof that the perpetrator chose the most efficient method to accomplish his objective of destroying the targeted part. Even where the method selected will not implement the perpetrator's intent to the fullest, leaving that destruction incomplete, this ineffectiveness alone does not preclude a finding of genocidal intent.

In short, there needn't be a Nazi-like efficiency in killing or destroying, in whole or in part, the African peoples of Darfur. That the methods previously and presently deployed by Khartoum will accomplish enough to meet the "substantiality" criterion is all that must be established for the purposes of finding that these methods may constitute genocide.

The Appeals Chamber review stated in Paragraph 33 that "genocidal intent may be inferred, among other facts, from evidence of 'other culpable acts systematically directed against the same group.' " In other words, Khartoum's systematic denial of humanitarian access to the African populations of Darfur may be considered in the context of the systematic destruction of African villages, now numbering in the thousands; the systematic destruction of African agricultural capacity in the form of poisoning and blowing up water wells and irrigations systems; in the form of destruction of seeds, fruit trees, agricultural implements, and critical agricultural livestock; and the widespread practices of execution, rape, abduction, and torture systematically directed against the African populations of Darfur.

The process of inferring genocidal intent from particular atrocities, atrocities such as have been reported in great number, for example, by Human Rights Watch, Amnesty International, the UN High Commission for Human Rights investigation of April 2004, the UN inter-agency investigation of the

Kailek concentration camp April 24 2004, is also illuminated in a discussion of legal precedent by the Appeals Chamber review Paragraph 34,

> Where direct evidence of genocidal intent is absent, the intent may still be inferred from the factual circumstances of the crime. The inference that a particular atrocity was motivated by genocidal intent may be drawn, moreover, even where the individuals to whom the intent is attributable are not precisely identified. If the crime committed satisfied the other requirements of genocide, and if the evidence supports the inference that the crime was motivated by the intent to destroy, in whole in part, a protected group, a finding that genocide has occurred may be entered.

We need not know the particular perpetrators of individual atrocities to reach a finding of genocide. But to the degree that such genocidal atrocities can be tied to specific individuals in the *Janjaweed* command structure, or in the intelligence, military, or political structure of Khartoum's NIF regime, this becomes cumulative evidence of responsibility for genocide.

Moreover the nature of this responsibility is specifically articulated by the Appeals Chamber review in paragraph 140,

> The Appeals Chamber has previously explained, on several occasions, that an individual who aids and abets a specific intent offense [e.g., genocide] may be held responsible if he assists the commission of the crime knowing the intent behind the crime.

In considering responsibility for genocide on the part of individual members of the Khartoum regime, actions such as heavily arming the *Janjaweed*, coordinating militarily with the *Janjaweed*, bombing and helicopter gunship missions in support of the *Janjaweed*, inciting the *Janjaweed* – all constitute acts of genocide, given the known nature and intention of *Janjaweed* attacks against African civilian populations.

The scale of intentional destruction of African tribal groups in Darfur, and the clear intent to destroy these groups as such, mark Khartoum's actions in Darfur as unambiguously genocide. This is clear not only from a common-sense reading of the language of the 1948 UN Convention on the

Prevention and Punishment of the Crime of Genocide, but from the vantage of a fully legally and historically informed analysis of the sort offered recently by the Appeals Chamber of the International Tribunal for the former Yugoslavia.

To be sure, skepticism about genocide can always be contrived on a temporary basis – especially, in the case of Darfur, by those whose inaction has done so much to allow a ghastly slide into the present abysm of suffering and destruction. But the truth will out, and the clarity that some now profess to be beyond them will be brought home with searing force.

There simply can be no reasonable skepticism or agnosticism about the genocidal realities in Darfur, much less about the responsibility of Khartoum for deliberately engineering massive displacement, famine, and epidemic disease among the African peoples of Darfur, especially by denying humanitarian access to these desperately needy civilians. There remains only a decision – daily more costly so long as it is not made – about how much we will to do mitigate the massive and now unavoidable genocidal catastrophe.

June 25, 2005 – "In Darfur, rape is systematically used as a weapon of warfare," Jan Egeland

Egeland's recourse to the present tense in describing the use of rape as an ongoing weapon of war in Darfur is entirely appropriate. The *Janjaweed* are continuing a brutal campaign of systematic sexual violence directed against the women and girls of non-Arab or African tribal groups. Khartoum for its part remains deeply complicit in this campaign, now in its third year, as Egeland made clear in his characteristically forthright statement in a June 21, 2005 Reuters dispatch,

> [Egeland said] the impact of [sexual] violence was compounded by Sudan's failure to acknowledge the scale of the problem and to act to stop it. "Not only do the Sudanese authorities fail to provide effective physical protection, they inhibit access to treatment." He said in some cases unmarried women who became pregnant after being raped had been treated as criminals and subjected to further brutal treatment by police. "This is an affront to all humanity," Egeland said.

The consequences of systematic, racially/ethnically-animated sexual violence in Darfur are enormous. Rape as a weapon of war is one the largest elements of the insecurity defining most of Darfur; sexual violence increasingly paralyzes civilian movement and powerfully circumscribes the grim lives within overcrowded and under-served camps for displaced persons. More broadly, insecurity continues to attenuate humanitarian reach and efficacy.

The threat of rape severely inhibits the gathering of firewood, water, and animal fodder. The collapse in Darfur's food production is also directly related to the ongoing intimidating effects of sexual violence. More generally, rape – and the impunity with which it is committed by Khartoum's proxy military force in Darfur – contributes to a desperate decline in morale within many camps and among displaced persons, some now entering their third year in this debilitating condition.

A powerful study of sexual violence in Darfur was published in October 2004 and deserves the closest attention. Written by Tara Gingerich, JD, MA and Jennifer Leaning, MD, SMH, *The Use of Rape as a Weapon of War in the conflict in Darfur, Sudan* was prepared for the USAID/OTI under the auspices of the Harvard School of Public Health and the Francois-Xavier Bagnoud Center for Health and Human Rights. Virtually all of the conclusions and assessments made in this detailed and historically informed study continue to be borne out by realities on the ground more than half a year later.

Certainly the central claim of the report stands without meaningful challenge (from page 1),

> Our findings suggest that the military forces attacking the non-Arab people of Darfur, the *Janjaweed* in collaboration with forces of the Government of Sudan, have inflicted a massive campaign of rape as a deliberate aspect of their military assault against the lives, livelihoods, and land of this population. . . .
>
> The highest priority now is to introduce a measure of real protection for the populations now displaced in Darfur and Chad in order to reduce the ongoing risk of rape to women and girls as they move outside camps and villages to find firewood and water.

But again, more than half a year later, such protection is nowhere in sight. Indeed, June 22, 2005 Congressional testimony by US Deputy Secretary of State Robert Zoellick as reported by the Associated Press on the same day works to ensure that current plans for an expanded but still wholly inadequate AU deployment will constitute the full extent of international response to ongoing genocidal violence and destruction,

> The Bush administration is opposed to the dispatch of US or European forces to help enhance security in Sudan's Darfur region because they could be vulnerable to attack by terrorists, [Zoellick] said Wednesday. "The region is populated by some bloodthirsty, cold-hearted killers," Zoellick said, mentioning Somalia in particular as one possible source.

Leaving aside the disgracefully lazy geography invoked, Zoellick is apparently unaware of the grim irony in declaring that Western troops cannot be deployed to Darfur because of "bloodthirsty, cold-hearted killers" in Somalia well over 1,000 miles away – even as defenseless women and girls in Darfur are daily and directly vulnerable to the "bloodthirsty, cold-hearted killers" that are the *Janjaweed*. Genocide is a brutal, ongoing reality in Darfur – an assessment recently confirmed in the abstract by President Bush. Yet the US remains content with an "Africa only" response, despite the clear inadequacies of the AU, even with NATO logistical and material support. Zoellick offered nothing in his Congressional testimony that suggests how the deployment of even 7,700 AU personnel by September 2005, a suspiciously optimistic time-frame, can address the multiple security tasks all too conspicuous in Darfur – including the protection of women and girls from sexual violence.

Though there can be no denying the significant physical risks associated with humanitarian military intervention augmented by American, European, Australian, or Canadian troops, these risks are almost certainly less than those confronted in Iraq and Afghanistan, even as the basis for participation in such military action is morally and legally much less ambiguous: halting genocide, halting the deliberate destruction of the African ethnic groups in Darfur because of who they are, "as such." Here we should bear in mind two of the acts of genocide specified in Article 2 of the 1948 UN Convention on the Prevention and Punishment of the Crime of Genocide,

[b] Causing serious bodily or mental harm to members of the group;

[d] Imposing measures intended to prevent births within the group.

Considerable international jurisprudential thought has been given to the particular meaning of these phrases, but both have a clear bearing on how we consider the implications of systematic, ethnically-targeted rape in Darfur. Rape causes extremely serious bodily harm, particularly the gang-rape so characteristic in Darfur, as does rape accompanied by non-sexual violence, also typical in Darfur. Rape causes excruciating mental trauma. And for a variety of reasons, rape also serves as a means of preventing births on the part of women within the targeted African groups. Those girls and women raped are often socially ostracized, and become much less valued as potential wives; violent rape often leads to medical complications that make further child-bearing impossible or much riskier; and rape often carries the threat of disease and infection, including direct threats to the lives of potential mothers.

Rape as committed by Khartoum's military proxy in Darfur is entirely consistent with the genocidal ambitions that have been in evidence for over two years, and contributes significantly to the current genocide by attrition that has succeeded the previous campaign of large-scale violent destruction of the lives and livelihoods of Darfur's African tribal groups. That sexual violence continues on a significant and consequential basis has been confirmed by UN reports, including the June 2005 report by the Secretary-General, and by reports from human rights observers and humanitarian organizations on the ground in Darfur.

But for Zoellick and the Bush administration – and clearly with the support of the European Union and officials within NATO – there is no willingness to contribute US or European personnel to this most urgent humanitarian intervention. Genocide, including rape as a weapon of war in Darfur, will as a consequence proceed at a pace limited only by the drastically inadequate AU deployment, currently operating without a mandate for civilian or humanitarian protection.

"Time must be given for an African solution to work," Zoellick declared in his Congressional testimony as a Voice of America broadcast reported on June 22, 2005. But as Zoellick well knows, the AU has been shamefully reluctant to admit its own fundamental limitations, has failed to secure a mandate for civilian protection, and has deployed, in well over half a year, only about two thirds of the 3,500 personnel planned for early autumn 2004. The AU has no capacity – either in material, manpower, or logistics – to reach the 7,700 target figure for September 2005, a date much too far in the future given critical current needs for protection.

NATO logistics and other assistance will help, but in fundamentally limited ways. Most significantly, 7,700 personnel are still far too few to address the insecurity that now claims thousands of lives every month. A force at least four times as large is required on an extremely urgent basis to halt the human destruction. Without such intervention, human mortality is poised to increase dramatically during the current rainy season.

Certainly a meaningful political settlement is nowhere in sight. Stalemated peace talks in Abuja, Nigeria may be on the verge of breakdown, with the largest of the two insurgency movements declaring that Khartoum is again engaged in a significant military offensive during negotiations, as was the case during the last round of talks in December 2004. Moreover, violence in eastern Sudan is cause for ever greater concern. Not only has JEM joined cause with the Eastern Front – the Beja Congress and the Rashaida Free Lions – but Khartoum has reportedly responded to recent military actions with Antonov bombing attacks. The insurgents have demanded that the international news media inspect the sites of reported bombings. These tactics have been integral to Khartoum's genocidal campaign in Darfur. Now it appears that the NIF regime is once again resorting to aerial bombardment of civilians as a counter-insurgency weapon.

So long as the international community fails to supplement the AU in Darfur, fails to put a robust force in place with an explicit mandate for civilian protection, an intolerable number of women and girls will be raped. This will compound the ongoing failure of the international community, in particular that of the UN Security Council. For the Council has failed to secure from Khartoum compliance with the only significant "demand" made to date, contained in Resolution 1556 of July 30, 2004, that the regime disarm the *Janjaweed* murderers and rapists, and bring their leaders to justice.

A LONG DAY'S DYING

In a region the size of France, with some 2.5 million internally displaced persons and refugees, including eastern Chad, many hundreds of thousands of women and girls are daily at risk of the sort chronicled by MSF in its immensely powerful and clinically informed March 8, 2005 study, *The Crushing Burden of Rape: Sexual Violence in Darfur*. Without international protection, girls as young as eight will continue to experience the most vicious form of sexual violence. MSF provides all too many horrific examples from its study,

> Five women, 2 young girls (13 and 14 years old) and 3 older women, went to collect grass for their donkeys. The group got ambushed by three armed men. "I was taken to the near-by river bed away from the other women. One man took me in one direction. The other man took the other girl. . . . The man who took me told me to sit on the ground. But I refused. He hit me twice on my back with a stick. Then he took out a knife and threatened me by pointing the knife at me. I sat down. And then he told me to take off my underwear. I refused, but he threatened me again with his knife. He pulled his trousers down and raped me. He left without saying anything or even looking at me." (Young girl, 13, February 2005, South Darfur)
>
> "One of the three man took me away from the other women. He threatened me with his knife by pinching my chest with it. He pushed me on the ground and took off my underwear. He raped me and was repeating I will kill you all the time to intimidate me." (Young girl, 14, February 2005, South Darfur) (Page 4)

Page 1 reports the hateful racial/ethnic animus that is all too often in evidence in these violent rapes,

> "We saw five Arab men who came to us and asked where our husbands were. Then they told us that we should have sex with them. We said no. So they beat and raped us. After they abused us, the told us that now we would have Arab babies; and if they would find any Fur [one of the non-Arab or African tribal groups of Darfur], they would rape them again to change the colour of their children." (Three women, 25, 30 and 40, October 2004, West Darfur)

Gingerich and Leaning also report on the racial/ethnic animus in the accounts of rape coming from non-Arab or African women, accounts that make clear the genocidal nature of these assaults on Page 15,

> It is widely reported that during the attacks, the *Janjaweed* often berated the women, calling them slaves, telling them that they would now bear a "free child," and asserting that they (the perpetrators) are wiping out the non-Arabs.

Gang-rape is, as MSF has established beyond doubt on Page 5, a characteristic feature of sexual violence in Darfur,

> [A number of] women described that the rapists abducted them and held them captive for several days and during that period they were raped regularly by several men. One woman reported that her abduction lasted 6 days and she was raped by 10 men. In addition, almost half of the survivors report that there was more than one victim in the attack.

The MSF report includes many accounts by individual women of unsurpassable horror. Page 5 offers this first-person narrative,

> "I was walking with a group of nine women and two men. We met some armed men along the road. They took the nine women and held us under a tree in their camp. They released us after three days. During all this time, I was raped every night and every day by five men." (Woman, 30, October 2004, South Darfur) (Among the nine women, only three came to the clinic, among which two girls were 12 and 13 years old.)

This authoritative MSF report was the reason given by Khartoum for the recent arrest of the two most senior officials of MSF working in Sudan and Darfur. Aware of the clinical authority of MSF's report, and the international respect for the organization, which won the Nobel Peace Prize in 1999, the regime clearly fears the impact of reports of rape within the Muslim world. For while all too much of the Muslim world has shown a disgraceful willingness to countenance mass murder in Darfur in the name of "counter-insurgency," as promulgated by Khartoum, rape has proved to be much more difficult to justify as a tool of war.

But sexual violence has undeniably been an essential tool of war from the beginning of Khartoum's barbarous counter-insurgency war in Darfur and continues to be so today, as MSF insists on Page 1 of the report that so angered the regime,

> Since early 2003, the people of Darfur have endured a vicious campaign of violence, which has forced almost 2 million people to flee from their destroyed villages in search of safety. Rape against women, children, and men has sadly been a constant factor in this violence throughout this campaign of terror. More tragically, it continues to this day even long after people have fled from their villages. The stories of rape survivors give a horrific illustration of the daily reality of people in Darfur and especially of women and young girls, the primary victims of this form of violence. [The] first waves of people in flight repeatedly recounted to our teams how armed militias attacked their villages, killing and raping the inhabitants.
>
> The hundreds of thousands who fled the destroyed villages have now sought refuge in makeshift camps with little but rags and sticks as shelter. But they have found no safety there. In spite of high-profile visits of the world's leaders, people still face persecution and intimidation inside the camps. Rape, a feature of the attacks on their villages, has now followed them insidiously into their places of refuge. Families, in order to sustain themselves, have to continue collecting wood, fetching water or working their fields. In doing so, women have to make a terrible choice, putting themselves or their children at risk of rape, beatings or death as soon as they are outside the camps, towns or villages.

MSF has quantified a number of their findings, and it was for uttering these terrible truths that Khartoum arrested the senior MSF officials in Sudan. Page 3 highlights a few,

The majority (82%) were raped while they were pursuing their ordinary daily activities. Only 4% of women reported that the rape occurred during the active conflict, while they were fleeing their home village. Almost a third (28%) of the victims reported that they were raped more than one time, either by single or multiple assailants. In more than half of the cases, physical violence was inflicted beyond sexual violence; women are beaten with sticks, whips or axes. Further, some of the raped women were visibly pregnant at the time of the assault, sometimes up to eight months.

But MSF is far from alone in reporting on the realities of rape. There have long been numerous accounts from the UN as well as international and Sudanese human rights organizations. The scale and viciousness of rape, especially in the more violent phases of the Darfur conflict, are suggested by a March 22, 2004 IRIN dispatch following an attack in the Tawilla area of North Darfur, one in which the notorious *Janjaweed* leader Musa Hilal is clearly implicated,

> In an attack on 27 February [2004] in the Tawilah area of northern Darfur, 30 villages were burned to the ground, over 200 people killed and over 200 girls and women raped – some by up to 14 assailants and in front of their fathers who were later killed. A further 150 women and 200 children were abducted.

This was but one of countless such attacks.

We have no clear idea about the number of women and girls who have been raped in Darfur, in part because of the extraordinary reticence – for cultural and religious reasons – on the part of the women assaulted. We may be sure that UN Under-secretary for Humanitarian Affairs Egeland is correct when in a June 21, 2005 Reuters dispatch, he refers to the implications of the MSF study and its clinical recording of the experience of rape victims: "this [MSF figure of 500 rape victims] is just a fraction of such attacks."

Gingerich and Leaning report in footnote 72 (interview, October 12, 2004) and footnote 73 (interviews, September 21, 2004) on Page 16 that,

[A] Darfurian nongovernmental organization has documented 9,300 cases of rape, although other observers on the ground have argued that the number of rapes is closer to double that figure.

Given the enormous reticence of raped women and girls, and the extreme limitations in reporting range and access on the ground, such estimates clearly intimate the possibility that many tens of thousands of rapes have occurred in Darfur.

It is in such a statistical context that we must understand the implications of Gingerich and Leaning's account of "the strategic use of rape," and its particular relevance for Darfur, as described on Page 8,

Rape in the context of war serves to create fear, shame, and demoralization among many others in addition to the individual who has been directly assaulted. Communities threatened by mass rape in war may well be more likely to choose flight in advance of the enemy attack and may delay return to captured areas. Further, if a war aim is to take territory and resources and prevent the return of the target population, systematic rape can be seen as a potentially effective means to sap the capacity of groups and societies to reconstitute themselves and organize a sustained return. . . .

In extreme circumstances, mass rape has been used to further an agenda of cultural and ethnic destruction, by polluting bloodlines and preying upon deeply instilled prejudices about victims of rape to weaken marital and communal relations. The poisonous power of rape to drain capacity for explanation or re-organization of self and community makes it a uniquely effective tool for undermining the social order. When the war aims include the ethnic cleansing or annihilation of a particular identified group, systematic rape could arguably be deployed to manipulate norms of honor, chastity, virginity, femininity, masculinity, loyalty, marriage, and kinship, and insert an emanating set of experiences and memories that destroy group bonds through time. . . .

"Raped women become pregnant by the enemy, they may suffer grievous physical and psychological injuries, they may die, they may be abandoned or disavowed by shamed families and husbands, all of which degrade the ability of a culture to replenish itself through sexual reproduction" [footnote 29, Jonathan Gottschall, "Explaining Wartime Rape"].

It is impossible to do full justice to either the data or accounts of rape as a weapon of war. The number of studies available is considerable. In addition to the reports by MSF and Gingerich and Leaning, Amnesty International's July 19, 2004 *Sudan, Darfur: Rape as a Weapon of War* cannot be overlooked. What is clear from all extant accounts, surveys, and data is that rape has in fact been deliberately deployed as a weapon of war, indeed as a weapon in service of genocidal assault. The subsiding of large-scale conflict has not diminished the ongoing significance or extent of this weapon.

Here we must bear in mind the highly significant finding on Page 4 of MSF's report,

> The majority (82%) [of women and girls] were raped while they were pursuing their ordinary daily activities. Only 4% of women reported that the rape occurred during the active conflict, while they were fleeing their home village.

As women have continued to be forced into camps for displaced persons, or trapped in besieged villages, this statistic is terrifying in its implications. There is no hiding or respite from rape. The UN, in *Darfur Humanitarian Profile No. 14* of May 1, 2005, estimates that 1.88 million Darfuris are now internally displaced. The UN estimates another 200,000 are refugees in eastern Chad. This figure for human displacement represents only those persons to which the UN has access, mainly through UN World Food Program registration. It does not represent a huge and inaccessible rural population that is either displaced or acutely vulnerable *in situ*. In short, the extreme threat of rape continues for as many as 1.5 million women and girls. This has immense implications for the populations of Darfur, as Gingerich and Leaning make clear on pages 17 and 18,

> Aspects of the underlying strategic rationale for these rapes can be discerned as follows:

Create a sense of fear in the civilian population in order to restrict freedom of movement and economic activity. The consistency and implacability of the *Janjaweed* attack pattern has cast a massive shadow of fear across Darfur. Word of the rapes of the non-Arab population has spread to all those who have not yet been struck. This fear translates into a siege situation, whereby no one ventures outside the confines of the village unless it is absolutely necessary. (page 17)

Instill flight to facilitate capture of land and killing of male civilians. The modus operandi of the *Janjaweed* and Government of Sudan military attacks on Darfurian villages has become known across the region. Defiance in the face of the onslaught simply leads to death. Over these months of war, the military aims of these forces have become easier to accomplish: they ride up to the horizon of a settlement and everyone before them tries to flee. (page 18)

Demoralize the population to reduce their will to resist and prolong their forced exit from the land. Mass rape in war ruptures community ties and disorganizes family structure, behavior, and expectations through time. In a culture that places such high value on virginity and chastity as Darfur, the burden inflicted by rape is particularly devastating and enduring. (page 18)

Tear apart the community, by breaking family and community bonds and by engaging in ethnic cleansing through "pollution" of the blood line. A key motive of the *Janjaweed* use of rape as a weapon of war appears to be to destroy the non-Arab Darfurian society as a separate ethnic entity. Reports of rapes are replete with statements made by the *Janjaweed* perpetrators suggesting their intent to make a "free baby" (implying that the non-Arabs are slaves) and to "pollute" the tribal blood line, which is patrilineal in the Darfurian tribes. (page 18)

The strategic use of rape as a weapon of war is also evident in the numerous reports of women deliberately scarred or branded as part of sexual violence, this in order to make them more conspicuously victims of rape and thus less desirable as prospective wives or mothers. Even women who will under no circumstances speak of their brutal experience must nonetheless bear the cruelly and purposefully inflicted marks of that experience.

As we are counseled by the Bush administration "to give time for an African solution to work," the transparent inability of the AU – now or in any foreseeable future – to provide civilian protection ensures that rape will continue to be deployed as a strategic weapon of genocidal war.

Current Darfur peace talks in Abuja are deeply imperiled and could collapse rapidly. The African Union clearly lacks the political and diplomatic leverage to move either the insurgents or Khartoum toward substantive peace talks; their role is narrowly limited to mediation. The Associated Press reported on June 22, 2005 that the SLA/M, by far the larger of the two main Darfuri insurgency movements, has accused Khartoum of current and significant military attacks in Darfur of sufficient seriousness to end negotiations. Though this may be a disingenuous means of obscuring the serious differences that exist between the leaders of the two insurgency groups – the other is the smaller JEM – it is certainly a distinct possibility that Khartoum has chosen to provoke a collapse through military action, as it did during the last negotiating session in December 2004.

Abuja makes terribly clear that the women and girls who will be the future victims of rape in Darfur cannot wait for a negotiated agreement to provide them protection. Nor can they count on an adequate AU force deploying, in timely fashion, with sufficient numbers and a meaningful mandate for civilian protection. The most vulnerable of civilians have been left with only the callous words of the Bush administration, as well as a silent complicity on the part of leaders in Europe, Canada, and other nations with the power to stop genocide in Darfur, "Time must be given for an African solution to work."

But time is on the side of Khartoum's génocidaires and their brutal militia proxy, the *Janjaweed*. And though there are a number of reports, including Gingerich and Leaning, page 19, that Khartoum's regular forces have also participated in the mayhem of sexual violence in Darfur, it is the *Janjaweed* – still unconstrained by Khartoum in any meaningful sense – that continue to rape on a massive, systematic basis. This is so despite the UN Security Council Resolution 1556's futile "demand" that the regime disarm the *Janjaweed* and bring its leaders to justice.

Nor is there any prospect of justice for these girls and women. Violations of international law, including the use of rape as a weapon of war, have nominally been referred by the UN Security Council to the International

Criminal Court (ICC). But Khartoum continues to evince nothing but contempt for the ICC, insisting both that no Sudanese will be extradited to The Hague and that preposterous domestic show trials, hastily contrived by its Justice Ministry, will have sole jurisdiction for all of Sudan.

The NIF regime in Khartoum has no interest in seeking and sustaining a just peace for Sudan, or for any of the marginalized populations of this vast country, including those in the increasingly explosive east. The regime's génocidaires seek only political survival on the most favorable terms. They will make no peace with the people of Darfur that threatens them more than the January 9, 2005 Comprehensive Peace Agreement with southern Sudan already does.

Those women seeking justice from this regime will seek in vain. And those in the international community who refuse to see this regime for what it is, who refuse to see that the regime seeks neither a just peace for the people of Darfur nor justice for the most aggrieved civilian survivors of ongoing genocide, are complicit in condemning the women and girls of Darfur to an indefinite future of the most heinous crimes of sexual violence.

July 6, 2004 – Current Mortality from violence, Malnutrition, Disease in Darfur – Statistical Inferences

What is the level of current human destruction in Darfur? How many people have already died? For months the UN has offered the figure of 10,000 – with no account of methodology or explanation of the meaning of this figure. Given the vast numbers defining the crisis in Darfur and Chad, this seems both implausibly low and disturbingly static. 2.2 million people are now defined by the US, the UN, and the European Union as "war-affected." The UN High Commission for Refugees's internal documents indicate a refugee population in Chad of over 180,000 people, and this almost certainly still understates the population significantly. 1.1 million have been internally displaced in Darfur.

How likely is it that following 17 months of conflict, vast violent displacement, mass executions, and growing severe malnutrition and disease, a figure of 10,000 dead is of any real use in quantifying realities in Darfur? We may ask this question in the context of a number of reports, findings, and other data. Some of the most significant are briefly noted and assessed below.

Asma Jahangir, the UN Special Rapporteur on extrajudicial, summary or arbitrary executions, reported in a June 29, 2004 UN News Centre dispatch that the "number of black Africans killed by Arab militias in the Darfur region of Sudan is 'bound to be staggering.'" And,

> Ms. Jahangir said that during her visit, "nearly every third or fourth family" she spoke to in the camps for internally displaced people (IDPs) within Darfur had lost a relative to the militias. "It's very hard to say [accurately] how many people have been killed," she said, but interviews with IDPs indicated it would be "quite a large number. They are bound to be staggering."

This finding alone indicates a huge number of dead – certainly many times the figure of 10,000 if we may take as statistically representative Ms. Jahangir's finding that, "'nearly every third or fourth family' she spoke to in the camps for internally displaced people within Darfur had lost a relative to the militias."

MSF has also recently released important epidemiological research on violence committed against the African populations of Darfur in their June 21, 2004 *Emergency in Darfur, Sudan: No Relief in Sight*,

> A recent survey conducted by MSF and the epidemiological research center Epicentre in the town of Mornay, West Darfur State, where nearly 80,000 people have sought refuge, found that one in 20 people were killed in scorched earth attacks on 111 villages from September 2003 until February 2004. Adult men were the primary victims, but women and children were also killed. Today, one in five children in the camp are severely malnourished while irregular and insufficient food distributions do not come close to meeting the basic needs of people weakened by violence, displacement, and deprivation.

If we make the very conservative assumption that the Mornay region has been especially violent, and that the 1 in 20 figure overstates by 50% the global death rate for armed killings in Darfur, this still implies, for a displaced population of 1.3 million, that over 40,000 people had been violently killed between September 2003 and February 2004, a weekly casualty figure of approximately 1,600. In the more than four months since the end of February 2004, violent killings have continued to be reported on a very wide-scale throughout Darfur, especially in March and April, subsiding recently only because the destruction of African villages is now largely completed. Many people were of course killed violently before September 2003. The insurgency conflict broke out in February 2003 and *Janjaweed* attacks on civilians accelerated dramatically in the late spring of 2003. These data aggregated, including the implied weekly casualty rate, suggest a very approximate figure of 80,000 killed violently in the course of the war.

For the past three months, according to data from the USAID's Chart, *Projected Mortality Rates in Darfur, Sudan 2004-2005*, mortality from malnutrition and disease has been rising for the larger population of "war-affected," approximately 2.2 to 2.3 million. The Global Mortality Rate has moved from 1 death per day per 10,000 in early May 2004 to 3 per day per 10,000 in early June 2004 to 4 deaths per day per 10,000. During these approximately thirteen weeks alone, mortality from malnutrition and disease in the larger "war-affected" population is approximately 40,000.

These data and the numerical conclusion are supplemented by recent predictions of disease mortality from the UN's World Health Organization (WHO), predictions that are already relevant to estimates of current mortality levels that Reuters reports on July 2, 2004,

> Some 10,000 people in Darfur could die of cholera and dysentery in July alone unless a massive aid operation can be set up to helicopter in food and medicines. "We anticipate that if things go ahead as at the moment, 10,000 people will die in the next month," David Nabarro, head of the World Health Organization's unit for health action in crises, told a news briefing in Geneva after a trip to Darfur.

WHO also warned in a July 2, 2004 Reuters dispatch that,

> A cholera epidemic could break out within weeks now that heavy rains have begun, striking 200,000 to 300,000 of the more than one

million displaced in the troubled western area of Sudan, a top WHO official told a news briefing. Cholera is an extreme form of watery diarrhoea which killed tens of thousands of Rwandans who fled genocide in 1994, according to the WHO. Dysentery, a bloody form of diarrhoea which is harder to treat, and malaria, a mosquito-borne disease, would be expected to follow in August.

Malaria – an often fatal disease among weakened populations – is also already claiming lives, as the rains have produced numerous ponds that are the breeding grounds for the mosquitoes that carry the disease and much more readily in crowded camp conditions. The UN has recently reported a sharp uptick in malaria cases.

Given the severe limits on humanitarian access, more global assessments of various populations in the three Darfur states have not been undertaken. The data above are representative of all that we have. But given the scale of the human catastrophe in Darfur, and the thoroughly implausible figure of 10,000 offered by the UN, statistical inferences concerning current total mortality are demanded.

The data above, in aggregate, yield a total civilian mortality figure to date of approximately 120,000.

3

RWANDA REDUX

June 7, 2004 – Without Intervention, The Dying Will Continue
Indefinitely – Thousands To Die Daily

INTERNATIONAL MORAL FAILURE is now compounding rapidly, as
the long-predicted effects of Khartoum's genocidal war against the
African peoples of Darfur have begun to take hold ever-more destructively.
For despite the human suffering and destruction already authoritatively
chronicled – reaching to the tens of thousands of deaths and more than 1.2
million displaced – acute malnutrition and mortality figures are now skyrocketing. A June 7, 2004 Agence France-Presse noted the ominous words
of Ramiro Lopes da Silva, UN World Food Program (WFP) Country
Director for Sudan,

> "The worst is still to come" for the people of Sudan's strife-torn
> Darfur region, where millions have been displaced by 15 months of
> rebellion, the UN World Food Programme (WFP) warned today.
> "The situation in Darfur is becoming more critical every day; the
> worst is still to come," WFP Country Director for Sudan, Ramiro
> Lopes da Silva said.

This comes on the heels of a June 3, 2004 extraordinarily grim prediction by Andrew Natsios, USAID Administrator, who noted in a June 3, 2004 Agence France-Presse dispatch,

"We estimate right now if we get relief in, we'll lose a third of a million people, and if we don't the death rates could be dramatically higher, approaching a million people," said US Agency for International Development (USAID) chief Andrew Natsios after a high-level UN aid meeting [in Geneva].

Annette Weber, an Amnesty International Sudan researcher just back from the Chad-Darfur border, who also attended the Geneva donors meeting, echoed Natsios' assessment in a June 4, 2004 dispatch from *The Guardian*,

"There are 350,000 people who are most likely to die in this period [the rainy season]."

The rainy season will run about another 120 days. These figures suggest that, on gruesome statistical average, 3,000 people will die every day during this time.

And casualties from famine and disease may rise to even higher levels: nutritional analyses in Darfur by MSF (Holland) actually suggest a steeper increase in Global Acute Malnutrition than is represented in the April 2004 USAID *Projected Mortality Rates in Darfur, Sudan 2004-2005*.

Moreover, the mortality rate may continue to increase indefinitely if the number of war-affected continues to rise as rapidly as it has in recent weeks and months, if humanitarian access continues to be impeded by Khartoum, and if the regime continues to create conditions of insecurity that prevent resumption of agricultural production.

For despite signing a cease-fire agreement, Khartoum continues to bomb civilian targets in Darfur. Agence France-Presse reported on June 4, 2004, citing Chadian diplomats, that on June 4, 2004 the town of Tabet was again bombed. In the same dispatch, a Chadian diplomat speaks of " 'inordinate Sudanese troop movements towards rebel positions.' " And there are many highly authoritative reports of the *Janjaweed* militia continuing their savage predations throughout Darfur, especially southeast of Nyala in South Darfur.

Jan Egeland, UN Under-Secretary General for Humanitarian Affairs, also said in a June 4, 2004 BBC dispatch that despite the ceasefire agreement to which Khartoum has nominally committed, the regime's orchestrated violence was continuing to be directed against civilians in what Egeland has previously described as "a scorched-earth campaign of ethnic cleansing,"

"These are totally defenseless people," he said. "Women and children for the most part, and those who kill them are grown men with Kalashnikov automatic rifles."

The deployment of a ten-person monitoring team from the African Union (AU), with no military protection, can do virtually nothing to enforce the April 8, 2004 cease-fire, even if augmented by another 100 or so unprotected monitors. Indeed, Khartoum will certainly test the viability of this monitoring force as soon as it is deployed. Access for investigating cease-fire violations will be restricted as fully as possible, with Khartoum granting only what is required to have this woefully inadequate force stand, at least for the expedient, as an "international response" to Darfur's catastrophe.

However shocking Darfur's casualty figures may be, there is nothing surprising about them. They have grown relentlessly, remorselessly, inexorably from Khartoum's genocidal conduct of war over many months. There is nothing surprising about the USAID figure of 2.2 million war-affected. The UN figure is now 2 million. The number is a function of the violent displacement of African civilian populations, primarily the Fur, the Massaleit, and the Zaghawa. Displacement has been engineered by the systematic, widespread destruction of African villages, water sources, food stocks, seeds and agricultural implements. Mass executions of men and boys, the gang-raping of girls and women, and the use of torture have all contributed to the displacement of over 1.2 million people. Terrorized civilians have fled in ever-greater numbers into concentrations camps.

Of the more than 1 million internally displaced persons, with another 200,000 made refugees in Chad, more than half are in camps – most with no humanitarian access whatsoever. Conditions in these inaccessible camps are utterly appalling, with little food and water, and no sanitary facilities.

Kailek, in South Darfur, offers a terrible example. This was the site of a camp assessed by on April 24, 2004 by the *United Nations Inter-Agency Fact Finding and Rapid Assessment Mission: Kailek Town, South Darfur,* which published its report on April 25, 2004. The team found "a strategy of systematic and deliberate starvation," a policy of "imprisonment," a "policy of forced starvation," an unreported catastrophic "child mortality rate of 8-9 per day," and the continued obstruction of humanitarian aid for this critically distressed, forcibly confined population. This assessment led these professional humanitarian aid workers to make explicit comparison to the Rwandan genocide.

And those camps to which there is humanitarian access are hardly havens of safety. UN officials reported to the BBC on June 4, 2004 BBC that, "In some refugee camps, the infant mortality rate is already 25 times the international average." Doctors Without Borders/Médecins Sans Frontières (MSF) said in their May 20, 2004 report from New York, *On the Brink of Mass Starvation in Darfur,* that a "recent nutritional survey shows dangerously high levels of malnutrition and mortality and a rapidly deteriorating food security situation. With already high levels of excess deaths and malnutrition, the whole population is teetering on the verge of mass starvation."

WHO Director-General Lee Jong-Wook declared in a June 2, 2004 CNN report,

> "Death and disease spiral upwards when there is inadequate food, unsafe water, improper sanitation and shelter, widespread violence, lack of public health inputs like vaccinations and insufficient access to medical care. These are the realities of the current crisis in Darfur."

And the seasonal rains have begun. Road corridors are more frequently severed, and recent heavy rains in the southernmost part of the refugee-hosting area of Chad cut several transport roads. The rains began in Nyala, South Darfur on June 6, 2004. Water-borne diseases are poised to explode, even as many lives are now being lost to disease and the effects of malnutrition. These deaths are in addition to the perhaps 40,000-60,000 who have already perished. Camp populations will be more and more vulnerable as the rainy season advances and humanitarian road access is largely severed. Violence continues to create insecurity that makes resumption of productive agricultural lives impossible to imagine for the foreseeable future.

Despite the urgency and moral clarity of the crisis in Darfur, there are too few voices calling for humanitarian intervention – and fewer still declaring their willingness to act without UN authorization. Since the UN Security Council gives every sign of acquiescing in Darfur's genocide, it is no longer enough to speak simply of UN authorization of the sort that exists in Chapter VII of the UN Charter, which permits the Security Council to take all actions necessary to "maintain or restore international peace and security," clearly threatened on many counts in both Chad and Darfur.

It is certainly notable that Human Rights Watch in a June 3, 2004 Press Release has called for such UN action to halt Khartoum's "campaign of 'ethnic cleansing,' " and that the International Crisis Group in its May 23, 2004 report *Sudan: Now or Never in Darfur Africa Report No. 80* has called for even more robust UN actions, including enforcing a "no-fly zone" to prevent further attacks on civilians by Khartoum's military aircraft.

But the likelihood of UN Security Council inaction is exceedingly high. Spokesman Adam Ereli highlighted this in a US State Department June 7, 2004 Briefing. For even as the US and the UK are trying to pass a Security Council resolution on the Naivasha peace agreement, they are facing opposition over any mention Darfur. Ereli announced, "some Council members are opposed to mentioning Darfur in the resolution. But we are pushing back strongly that not mentioning Darfur would be unconscionable." Security Council objection extended even to referring to the previous Council Presidential statement on Darfur.

If the Security Council is opposed even to mentioning Darfur, and in such a context, how likely is it to move beyond its May 25, 2004 generic expression of "grave concern?" This in turn forces the critical question: what is the international community prepared to do in the absence of UN authorization? To be sure, Iraq has made such a question a great deal more difficult. But obligations incurred by the contracting parties to the 1948 UN Convention on the Prevention and Punishment of the Crime of Genocide cannot be avoided simply because of difficult political circumstances. If the UN fails to respond adequately to human destruction in Darfur, destruction representing the ever-fuller accomplishment of Khartoum's genocidal ambitions, obligations under the Genocide Convention nonetheless remain fully exigent.

The US Congress, under the leadership of Congressman Frank Wolf, sent a bluntly worded letter dated June 4, 2004 to UN Secretary-General Kofi Annan, urging him to undertake high-profile and urgent action. Co-signed by 44 other members of Congress, the bipartisan letter declared,

> Urgent, immediate action is needed to prevent the deaths of hundreds of thousands of innocent civilians. . . . The international community must act swiftly. Failure to act will bring certain death to the thousands languishing in camps. The world will wake up 10 years from now and wonder why more was not done to protect humanity. The evidence is clear. We cannot say we did not know.

Among the signatories to the letter are Congressmen Henry Hyde and Tom Lantos, Chair and Ranking Member respectively of the House International Relations Committee; also among the signatories are Congressmen Edward Royce and Donald Payne, Chair and Ranking Member respectively of the African Subcommittee of the House International Relations Committee.

But the evidence available strongly suggests that Mr. Annan has decided not to take a leadership role in responding to the Darfur crisis. This is so despite his apparently tough-minded words, on the grim anniversary of the Rwandan genocide, when he explicitly invoked Darfur in an April 7, 2004 Reuters dispatch from Geneva,

> UN Secretary-General Kofi Annan warned on Wednesday that outside military action may be needed in western Sudan to halt "ethnic cleansing" in the strife-torn Darfur region. Annan said humanitarian workers and human rights experts needed to be given full access to Darfur to administer aid to hundreds of thousands of people driven from their homes, many into neighboring Chad.

Annan went on to declare, in an April 7, 2004 UN Press Release,

> "It is vital that international humanitarian workers and human rights experts be given full access to [Darfur], and to the victims, without

further delay. If that is denied, the international community must be prepared to take swift and appropriate action. By 'action' in such situations I mean a continuum of steps, which may include military action.

Let us, Mr. Chairman, be serious about preventing genocide."

Two months later, humanitarian access is still far from full, ethnic cleansing, indeed genocide continues unabated – and Annan has not once returned to the crisis in Darfur with the urgency or "seriousness" of his April 7, 2004 words. The international community must, as a consequence, prepare for the moral failure of the UN Secretary-General and the UN Security Council. As Susan Rice, former Assistant Secretary of State for African Affairs, and Gayle Smith, former Senior Director for African Affairs at the National Security Council, wrote with courageous honesty in the *Washington Post* on May 30, 2004,

> The United States should press European and capable African countries to lead this humanitarian intervention with US support. Given the demands on US forces in Iraq, Afghanistan and Haiti, it is reasonable to ask Europe and Africa to play a key role.
>
> Finally, the United States should begin urgent military planning and preparation for the contingency that no other country will act to stop the dying in Darfur. The administration has worked hard to end Sudan's long-running civil conflict. But this effort will have been wasted if we allow the Sudanese government to continue committing crimes against humanity. Not only will the international community have blood on its hands for failure to halt another genocide, but we will have demonstrated to Khartoum that it can continue to act with impunity against its own people. In that case, any hard-won peace agreement will not be worth the paper it's signed on.

Is the world prepared to allow 3,000 innocent civilians to die every day . . . for the foreseeable future? Has deliberate, genocidal destruction on a massive scale again been found acceptable in Africa?

June 9, 2004 – If the UN won't save hundreds of thousands in Darfur, who will? NGO proposals.

A rapidly growing body of evidence suggests that the UN will not respond with appropriate urgency or forceful resolve to end the massive human destruction in Darfur. Indeed, there is at present no indication that the UN – either the office of the Secretary-General or the Security Council – will act in a timely and robust fashion. Rather, the issue of humanitarian intervention in Darfur is daily becoming more politicized at the UN, making meaningful action extremely unlikely.

This leaves the international community with a stark choice: begin urgent planning for a multilateral, non-UN humanitarian intervention in Darfur – or acquiesce in the genocidal destruction of hundreds of thousands of innocent human beings. Though the war in Iraq has made the political challenges of such non-UN intervention extremely difficult, there is no alternative. Presently unacceptable mortality rates, running to over 600 per day according to data from the USAID and humanitarian organizations doing malnutrition sampling, and the rapid onset of catastrophic mortality rates reaching to the thousands per day, make humanitarian intervention imperative. Delay at this point is countenancing continuing genocidal destruction that may reach 1 million human beings.

Those who have called for action through the UN – including the International Crisis Group (ICG) and Human Rights Watch – are to be commended for their forthright statements and their powerful accounts justifying UN military intervention for humanitarian purposes in Darfur. But these organizations must take the next step and declare a near-term deadline for UN Security Council action, and – critically – what action they will call for when it becomes fully clear that there will be no enabling resolution from the UN.

The same is true of the Bush administration and the John Kerry Democratic presidential campaign. Both must answer now, while their voices can still shape events, with clarity and decisiveness, the following question,

Are you prepared to support, vigorously and publicly, multilateral humanitarian intervention in Darfur without UN authorization?

Obviously a failure to answer this question, now overwhelmingly exigent, is a refusal to support humanitarian intervention. It is acquiescence in genocidal destruction whose death toll may surpass that in Rwanda precisely ten years ago.

The State Department has taken strong exception to a June 7, 2004 *Washington Post* editorial rightly criticizing the Bush administration for muting its comments about Darfur while trying to conclude north-south peace negotiations in Naivasha, Kenya. And to be sure, the US has begun to find its voice on Darfur, as Adam Ereli, State Department spokesman, made clear the same day in an account offered to Voice of America. But there was no comment from Ereli on the obligations of the US as a contracting party to the 1948 UN Convention on the Prevention and Punishment of the Crime of Genocide. Such obligations to prevent genocide do not require an actual finding of genocide – only sufficient evidence that genocide is impending. There is no intellectually respectable basis for denying such a threat of genocide, especially given the numerous findings – by the US, the UN, Human Rights Watch, the International Crisis Group, and many others – of ethnic cleansing in Darfur.

In fact, despite the semantic and institutional diffidence too frequently in evidence, genocide is clearly the appropriate term for what is underway in Darfur – the deliberate, systematic destruction of the African peoples of the region, as such. We now have overwhelming evidence that the Khartoum regime and its Arab militia allies are "deliberately inflicting on the [African] group[s] [of Darfur] conditions of life calculated to bring about [their] physical destruction in whole or in part," using the 1948 Genocide Convention, Article 2, Clause C, as a standard.

But the clarity of genocidal destruction also obliges that the Kerry campaign be forthright and honest, both in assessing the extreme improbability of adequate UN action and in declaring what action Senator John Kerry will call for in the all too likely context of UN moral failure. On Monday June 7, 2004 in a Kerry Campaign Press Release, Senator Kerry said,

I believe that the United States and the international community must act immediately to apply effective pressure on the Government of Sudan to rein in its militia proxies and to immediately provide unrestricted access for humanitarian aid and aid workers. We must also act swiftly to initiate negotiations aimed at securing a political settlement to the conflict. And because there is no guarantee that the Sudanese government will relent, we must also start planning now for the possibility that the international community, acting through the United Nations, will be forced to intervene urgently to save the lives of the innocent.

But what if the UN will not authorize "the international community . . . to intervene urgently to save the lives of the innocent"? This is a difficult question, but one Senator Kerry cannot skirt – not having in the same press release invoked the genocidal slaughter in Rwanda,

> The world did not act in Rwanda, to our eternal shame. Now we are at another crisis point this time in Sudan. The Sudan's western Darfur region demands the world's immediate attention and action.

Both the Bush administration and the Kerry campaign are obliged – if they are honest, if they genuinely care about the hundreds of thousands of lives at risk in Darfur – to answer the critical question,

> If there is no UN authorization for humanitarian intervention in Darfur, are you prepared to support – publicly, vigorously – multilateral intervention without UN auspices?

What is the evidence that the UN Security Council will not act? Part of the answer lies in the woefully inadequate leadership of UN Secretary-General Kofi Annan. Despite the powerful words in his speech, *Action Plan to Prevent Genocide*, which referred to the Darfur crisis on the occasion of the tenth anniversary of the Rwandan genocide (April 7, 2004), Annan has subsequently said nothing that represents either appropriate urgency or resolve. This strongly suggests that his words, entirely appropriate to the crisis in Darfur, met with stiff political resistance – from Khartoum, from the Arab League, from the Organization of the Islamic Conference, from UN Security Council permanent member China, and from others within the UN bureaucracy.

Indeed, unhelpful comments from the UK and Germany also suggest that Annan has failed to speak out following his appropriately urgent April

7, 2004 statement because of a lack of political support from influential European countries. But this does nothing to justify the shameful silence that has followed his earlier exhortation, reported in a UN Press Release of April 7, 2004,

> "It is vital that international humanitarian workers and human rights experts be given full access to [Darfur], and to the victims, without further delay. If that is denied, the international community must be prepared to take swift and appropriate action. By 'action' in such situations I mean a continuum of steps, which may include military action.
>
> Let us, Mr. Chairman, be serious about preventing genocide."

But Mr. Annan is not being "serious about preventing genocide." On the contrary, knowing full well that two months after his solemn statement, Khartoum is still seriously impeding humanitarian access, Mr. Annan is bending to political pressures rather than demonstrating the necessary leadership. To be sure, these political pressures and difficulties are intense and various. But without Mr. Annan regaining his original moral clarity on Darfur, the Security Council will not act, indeed is unlikely to do so in any event.

A fundamental problem is that permanent UN Security Council member China, with veto power over any Security Council resolution, regards Sudan almost exclusively as its premier source of offshore oil. China has been a net importer of oil for the last decade, and economic growth in China is fueled by an annual 10% increase in petroleum consumption. Genocide in Darfur is a political inconvenience, not a moral issue. We can glean the essence of China's response to any meaningful Security Council resolution on Darfur from a Xinhuanet wire report from Beijing, June 8, 2004,

> China welcomes the positive efforts made by the Sudanese government to solve the humanitarian crisis in Darfur, western Sudan, said Chinese Foreign Ministry spokesman Liu Jianchao here Tuesday. Liu made the remarks when asked to comment on China's position on the humanitarian crisis in Sudan's Darfur.

He said China welcomes the positive efforts made by the Sudanese government on this issue. China hopes relevant parties continue to make joint efforts to settle the crisis through negotiation, so as to realize peace, stability and development in this region.

Such blandly disingenuous commentary publicly positions China to reject any UN effort to authorize humanitarian intervention, despite massive evidence that supposedly "positive efforts made by the Sudanese government" amount to continuing the violence in Darfur by various means and substantially impeding humanitarian access.

But opposition comes from European countries as well. Two senior British officials have publicly and emphatically rejected the option of humanitarian intervention, making the political task of securing UN authorization that much more difficult. Alan Goulty, the UK's special Sudan envoy, callously dismissed the notion of humanitarian intervention, as reported in a May 31, 2004 *Telegraph* (UK) dispatch,

[Humanitarian intervention in Darfur] would be very expensive, fraught with difficulties and hard to set up in a hurry.

And *The Guardian* (UK) reported on June 9, 2004 that Hilary Benn, Great Britain's International Development Secretary, yesterday also ruled out humanitarian intervention, despite characterizing Darfur as "the world's worst humanitarian emergency,"

The British government ruled out international military intervention yesterday in the face of the impending humanitarian catastrophe in Sudan and is instead placing its faith in a small African Union contingent sent in to monitor the shaky ceasefire. . . . "I do not think it is a helpful suggestion. I think we should let the monitors do their work. I think they will make a difference."

The monitors Benn refers to are the 10 unprotected African Union ceasefire monitors to have been deployed to Darfur, a region the size of France, on June 9, 2004. With rampant violence continuing to be reported by numerous humanitarian and UN officials on the ground, the usefulness of the work of these monitors is quite impossible to see. Khartoum can restrict their travel at will, always able to cite "security concerns." This will not change with the addition of a few score additional unprotected African Union monitors.

This team can do nothing to prevent violence of the sort reported in a June 4, 2004 USAID *Darfur: Humanitarian Emergency* fact sheet,

> Several humanitarian agencies reported a [Government of Sudan] air attack on the village of Thabit, 25 kilometers southwest of El Fasher on May 28 [2004].

Thabit was the site of another air attack by Khartoum on June 4, 2004 according to Agence France-Presse, citing Chadian diplomats on June 4, 2004. USAID's fact sheet continues,

> Field reports also indicate the population movement near Kutum is extremely fluid, and large concentrations of [Internally Displaced Persons] are now living in rural areas [and thus beyond humanitarian access.] Civilians, especially women, report continued attacks and harassment in localities near Kutum.
>
> According to the US AID/DART, Jingaweit [*Janjaweed*] militias are active in the areas surrounding Nyala . . . [Internally Displaced Persons] told relief workers that they could not venture outside their camps or villages for fear of being assaulted, raped or murdered by Jingaweit.
>
> According to the US AID/DART, large numbers of [Internally Displaced Persons] have recently fled violence east of Geneina, West Darfur . . . and civilians in Selaya, north of Geneina, are virtual prisoners in the homes, fearful of attacks by Jangaweit if they travel outside the town.
>
> Sexual violence remains an enormous problem in all states of Darfur.

And this is but a glimpse, a very partial snapshot of current violence in the vast region of Darfur. A more global perspective on the unconstrained violence in Darfur was offered in a June 8, 2004 Press Release (AFR 54/064/2004) by Amnesty International,

> The failure of the justice system [in Darfur] cannot be ignored. Injustice is not just a consequence of the conflict, it is one of its causes. These abuses, like the fighting, will worsen if immediate preventative measures aren't taken. One reason the abuses have been so horrific and widespread in Darfur is that all members of the Janjawid [*Janjaweed*] militias who have killed, raped, looted and forcibly displaced people since April 2003 have benefited from complete impunity.

Khartoum still refuses to control or disarm the *Janjaweed*. The regime's primary weapon in the war on African civilian populations in Darfur remains fully deployed, creating insecurity that has brought nearly the entire agricultural economy of Darfur to a standstill. Food prices are reportedly skyrocketing in the markets that have any remaining commodities, a sure sign of impending famine.

The cease-fire committed to by the Khartoum regime on April 8, 2004 is clearly meaningless, and a small, militarily unprotected African Union team of monitors can have virtually no impact. Khartoum will merely direct its violence with slightly more care or deny access to places where evidence of atrocities and genocide is too conspicuous. For Hilary Benn and Great Britain to put so much stock in this force, with the human stakes so exceedingly great, is incomprehensible except as political expediency.

Nor is there any evidence that humanitarian access is improving, especially for the vast majority of the war-affected populations in Darfur, people who simply can't be reached by the limited humanitarian personnel and resources available. For while easing the most obvious travel restrictions imposed in the "systematic" impeding of humanitarian access, Khartoum has simply changed its obstructionist tactics, as the UN Integrated Regional Information Networks (IRIN) reported June 1, 2004,

> The advocacy group Refugees International (RI) said last week that "Khartoum was continuing to place obstacles" in the way of agencies seeking to respond to the Darfur crisis by requiring relief supplies

to be transported on Sudanese trucks and distributed by Sudanese agencies.

The capacity of these trucks and these agencies is by all accounts completely inadequate to the Darfur crisis. IRIN continues,

> A further problem was Khartoum's insistence that all medical supplies being shipped into Sudan needed to be tested before they were used, Refugees International added.

USAID reported in its June 4, 2004 *Darfur: Humanitarian Emergency* fact sheet,

> [Humanitarian organizations] continue to be frustrated by cumbersome [Government of Sudan] field travel notification requirements and clearance procedures for importing equipment into Sudan. . . . Bureaucratic delays persist, and the humanitarian community remains skeptical until new measures are fully adopted in Khartoum and translated into reality in the field.

Khartoum is clearly determined to finish the genocidal task, and obstructing humanitarian access at this moment is profoundly destructive of the targeted populations, primarily the Fur, Massaleit, and Zaghawa African tribal groups – as the regime well knows.

The spring planting season has now been missed – there will be no harvest in Darfur for autumn 2004. Given the extreme levels of fear, trauma, and terror on the part of the displaced African populations, there must now be concern there will be no fall/winter plantings for a spring 2005 harvest.

This is the context in which to understand the humanitarian imperative. The UN is presently using a figure of 2 million war-affected. the USAID is using a figure of 2.2 million. This number continues to grow, and explains why MSF (New York) is warning in its May 20, 2004 report, *On the Brink of Mass Starvation in Darfur*, that there are in Darfur "already high levels of excess deaths and malnutrition, [and] the whole population is teetering on the verge of mass starvation."

The figure of 2.2 million, one third of Darfur's total population, is the baseline number used by the USAID's *Projected Mortality Rates in Darfur, Sudan 2004-2005*. This is what USAID refers to as the "vulnerable group," the population that will see a "cumulative death rate of approximately 30%" between now and spring 2005, or approximately 650,000 deaths. This number of war-affected is still clearly growing at a substantial rate, however, which is the basis for the terribly grim forecasts from USAID and Amnesty International that Agence France-Press reported June 3, 2004.

> "We estimate right now if we get relief in, we'll lose a third of a million people, and if we don't the death rates could be dramatically higher, approaching a million people," said US Agency for International Development (USAID) chief Andrew Natsios after a high-level UN aid meeting [in Geneva].

Annette Weber, an Amnesty International Sudan researcher who recently spent time at the Chad/Darfur border, and who also attended the Geneva donors meeting, echoed Natsios' assessment in a June 4, 2004 article in *The Guardian*,

> "There are 350,000 people who are most likely to die in this period [the rainy season]."

In sum, without humanitarian intervention of a sort clearly not envisioned by the UN Security Council, the world will be acquiescing in a mortality rate that, on gruesome statistical average, will soon reach to 3,000 human beings a day, possibly every day for the foreseeable future.

Ideally, humanitarian intervention would have UN authorization. But however unlikely such authorization may be, the obligations of contracting parties to the 1948 UN Genocide Convention are pellucidly clear, even as there is no sign that they are being taken seriously. In a June 7, 2004 press release by the US Committee for Refugees, Lavinia Limón, executive director of the organization for the US Committee for Refugees, declared what must inevitably pertain to Presidential candidate Kerry until he clarifies his position on humanitarian intervention,

The failure of President Bush and UN Secretary General Kofi Annan to lead the world to stop the genocide is shameful and indefensible. It is not too late for the President to act to save hundreds of thousands of lives, but time is running out.

June 18, 2004 – Time Runs Out for Hundreds of Thousands. Will UN moral failure ensure genocide continues?

On June 17, 2004, Kofi Annan declared of Darfur that, "Based on reports that I have received, I cannot at this stage call it genocide. There are massive violations of international humanitarian law, but I am not ready to describe it as genocide or ethnic cleansing yet."

With these remarkably ill-informed words, UN Secretary-General Kofi Annan has dramatically reduced the chances for either UN or non-UN multilateral humanitarian intervention to stop the vast racially/ethnically animated human destruction currently accelerating in Darfur. Moreover, he has perversely given the National Islamic Front (NIF) regime in Khartoum an assessment that is all that the regime could wish for, and has indeed been soliciting in the form of absurd propaganda releases. Annan has given Khartoum breathing space in which to continue with its propagandistic assessments of the crisis in Darfur, as a June 16, 2004 Agence France-Presse release in Cairo reported,

> [NIF First Vice President Ali Osman Taha] accused the international media of deliberately magnifying the scale of the humanitarian problem in the region. He also claimed that the conflict was fabricated by the West.

By failing to give credence to the many authoritative and highly detailed findings from human rights groups and other investigators – of both ethnic cleansing and genocide in Darfur – Annan reveals either profound ignorance or shameful expediency. Given the scale of human destruction and suffering to date, and the massive impending loss of life, this is unforgivable . . . again.

For of course it is Kofi Annan who bears so much shameful responsibility for the UN failure to intervene in the Rwandan genocide of spring 1994, which occurred during Annan's tenure as head of UN peacekeeping operations. Now Annan has done much to ensure that the genocide in Darfur will also not receive the timely intervention that is so clearly and desperately needed. He has given Khartoum precisely what it wants, even as there continue to be scores of reports indicating that the regime is deliberately impeding humanitarian access to the many hundreds of thousands of African tribal peoples of Darfur who are most at risk. He has given a scandalously inert UN Security Council more than enough excuse for continuing its morally slothful ways. And he has critically weakened the diplomatic force of last week's announcement by US Secretary of State Colin Powell in the June 12, 2004 *New York Times* that the US was undertaking a legal analysis to see whether what is now officially described as ethnic cleansing rises to the level of genocide.

This is Kofi Annan's Rwanda redux. See, for example, Philip Gourevitch's "The Genocide Fax" in *The New Yorker*, May 11, 1998, for brilliant reporting on Annan's appalling response to an infamous fax of January 11, 1994, from Lieutenant-General Roméo Dallaire, UN force commander in Rwanda. That fax decisively warned Annan of impending "extermination" of the Tutsis, and the highly ominous "ordering of the registering of all Tutsis" in Kigali, capital of Rwanda."

What, more specifically, follows from Annan's declaration, on the basis of "reports that I [Annan] have received" that he is not "ready" to describe realities in Darfur as ethnic cleansing or genocide?

Annan has undermined his own UN Undersecretary for Humanitarian Affairs, Jan Egeland, who has repeatedly and emphatically referred to the catastrophe in Darfur as ethnic cleansing. Indeed, Egeland referred in a May 27, 2004 Reuters dispatch to a "scorched-earth campaign of ethnic cleansing" in Darfur. Since Egeland first referred to the actions of Khartoum and the *Janjaweed* as ethnic cleansing in an April 4, 2004 Reuters dispatch, we must wonder whether Secretary-General Annan and Undersecretary for Humanitarian Affairs Egeland are reading the same reports, or even assessing the same evidence.

Perhaps we gain a glimpse into Annan's motives if we recall that Khartoum deliberately refused to grant Egeland permission to accompany the recent UN humanitarian assessment mission to Darfur by refusing to grant access to the UN mission on dates that were available to Egeland.

Egeland was clearly being punished for daring to use the phrase "ethnic cleansing." Perhaps Annan, in the attempt to gain symbolic access to Darfur, has paid the price of admission with his refusal to characterize the crisis as ethnic cleansing or genocide. If so, this expediency – like all expediency in dealing with the Khartoum's NIF regime – will backfire badly.

Whatever Annan's motives, his comments were clearly not informed by the professional assessments of Darfur offered by the seasoned UN humanitarian coordinator for Sudan, Mukesh Kapila – or the reports presented to Kapila in his capacity as humanitarian coordinator for Sudan. Such ignorance, or expediency, again echoes the fate of Rwanda, especially insofar as these reports and assessments are in many cases several months old, as the following dispatches report.

Reuters on March 26, 2004 reported from Khartoum,

> [Kapila] said the violence, which he described as "ethnic cleansing," was mostly carried out by Arab militias known as *Janjaweed* who were supported by government forces. "Under those circumstances one can only conclude that it is state-sanctioned."

Kapila's statements were at least in part a response to the Khartoum regime's characterization of his previous remarks concerning Darfur as "a heap of lies," which the BBC reported on March 23, 2004. In these remarks Kapila likened the deliberate human destruction in the region to what occurred ten years ago in Rwanda, as IRIN reported on March 22, 2004,

> "The only difference between Rwanda and Darfur now is the numbers involved" [said Kapila]. "[The slaughter in Darfur] is more than just a conflict, it is an organised attempt to do away with a group of people."

Indeed, as Kapila had said in a March 19, 2004 BBC report,

> "I was present in Rwanda at the time of the genocide, and I've seen many other situations around the world and I am totally shocked at what is going on in Darfur. . . . This is ethnic cleansing, this is the world's greatest humanitarian crisis, and I don't know why the world isn't doing more about it."

Despite claims by Khartoum in early February to have brought the situation in Darfur under "total military control," IRIN on March 22, 2004 reported that Kapila insisted,

> The pattern of organised attacks on civilians and villages, abductions, killings and organised rapes by militias was getting worse by the day, [Kapila] said, and could deteriorate even further. "One can see how the situation might develop without prompt [action] . . . all the warning signs are there."

This led to the only appropriate conclusion, though one that Kofi Annan has chosen either to refuse to comprehend or expediently ignore, as Reuters reported from Khartoum on March 26, 2004,

> War crimes tribunals must be held to try those responsible for raping, looting and killing in African villages in Sudan's western Darfur region, a senior UN official said, accusing the state of complicity. "There are no secrets," UN Humanitarian Coordinator for Sudan Mukesh Kapila said. "The individuals who are doing this are known. We have their names. The individuals who are involved occupy senior positions [of the government of Sudan]."

This larger assessment of the situation in Darfur in March 2004 was far from being Kapila's alone. A group of concerned humanitarian workers in Darfur submitted on March 26, 2004 *A Briefing Paper on the Darfur Crisis: Ethnic Cleansing,* a "[report] prepared by a group of concerned humanitarian workers in Darfur who requested the UN Resident and Humanitarian Coordinator to bring this to the attention of the international community."

By what conceivable authority, intellectual or moral, can Kofi Annan pronounce on the issues of ethnic cleansing and genocide in Darfur without taking note of such reports? Further, how can he ignore the meticulous May 2004 Human Rights Watch report, *Darfur Destroyed: Ethnic Cleansing by Government and Militia Forces in Western Sudan*? Page 39 declares,

> In this report, Human Rights Watch has documented a pattern of human rights violations in West Darfur that amount to a government

policy of "ethnic cleansing" of certain ethnic groups, namely the Fur and the Masalit, from their areas of residence.

The Human Rights Watch report acknowledges in footnote 114 at this point,

> While a similar pattern may be in effect in North Darfur, the Zaghawa homeland, the scope of this report is limited to West Darfur.

Other credible sources, in particular the Emergency Relief Coordinator of the UN system, and the former Resident Coordinator of the UN system in Sudan, Mukesh Kapila, have made similar claims as Human Rights Watch notes on page 39.

Human Rights Watch's report, based on extensive field research both along the Chad-Darfur border and in West Darfur itself, provides utterly compelling evidence for all its claims. Its documentation is extraordinarily detailed. Is this another report that Kofi Annan has not read ("based on reports that I have received . . .")? Again, there are only two possible explanations for Annan's highly consequential declaration: ignorance or expediency. It is not clear which is more destructive in the context of Darfur.

What other reports are among those Annan has not received or has chosen not to read or regard? Certainly the compelling analyses from the Brussels-based International Crisis Group (ICG) can have played no part in Annan's declaration. In the most recent in a series of highly informed reports, ICG declares in its May 23, 2004 report, *Sudan: Now or Never in Darfur Africa Report No. 80,*

> A month after the international community solemnly marked the tenth anniversary of the Rwandan genocide in April 2004 with promises of "never again," it faces a man-made humanitarian catastrophe in western Sudan (Darfur) that can easily become nearly as deadly. It is too late to prevent substantial ethnic cleansing, but if the UN Security Council acts decisively – including by preparing to authorise the use of force as a last resort – there is just enough time to save hundreds of thousands of lives directly threatened by Sudanese troops and militias and by looming famine . . .

On the basis of numerous reports, analysis, and research – going back over a year – ICG finds that "it is too late to prevent substantial ethnic cleansing." Clearly this is another report that Annan has not received or has chosen not to read. But his pronouncement June 17, 2004 on this most consequential of issues in Darfur ensures that the UN Security Council is much less likely to "act decisively – including by preparing to authorise the use of force as a last resort" – and thus much less likely to "save hundreds of thousands of lives directly threatened by Sudanese troops and militias and by looming famine."

Kofi Annan has also clearly given no credence to the finding of ethnic cleansing by Roger Winter, Assistant Administrator at the USAID, and one of the world's most distinguished and long-serving advocates for peace and justice in Sudan. There are very few, if any, voices in the world that carry the moral authority and breadth of knowledge possessed by Mr. Winter, formerly executive director of the US Committee for Refugees. In the "Statement of Roger Winter, Assistant Administrator USAID," before the Senate Committee on Foreign Relations, Subcommittee on Africa, on June 15, 2004, Winter declared, on the basis of extensive USAID research and his own repeated travels to Darfur over the last year,

> That men, women, and children uprooted by the war and ethnic cleansing will die in enormous numbers is no longer in doubt due to advanced stages of malnutrition and disease that cannot be reversed in time. What remains in doubt is how high the body count will climb, and whether or not the Sudanese government will finally make saving lives in Darfur the priority rather than a chit for negotiation.
>
> As the [Government of Sudan] and its Jingaweit proxy forces continue a campaign of ethnic cleansing in Darfur that has forced an estimated 1.1 million people from their homes while inflicting widespread atrocities, serious food shortages, deliberate blockages of humanitarian aid, and destruction of shelter and medical care, it is possible to conceive of chilling scenarios that could push the death toll far higher than even the astounding level of 300,000. Some 2.2 million Darfurians are directly affected by the crisis.

At US AID, we are vitally aware that if thousands of lives and an entire society and way of life are to be saved in Darfur, greater international pressure must be brought to bear upon the Government of Sudan to halt the killing and rapes, reverse the ethnic cleansing and forced displacement, and eliminate [Government of Sudan] policies that obstruct relief efforts. We should avoid the trap of negotiating with the [Government of Sudan] for token, incremental concessions on the humanitarian front that leave overarching [Government of Sudan] policies of devastation in Darfur unchanged and undisturbed.

The countless USAID reports, fact sheets, and public testimony on Darfur are also among the material that Kofi Annan has failed to consult or give credence to with yesterday's statement. Also unheeded is testimony of US Assistant Secretary of State for African Affairs Charles Snyder before the Senate Committee on Foreign Relations Subcommittee on Africa, June 15, 2004, whose remarks comport fully with those of Human Rights Watch, ICG, and Amnesty International:

As a major part of [its counterinsurgency war] effort, the [Khartoum] government armed and supported Arab-based "jingaweit" militias have attacked and displaced civilians. These attacks are coordinated and supported by government security forces. African villages have been systematically attacked in a scorched-earth type approach. Villages are burned to the ground, water points destroyed, crops burned, and the people are forced from their land. The African population has been brutalized by the jingaweit through widespread atrocities including mass rape, branding of raped women, summary killings, amputations, and other atrocities. Estimates of civilians killed range between 15-30,000. As many as one million people have been displaced, and tens of thousands have sought refuge across the border in Chad. All of this amounts to "ethnic cleansing" on a large scale.

At this same Senate hearing, John Prendergast, representing the ICG, spoke of evidence revealing "conditions of genocide in Darfur." Julie Flint, representing Human Rights Watch, and the only other witness at the Senate hearing, also spoke unambiguously about the realities she encountered during her recent assessment mission inside Darfur,

> The political lead must be taken by the US and the [UN] Security Council to end abuses and reverse ethnic cleansing in Darfur.

Nicholas Kristof, columnist for the *New York Times*, has traveled twice to the Chad-Darfur border. He has filed a series of compelling accounts of what he explicitly finds to be genocidal destruction. Numerous editorials and editorial page commentaries have been just as explicit in declaring Darfur's realities to be genocidal in nature. Africa Action (Washington, DC), in a June 15, 2004 press release, forcefully announced in a petition drive launch that,

> the term "genocide" not only captures the fundamental characteristics of the Khartoum government's intent and actions in western Sudan, it also invokes clear international obligations. Africa Action notes that all permanent members of the United Nations Security Council – including the US – are parties to the 1948 Convention on Genocide, and are bound to prevent and punish this crime under international law.

Despite all this, Kofi Annan apparently cannot discern his own ghastly role in the chronology of unfolding genocide in Africa. Fortunately, the *Washington Post* provides guidance in a superb editorial of June 6, 2004,

> The early preparation for the genocide in Darfur, Sudan's vast western province, played out behind a veil of ignorance: almost no foreign aid workers operated in the region, and the world failed to realize what was happening. Stage two of the genocide, the one we are now in, is more acutely shameful: a succession of reports from relief agencies, human rights groups and journalists informs us that hundreds of thousands of people are likely to perish, yet outsiders still cannot muster the will to save them. Unless that changes, we are fated to live through the genocide's third stage. There will be speeches,

commissions of inquiry and sundry retrospectives, just as there were after Cambodia and Rwanda. Never again, we will be told.

And as Amnesty International reminded us on June 9, 2004 in a Memorandum to the Government of Sudan,

> On 7 April [2004], on the 10th anniversary of the Rwanda genocide, UN Secretary General Kofi Annan announced that he was sending a high level team to Darfur "to gain a fuller understanding of the extent and nature of this crisis."

It is now more than two months later. But even with the report from this "team" in hand, as well as several other intervening UN reports, from various levels within the UN organization, Annan still declares he hasn't found evidence of genocide or ethnic cleansing in Darfur. Has he bothered to look?

Indeed, despite Annan's somber words on April 7, 2004, despite the fact that this grim anniversary marked his own terrible failures in 1994, he has shamefully retreated from his frank words on this occasion. On April 7, 2004 in a UN News Centre report, Annan declared, having explicitly invoked the context of Rwanda's genocide, that reports on atrocities in Darfur "leave me with a deep sense of foreboding." He concluded with the declaration that, "wherever civilians are deliberately targeted because they belong to a particular community, we are in the presence of potential, if not actual, genocide."

As effective and timely humanitarian intervention in Darfur becomes less and less likely, the more so because of Kofi Annan's statement, we are – in the face of massive, deliberate, and now unavoidable human destruction – forced to cleave only to moral clarity. But let us at least have this much decency. The more than 80,000 who have already perished from Khartoum's genocidal conduct of war; the countless thousands who have endured rape, torture, and terrible privation; the more than 1.3 million people who have been driven from their homes; the 2.2 million people who are now war-affected; and the hundreds of thousands who are doomed to perish – these people are owed the decency of our honesty.

We know full well that genocide is underway. We know at the very least that ethnic cleansing – a "euphemistic halfway house" for genocide, in the words of Samantha Power – in Darfur entails the deliberate destruction of the African tribal peoples because of who they are, "as such." The means of destruction are the continuing targeted obstruction of humanitarian aid; the continuing military deployment of the savage *Janjaweed* militias to destroy all African agricultural production; the ongoing use of concentration camps, most with no humanitarian access, in which people are exterminated through the denial of food, water, and all sanitary facilities; and the deliberate mass executions of African peoples, especially men and boys.

Kofi Annan has refused to acknowledge the significance of these realities, and has thus significantly diminished the chance for marshalling international support for the humanitarian intervention that might halt them, and thus mitigate vast human destruction. But Mr. Annan's refusal, whether deriving from ignorance or expediency, does nothing to change these terrible realities. It merely completes a reprise of his failure in Rwanda.

July 1, 2004 – Annan and Powell Visit Sudan – Mortality Figures Rise – No Sense of Urgency

For all the symbolic importance of the June 30 and July 1, 2004 trips by Kofi Annan and Colin Powell to Khartoum and Darfur, there is only one way to measure the significance of these well-choreographed events. Do they move the international community closer to the humanitarian intervention that alone can significantly mitigate massive genocidal destruction? Judging by the exceedingly weak resolution floated by the US in the United Nations Security Council, and by Kofi Annan's relentlessly nebulous comments on a UN response to the Darfur crisis, the answer must be no.

As reported by the Associated Press July 1, 2004, the resolution proposed by the US would have the UN Security Council "impose an arms embargo and travel ban on Arab militias blamed for attacks on African villagers in Darfur." The BBC July 1, 2004 also reported that the draft resolution requires that the Security Council "decide after 30 days whether the arms embargo and travel ban against the militias should be extended to others 'responsible for the commission of atrocities in Darfur.'"

It is difficult to imagine a more inconsequential resolution. The *Janjaweed* militia have already been heavily armed by Khartoum, and as Human Rights Watch has insistently pointed out, have increasingly been coordinating with and incorporated into Khartoum's regular military forces. An arms embargo that does not include the Khartoum regime, that does not include those who supply arms to these brutal militia forces, is worse than useless. For this conveys a sense, through the authority of the Security Council, that something meaningful is being done when this is patently not true.

A travel ban on the *Janjaweed* militia leaders is even more pointless. Most of these men have no ambition to travel. Many have already been moved within Sudan and if necessary can be given new identification, and identity documents. These will be provided by the very security organs within the Khartoum regime that have overseen the *Janjaweed*'s destruction and atrocities in Darfur.

Moreover, the expansive 30-day time frame for deciding whether further action should be taken makes a mockery of the urgency defining the unfolding catastrophe in Darfur. Recent data from MSF help to substantiate a gross mortality figure of over 100,000 for the past 16 months. Asma Jahangir, the UN Special Rapporteur on extrajudicial, summary or arbitrary executions, reported that the "number of black Africans killed by Arab militias in the Darfur region of Sudan is 'bound to be staggering.'" The UN News Centre reported on June 29, 2004,

> Ms. Jahangir said that during her visit, "nearly every third or fourth family" she spoke to in the camps for internally displaced people (IDPs) within Darfur had lost a relative to the militias. "It's very hard to say [accurately] how many people have been killed," she said, but interviews with IDPs indicated it would be "quite a large number. They are bound to be staggering."

It is indeed difficult to extrapolate from Jahangir's statistical generalization about affected families in Darfur, but it strongly suggests a number in excess of 100,000 violent deaths.

Mortality figures and projections from the USAID continue to be ignored by most wire services and news media reports on Darfur, despite the authoritative research that lies behind them. Assuming with the UN, the

European Union, and the US a figure of 2.2 to 2.3 million war-affected persons in Darfur, and assuming the current USAID Crude Mortality Rate (CMR) of 4 people per day per population of 10,000, then the weekly mortality total is approximately 7,000. This suggests that even if a Security Council resolution were to pass within the week, more than 30,000 will have died before the Security Council considers follow-up action. By that time, USAID data indicate that the Crude Mortality Rate will be 10 persons per day per population of 10,000, or more than 15,000 people dying every week.

This will be the height of the rainy season, which has almost fully arrived. Transport difficulties will be at their greatest; humanitarian intervention will then be most difficult.

What accounts for US willingness to support such an exceedingly weak resolution? Much of the answer apparently lies in the US understanding that no stronger resolution would have a chance in the Security Council. Indeed, it is reliably reported that Permanent Member China, with its veto power, is unhappy with any resolution that is specific to Darfur. Russia is similarly disposed, as are Algeria and Pakistan. No one following the internal deliberations at the Security Council feels that any form of humanitarian intervention will be agreed to by China – certainly not for the foreseeable future.

Colin Powell may believe, as the Associated Press reported July 1, 2004, that a Security Council resolution will get the attention of Khartoum's leadership,

> As a stick, Powell warned that the United States might take the issue to the UN Security Council if Sudan ignored the problem. He believes that got [National Islamic Front President Omar] Bashir's attention because no government wants the stigma of Security Council sanctions.

But this is merely wishful thinking. Khartoum has endured international opprobrium on many occasions, and has always outlasted all who have attempted to rebuke this evil. The regime, without the clear prospect of international humanitarian intervention, will do what it has done for the past fifteen years of brutal tyranny, persisting in a ruthless and resourceful survivalism.

In Darfur, Khartoum's efforts will likely entail marginally improving some features of humanitarian access, and promising much more. But we should recall what NIF Foreign Minister Mustafa Ismail declared in a June 29, 2004 Associated Press dispatch on the eve of Colin Powell's arrival, " 'there is no famine, no malnutrition and no disease [in Darfur].' " Such gross and shameless dishonesty tells us all we need know about the worth of Khartoum's promises. There may also be a few symbolic arrests of *Janjaweed* scapegoats or stage-managed disarming ceremonies. But again, we should recall that President al-Bashir promised on May 25, 2004 to rein in the *Janjaweed*; as numerous reports from the ground make clear this simply has not happened, and the massive violence that has claimed many tens of thousands of civilian lives continues remorselessly.

With the UN Security Council so unlikely to provide the Chapter VII authority for such intervention, the only authority for international action comes in the form of the obligations deriving from the 1948 UN Convention on the Prevention and Punishment of the Crime of Genocide. It is of particular consequence, then, that Colin Powell offered such a deeply misleading and confusing explanation concerning a determination of genocide in Darfur in an interview with National Public Radio, June 30, 2004, from Sudan,

> [There are] some indicators [of genocide in Darfur] but there was certainly no full accounting of all indicators that lead to a legal definition of genocide, in accordance with the terms of the genocidal [sic] treaties.

This sentence is suspiciously opaque. Listeners and readers may be forgiven for failing to understand what is meant by "full accounting of all indicators" or even "indicators." There is in any event only one "genocidal treaty" to which the US is party, and crucially it demands that the US undertake to "prevent genocide." It is not clear what other "genocidal treaties" Secretary Powell had in mind, but the language of the 1948 UN Convention on the Prevention and Punishment of the Crime of Genocide includes "deliberately inflicting on the group conditions of life calculated to bring about its physical destruction in whole or in part." All available evidence, now voluminous, makes clear that this clause describes, with terrifying precision, Khartoum's intention and relentless actions in Darfur.

It is thus incumbent upon the Bush administration State Department to answer much more clearly a series of questions that have grown steadily more exigent since the announcement on June 11, 2004 that a genocide determination had begun.

When did the effort at a determination begin? When is it expected to be made? Is there any relation between the timing of this determination and actions at the UN Security Council? Of course there should not be, but there is more than a whiff of expediency in the air.

What evidence is missing? What evidentiary threshold(s) has not been met?

Is there doubt about Khartoum's intent to "deliberately inflict on the African tribal groups of Darfur conditions of life calculated to bring about their physical destruction in whole or in part?" What is any such skepticism based upon?

Both the Assistant Secretary of State for African Affairs and senior officials of the USAID have described the human destruction in Darfur as ethnic cleansing. What is the difference between ethnic cleansing and genocide? What does the latter term comprise that the former term does not? Is there any reason to believe that the phrase "ethnic cleansing" is anything other than a euphemistic halfway house between crimes against humanity and genocide, as Samantha Power has put the issue?

US Ambassador at large Pierre-Richard Prosper declared in June 25, 2004 Congressional testimony before the House International Relations Committee that, "We see indicators of genocide, and there is evidence that points in the direction [of genocide]."

Why are such indicators and evidence of genocide not enough to obligate us according to Article 1 of the Genocide Convention to prevent genocide now, rather than waiting for a full legal determination? How far short of the threshold for prevention are we? What further evidence or indicators are required to reach this threshold?

Secretary Colin Powell also declared in his June 30, 2004 interview with National Public Radio that,

> To spend a great deal of time arguing about the definition of what the situation is isn't as important as identifying where the people are who are in need.

But the argument isn't over "definition" but whether the realities of Darfur match the specific definition offered in the UN Genocide Convention. And to suggest that such determination is unimportant or unrelated to the humanitarian task at hand is either ignorance or disingenuousness. Certainly Powell's comment forces another question: Is there some basis for international humanitarian intervention in Darfur other than a Security Council resolution or fulfillment of obligations under the UN Genocide Convention?

These questions require answers, and the urgency must be commensurate with the scale of human destruction – achieved and impending. That urgency is at least declared by Kofi Annan in a July 1, 2004 Associated Press dispatch on the occasion of his own trip to Darfur: "UN Secretary-General Kofi Annan told Sudan's government that he wants to see progress within 48 hours resolving a bitter conflict in the Darfur region." But what does this mean? What are the consequences if there is no progress within the next 48 hours? And what constitutes progress? What are the benchmarks by which we can measure it?

Annan seems now to have determined upon a course of saying the right things, making the requisite appearance in Darfur – and then leaving the real work to others. While invoking again the threat of military force to protect the civilians of Darfur, this threat was first sounded on April 7, 2004 on the grim anniversary of the Rwandan genocide. It has a conspicuously hollow sound when issued again only after three long months of a deepening crisis have passed. Informed sources at the UN in New York indicate that Annan has done none of the urgent lobbying of Security Council members that is dictated by the crisis.

Indeed, Annan still cannot bring himself to use the terms genocide or ethnic cleansing to describe Darfur's realities, despite the emphatically repeated statements by Undersecretary for Humanitarian Affairs Jan Egeland that Khartoum's orchestrated violence continues to be directed against civilians in a "scorched-earth campaign of ethnic cleansing."

The June 21, 2004 MSF report *Emergency in Darfur, Sudan: No Relief in Sight* released important epidemiological research on violence committed against the African populations of Darfur,

A recent survey conducted by MSF and the epidemiological research center Epicentre in the town of Mornay, West Darfur State, where nearly 80,000 people have sought refuge, found that one in 20 people were killed in scorched earth attacks on 111 villages from September 2003 until February 2004. Adult men were the primary victims, but women and children were also killed. Today, one in five children in the camp are severely malnourished while irregular and insufficient food distributions do not come close to meeting the basic needs of people weakened by violence, displacement, and deprivation.

If we make the very conservative assumption that the Mornay region has been especially violent, and that the 1 in 20 figure overstates by 50% the global death rate for armed killings in Darfur, this still implies, for a displaced population of 1.3 million, that over 40,000 people had been violently killed between September 2003 and February 2004. This represents a weekly casualty figure of approximately 1,600. In the four months since the end of February, violent killings have continued to be reported on a very wide-scale throughout Darfur, subsiding recently only because the destruction of African villages is now almost completed. Many people were of course killed violently before September 2003, as the insurgency conflict broke out in February 2003. *Janjaweed* attacks on civilians accelerated dramatically in the late spring of 2003. These data aggregated suggest a figure of 80,000 killed violently in the course of the war.

For the past two months, according to the USAID data, mortality from malnutrition and disease has been rising for the larger population of war-affected estimated to be 2.2 to 2.3 million. The Crude Mortality Rate has moved from 1 death per day per 100,000 in early May, to 3 per day per 10,000 early June, to 4 deaths per day per 10,000 by July 2004. During these approximately nine weeks alone, morality from malnutrition and disease in the larger war-affected population has likely been approximately 40,000.

This yields a total civilian mortality figure to date of 120,000 – growing at a rate of 7,000 per week.

Have the visits to Darfur by US Secretary of State Colin Powell and UN Secretary-General Kofi Annan made any substantial headway in mitigating this genocidal destruction? The high profile of the visits ensures greater financial support for UN agencies and humanitarian organizations; it also increases the visibility of the Darfur catastrophe. But nothing has been done to address the gross mismatch between humanitarian need and current humanitarian capacity without military intervention. The UN's World Food Program (WFP) declared in its Rome Press Release of June 29, 2004 that the organizations fell short of feeding half a million people in June. It claims to have provided food to 700,000, but the organization admits that 1.2 million are in need of food assistance. Transport access is diminishing because of the rains, and the number of people in need of food aid will, according to WFP, rise to 2 million in three months.

Just as significantly, nothing has been done that will provide security for the hundreds of thousands in camps for the displaced to which there is no meaningful humanitarian access; this represents at least half the displaced population in Darfur. These are desperate and weakened people, without food and water, without latrines or sanitary facilities of any kind. They are without medical assistance even as diseases like cholera, dysentery, and mosquito-borne malaria are beginning to explode with the rains. They are completely at the mercy of the brutal and heavily armed *Janjaweed*.

In short, despite the opportunities of the moment, and the significance of these high-profile visits, nothing has been done to give this cataclysm of human destruction its proper name – or to begin the actions that can mitigate vast human destruction. The descent into the abyss – the abyss of human suffering and death, the abyss of moral failure – continues to gather pace.

August 24, 2004 – Impending Failure in Abuja, UN Security Council Inaction, Dying in the Camps

As Darfur enters a moment of supreme crisis, as engineered genocidal destruction is poised to accelerate uncontrollably during the August rains, the Khartoum regime remains intransigent. The international community, for its part, is failing both in diplomacy and in bringing pressure to bear on an obdurate National Islamic Front. At the same time, international humanitarian efforts are falling far short in providing for huge numbers of the increasingly desperate displaced populations of this vast region.

At the UN in New York, there is no sign that meaningful action will follow upon the expiration of the August 29, 2004 deadline set by Security Council Resolution 1556, passed July 30, 2004. Permanent Security Council member Great Britain has signaled that the Security Council is set to accept the status quo in Darfur. This is in large part because Kofi Annan and his special representative for Sudan, Jan Pronk, have negotiated away the only meaningful demand in Resolution 1556, viz. that within 30 days Khartoum must "disarm the *Janjaweed* militias" and bring to justice those guilty of "human rights and international law violations."

Pronk and Annan evidently hope that their renegotiation of this key demand can be muffled or obscured by vague commitments from Khartoum, part of a nebulous "Plan of Action" that Pronk signed on August 5, 2004. But the "Plan of Action" is without sufficiently clear deadlines or benchmarks, and is susceptible of various interpretations on key issues. The document certainly provides Khartoum with all the maneuvering room it could have hoped for.

To be sure, Annan and Pronk hoped that a substantial African Union force might be deployed to obscure the inability of the Security Council to act under Chapter VII of the UN Charter (Resolution 1556 has Chapter VII authority). But this hope has also been thwarted, largely because the evisceration of Resolution 1556 ensures that there are no effective means for bringing UN pressure to bear on Khartoum. Thus in peace talks in Abuja, Nigeria, Khartoum is refusing to countenance an African Union force of several thousand peacekeepers.

This in turn creates an insuperable obstacle in negotiations with the two Darfur insurgency groups, the SLA/M and JEM. They understand full well that insecurity in Darfur cannot be diminished without a forceful international presence of precisely the sort that Khartoum is blocking. UN expediency has perversely worked to create a diplomatic stalemate, despite the clear willingness of African Union members Nigeria and Rwanda, and perhaps Tanzania, to work to bring security to Darfur.

Meanwhile, misleading and disingenuously optimistic comments from some quarters in the UN about an "improving" humanitarian situation in Darfur also work to lessen pressure on Khartoum. Indeed, the effect of these comments is to give credence to a series of preposterous claims about Darfur by regime officials intent on downplaying the scale of the catastrophe. Such comments also encourage Khartoum's ominous plans to empty the camps of displaced persons, forcing them to return to burned-out villages and a countryside that remains highly insecure because of *Janjaweed* predations.

But despite such skewed UN pronouncements, other voices from the UN and humanitarian organizations – especially when recorded off-the-record and without fear of running afoul of the UN political line on Darfur – make clear that the situation continues to deteriorate badly, and that the scale of human suffering and destruction is expanding.

Present failures are compounding egregious previous failures, and the consequences will inevitably be measured in Darfuri lives. Whether we look at diplomatic efforts, especially in supporting deployment of African Union forces with a true peacekeeping mandate, efforts at forcing Khartoum to improve security in Darfur, or efforts to improve overall humanitarian capacity and delivery, we see dangerous failures. The successes of the intrepid and courageous humanitarian organizations with a real presence on the ground in Darfur are being overwhelmed by the size of the catastrophe, by the paralyzing seasonal rains at their August maximum, and by the slow withering of human resources among those displaced and traumatized by violence.

This analysis looks at diplomacy in Abuja, at the security situation as revealed by a flurry of recent dispatches from Darfur and Chad, and briefly at the realities of humanitarian need and the still-growing mismatch between need and capacity.

Unless the international community commits to humanitarian intervention in Darfur – an increasingly unlikely prospect – or at the very least commits to full support for the deployment of an African Union peacekeeping force of at least several thousand troops, it is unclear how progress can be made in saving the many hundreds of thousands of civilian lives at acutest risk in Darfur. The huge transport and logistical resources for more than 2 million war-affected persons are nowhere in sight, and security issues – both in the camps and the rural areas – compound an already catastrophic humanitarian crisis. The only way forward is to secure agreement from Khartoum on the deployment of African Union peacekeeping forces, and a commitment from the international community to do all that is necessary to provide adequate transport capacity into and within Darfur.

But meaningful agreements from Khartoum do not exist, nor are they in prospect. Khartoum, which has an extremely long history of violating or reneging on every agreement ever signed with a southern Sudanese party, is preserving this record of bad faith in Darfur. The regime has now reneged on various agreements: the April 8, 2004 "Humanitarian Cease Fire Agreement on the Conflict in Darfur," signed in N'Djamena, Chad; the commitments in a joint communiqué signed in the presence of UN Secretary General Kofi Annan on July 3, 2004 in Khartoum; and the commitments made to US Secretary of State Colin Powell in Khartoum.

Subsequently, the UN Security Council would incorporate the demand that Khartoum fulfill its commitments to disarm the *Janjaweed* militias and apprehend and bring to justice *Janjaweed* leaders into the July 30, 2004 UN Security Council Resolution 1556, Section 6. This "demand" has also been contemptuously ignored by Khartoum, without consequence. The predictable response of the Council has been to pass two weaker and more meaningless resolutions, No. 1564, dated September 18, 2004, and No. 1574, dated November 19, 2004.

Khartoum was certainly encouraged in its intransigence by the willingness of Kofi Annan and his special representative, Jan Pronk, to negotiate away the July 30, 2004 Security Council Resolution 1556 demand, the same demand in the original April 8, 2004 cease-fire agreement. Instead of pressuring the regime to disarm the *Janjaweed* and bring its leaders to justice, Pronk substituted a request that Khartoum provide a list of *Janjaweed* leaders. This request, and a disastrously conceived scheme for so-called safe areas, were the essential features of the August 5, 2004 "Plan of Action" negotiated by Pronk. Khartoum has not provided the requested list. And the "safe-areas" plan was so conspicuously a disaster that Pronk and UN officials have quietly – very, very quietly – abandoned it.

This is the context in which to assess current negotiations in Abuja, Nigeria, which commenced on August 23, 2004. As of this writing, Khartoum is predictably holding fast to its refusal to allow an African Union peacekeeping force into Darfur. All the regime will permit is a force with a mandate to protect the 120 planned "cease-fire" observers. Lead NIF negotiator, Agriculture Minister Majzoub al-Khalifa made Khartoum's position perfectly clear on the opening day of the negotiations, and echoed previous statements by senior NIF officials, including the especially hard-line army official, General Mohamed Bashir Suleiman. The Associated Press on August 23, 2004 reported from Abuja, Nigeria,

"Nobody agreed about that (a peacekeeping force). There was an agreement about a force to protect observers," Agriculture Minister Majzoub al-Khalifa Ahmad said. "The security role is the role of the government of Sudan and its security forces." He said Sudan might consider an expanded African Union role later. "If there's a need, it will be discussed."

This vague promise to revisit the issue of an African Union peacekeeping force in the unspecified future is the direct result of insufficient international pressure on Khartoum. The diminishment of pressure, in turn, is primarily the responsibility of Kofi Annan and Jan Pronk, who expediently negotiated away the singular demand of Resolution 1556.

For their part, the insurgency groups refuse to disarm so long as the *Janjaweed* remain a force of terror and continuing human destruction and displacement, as the Associated Press reported from Abuja, Nigeria August 23, 2004,

"We're an independent movement and we're fighting for our people and our rights. This force is our guarantee. How can we disarm them?" said Abdelwahid Muhamed El Nur, chairman of the Sudan Liberation Army rebel group.

Khartoum won't permit a peacekeeping force into Darfur to disarm the *Janjaweed*, or at least protect civilians from ongoing attacks by these brutal militia forces. At the same time the regime – which previously had refused to acknowledge the reality of the *Janjaweed*, let alone their military coordination with the militia forces – admits it can't do so itself in the foreseeable future. And the rebels won't disarm as long as the *Janjaweed* remains such a potent threat. This is again a diplomatic stalemate.

Either the international community devises means of pressuring Khartoum in highly concerted fashion, without UN support, or this stalemate will continue indefinitely. Extreme insecurity will continue to be a major source of displacement and death, and will prevent a resumption of agricultural production in Darfur. Insecurity will also continue to pose major threats to humanitarian aid workers, as well as humanitarian operations and transport.

The connection between insecurity and humanitarian operations is on vivid display in various camps. There are numerous and continuing reports of forcible expulsions from camps, as well as violent treatment, including torture of those resisting expulsion. Aid workers are also confronting the effects of insecurity. Khartoum's security forces shut down the huge Kalma Camp near Nyala for several days in mid-August 2004 following the killing of a worker identified by camp residents as a *Janjaweed* collaborator. Khartoum's soldiers prevented aid workers from entering, even as many people within the camp – especially severely malnourished infants – were put at extreme risk by this action.

The camp at Kass was also closed by Khartoum's security forces on August 17, 2004. And there are reports that the normally intrepid MSF has been forced to withdraw from Mukjar Camp in West Darfur. If true, this would be an especially disturbing development, given MSF's early and courageous presence in Darfur.

A British official traveling with UK Foreign Minister Jack Straw gave a terse but telling account of insecurity in the immediate environs of the Abu Shouk Camp in North Darfur. An August 24, 2004 Reuters dispatch from the Abu Shouk Camp reported,

> A British official traveling with Straw described the area around the Abu Shouk camp as "bandit country" and said the *Janjaweed* were "doing what they want, where they want, when they want to non-Arabs."

The *Janjaweed* are "doing what they want, where they want, when they want to non-Arabs." This tells us far too much about the reality confronting displaced Darfuris and the risks facing those who do not enjoy even the tenuous security of the camps. Other recent global assessments are just as discouraging. Kitty KcKinsey, spokesperson for the UN High Commission for Refugees in Chad, noted in an August 17, 2004 Voice of America broadcast that,

> "We have seen some people who have tried to go home to their villages, but when they go home, they said the security was very bad and they either flee to be displaced once more inside Darfur or they cross over into Chad."

The UN is reported by an August 18, 2004 Reuters dispatch as "concerned by Sudan's lack of progress in bringing security to Darfur," noting insecurity in the camps for the displaced in particular,

> "We are still concerned, very much so, by the lack of progress on the ground," [UN] spokeswoman Radhia Achouria told reporters in Khartoum, referring to camp security.

An August 18, 2004 IRIN dispatch continues this grim assessment,

> "Protection and security remain of paramount concern to Internally Displaced Persons," [UN spokeswoman Jennifer] Abrahamson noted. "General insecurity persists on the ground with continued violence carried out by various armed groups in addition to incidents of banditry and ongoing lawlessness," she added. She quoted Internally Displaced Persons as telling a UN team that visited Zam Zam camp [North Darfur] on 16 August [2004], that Janjawid militias had moved closer to El Fasher town and were hiding at Jamena village, 4 km south of the town.

Another dispatch, from Agence France-Presse, reports on the sexual violence and exploitation of women in camps for the displaced. AFP focuses in particular on the "police" charged with providing security in the camps. As many reports from the ground have made clear, the ranks of these police have been greatly increased as Khartoum simply gives paramilitary or police uniforms to the *Janjaweed*. According to a UN report released August 14, 2004, women in the camps are "reporting increasing incidents of sexual abuse and exploitation in Abu Shouk Camp near El Fashir committed by police officers . . ." "the police are exploiting women's inability to venture outside of the camp to collect firewood out of fear of *Janjaweed* attacks, by collecting firewood for the women in exchange for sexual favours,'" the UN report said. Agence France-Presse continued in an August 15, 2004 dispatch, "'[the displaced women] further report that some police officers had followed the women to the forests and threatened to beat them unless they succumb to their demands.'"

The *New York Times* on August 16, 2004 reported that even the expedient Jan Pronk has been forced by the undeniable realities of Darfur to admit that "there is no improvement in terms of safety, there is more fighting, the humanitarian situation is as bad as it was."

Moreover, there are a growing number of camps, spontaneously created by the most bereft of the displaced, to which no humanitarian organizations are permitted and in which security is non-existent. And there will be more of these camps as Khartoum continues with its announced policy of forcing displaced persons to return to their burned-out villages. Encampments like Otash and Siref, near Nyala (South Darfur), are "unauthorized," according to Khartoum, and the NIF regime's Humanitarian Affairs Commission has, according to an August 14, 2004 article from *The Independent* (UK), dateline Nyala,

> refused permission for the international agencies to operate [in these camps]. That decision is being partly modified, but apart from the charity CARE putting in water at Otash, there has been no change to the appalling conditions.

There are also a great many concentrations of displaced persons – in squalid squatter camps around Khartoum and in insurgency-controlled territories – that are completely unregistered and unassessed. These are the people dying helplessly and invisibly.

Further, as underscored in the ICG's superbly authoritative report of August 23, 2004, *Darfur Deadline: A New International Action Plan*,

> Many of the displaced [persons in Darfur] are restricted from relocating and are effectively trapped, often in poorly run government camps, without their normal means of survival in difficult times.

This raises the issue of the so-called "safe areas" that were negotiated by Pronk in the August 5, 2004 "Plan of Action." What sort of security will be afforded these areas, reminiscent in all too many ways of the "safe area" that was Srebrenica? We catch a glimpse in an August 16, 2004 Reuters dispatch reporting on conditions at Sani Deleiba in South Darfur – one of the places NIF Foreign Minister Mustafa Ismail designated a "safe area" on August 16, 2004,

> Villagers returning to their homes in Sudan's Darfur region are living in fear of the Arab militiamen who initially drove them away, the UN says in a report received by Reuters. . . . "A UN team reported on August 12 [2004] that it found approximately 2,700 returnees in Sani Deleiba that lived in fear due to heavy *Janjaweed* presence in the area," the UN said in a weekly report on the situation in Darfur.

Camp insecurity is also an issue that may send tens of thousands of already displaced Darfuris fleeing into Chad. The Masteri Camp in West Darfur is a site of particular concern for the UNHCR, as reported in an August 22, 2004 Agence France-Press dispatch,

> The UN High Commissioner for Refugees warned Friday [August 20, 2004] that a further 30,000 displaced people were poised to flee over the border into neighboring Chad, joining 200,000 refugees already there, because of the continuing depredations by the militias. "We are concerned that such an influx of 30,000 refugees in one single spot along the Chad-Sudan border, if it were to materialize, would put a strain on our ability to care for and feed refugees in our camps there," the UN agency said.
>
> "This group of displaced people said they want protection from UN peacekeepers," the agency's statement said. "If they do not get international security guarantees, they said they will all cross to Chad as soon as the rain-swollen river that marks the border with Sudan dries up." Most of the displaced people in the Masteri camp fled attacks on their own villages earlier this year, but are still prey to state-sponsored Arab militias, the UNHCR said.

These huge numbers of refugees would be in addition to the many hundreds who have very recently entered Chad. Approximately 500 Darfuris crossed the border close to the Chadian village of Berak as a result of "renewed violence in the Darfur region" according to the BBC, August 16,

2004. Further north, in the Bahai region, additional new refugees "describe attacks by Sudanese government planes and militia on horseback," and their testimonies indicate "the campaign against Sudanese of African descent continues," as the BBC reported on August 16, 2004.

We must bear in mind that conditions for the more than 200,000 refugees in Chad, as well as their Chadian host communities are extremely difficult. Indeed, in many ways conditions are worse in Chad than in Darfur itself – "appalling" is the word used most frequently by camp workers. Child malnutrition rates are 36-39%, while the range in Darfur is 16% to 39%. A very high percentage of women are no longer able to breast-feed their infants; and transport and logistics are extraordinarily difficult, even judged by the standards of this crisis. As Mark Zeitoun, a water engineer for Oxfam, noted in a dispatch from the *International Herald Tribune* on August 15, 2004, "the situation is slipping out of control."

The reality is that insecurity in and around camps for the displaced in Darfur remains extremely severe and threatens the survival of hundreds of thousands. This is so despite the comment by Jan Pronk, reported by IRIN August 5, 2004, made the same day he signed, on behalf of Kofi Annan and the UN, the "Plan of Action,"

[Pronk] said that security in the Internally Displaced Persons camps had generally improved.

We may be sure that so long as Khartoum believes the UN capable of such absurd and expedient statements, it will be commensurately less responsive to international demands, confident that the UN political leadership is not serious about bringing meaningful pressure to bear.

Reports from displaced persons on insecurity in the rural Darfur areas are numerous, terrifyingly consistent – and ominous in the extreme. They make clear that Khartoum has not begun to make good on the demand of Resolution 1556 that it "disarm the *Janjaweed*." Instead of such effort, Khartoum has made a series of promises; first 6,000 "police," then 10,000 – then for good measure 20,000. It has promised to reduce its paramilitary forces in the region by 30%, a tacit admission that these have been part of the security problem. But there is nothing that responds meaningfully to the extreme violence of the *Janjaweed* militia and the general lawlessness that follows in its wake of widespread destruction.

The refugees that have newly fled to Chad report that they "have tried to go home to their villages, but when they go home they said the security was very bad and they either flee to be displaced once more inside Darfur or they cross over into Chad," as the Voice of America reported on August 17, 2004. Obviously with every forced movement these populations of civilians become weaker and more traumatized.

The same August 17, 2004 Voice of America dispatch reports that instead of improving security, Khartoum is employing violent means to create an appearance of restored order,

> Aid workers in Chad and Darfur say the situation appears to be deteriorating, not improving. Unnamed sources within UN relief organizations have been quoted as saying they believe [Khartoum's] government troops are preventing many more terrorized civilians from fleeing Darfur in an effort to show the government is restoring stability in the region.

The fact that Khartoum continues to coordinate militarily with the *Janjaweed* has been reported in many news dispatches, including this August 20, 2004 *New York Times* report from Bahai, Chad,

> The latest refugee influx . . . is an alarming barometer of continuing violence inside Darfur. . . . United Nations officials here, relying on accounts by refugees, have been documenting new attacks by the Sudanese military and their proxy Arab militias, the *Janjaweed*. On August 6 [2004], these [UN] officials said, *Janjaweed* forces attacked a displaced peoples camp near the Darfur village of Ardjah. On August 10 [2004], the [UN] agency said, cargo planes dropped bombs on a section of the Djabarmoun mountains commonly used as a hiding place for villagers trying to flee the fighting.

The date August 6 reported above is the day after the Khartoum regime signed the "Plan of Action" that Jan Pronk had presented on behalf of the

UN. Aerial attacks on civilians by Khartoum's air force, one day after the "Plan of Action" went into effect, make clear how much meaning this Plan has for the regime.

Especially disturbing is the UN suggestion that the number of war-affected persons has declined from 2.2 million to under 1.5 million. In fact, the number of war-affected persons has grown considerably since the UN, the EU, and the US expressed deep concern for 2.2 million war-affected persons in a joint communiqué from Geneva on June 3, 2004. Further, a preposterously low total mortality figure of 363 deaths among over 800,000 displaced persons, over a five-week period to August 17, 2004, has been put forward by the UN World Health Organization. This figure will be subjected to vigorous scrutiny.

The general assessment offered by Mike McDonagh, who manages the Darfur relief effort for the Khartoum office of the UN's OCHA, offers a clear, if troubling, point of reference in a Knight-Ridder new service dispatch from Khartoum, August 19, 2004, "I feel we are slowly but surely getting on top of the health crisis." For a realistic look at the health crisis and the humanitarian situation, we must leave the Khartoum office of OCHA and hear the comments coming from those unencumbered by either UN bureaucracy or politics. These voices, guided by no ulterior motives, are our best means of understanding what the situation is currently.

The outbreak of Hepatitis E in camps in both Darfur and Chad continues to be cause for extreme concern, especially given the very high weekly rates of increased infection. Hepatitis E – a disease for which there is no vaccine, cure, or treatment – has an incubation period of 28-40 days; the feces of an infected person can carry the virus for over 2 weeks as Gerald Mandell, et al, note in *Principles and Practice of Infectious Diseases*. This suggests that the outbreak of Hepatitis E that we are seeing, which is rare in epidemic form, especially for a region in which the disease is not endemic, may prove a major health catastrophe.

Mortality among pregnant women can be 20-25%. But even the lower mortality rates of 1 to 4% suggested by medical personnel in the humanitarian theater are of extreme concern, given the incubation period and the duration of fecal infection. This may not be one of the major killers, such as cholera and dysentery, which still lurk as camps have become open sewers following the near daily rains. But it could claim a great many lives beyond those it has already, and could spread much more widely. There are already concerns that the disease has jumped from refugee camps in Chad to host communities, as IRIN reported on August 20, 2004. The UN Population Fund (UNFPA) warned that,

> unless immediate action was taken to avert the spread of the disease [Hepatitis E] in Darfur, it could spread quickly among the hundreds of thousands of Internally Displaced Persons living in camps with poor sanitation.

But of course there are no additional resources in place to make possible this "immediate action." The disease seems destined to become yet another source of trauma, another factor in the general debilitation of the huge populations of displaced persons.

Darfur and Chad have also entered the high malaria season and between July 3 and August 6, 2004 the World Health Organization reported "104,859 cases in Internally Displaced Persons camps," in an August 20, 2004 IRIN report. Malaria, too, is a debilitating disease that even among survivors can mean increased vulnerability to other diseases.

Polio represents yet another threat, especially since so many children in Darfur were not part of the recent vaccination campaign because of insecurity. The Associated Press reported on August 24, 2004 that "epidemiologists fear a major [polio] epidemic this fall – the start of the polio 'high season' – leaving thousands of African children paralyzed for life, [the UN] World Health Organization has said." This is yet another grim feature of the terrible autumn of suffering and dying in Darfur and Chad that is so clearly in prospect.

More globally, *The Independent* on August 15, 2004 reported that Barbara Stocking, director of Oxfam/Great Britain, declared following an assessment trip to Darfur that, "large swathes of north-western Sudan still remain inaccessible to aid organizations." This key issue – the huge numbers of inaccessible people in the very large areas with no humanitarian presence – must loom large in any comprehensive understanding of Darfur's crisis.

Richard Lee, a spokesman for the UN World Food Program, in an

August 18, 2004 Voice of America report, gives a sense of the magnitude of the key task by noting that the number of people assessed as in need of food assistance "is expected to rise to two million by September [2004]." Lee also declared in an August 18, 2004 IRIN dispatch that the heavy rains had contributed to the creation of a "logistical nightmare," and that "more areas [are becoming] inaccessible." This should not be surprising, since this is typically the month of heaviest rains in Darfur; it does highlight yet again the failure of the World Food Program in not pre-positioning large stocks of food in Darfur before the rainy season.

The Knight-Ridder news service on August 19, 2004 reported that another World Food Program spokesman, Peter Smerdon, said that WFP fell short of its target of 1 million people in July 2004, and that the organization would have trouble in August reaching even July's total because of difficulties in reaching West Darfur. This augurs extremely poorly for the 2 million people the WFP estimates will need food assistance in September, another very rainy month.

Significant shortfalls have defined the WFP response in Darfur for months now, with a number of gaping holes in the delivery system that have been only very partially closed, as *The Telegraph* reported on August 18, 2004,

> The world's biggest international relief effort has delivered less than one third of the special food needed for acutely malnourished children in Darfur, the United Nations said yesterday. . . . According to [the UN] World Food Program figures, 8,220 tons of corn and soya blend were needed to feed malnourished children between April and last month. But only 2,455 tons were delivered, barely 30 per cent.

MSF reported in a July 26, 2004 release that,

> in one big camp around El Geneina, only 35% of the displaced people even have a card entitling them to food from the UN. And the last time they received any was at the end of May – over seven weeks ago.

The *Washington Post* reported on August 22, 2004 from Bahai, Chad that a recent survey by the US Centers for Disease Control and Prevention found that "four out of ten Sudanese refugee children younger than five in Chadian camps are acutely malnourished."

On top of all this, Khartoum continues to impede humanitarian relief – deliberately increasing both morbidity and mortality among these terribly weakened populations. The most recent fact sheet from the USAID's August 20, 2004 *Darfur – Humanitarian Emergency* records several UN and other aid group findings on this score,

> On August 17 [2004] the UN reported that the Government of Sudan [GOS] had imposed additional bureaucratic obstacles that limit humanitarian access and relief agencies' capacity to respond to the emergency. The GOS recently denied access to an aircraft carrying relief supplies on the basis that the aircraft was more than 20 years old. A non-governmental organization already working in Darfur reported that one of its vehicles was denied customs clearance by the GOS Humanitarian Aid Commission. Other nongovernmental organizations reported restrictions on the hiring of national medical staff and additional delays in customs clearance for essential equipment.

This is genocide by attrition – no less destructive ultimately than attacks on civilians of the sort reported by the intrepid journalist Kim Sengupta, whose dispatches from Nyala have been some of the most revealing by any news reporter working in Darfur. She reported in *The Independent* (UK) on August 22, 2004,

> On 30 July [2004], three weeks after the United Nations Secretary-General, Kofi Annan, announced that he had reached agreement with the Sudanese President, Omar al-Bashir, on ending the violence, the village [of Silaya] came under sustained and murderous attack from government troops and their *Janjaweed* allies. . . . More than 100 people were killed in one raid. Most of them were shot, but 32 were tied up and burned alive. Twenty-five young women and girls were taken away; the bodies of some were found later. Also discovered were the remains of many who fled the onslaught but were pursued and slaughtered.

Survivors say that the raiders had specific, targeted victims whom they hunted down and set alight – teachers, clerics and those who had returned after further education in the cities.

Genocide by attrition amidst the world's greatest humanitarian crisis, genocide by violent destruction and cultural obliteration, genocide by means of diplomatic and political intransigence. Khartoum's regime presents all aspects of genocidal ambition.

November 29, 2004 –A Year's Failure to Intervene – Khartoum emboldened. Villages Gone. People Next?

As violence intensifies in the Darfur region of western Sudan, and as growing insecurity restricts humanitarian access in ever more consequential fashion, there is a revealing failure on the part of UN officials, the US State Department, and other international actors to see present realities within the historical context of the past year. Though conflict has raged in Darfur for almost 22 months, and grew in many ways out of antecedent lawlessness and abusive neglect by Khartoum, the last year of violence in particular has defined the present nature of the crisis. Historical myopia may simplify matters here for diplomats and political officials, who seem incapable of doing more than decrying present disastrous trends. But such myopia badly distorts the meaning of increasing violence, and all too conveniently serves to obscure the now conspicuous failure to plan for and mount a timely international humanitarian intervention, with a broad mandate to protect humanitarian aid efforts and increasingly vulnerable, badly weakened civilian populations.

International refusal to act upon the clear historical evidence of the past year also continues to embolden Khartoum. Thus the BBC on November 29, 2004 reported that the regime has ordered the expulsion of senior aid officials from two of the most distinguished international humanitarian organizations operating in Darfur,

country directors of British Oxfam and Save the Children were told [by the Sudanese government] to leave within 48 hours. The Sudanese government accused both organisations of prolonging the conflict rather than helping it.

What should be a shocking event is simply another episode in Khartoum's testing the resolve of the international community, only to find that there is none.

In the case of Save the Children/UK, the issue seems to be that dozens of the organization's workers were in the Tawilla area when Khartoum used its aerial military assets to bomb targets very close to Save the Children operations. The organization then had the temerity to report publicly this egregious breach of the terms of the November 9, 2004 cease-fire agreement in Abuja, Nigeria, which committed Khartoum to "refrain from conducting hostile military flights in and over the Darfur region." The BBC reported on November 29, 2004 that,

> Save the Children said that field workers were forced to flee from Tawilla when government warplanes bombed a site close to a feeding centre run by the organisation. . . . Save the Children is one of the largest food distributors in Darfur. It provides food to more than 300,000 of around 1.5 million refugees in the troubled region.

Oxfam has also been punished for speaking honestly, in particular about the meaninglessness of recent UN Security Council resolutions, the last of which Khartoum found fully satisfying in its vacuity. Oxfam, which has been working throughout northern Sudan for more than 20 years, stands accused by Khartoum's "Humanitarian Affairs Commission" of "breaking laws on non-intervention in Sudan's political, ethnic or sectarian issues," as the BBC reported November 9, 2004.

Continuing international failure to bear in mind the actions by Khartoum over the past year ensures only that there will be more such outrages, targeting the very humanitarian relief that is increasingly essential for a conflict-affected population that reaches to approximately 3 million.

More than eight months after UN Humanitarian Coordinator in Sudan Mukesh Kapila's bluntly honest and explicit March 2004 warning, total mortality in Darfur has climbed to more than 300,000 human beings; as many as 2.5 million have been displaced; and as many as 3 million are in need of urgent humanitarian assistance – the very assistance that Khartoum has previously, and now again, obstructed. Moreover, humanitarian personnel and operations currently face unacceptable security risks.

Such insecurity was clearly in prospect in 2004. The UN's Egeland openly worried about the nightmare scenario for humanitarian operations that is now so evident. The BBC on July 14, 2004 reported Egeland expressing concern that "Darfur was becoming too dangerous for aid workers." And in a chilling moment of speculation, Egeland described, "'my worst scenario [is that] that the security will deteriorate, that we will step back at a moment we have to actually step up [emergency relief].'"

At this inexcusably belated point in the Darfur catastrophe – despite the manifest bad faith of the Khartoum regime and the clear threat of massive additional human mortality – there has been no planning for meaningful humanitarian intervention; there has been no planning for an international effort that will protect humanitarian workers and operations, as well as undertake the daunting civilian-protection tasks that have grown exponentially more difficult.

Rather, the international community remains content with what can be achieved by an African Union (AU) force that is deploying without adequate equipment, especially transport and communications capacity, and without a mandate to do more than observe the ongoing disintegration of the April 8, 2004 cease-fire that was subsequently re-iterated at Abuja, Nigeria on November 9, 2004, with only the very slightest augmentation of mandate for AU forces. In the end, this deployment will become another casualty of Darfur's conflict, saddling the important but still fledgling African Union Peace and Security Commission with a conspicuous and ignominious inaugural failure.

For even when fully deployed, perhaps not until February 2005 or later, the 3,500 to 4,000 AU troops, including monitors, police, and support personnel, will be hopelessly inadequate to the security tasks so urgently in evidence. This is not a matter of dispute, though it is a source of abundant disingenuousness and excuse-making. All evidence, past and present, makes clear that absent a robust, very substantial international humanitarian intervention, with all necessary military support, hundreds of thousands of additional human beings will die in the coming months and years. Perhaps 30,000 are now dying monthly, and growing food shortages ensure that this number could rise rapidly.

This massive genocide by attrition gives no sign of ending, nor can it end until the instruments of genocide have been militarily neutralized and

Khartoum held meaningfully accountable for its actions. Evidently aware of such reports, though he would later expediently deny the fact, Annan declared in his Rwandan Genocide 10th Anniversary speech, reported by an April 7, 2004 UN News Centre dispatch,

> "Such reports leave me with a deep sense of foreboding," said the Secretary-General. "Whatever terms it uses to describe the situation [in Darfur], the international community cannot stand idle."

Almost eight months later, despite Annan's "deep sense of foreboding," "the international community" has essentially "stood idle," relying exclusively on a woefully inadequate African Union force and humanitarian relief that is increasingly inadequate and endangered. And still the destruction of the African tribal populations of Darfur proceeds at a horrifying rate.

In a moment of characteristic bluster, Annan went on to say in the same April 7, 2004 speech,

> "It is vital that international humanitarian workers and human rights experts be given full access to the region, and to the victims, without further delay," he said. "If that is denied, the international community must be prepared to take swift and appropriate action," he warned.

But of course Khartoum would contrive months of further delay in humanitarian access, and severely constrain UN human rights officials. There certainly was no "swift" or "appropriate" response.

> "Let us not wait until the worst has happened, or is already happening," the Secretary-General Annan concluded in his April 7, 2004 speech, "Let us not wait until the only alternatives to military action are futile hand-wringing or callous indifference. Let us be serious about preventing genocide."

Annan, with unintended accuracy, was describing precisely the situation that now prevails in Darfur. His own response seems to alternate fitfully between "hand-wringing" and "indifference," for he would say nothing significant about Darfur for two months following his April 7, 2004 speech.

And though he himself explicitly evoked the threat of military intervention on April 7, there is still no sign – almost eight months later – that any planning for such intervention has even begun.

Instead, Annan disingenuously and expediently manipulates the issue of genocide in Darfur as a means of obscuring his own failure to provide moral and political leadership at the UN. The most egregious example comes from an interview Annan provided to the US Public Broadcasting System's October 15, 2004 "The News Hour,"

> ANNAN: The impression . . . which has been gained in some quarters, that if you were only to label it genocide things will fall in place, I'm afraid, is not really correct. We know what needs to be done. We need to have the will and the resources and go in and do it.

This is of course utterly specious. No one has argued that "if you were only to label Darfur genocide things will fall in place" – no one. And Annan knows this perfectly well. By setting up what is transparently a straw-man to be knocked down, Annan is attempting to avoid responsibility for his own failure to accept the truth of his words of April 7, 2004. There can be no more disgraceful betrayal of the meaning of this somber anniversary.

To be sure, Annan's expediency was widely shared in early April of this year. From late 2003 through May of 2004, north-south peace talks preoccupied the US, the UK, and Norway – the "troika" – and there was no inclination to speak honestly about the discomfiting realities in Darfur. Troika members were seeking an expeditious conclusion to the Naivasha peace negotiations between Khartoum and the southern Sudan People's Liberation Movement under the auspices of the East African Intergovernmental Authority for Development (IGAD). As a result of their attempt to secure completion of the Naivasha agreement, which, notably by November 29, 2004, has still not been concluded, these countries muted their criticism of Khartoum's genocidal destruction in Darfur and ongoing obstruction of humanitarian aid. Because the "troika" represented a larger consortium of Western nations, the IGAD Partners Forum, there was little willingness in other quarters to challenge this expedient silence.

Ultimately, Khartoum triumphed diplomatically both in refusing to complete the Naivasha agreement, despite signing protocols dealing with all issues of substance on May 26, 2004, and in refusing to rein in the *Janjaweed*, or allow for timely humanitarian response to the urgent crisis in Darfur. Indeed, even now the regime is playing off the uncoordinated negotiating venues of Naivasha and Abuja, as well as Cairo, site of putative negotiations between Khartoum and the umbrella organization for northern opposition groups, as well as the SPLM, the National Democratic Alliance (NDA).

There has been a good deal of reporting on violence in the Tawilla (also Tawilah) area in the first week of November 2004. Much blame has fallen on one of the insurgency groups, the SLA/M for "violating" the "cease-fire" nominally put into effect at Abuja on November 9, 2004. The full nature of a series of incidents beginning on September 16, 2004 is still not entirely clear, but a November 29, 2004 dispatch from the *New York Times*, from Tawilla, comports with a number of wire-reports and other accounts. Excerpts offer a crude time-line; but again, we should remember the extraordinary levels of ethnically-animated violence endured by the people in this area for many months. With this as our context, the unseemly haste of the UN and others to blame the insurgents for a "cease-fire" violation seems yet another example of international failure to accept the ghastly historical realities of the past year and more. The November 29, 2004 *New York Times* article reported one violation,

Few people in North Darfur were surprised by the violence in Tawila on November 22 [2004]. Tensions between the townspeople, largely members of African tribes, and Arabs from nearby villages had been building. The pivotal event, townspeople said, was a brawl on market day, November 16. A group of Arabs had come to the market, as they normally did. This time, they picked out a pile of women's clothes, stuffed them in their sacks and refused to pay. Instead, they brandished guns.

Frustration was running high from similar incidents in the past, and the town was still recovering from an attack by government forces and allied Arab militias earlier this year. So this time, when the Arabs refused to pay, the Africans retaliated. The entire market took part. People grabbed sticks and stones from the market stalls and began pummeling the Arabs, killing four of them on the spot and injuring as many as seven. By the time the police arrived, the Arab bodies lay bashed and disfigured in the market.

Revenge begot revenge. That night, Arabs returned, firing randomly at the houses and looting from the market. . . .

Then, just after dawn prayers on November 22, [SLA] rebels attacked the town, killing nearly 30 government police officers and pocking the garrison with bullet holes. The government retaliated with airstrikes. People ran any way they could. Like so many other towns in Darfur, Tawila virtually emptied.

Khartoum's characteristically indiscriminate bombing attack, which came within 50 meters of Save the Children operations, was meant to be inflammatory. The point was not merely to retake Tawilla militarily, but to provoke further military action by the insurgents, giving the regime excuse to unleash its aerial weaponry in other places. For their part, the insurgents continue to give evidence of poor communications capacity. Mid-November 2004's wildly contradictory statements from the SLA concerning respect for the Abuja cease-fire agreement is the most striking example, as command-and-control deteriorates and fissures appear within the broader insurgency movement. In turn, Khartoum senses that it has the upper hand militarily and will eagerly seek means to exploit this advantage. Where possible, the regime will use insurgency attacks as pretext; where not, the *Janjaweed* remain as potent as ever, with a now thoroughly cultivated sense of impunity.

Though there are some organizations and many governments that continue to profess agnosticism about whether the massive crimes against humanity and ethnically-animated violence in Darfur rise to the level of genocide, such agnosticism has become thoroughly irrelevant. For in their very different ways, Colin Powell and Kofi Annan have ended the debate about genocide. Powell declared unambiguously that genocide is occurring in Darfur in his September 9, 2004 Senate testimony, basing his determination on the most authoritative report that we will have on the issue, that of the Coalition for International Justice in *Documenting Atrocities in Darfur*, September 2004. But Powell then proceeded to declare further that "nothing new follows from this [genocide determination]," other than referral of the US finding to an obviously paralyzed UN Security Council.

Annan has, perhaps more contemptibly, simply ridiculed the notion that a genocide determination makes any difference for Darfur. Despite his sanctimonious remarks of April 7, 2004, genocide seems not a word that carries much real moral or political weight with the Secretary-General. It is difficult to imagine a more obscene compounding of the failure to intervene in Rwanda ten years ago.

Both Annan and Powell have transparent motives for their respective positions on genocide in Darfur. Powell knows the Bush administration has no intention of undertaking to prevent genocide in Darfur, a contractual obligation for the US under Article 1 of the 1948 UN Convention on the Prevention and Punishment of the Crime of Genocide. Insisting that US contractual obligations are fulfilled by sending a determination to the Security Council is simply a way for the administration to wash its hands of greater responsibility.

Annan wishes to preserve the appearance of working practically on Darfur, even as he hopes to minimize how conspicuously the UN Security Council is incapable of responding to Sudan. But China's veto threat alone ensures paralysis, and thus a further move toward appeasement, recently enthusiastically endorsed by John Danforth, US ambassador to the United Nations. In the expedient arena of geopolitics, in which Darfur has already been traded out, there is a perverse convergence of US and UN political interests. For its part, a docile and impotent European Union desperately seeks to substitute exhortation for action, but only succeeds in making failure more conspicuous. Japan and the Arab world are silent.

If we wish to see Darfur's future, we need only look to the past year. To be sure, violence will abate, as so many of the tasks of genocidal destruction have now been completed. 80 to 90% of African villages in Darfur have been destroyed. But 2.5 million people have been displaced, and even more are dependent on international humanitarian assistance, which in turn will lead to ever greater civilian concentrations. Agricultural production has been virtually ended, with no prospect of resumption – and a way of living is in the process of disappearing. We no longer need wait for history's judgment of our failure; too many judgments have already been clarified by the actions and inaction of the past year.

December 6, 2004 – Genocide in Darfur – No Humanitarian Intervention – Equivocation – Avoidance of Moral Responsibility

Though genocide by attrition daily claims perhaps a thousand lives in Darfur, adding to a total morality figure of approximately 350,000 human beings, the once austerely clear moral character of this human destruction is slowly dissipating. In its place, we are being encouraged in various quarters to believe that the non-Arab or African populations of Darfur are dying and suffering because of insecurity that is increasingly attributed to the Darfuri insurgency groups. The central role of the *Janjaweed* – Khartoum's savage militia proxy – is highlighted less often, and is frequently conflated with an unspecified mélange of armed militias. The compelling underlying grievances that originally gave rise to the insurgency are also discussed less often, especially by Kofi Annan and his special representative for Sudan, Jan Pronk. But neither is there much stomach for historical truths in Washington, European capitals, or in other quarters.

Much of this expedient change in subject is captured in the increasingly cited analogy to Somalia, symbol of an ungovernable land degenerating into chaos, uncontrollable violence, and warlordism, a term heard more often in connection with the insurgency leaders. But the differences are distinctly greater than the similarities, and the "Somalia analogy" ultimately obscures the essential agency, the animating genocidal evil, responsible for human destruction in Darfur.

The upshot is that Darfur is being transformed – from an episode in massive, ethnically-targeted human destruction into a humanitarian crisis that is being impeded by an impersonal, almost abstract insecurity. There are no longer non-Arab or African victims of genocide and Arab génocidaires, but rather generic civilians at risk. Correspondingly, in place of the clearly demanded humanitarian intervention, many in the international community are content to discuss political, diplomatic, and funding challenges. The focus is not on Khartoum's past actions and serially broken agreements, but on present cease-fire violations and a perversely equitable distribution of responsibility for insecurity. Ultimately, the moral equivalence that has emerged from various pronouncements by Annan and Pronk is a sign of capitulation, a refusal to judge Khartoum's actions or those of the *Janjaweed* except in the context of a morally bankrupt neutrality. This is especially apparent in the December 3, 2004 *Report of the Secretary-General on the Sudan pursuant to UN Security Council Resolutions, 1556, 1564, and 1574.*

The *Report* is the inevitable culmination of a steadily weakened series of UN Security Council resolutions, which collectively represent a policy of appeasement. Indeed, Resolution 1574 dated November 18, 2004 was so utterly inconsequential in speaking of Darfur's catastrophe that Khartoum publicly and enthusiastically welcomed this international response.

It has not always been so within the UN. It is worth repeating Mukesh Kapila's comments that skated very close to an actual accusation of genocide, without using that word. Kapila, the outspoken former UN humanitarian coordinator for Sudan, declared as he approached the end of his tenure in a March 22, 2004 IRIN dispatch,

> "The only difference between Rwanda and Darfur now is the numbers involved" [said Kapila]. "This is more than just a conflict, it is an organised attempt to do away with a group of people." . . .
>
> The pattern of organised attacks on civilians and villages, abductions, killings and organised rapes by militias was getting worse by the day, [Kapila] said, and could deteriorate even further. "One can see how the situation might develop without prompt [action] . . . all the warning signs are there."

Kapila continued in a March 26, 2004 Reuters dispatch from Khartoum,

> "There are no secrets," U.N. Humanitarian Coordinator for Sudan Mukesh Kapila said. "The individuals who are doing this are known. We have their names. The individuals who are involved occupy senior positions [in the government of Sudan]."

Over seven months later, Kapila's words, which infuriated Khartoum, have proved all too prescient. 350,000 have died and perhaps another 30,000 die every month. By the end of the year, Darfur's genocide may have claimed half as many lives as Rwanda's genocide in 1994. And there are no signs that this genocidal destruction will diminish.

Forward-looking food assessments by the International Committee of the Red Cross (ICRC) and USAID, appalling conditions in the camps, huge numbers of people beyond all humanitarian access, and continuing insecurity deriving primarily from Khartoum's refusal to disarm or militarily neutralize the *Janjaweed* all suggest that mortality rates will continue to rise. Because the African tribal populations concentrated in camps cannot return to their villages, or the sites of their former villages, agricultural production remains at a standstill. Indeed, it has become increasingly difficult to see how the agricultural economy of Darfur can be revived. There is virtually no chance that there will be a meaningful spring 2005 planting, and thus no fall 2005 harvest. This huge food-dependent population of between 2 and 3 million human beings will require humanitarian assistance for at least two years. During that time, the lands of Darfur will likely be distributed to those who have backed the Khartoum regime's genocide, and the camp populations will slowly die or migrate from the region. Many young men will join the insurgency movements, continuing a cycle of violence and retribution.

Here we must bear in mind how directly responsible Khartoum and the *Janjaweed* are for the current state of affairs, and how relatively little responsibility falls upon the insurgents. For the NIF regime's counter-insurgency policy of systematically destroying the African villages throughout Darfur, as a means of eliminating the civilian base of support for the insurgents, has been in evidence for over a year. We know from a great many highly authoritative reports by Amnesty International, the International Crisis Group, Human Rights Watch, and other human rights investigations that Khartoum's policy of comprehensive village destruction began in summer 2003, and has continued unabated, with the *Janjaweed* the primary instrument of civilian destruction.

Human Rights Watch announced in its July 20, 2004 *A Human Rights Watch Briefing Paper - Darfur Documents Confirm Government Policy of Militia Support* that it obtained Sudan government internal documents that reveal a "government [of Sudan] policy of militia recruitment, support and impunity that has been implemented from high levels of the civilian administration."

Human Rights Watch also established in an August 27, 2004 report *Janjaweed Camps Still Active* that,

Despite repeated government [of Sudan] pledges to neutralize and disarm the *Janjaweed*, Human Rights Watch investigators in West and North Darfur were able to gather information on the militias' extensive network of bases. Five of the 16 camps, according to witnesses, are camps the *Janjaweed* share with the Sudanese government army. Even more ominous, the Sudanese government has incorporated members of the *Janjaweed* militia and its leaders into the police and the Sudanese army, including Islamist militia the Popular Defense Forces (PDF), which is under army jurisdiction.

Clearly Khartoum has not disarmed the *Janjaweed* – as promised in the "Joint Communiqué" of July 3, 2004, and as "demanded" in UN Security Council Resolution 1556, July 30, 2004 – and has not brought *Janjaweed* leaders to justice, also demanded in Security Council Resolution 1556. Indeed, the regime has not even provided a list of *Janjaweed* leaders, per the terms of the August 5, 2004 "Plan of Action" negotiated by Kofi Annan's special representative Jan Pronk. Nor has Khartoum provided any information on its "arrest or disarmament of *Janjaweed* and other armed groups," per the terms of Security Council Resolution 1564 dated September 18, 2004. Such information was to have been provided to the African Union Ceasefire Commission, but even Kofi Annan acknowledged in his December 3, 2004 report to the Security Council, S/2004/947 Section III paragraph 12, that "no progress was made [in November]" on this score.

And still the UN and the international community acquiesce before an ongoing policy of ethnic destruction that has been systematic. Arab villages, even when proximate to non-Arab villages, have typically been spared. This systematic destruction has entailed consistently close military coordination between Khartoum's regular ground and air military forces and the *Janjaweed*, and has been relentlessly thorough. People are killed, particularly men and boys, children are abducted, and women are raped. Dwellings and mosques are burned, Korans are desecrated; food- and seed-stocks are destroyed, along with fruit trees and agricultural implements; precious water wells are poisoned with human and animal corpses, and irrigation systems broken apart. Those who flee often die for lack of water and food in this harsh arid land. These are the searing realities that are now increasingly obscured by an international community that has no means of responding effectively.

Even humanitarian organizations have become complicit. MSF, which has performed superbly in the field, has not only made extremely ill-considered public comments on the issue of ethnic crimes in Darfur, but continues to bleach out of its reports virtually all data and observations that reflect the ethnic character of human destruction. The exceedingly rare references to ethnicity are typically disingenuous. In an October 2004 study by MSF Holland, *Persecution, Intimidation and Failure of Assistance in Darfur*, the organization can bring itself to say on page 7 only that "the majority of patients treated in MSF clinics and feeding centres are of Fur, Massaleit, and Zaghawa tribal origin." But of course the truth is that the overwhelming majority of people seen by MSF are members of the targeted African tribal groups – certainly over 95%. This self-censorship is evidently the price MSF is willing to pay to retain humanitarian access, though this seems not to preclude ignorant and presumptuous statements about the issue of genocide. Comments by Jean-Hevré Bradol, head of MSF-France, in "Thousands Die as World Denies Genocide," *The Financial Times* (London), July 6, 2004, work to deny genocide in Darfur,

> "Our teams have not seen evidence of the deliberate intention to kill people of a specific group. We have received reports of massacres, but not of attempts to specifcally eliminate all the members of a group."

Bradol's comments and tendentiously implied definition of genocide are a particular disgrace to an organization that was born out of a refusal to accept international protocols of neutrality during the genocide in Biafra (Nigeria) in the late 1960s.

The primary means by which the scale and nature of genocide in Darfur is obscured continue to be a refusal to acknowledge recent history, which has been amply recorded. At the same time that Mukesh Kapila was declaring that "the only difference between Rwanda and Darfur now is the numbers involved," and that, "one can see how the situation might develop without prompt [action] . . . all the warning signs are there," Amnesty International declared that,

"The government of Sudan has made no progress to ensure the protection of civilians caught up in the conflict in Darfur" Amnesty International said today. "This is not a situation where the central government has lost control. Men, women and children are being killed and villages are burnt and looted because the central government is allowing militias aligned to it to pursue what amounts to a strategy of forced displacement through the destruction of homes and livelihood of the farming populations of the region," Amnesty International said.

In the more than eight months since these emphatic press releases, nothing has changed. To be sure, many more hundreds of thousands of displaced people are now concentrated in camps characterized by appalling conditions, widespread shortages of clean water, shelter, sanitary facilities, and food. But even in these camps, the same ethnically-targeted violence and destruction – rape, murder, torture, abduction – continue with full sanction by the Khartoum regime. Amnesty International published a December 2, 2004 study of conditions in Darfur, *No One to Complain to: No Respite for the Victims, Impunity for the Perpetrators*, and the all too familiar patterns are here articulated on the basis of current evidence. Indeed, in some ways conditions have deteriorated, and this is especially clear in the growing hesitation of displaced Darfuris to speak to members of the international community. Page 1 of the study notes,

> While in June 2004 there was an urgency to speak to foreigners about the massive abuses committed in Darfur among the displaced community, it seems that since September the displaced have become afraid of talking. They are being watched by the security forces and the police within the camps for internally displaced persons, and fear being arrested after being seen speaking to foreigners.

The relentless failure of their stories to make a difference in camp conditions and the overall deterioration in the security situation has increasingly had the effect of silencing the voices of the victimized. And as these extremely vulnerable voices go silent, it becomes easier for their plight, and its causes, to be ignored by the international community, which is increasingly engaged in an expedient suggestion of moral equivalence between Khartoum and the insurgents, between the génocidaires and those resisting abusive tyranny.

Amnesty International declared on page 2 in its December 2 study that the Khartoum regime "continues to undermine the rule of law and the very concept of justice." In commenting on the "harassment and arrests of lawyers and human rights activists," Amnesty International noted that the detention and harassment of certain lawyers and activists "is a warning to the population that humanitarian, human rights and legal activities, particularly on behalf of the victims of the conflict in Darfur, are often considered subversive by the [regime's] authorities."

During the Darfur conflict, Amnesty International noted on page 6, "arbitrary arrests and prolonged incommunicado detention without charge or trial have increased." On page 8, Amnesty reported that "many arrests carried out by the security forces do not seem to be for any other reason than belonging to particular ethnic groups, usually those represented in the Darfur armed opposition groups (Zaghawa, Fur, Masalit, and other smaller groups)." And on page 13 Amnesty ominously notes, "persons arrested by the Sudanese security forces have been routinely tortured." On page 15, this alarming observation continued, "sometimes torture by the security forces is so severe that it causes the death of detainees." ... "torture is encouraged to continue because of the overwhelming impunity enjoyed by the perpetrators."

Amnesty International on page 21 draws the appropriate conclusion, "an international presence in every district of Darfur is needed." But there is no chance that present deployment of the contemplated African Union force and international human rights monitors can possibly take up this task without an immense augmentation of personnel and resources. Moreover, Khartoum for its part continues to refuse to accept any presence other than the current very small contingent of UN human rights monitors and an African Union force that has as its only mandate monitoring a ceasefire that has been in tatters since first negotiated in early April 2004.

This is the context in which Secretary-General Annan devotes inordinately particular attention, in his December 3, 2004 *Report to the Security Council (S/2004/947)*, to assessing very recent actions, but with almost no attention to the historical context of the past 22 months of genocidal destruction. Indeed, Annan's last explicit words on the issue of genocide, on June 17, 2004 were that he has "seen no reports that indicate ethnic cleansing or genocide." Jan Pronk for his part declares simply that a genocide finding is "premature," a full year after evidence of the ultimate human crime became unignorable.

Annan, following his assertion that "the Sudan Liberation Movement/ Army has aggressively violated its commitments to the November 9, 2004 Abuja protocols November 9, 2004," blandly observes in Section II paragraph 11 of S/2004/947 that the recent fully established aerial bombing attacks by Khartoum "may mean that the bombing took place despite Government instructions to the contrary." Annan ignores both the context for the intense fighting in the Tawilla area of North Darfur, the primary focus of his comments, and ludicrously suggests that acts as consequential as aerial bombing attacks, in clear violation of a recently signed cease-fire agreement, might be the work of rogue elements within Khartoum's military establishment. Whatever dissension among the NIF génocidaires in Khartoum, this notion of bombing taking place "despite Government instructions to the contrary" is simply not credible, and serves only as a means of asserting moral equivalence with the insurgents, who clearly do have both communications and command-and-control problems.

In Section III paragraph 12 of S/2004/947, Annan again blandly notes that,

> No progress was made with the disarmament of the *Janjaweed* in November. In accordance with paragraph 9 of Security Council Resolution 1564 (2004), any information on the arrest or disarmament of *Janjaweed* and other armed groups is to be provided by the Government [of Sudan] to the AU Ceasefire Commission (AUCFC). However, the AUCFC confirmed that it had not yet been invited to verify any disarmament activities by the government.

Annan goes on to remark in S/2004/947's Section IV paragraph 16, "there has also been no indication of the Government apprehending and bringing to justice *Janjaweed* leaders, which has been a central demand of the Security Council since its adoption of resolution 1556 (2004)."

Honesty dictates that this deferential and disingenuous diplomatese be translated. Khartoum continues to flout – brazenly and contemptuously – clear international demands, demands that have taken many forms over the past five months. Instead of condemning this obduracy, instead of reiterating UN demands in more forceful terms, Annan's simply registers Khartoum's non-compliance. There is no judgment, no condemnation, and certainly no honest acknowledgement that any meaningful response to current insecurity and cease-fire violations must entail ending impunity for the *Janjaweed*. For ongoing *Janjaweed* predations provide the essential context in which to understand the fighting in Tawilla and surrounding villages in North Darfur, as well as the reported attacks on police in Kalma camp in South Darfur. The continuing recycling of *Janjaweed* into the ranks of police, and the close coordination between police and Khartoum's brutally efficient security forces, are essential elements to any understanding of current violence in the camp environs, and yet Annan makes no mention of these key facts.

Finally, as if commenting on the mutual violation of rules at some sporting event, Annan makes the assertion of moral equivalence fully explicit in his concluding "Observations" in paragraph 55,

> The rebel movements must realize that their recent aggression cannot be justified on the basis of self-defence or grievances that predate the 9 November [Abuja] agreement to cease hostile actions. For its part, the government should note that any military advantage it might reap from the use of aerial bombing is more than outweighed by the negative political consequences of breaking its commitments under the ceasefire agreement.

It would be exceedingly difficult to parse fully the disingenuousness of these comments, or their deliberate omissions and highly partial nature. But the suggestion that Khartoum might fear negative political consequences as a result of violating the Abuja reiteration of previous ceasefire commitments is nothing short of shameless mendacity. Annan knows full well that Khartoum, on the contrary, has been considerably emboldened by the international community's failure to hold the regime to numerous previous agreements. To suggest that there might now be some fear-inducing political fallout for Khartoum as a result of its continuing use of military resources is simply absurd. The regime will use, as circumstances permit, all its military resources; and it will certainly continue to accord full impunity to the brutally predatory *Janjaweed*.

Even in commenting on humanitarian issues, Annan's inclination is to mislead. He declares, for example, in Section VII, paragraph 26 that "[in November] the percentage of vulnerable persons accessible in Darfur as a whole fell from 90 to 80 percent." But humanitarian access extended to nothing approaching 90% of the vulnerable populations in Darfur in October. Indeed, recent UN *Darfur Humanitarian Profiles* make clear that there is a huge conflict-affected population that is both inaccessible and unassessed. In early October 2004, the UN claimed access to 87% of the estimated 2 million conflict-affected persons in known camps and communities. However, the UN's September 6, 2004 *Darfur Humanitarian Profile No. 6* did not include the more than 500,000 conflict-affected persons estimated to be surviving beyond the reach of any humanitarian agencies. Counting both populations of conflict-affected persons yields a total of 2.5 million. The UN was able to reach only 1.8 million in October 2004, and in many cases very superficially. But even using the figure of 1.8 million, this is only 72% of the total conflict-affected population.

And it is from this level that we saw a further 10% decline in November 2004 to approximately 62%. A more accurate census of conflict-affected persons beyond humanitarian reach may very well reduce the figure for those reached to approximately 50%. And in all too many cases, those reached are provided with deeply inadequate supplies of food and critical non-food items, shelter, provision for clean water, sanitary facilities, basic medical care. A telling example appears on page 3 in the World Food Program and Center for Disease Control and Prevention's study, *Emergency Nutrition Assessment of Crisis Affected Populations, Darfur Region*, based on data collected between September 2 and September 20, 2004,

> Of those households with a ration card [troublingly, only 78% – ER] that received a ration in September [2004], more than half did not receive oil or pulses [legumes] (64.5% and 72.8% respectively). . . . More than half of households (57%) only received a cereal in the general ration in September.

This is simply not a diet that can sustain human beings for any extended period of time.

The National Islamic Front sees clearly the lack of resolve, the expediency, the disingenuousness that have consistently marked the international response to the regime's bad faith. Certainly Khartoum welcomed the change of subject from Darfur to the north-south peace talks in the November meeting of the Security Council in Nairobi and the passage of Resolution 1674 on November 19, 2004, a resolution so meaningless that Khartoum could do no less than welcome it. Nor was the shift in diplomatic strategy – from threats and demands to cynical financial inducements – lost on this group of ruthless survivalists.

This international encouragement of Khartoum's current behavior no doubt lies behind the steadily more menacing threats to humanitarian organizations operating in Darfur. The expulsions, noted earlier, of the country heads of operations for Oxfam International and Save the Children – for daring to criticize UN Security Council action and for reporting on Khartoum's military bombing attacks – are only the first step. Though it was widely reported that the expulsion orders had been "suspended," there can be little doubt about Khartoum's determination to see its will done, if by more devious means. Associated Press reported on December 2, 2004 on the de facto expulsion of the head of Oxfam's operations,

> In a letter obtained by The Associated Press, the Ministry of Humanitarian Affairs told the Oxfam director that although his expulsion was postponed, he had to leave Sudan because he had applied for an exit visa. "You have to depart as soon as possible, so that you will not find yourself in breach of Sudanese immigration laws and procedures," the letter said.

Even Kofi Annan is obliged to note in Section VII, paragraph 28 of his *Report* to the Security Council that,

> during the last two weeks [of November], [Khartoum's] process of issuing visas has slowed down for the nongovernmental organizations [NGOs] compared to previous months. In addition, some

Government authorities seem to have hardened their position towards international NGOs in allowing them to continue their work unconditionally. The ability of NGOs to speak out about aspects of the crisis that affect their activities, as well as threats to the civilian populations from either side, should be preserved and fully respected.

But there is no sign that Annan, the UN, or the international community is prepared to guarantee this respect. On the contrary, Khartoum seems to be gearing up for more expulsions and visa denials.

Moreover, there are strong signs that the regime may be on the verge of consolidating some of the geographic and demographic consequences of its genocidal assault on the African peoples of Darfur. The *Washington Post* reported on December 3, 2004 from Darfur,

> More than a million Darfurians, driven from their ancestral home-lands by government-backed Arab militias, could lose their land if authorities invoke a little-known law that allows the government to take over land abandoned for one year, relief officials and human rights groups said.
>
> For centuries, Darfur residents have been allowed to own and dis-tribute their land according to tribal customs. The rest of Sudan, however, is governed by the 1984 Sudan land tenure law. If imposed on Darfur, it would have dire implications for . . . displaced inhabi-tants now living in squalid camps in Sudan or neighboring Chad. As tens of thousands of Darfurians approach the anniversary of fleeing their villages, there is growing suspicion among UN observers and international human rights groups that the Sudanese government plans to use the obscure law to keep the displaced – mostly African farmers – from reclaiming their land.
>
> Tony Hall, the US ambassador to the UN World Food Program, who visited Nyala, the capital of South Darfur, last week. "The effects of this could be horrendous. Even if you get the displaced to go home, they would not own their land anymore. They might have to rent it or be forever homeless. I think we would then see a conflict and death toll that would be horrifying."

The *Washington Post* continued and provided appropriate historical context for those who are skeptical that Khartoum would proceed in such a fashion,

> Analysts said official efforts to move populations, part of a plan to solidify power and control resources, have been going on for decades. "Moving people off of land is part of a long pattern on the part of the government of Sudan," said John Prendergast of the nonprofit International Crisis Group. . . . In the 1980s, the government forcibly moved the Dinka population from the Bahr al-Ghazal area of southwest Sudan, where slave raiding, mass displacement and bombings became the norm, he said. In the early 1990s, government-backed militias burned huts and seized fertile land in the central Nuba Mountains region. Later in the decade, longtime residents of the Upper Nile oil fields were trucked off their land when the government wanted to start drilling for oil, human rights groups have reported. Now, international observers say, the same thing could easily happen in Darfur.

These are historical facts that provide essential context for understanding present human destruction and displacement in Darfur. Those ignorant of Khartoum's previous genocidal ambitions are likely to fail in recognizing these same ghastly ambitions in Darfur.

Kofi Annan and others may wish to promulgate the notion of "moral equivalence" despite the genocidal realities so fully and authoritatively chronicled by human rights organizations and other reporting bodies. But recent evidence strongly suggests the terrible asymmetry in violence throughout Darfur. For example, the recent shooting of an African Union peacekeeper that IRIN reported on December 3, 2004, "occurred as a team of ceasefire monitors were travelling to the village of Adwah in north Nyala, to investigate an alleged bombing by the government in breach of a ceasefire agreement with rebels." Which party in the conflict has a motive for such an unprecedented shooting incident and the obstruction of this investigation?

IRIN's December 3, 2004 dispatch noted another incident where the role of the *Janjaweed*, though not explicitly stated, seems beyond doubt:

On Tuesday [November 30, 2004], armed men had attacked a village in the western Sudanese state of North Darfur forcing about 2,000 internally displaced persons to flee from their homes, the medical charity Médecins Sans Frontières reported. "We are not sure who was behind the attack," Wyger Wentholt, MSF regional information officer told IRIN. "What our people on the ground were told by the IDPs was that the attackers were suspected to be a pro-government militia."

It is simply impossible to account for such an attack except as another episode of *Janjaweed* destruction. The Sudan Organization Against Torture (SOAT) reported a very similar attack in North Darfur, explicitly attributed to the *Janjaweed*, in its December 3, 2004 human rights report,

On 28 November 2004, a group of *Janjaweed* militia composed of 300 fighters on horse back allegedly launched an attack on Jenjanat village, 20 km east of Taweela [Tawilla] in Northern Darfur state and destroyed 200 houses and looted the villagers' livestock. During the attack, around 17 people were killed and 3 wounded.

Clearly Khartoum is continuing to use the *Janjaweed* as a military force, one not formally bound by any cease-fire agreement. And because there have been no consequences for its contemptuous refusal to respect international demands and agreements, the regime is now fully convinced that there will be no future consequences.

The movement toward moral equivalence, on the part of the UN, the US, and various other international actors is – in the context of ongoing genocide – the ultimate betrayal of justice and moral responsibility. Though some actions by the insurgents must be strongly criticized, there is nothing that can be measured against the massive, deliberate destruction of the African peoples of Darfur. They are the victims of genocide. A failure to acknowledge their suffering and terrible losses is the only betrayal left to the international community. This betrayal has begun.

February 17, 2005 – Darfur's Genocide – Faces of International Failure: A "Perfect storm" of Disingenuousness

Despite the current rhetorical sound and fury at the UN, nothing of substance has yet emerged to signify that the situation on the ground in Darfur will change soon. Genocide by attrition continues unabated, with staggering total mortality to date. The humanitarian crisis deepens, especially in the provision of food to badly weakened populations, foreshadowing even greater mortality in the longer term. No significant pressure has been exerted on Khartoum, pressure that might fundamentally change the NIF regime's behavior on the ground in Darfur. Meaningful peace negotiations, which address key issues of severe political and economic marginalization in Darfur, cannot be achieved under current African Union auspices; and the intense politicization of a possible International Criminal Court referral for Khartoum's génocidaires has too often been at the expense of meaningful discussion of humanitarian intervention.

Indeed, despite strong language from UN Secretary-General Annan and UN High Commissioner for Human Rights Louise Arbour on February 16, 2005, despite yet another US-proposed resolution for UN Security Council consideration, and despite the peculiar optimism of the belated January 1, 2005 *Darfur Humanitarian Profile No. 10*, which speaks to developments only through January 1, 2005, Darfur's crisis continues to deepen. Any global assessment of recent commentary and developments must discern a pattern of disturbing disingenuousness, an expedient reaching for the lowest common denominator of international agreement, and a profound moral failure to value, as fully human, Darfuri lives – daily lost in huge numbers amidst what Annan has accurately described as "little short of hell on earth."

Lieutenant-General Roméo Dallaire, UN force commander in Rwanda during the 1994 genocide and author of *Shake Hands with the Devil: The Failure of Humanity in Rwanda* (2003), cited the US commitment in Iraq and drew an ominous historical parallel in an Inter Press Service (IPS) dispatch of February 15, 2005,

> The Western world did not put enough resources into preventing the Rwandan genocide because it was focused on tensions in Yugoslavia, said Dallaire. Likewise, said Dallaire, Sudan is being sacrificed for

another conflict. "We're not going to Darfur (because) we're so involved in Iraq. There are no lessons learned in stopping the violence and rape and decimation of an ethnic group."

Although Annan appears, and merely innocuously, on only four pages of Dallaire's 560-page book, Dallaire spoke with unprecedented frankness about the duplicitous role of Annan and the UN in the Rwandan genocide, as Inter Press Service reports,

> Dallaire says he was told by Kofi Annan, then under-secretary-general for peacekeeping operations, not to act on the information [i.e., intelligence about Hutu extremist plans for genocide]. Further, Annan told him to give the data [from his confidential source "Jean-Pierre"] to the leader of the official Hutu political party – and one of the orchestrators of the secret plot. Dallaire deeply regrets not acting on "Jean-Pierre's" advice and preventing the genocide, "My failure to persuade (UN headquarters in) New York to act on Jean-Pierre's information still haunts me."

We might wish for a fuller transcript of Dallaire's actual words, so important is this assessment of Annan's role before and during the Rwandan genocide; Inter Press Service, however, is the only news-wire reporting on these extraordinary remarks.

But we do have Annan's words concerning the current genocide in Darfur, and though they have finally achieved an appropriate level of expressed outrage, there is deep disingenuous in his suggested time-line for what the world has known about Darfur, and the authority with which we have known it. For using the the January 25, 2005 *Report of the International Commission of Inquiry on Darfur to the United Nations Secretary-General - Pursuant to Security Council Resolution 1564 of 18 September 2004*, Annan is clearly attempting to suggest that this Report marks a *terminus a quo*, some point of departure in our understanding of Darfur's horrific realities. This is not true, and Annan's suggestion to the contrary is motivated at least in part by his desire not to be seen as having stood idly by for so many months during which these realities were unfolding. Annan is reported by Reuters as declaring on February 16, 2005,

"This report is one of the most important documents in the recent history of the UN," Annan said.

Agence France-Press amplified Annan's position in its February 16, 2005 dispatch,

"This report [of the International Commission of Inquiry] demonstrates beyond all doubt that the last two years have been little short of hell on earth for our fellow human beings in Darfur," Annan said.

But Annan's reference to the "recent history of the UN" is deliberately misleading; certainly such "doubt" as Annan suggests in this comment was incinerated long ago, indeed over a year ago, by continuous reports from Amnesty International, Human Rights Watch, the International Crisis Group, as well as subsequent reports from Physicians for Human Rights, various UN human rights investigations, and the Coalition for International Justice. There is virtually nothing new in the Report of the Commission of Inquiry; indeed, it did scandalously little forensic work, despite having forensic specialists on the Commission team, and failed badly in not investigating the sites of specifically reported mass executions of non-Arab/African men and boys.

Annan declared in a February 16, 2005 UN News Centre dispatch, as if revealing something heretofore in doubt,

The Commission has established that many people in Darfur have been the victims of atrocities perpetrated on a very large scale, for which the Government of Sudan and the *Janjaweed* are responsible.

But again, these atrocities and Khartoum's responsibility were long ago established with full authority by numerous human rights investigations, including investigations by UN human rights experts. Human Rights Watch, Amnesty International, MSF, International Crisis Group, and the ICRC among others have generated numerous reports detailing conditions that make clear the existence and extent of the genocide occurring in Darfur. Here we must recall that Annan declared on June 17, 2004 – reported that day by Voice of America, and on June 19, 2004 in *The Globe and Mail*, when many of these reports were already extant – that "'based on reports that I have received, I am not ready to describe [Darfur] as genocide or ethnic cleansing yet.' " These remarks, either remarkably ignorant or deeply disingenuous, stood in the starkest contrast to assessments coming earlier from the UN humanitarian coordinator for Sudan, Mukesh Kapila, who in March 2004 explicitly likened ethnically-targeted human destruction in Darfur to the Rwandan genocide, and from UN Under-Secretary for Humanitarian Affairs Jan Egeland, who had on a number of previous occasions insistently described the actions in Darfur as "ethnic cleansing."

We should be grateful that Annan is finally describing truthfully the nature of human destruction in Darfur; but this must not be the occasion for a re-writing of the historical time-line defining our understanding of this destruction. The belatedness of Annan's remarks cannot be expunged by merely rhetorical means.

We catch another glimpse of UN belatedness in comments on the January 25, 2005 *Report of the Commission of Inquiry* coming from UN High Commissioner for Human Rights Louise Arbour. Arbour commented in detail on the horrific conditions at Kailek during March and April 2004 in a February 16, 2005 UN News Centre report,

> In one of the most chilling examples catalogued by the commission, Government forces and Janjaweed militiamen twice attacked Kailek, a village populated mainly by members of the ethnic Fur group, in South Darfur. After the second attack, during which many civilians were shot and killed, about 30,000 villagers were confined for 50 days within a small area where they then endured "the most abhorrent treatment," Ms. Arbour said.
>
> ". . . some men were singled out and summarily shot. There are reports of people being thrown on to fires and burnt alive. Women and children were separated out, confined in a walled area, and periodically taken away by their captors to be raped, [with] some subjected to gang rapes."

But we learned of these realities long before the UN Commission of Inquiry reported on Kailek. And the suggestion by Arbour that the realities of Kailek are in any way new, or receive new authority from the Commission of Inquiry, appears but another disingenuous effort to obscure how much we have known and how long we have known it.

The author detailed conditions in Kailek in March 2004 on the basis of substantial reports in a series of emails from Eltigani Seisi Ateem, former Governor of Darfur and chairman of the Darfur Union in exile in Great Britain. Ateem's March 24, 2004 email noted,

> Two weeks ago the Janjaweed militia attacked the villages to the south of Kass. All the villages in the Shattaya and Hamiya areas have been torched and a number of innocent civilians have been killed. The attack on Sindo which I have reported earlier has led to mass displacement. Between 11,000 and 13,000 people have fled to Kailek area where they have been surrounded by the [Janjaweed] militia.
>
> These people have no access to water or food as the militia has prevented any supplies of water and food. We have just received information that those who are now surrounded in Kailek are dying of thirst and hunger. The situation requires immediate intervention to save the lives of about 13,000 innocent civilians trapped by the Janjaweed militia in Kailek, dying of thirst and hunger.

This email and a subsequent analysis by the author, included in Chapter 2 (see section *March 31, 2004 – the N'Djamena, Chad Peace Talks – Khartoum's Contempt*), helped to galvanize a UN inter-agency investigation of conditions at Kailek, the April 24, 2004 *Report: A UN Inter-Agency fact-finding and humanitarian needs assessment mission, Kailek, South Darfur,* an investigation whose conclusions were widely disseminated at the time, by the author among others.

The realities of the Kailek camp were established definitively over nine months ago. It is either culpable ignorance on the part of Arbour to suggest that these realities have been reported with new authority by the Commission of Inquiry – or an even more culpable disingenuousness. As Darfur's realities intrude themselves ever more forcefully into international awareness, their historical timeline must not be re-written over the blood of the many hundreds of thousands who have perished or been displaced and left totally bereft in this cataclysm of genocidal destruction.

The US draft proposal for a new UN Security Council resolution on Sudan faces almost certain defeat or major revision, given opposition from veto-wielding China and Russia. But it is important to understand that not only does this resolution fail to offer effective measures to halt genocide in Darfur, but in acquiescing before the proposed peace-support operation for southern Sudan, as fashioned by the UN Department of Peacekeeping Operations, the US proposal does positive harm. Even in the process, however, the draft proposal misleadingly attempts to suggest that such a southern Sudan peace-support operation will have significant implications for Darfur. This is untrue.

What is true is that the international community appears willing to contribute forces to a peace-support operation in southern Sudan, presumably because a cease-fire has largely held since October 2002, albeit with notable violations on the part of Khartoum and its militia allies. But the world refuses to intervene to halt civilian slaughter and ongoing genocidal destruction in Darfur. Let us at least be clear about the choice that is reflected here.

The force for southern Sudan is addressed by the "Agreement on Permanent Ceasefire and Security Arrangements Implementation Modalities." This became part of the Comprehensive Peace Agreement of January 9, 2005 in Nairobi, Kenya, signed on December 31, 2004 by the Khartoum regime and the Sudan People's Liberation Movement/Army (SPLM/A). This key protocol is the only language concerning a UN peacekeeping operation to which the SPLM/A has committed itself and on which it has been consulted. The Protocol stipulated in section 15.1,

> The Parties [Government of Sudan and SPLM/A] agree to request the UN to constitute a lean, effective, sustainable, and affordable UN Peace Support Mission to monitor and verify this Agreement and to support the implementation of the Comprehensive Peace Agreement as provided for under Chapter VI of the UN Charter.

There is no evidence that the proposed UN peace support operation for southern Sudan – United Nations Mission in Sudan (UNMISUD) – will be either lean or affordable for the purposes that should guide deployment. It is thus difficult to see how such an operation can be "sustainable." The force proposed in the US-drafted Security Council resolution, "up to 10,000 uniformed personnel, plus 715 civilian police, and an appropriate civilian component," could hardly be more vaguely described. Moreover, though articulated under the auspices of Chapter VII of the UN Charter, the proposed deployment of this force is not defined in terms that are specific to the particular military situation in southern Sudan.

There is no indication of how UNMISUD would confront military hostilities initiated by Khartoum-controlled militia forces, even as this is distinctly the most likely source of cease-fire violations and the greatest single threat to the peace agreement. The US proposal speaks of a mandate in Section 2, (a)(b)(c), to "monitor and verify the Ceasefire Agreement, and support implementation of the Comprehensive Peace Agreement," "to observe and monitor the movement of armed groups," and to "investigate violations of the ceasefire agreement," but not how the force would respond to violations that threaten the existence or viability of the ceasefire.

The mandate includes "assisting in the establishment of the disarmament, demobilization, and reintegration program as called for in the Comprehensive Peace Agreement and its implementation through voluntary disarmament, and weapons collections and destruction." But without very specific rules of engagement, and a much clearer role in the disarmament of the militias, the bulk of this vast UNMISUD force, in excess of 10,000, will have no role other than to protect the approximately 750 actual monitors on the ground.

Jan Pronk, in a February 7, 2005 briefing of the UN Security Council, outlined the details of UNMISUD. UNMISUD will have 750 military observers, a 5,000-strong "enabling force," and a "protection component" of 4,000. But despite the Chapter VII auspices specified in the US proposal, it is unclear how the mandate articulated can be fulfilled by a force of such composition – except in terms of observation and monitoring alone. Such observation and monitoring are certainly of fundamental importance, and must without question be provided. But a force well in excess of 10,000, costing over $1 billion per year, without a meaningful mandate other than observation, is the very opposite of lean and sustainable, especially in the context of the overwhelming transitional needs of civilian southern Sudan.

Here we should consider the almost total lack of funding for emergency transitional aid in southern Sudan, particularly in the context of returning displaced persons, as Secretary-General Annan noted in a February 3, 2005 UN News Service dispatch,

> Secretary-General [Annan] states that substantial aid is required to resettle refugees and Internally Displaced Persons [in southern Sudan], with between 500,000 and 1.2 million displaced people expected to return to their homes this year alone.

These 500,000 to 1.2 million returnees represent a huge financial challenge. How can a bloated and extremely expensive peace-support operation, with no meaningful mandate beyond monitoring, be justified in the context of such desperate human need? Unless a much clearer mandate is articulated, with specific goals and functions, this force will reflect not the needs of southern Sudan but the very worst of UN bureaucracy and inefficiency. It will be neither lean nor affordable in any meaningful context of cost effectiveness.

Moreover, there are deeply troubling features to the nature and composition of UNMISUD. Again, this force has been negotiated by the UN Department of Peacekeeping Operations exclusively with the same Khartoum regime that has been found by the UN Commission of Inquiry to be responsible for massive and ongoing "crimes against humanity" in Darfur, and which has been guilty of genocide in the Nuba Mountains and the southern oil regions of Sudan. The SPLM/A has not been consulted or included in the planning of the peace-support operation. This is short-sighted and invites conflicting views of the UNMISUD mandate, terms of deployment, and difficulties expected by the Parties to the cease-fire agreement.

Further, the makeup of presently committed forces is troubling. India, Malaysia, China, and Russia – all countries with very substantial investments in Sudan's oil sector – are among the relatively few nations that have volunteered forces. The presence of Pakistan and Jordan in this mix is also a concern. Pakistan proved to be an obstructionist force on the Security Council in 2004 in efforts to confront the crisis in Darfur. Jordan has supplied Khartoum with much of the ordnance used by the NIF regime's Antonovs in attacks on civilians during the 1990s. There has been far too little effort to secure the presence of countries that have not demonstrated a morally compromised solidarity with Khartoum and which are not interested parties in preserving oil development access.

Though the US proposal repeatedly refers to Darfur in the context of UNMISUD, there is never any indication of how deployment in southern Sudan will have any effect on the ground in Darfur. The proposed resolution speaks of UNMISUD carrying out its mandate in "continuous liaison with the AU Mission in Darfur"; but if the UNMISUD is exclusively to monitor the ceasefire in southern Sudan, the significance of "continuous liaison" is quite unclear.

Elsewhere the draft resolution speaks of UNMISUD in terms of "an effective public information campaign in coordination with the AU." This would seem to be the quintessence of UN "non-speak," and irrelevant to the desperately real security needs in Darfur, needs far beyond the capacity of the present, or contemplated AU force.

The closest the draft resolution comes to speaking meaningfully about the connection between Darfur and UNMISUD is,

[The Security Council] requests the Secretary-General to brief the Council within 60 days on options for how UNMISUD can reinforce the effort to foster peace in Darfur, including through appropriate capacity building assistance to the AU Mission.

But what does this mean? How are we to imagine that the "options" Kofi Annan will offer two months from now are different from the "options" now evident on the basis of months of slow and uninspired deployment by the AU?

The proposed US resolution is but another diplomatic placeholder. It is neither specific nor resolute in moving the international community towards humanitarian intervention in Darfur, the only option that gives any promise of slowing the massive, ethnically-targeted human destruction that has been clearly in evidence for well over a year. The proposed arms embargo will never be approved by China or Russia, Khartoum's two key arms suppliers. And the carefully hedged, targeted sanctions against Khartoum (Sections 11-13, Annex 1) – restrictions on travel and potential asset-freezes – are of little more than symbolic significance to a regime that has already declared it will strenuously resist any international effort to have Sudanese nationals tried abroad for crimes against humanity, genocide, and war crimes in Darfur.

It is easy for the resolution to declare in its penultimate paragraph in Section 19, that the Security Council is determined "that perpetrators of the crimes and atrocities identified by the International Commission of Inquiry [for Darfur] must be brought to justice through international accepted means and that the climate of impunity in Sudan shall end."

But without specifying the means for ending violence in Darfur, without providing expanded humanitarian capacity, without suggesting consequences for Khartoum's continuing flouting of the previous Security Council demand that the regime disarm the *Janjaweed* and bring its leaders to justice – the singular demand of Resolution 1556 dated July 30, 2004 – without committing to anything more than vague support for a clearly inadequate AU force, the US proposal seems little more than vacuous rhetoric.

The same must be said of the transparently empty threat of "actions relating to Sudan's oil sector" in Section 18. Though Kofi Annan is much given to this threat, as was former US Secretary of State Colin Powell, it is simply meaningless with China sitting on the Security Council. Not only has Beijing made clear that it will veto any sanctions provision that might include such actions, the Chinese economy could easily absorb every barrel of Sudanese crude available for export. Since the Chinese are the dominant player in southern oil development and production, and view Sudan exclusively as a strategic off-shore asset that must be protected diplomatically at all costs, threats of "actions" against Sudan's petroleum sector are far from threatening: they simply make plain that the international community is content with posturing.

Because insecurity in Darfur is not seriously addressed by the US draft proposal, nor by proposals from any other international actor, we must assess the future of humanitarian aid delivery on the basis of current conditions and capacity. The conclusions are unspeakably grim.

The WFP reached 1.5 million recipients in December 2004, a figure that defines the humanitarian situation as detailed in the UN's *Darfur Humanitarian Profile No. 10*. But this figure does not reflect the extremely ominous drop in food deliveries from January 1 to January 31, 2005. 300,000 fewer people received food, possibly as many as 1.2 million according to various

UN sources, even as food needs became globally more acute in the greater Darfur humanitarian theater. The ICRC declared in a February 9, 2005 report, *Darfur: A Deteriorating Situation*, that it, "concurs with WFP figures that estimate between 2.5 and 3 million people in Darfur will need food assistance this year."

In short, a massive food deficit and the threat of famine loom ever greater, and the UN's respected Food and Agricultural Organization (FAO) has declared as much explicitly in a February 7, 2005 *Wall Street Journal* article,

> "All the indicators are there for a famine," says Marc Bellemans, the Sudan emergency coordinator for the UN's Food and Agriculture Organization. In a report to fellow UN agencies late last year, the FAO warned "a humanitarian crisis of unseen proportions is unfolding in the Darfur region."

Despite these clear features of the humanitarian situation, *Darfur Humanitarian Profile No. 10* glibly suggests on page 3 that "the catastrophic mortality figures predicted in some quarters have not materialized." But there is no indication of what mortality data inform this assessment. There is certainly nothing that speaks to mortality assessments by the author or by Dr. Jan Coebergh in "Sudan: Genocide has Killed More Than the Tsunami," *Parliamentary Brief* Vol. 9, No. 7, February 2005. There is no account in this or any other UN Profile of violent mortality, mortality in inaccessible rural areas, mortality in Chad, mortality from February 2003 through March 2004. We are offered simply the bald assertion that catastrophic mortality has not materialized, despite the substantial number of reports and data suggesting that in fact mortality is well in excess of 300,000. Perhaps those assembling the monthly *Darfur Humanitarian Profiles* do not consider this figure catastrophic.

What cannot be concealed, even by the belatedness of *Profile 10's* appearance, are dimensions of the humanitarian crisis that ensure prospective human mortality in Darfur will certainly continue to be catastrophic, at least by most standards. An important factor in amplifying the effects of famine mortality will be what appears to be an impending second missed opportunity by international aid organizations to pre-position food in

Darfur prior to the June/July - September rainy season. Moreover, funding for food is far short of what is needed, and the appropriate mix of foods – a diet that can sustain human life – is clearly threatened. The UN World Food Program (WFP) reported from Geneva in a February 15, 2005 Reuters dispatch that any previous improvements in the provision of food would soon be reversed,

> The United Nations urged donors on Tuesday to speed the flow of food aid to Sudan's Darfur or risk worsening shortages in the conflict-ridden region.

WFP spokeswoman Christiane Berthiaume noted key deficiencies in the food provided, deficiencies with extremely serious health implications over the longer term as she continued, "In addition, much of the food aid received so far had been in the form of cereals, but other commodities, such as beans, sugar and salt, were in perilously short supply, she said."

And more details of the food program shortage emerged as Voice of America reported on February 16, 2005 another important part of Berthiaume's comments,

> [Berthiaume said] it is crucial that the agency pre-position food stocks before the rainy season that begins in July and August. "And the case is particularly critical in West Darfur where there are large areas that will be cut off by the rain," she said. . . . "The food aid requirement at the peak of the hunger season in July and August is estimated at just over 11,000 tons of food. So, that means that we need to pre-position 23,000 tons of food for July and August and that is on top of the monthly requirement."

There is nothing remotely approaching this transport or logistical capacity for West Darfur.

Refugees International (RI), in its important February 16, 2005 Sudan food-needs assessment, *Sudan: Food Shortages Spreading Beyond Conflict Areas*, detailed a number of deeply troubling contingencies and considerations that figure nowhere in *Darfur Humanitarian Profile No. 10* or its assumptions about mortality,

Without an increase in food commitments, WFP anticipates to run out of food at the end of March for the South, Eastern and Central regions of Sudan. If new commitments are not made for Darfur, food could run out this summer. Moreover, the food needs in southern Sudan could rise sharply if larger than expected numbers of refugees and internally displaced people decide to return following the signing of a peace agreement last month.

Assessing global acute malnutrition, the February 16, 2005 RI report noted that while rates in camps have improved,

Outside of camps, however, malnutrition rates may run between 20% and 25%, and wild foods are turning up for sale in markets in North Darfur, an indicator of severe food stress.

RI also notes with particular concern that "the WFP says that it doesn't currently have enough food in the pipeline to pre-position all the food it needs for the rainy season, when muddy roads make transportation and deliveries difficult." This will be most consequential for West Darfur, which has been spared much of the current violence, but may because of its geographic remoteness during the rainy season see the highest levels of mortality.

The US draft Security Council resolution does not meaningfully advance the international response to massive genocidal destruction in Darfur. The supposed connections between a bloated and vaguely tasked UN peace-support operation in southern Sudan and the urgent human security requirements in Darfur are facile and largely rhetorical. Though the cessation of hostilities agreement in southern Sudan has largely held since October 2002, more than 10,000 uniformed personnel are evidently likely to be deployed for essentially monitoring purposes.

In Darfur, where the AU has managed to deploy only about 1,500 troops over several months, violence directed against civilians continues unabated in a climate of virtually total impunity. Khartoum flouts the only meaningful demand that the UN Security Council has made, that it disarm the brutal *Janjaweed* allies and bring *Janjaweed* leaders to justice, and has accelerated its deliberate obstruction of humanitarian operations.

These realities cannot be changed by rhetoric, by newly contrived historical time-lines, by lowest-common-denominator UN resolutions, or by the threat of international criminal trials – despite the inflated claims by human rights organizations such as Human Rights Watch, which is using Darfur as an occasion to lobby for the International Criminal Court.

Absent robust humanitarian intervention, what is indeed catastrophic human mortality – animated by genocidal ambitions – will continue essentially unchecked.

March 17, 2005 – Failure to Confront Khartoum: Intervention Slips to Mere Relief – Consequences for Darfur

The situation in Darfur has taken an extremely ominous turn, as Reuters reported on March 16, 2005,

> The United Nations has withdrawn all international staff in part of western Sudan to the state capital after Arab militias said they would target foreigners and UN convoys in the area, the top UN envoy in Sudan said on Wednesday. "The Janjaweed militia have said that they will now target all foreigners and all UN humanitarian convoys, so we have withdrawn all people to El-Geneina [capital of West Darfur]," [the UN's Jan Pronk] said. The militias gave the warning to the drivers of seized UN trucks, he said.

The direct, ongoing relationship between Khartoum's regular military and intelligence forces and the *Janjaweed* has been established beyond any reasonable doubt by human rights groups, particularly Human Rights Watch, the UN Commission of Inquiry, the African Union monitoring force in Darfur, and by virtue of variously obtained internal regime documents. The full extent of the present *Janjaweed* threat to humanitarian workers in West Darfur is unclear but deeply ominous; the origin of this threat in Khartoum is unmistakable.

We must see this *Janjaweed* threat against humanitarian personnel in West Darfur both as a means of curtailing the international witnessing of Khartoum's accelerating military efforts in the area, and as an extension of Khartoum's resumed campaign to obstruct relief efforts, a development highlighted by Kofi Annan in his February 4, 2005 briefing *Report of the Secretary-General Pursuant to Security Council Resolution 1556*, Paragraph 21, to the UN Security Council,

> December and January saw increasing harassment of international nongovernmental organizations by [Khartoum's] local authorities [in Darfur], particularly in South Darfur. In a worrying sign that earlier progress is being rolled back, systematic arrest, false and hostile accusations through the national media outlets, and outright attacks were combined with renewed restrictions on travel permits and visa applications. Almost all NGOs operating South Darfur faced some form of intimidation that delayed and restricted their operations.

This obstructionism marks resumption of a strategy that was evident as long ago as December 2003, when UN Special Envoy for Humanitarian Affairs Tom Vraalsen reported Khartoum's "systematic" denial of humanitarian access to non-Arab or African tribal populations in Darfur. Even more insistently, in February 22, 2005 testimony before the International Development Committee of the British House of Commons, Mukesh Kapila describes what he witnessed as UN Resident and Humanitarian Coordinator for Sudan prior to being forced from his position by Khartoum in March 2004.

> [Kapila:] I would say that 75-80% of the problem we had on the humanitarian side [in responding to Darfur] was certainly due to the systematic obstruction by the Sudanese government of humanitarian access.

And this continues. It is almost impossible to conceive a more brazen defiance of the international community than Khartoum's renewed, calculated assaults on humanitarian efforts in the most distressed region in the world today. The direct human consequences, if this present tactic of genocidal destruction is not reversed, will be many tens of thousands of lives lost. In a statement reported by the December 15, 2004 *Financial Times*, UN Undersecretary for Humanitarian Affairs Jan Egeland declared that mortality in Darfur could reach to 100,000 deaths per month if insecurity forced the withdrawal of humanitarian assistance. What we are witnessing in West Darfur is the first step in that forced withdrawal.

For West Darfur is the most precariously situated of the three states that make up Darfur Province, and is the geographic region where the UN's World Food Program must work hardest to pre-position food before the advent of the rainy season in late spring/early summer. Every day of delay in this effort will add more casualties to the already unforgivably large current number, possibly as large as 380,000.

Peace will neither come to Darfur nor survive in southern Sudan without a fundamental shift in world attitudes towards the National Islamic Front regime in Khartoum, even when it is nominally succeeded in July 2005 by a "government of national unity" as a result of the January 9, 2005 Comprehensive Peace Agreement signed in Nairobi. For years the international community has behaved – despite all evidence to the contrary – as though this military junta is capable of fundamental reform, that it can be moderated in significant ways, and that it can be weaned of its recourse to genocidal domestic security policies.

In fact, the only shifts within the regime have been calculations about which of its policies must be accommodated to international pressures that wax and wane. The very same brutal men who came to power by military coup in June 1989 continue to rule the country, with the complex exception of Hassan al-Turabi. The senior members of the NIF now under sealed indictment for massive "crimes against humanity," per the January 25, 2005 UN Commission of Inquiry in Darfur, were all part of the regime that came to power in large measure to abort the peace process that was reaching towards culmination during the 1986-89 government of Sadiq el-Mahdi.

[*Africa Confidential* February 18, 2005, Volume 46, No. 4 has published an extensive list of members of the National Islamic Front who have been implicated in "crimes against humanity," and who have as a consequence increasingly little interest in accommodating international concerns about justice and "accountability." Included is First Vice-President Ali Osman Taha, with primary responsibility for Khartoum's Darfur policy.]

The process that produced the Comprehensive Peace Agreement between the National Islamic Front (NIF) and the Sudan People's Liberation Movement (SPLM) must be seen for what it is: a process that is still very much underway, and extremely vulnerable. For Khartoum assumes that the remarkable, and unprecedented, international pressure that sustained this process will inevitably diminish under the costly burdens of ongoing commitment to protecting the peace, both financially and militarily in the form of a UN peace-support operation. There is already considerable evidence that Khartoum's calculation is all too accurate.

Moreover, since the regime acceded to the agreement of January 9, 2005 so clearly under duress, so obviously needing to offer the international community something while it pursued a genocidal counter-insurgency policy in Darfur, it is difficult to see this context of "agreement" as auguring any but an ominous future. When the Darfur matter is resolved, Khartoum will be in a position to resume war in southern Sudan, the Nuba Mountains, and Southern Blue Nile if it wishes.

Certainly the massive human destruction and displacement already achieved in Darfur suggest that the genocide is so far along as to be unstoppable before there has been a fundamental shift in the region's demographics, as well as its economic and political power arrangements. Khartoum's counter-insurgency operation has achieved ghastly success. The rebel groups have fractured politically and militarily, and agricultural production among the non-Arab or African populations from which the insurgents have recruited has collapsed.

But why would the regime choose to resume war with the south? Why would the historic opportunity of peace be foregone? Because there is great oil wealth in the south that the NIF still believes it can control in its entirety, rather than share evenly with the people of southern Sudan. And because the regime remains committed to an Islamizing and Arabizing agenda, and because it calculates that the international consequences of resuming war, and reasserting full political control in Khartoum, will be manageable. It is no secret that a number of powerful voices within the regime have felt that in accommodating international pressure through the Naivasha peace process, too much was given away to the south. These voices, of a more brutally calculating survivalism, may very well prevail when Darfur is extinguished or becomes merely a chronic humanitarian warehousing operation.

And how can we gainsay such vicious calculation? If the world continues to conduct business as usual with this regime; if commercial and capital investment continues to come from European and Asian countries even at the height of the 21st century's first great episode of genocidal destruction, if the World Bank blandly declares it "expects to normalize relations with heavily indebted Sudan within a year," as Reuters reported on March 9, 2005, why should the regime believe that things will be any different after a carefully contrived breakdown of the peace agreement with southern Sudan? Certainly there will be ample opportunities for such contrivance; the regime-allied militias of Upper Nile Province are only the most conspicuous means available. For this reason alone the international community should be registering a great deal more concern about recent militia activities in the oil regions of Eastern Upper Nile, particularly the Akobo and Nasir areas.

At the same time, Khartoum is more than willing to use the peace agreement of January 9, 2005 as a means of deflecting or warning off greater international pressure over Darfur, declaring in effect that the north-south peace agreement is in danger if the world community decides to act more aggressively on Darfur. We have what is only the most recent installment in this pattern of behavior in comments by Khartoum's Justice Minister Ali Yassin, one of those who is under sealed indictment for "crimes against humanity."

Yassin was speaking on the convening of the UN Commission on Human Rights – the NIF regime holds a seat on this now disgraced international body – and his reference to Sudan's impending "government of national unity" was a clear invocation of the power-sharing agreement that was a central part of the January 9 Comprehensive Peace Agreement. A March 14, 2005 Agence France-Press dispatch from Geneva reported,

> "Unmeasured, uneven and unbalanced pressure and signals have exacerbated the already volatile situation in Darfur," Sudan's Justice Minister Ali Yassin said in a speech to the 53-strong committee [of the UN Commission on Human Rights] which began its 61st annual session here on Monday. "Any undue pressure on the government of national unity will retard its ability to implement the comprehensive peace agreement," he said.

This strategy of using as a threat the possible collapse of the completed north-south peace agreement is entirely continuous with the strategy the regime deployed for months in holding out the prospect of an impending agreement. In February 22, 2005 testimony before the International

Development Committee of the British House of Commons, former UN Resident and Humanitarian Coordinator for Sudan Mukesh Kapila offered an extraordinary moment of honesty. The Chair of the International Development Committee, Tony Baldry, pointedly asked,

> [Baldry:] Did you have any suggestion from the UK Government that you should ease up your comments and your criticisms on Darfur until the Naivasha agreement was concluded?
> [Mukesh Kapila:] Yes.

In other words, for well over a year, Khartoum used the southern peace process as a means of muting international criticism – especially by the UK, the US, and Norway – of genocide in Darfur. Now the regime's diplomatic manipulation has reversed itself. As criticism over Darfur mounts, Khartoum is resorting to clear threats to undermine the January 9, 2005 Comprehensive Peace Agreement. The assumption is that the international community will again find expediency the easiest way to respond to Sudan's ongoing agony, and make a series of trade-offs and concessions that will cumulatively compromise the effectiveness of any response to Darfur or to the urgent transitional needs of southern Sudan. This attitude on the part of the international community is perfectly reflected in comments attributed to a "senior US official," likely Charles Snyder, the chief State Department official working on Sudan, published in a March 14, 2005 *Financial Times* dispatch,

> A senior US official argued that the main US constraint [in considering humanitarian intervention in Darfur] was fear that too much pressure over Darfur would destroy the US-mediated agreement signed in January that ended Sudan's separate north-south conflict, Africa's longest-running civil war, which cost some 2 million lives.

In other words, despite the finding by the US State Department that genocide is occurring in Darfur – a finding nominally echoed by the White House – and despite hundreds of thousands of casualties to date, and with many more clearly in prospect, the US is worried about excessive pressure on the regime orchestrating this genocide.

The National Islamic Front is easily able to sniff out such expedient instincts and fashion responses accordingly. This is moral cowardice on the part of the US, which in its painful transparency constitutes very poor policy.

There are a number of deeply worrying signs and trends in southern Sudan. Some can be easily identified; others require closer examination of geography, recent history, the terms of the peace agreement, and the particular needs of a land ravaged by 21 years of brutally destructive civil war and scorched-earth clearances, particularly in the oil regions of Upper Nile Province.

The lack of financial commitment to emergency transitional aid is one obvious measure of the fragility of the peace process. Speaking of the agreement, UN Undersecretary for Humanitarian Affairs Jan Egeland declared in a March 7, 2005 Deutsche Presse-Agentur dispatch,

> "In the south of Sudan, the world has really achieved something fantastic in putting an end to the bloodiest war in this region. But it is not willing to foot the bill of building the peace and providing for the return of refugees," [Egeland] said. "My (UN) people have built up very dramatically in anticipation that the money will be coming because they simply cannot believe that the donor community will not assist them."
>
> [Egeland] told *The New York Times* in an interview that only 25 million dollars of the total 500 million dollars pledged by donors last October had been received by his office. The funds are destined to economic development and build a democratic system to support the peace accord.

Only 5% of the internationally pledged emergency assistance has been received, this as southern Sudan has entered into what will be the most precarious moment of a nascent peace. Even the food needs of southern Sudan have not been funded, as senior spokesman for the World Food Program Peter Smerdon noted in a March 9, 2005 IRIN dispatch,

> "The reality is that as of this week the 2005 [UN World Food Program] operation for south and east Sudan, totaling [US] $301 million, is less than 10% funded."

The failure to commit to substantial resources for emergency transitional needs in southern Sudan ensures that the means for accommodating the many hundreds of thousands of returning Internally Displaced Persons and refugees will not be in place in a timely fashion. The threats to stability created by such a large influx of bereft civilians, in regions that are destitute and bearing the terrible scars of war, are far too many.

At the same time, the UN Department of Peacekeeping Operations has proposed an exorbitantly expensive and very poorly conceived peace-support operation for southern Sudan – one that will cost over $1 billion per year and yet still fails to address in meaningful fashion the greatest military threat to the negotiated peace, viz. the potent Khartoum-allied militias, especially in Eastern Upper Nile (EUN). The Akobo and Nasir regions of EUN have seen heavy recent fighting between these militias and forces of the Sudan People's Liberation Army. Akobo has been captured and re-captured, and present insecurity prevents all humanitarian relief operations in the area, including Akobo, Nasir, Wandeng, Mandeng, Wanding, Kier, Thot Liet.

Citing "humanitarian sources," a March 11, 2005 IRIN report from Nairobi gives us an unusually good account of these under-reported developments,

> Recent movements of armed militias around the eastern Sudanese town of Akobo in Jonglei State have led to increased tension in the area, humanitarian sources told IRIN. "Some 700 militia were heading to Akobo from Nasir [near the Ethiopian border], during the first week of March," one source said on Wednesday. "The troops came very close, up to an hour's walking distance, and camped there for a day or so."
>
> On 17 February, fighting broke out when armed militias attacked Akobo. They were reportedly under the command of Taban Juoc, who was recently promoted to the rank of Brigadier by the Sudanese government. "The unprovoked attacks on SPLM/A positions in the town of Akobo by renegade Commander Taban Juoc are a direct violation of the Comprehensive Peace Agreement," Samson Kwaje, spokesman for the SPLM/A said in a 4 March [2005] statement. . . . The SPLM/A retook Akobo on 20 [2005] February and its Commander Dou Yaak said the armed group that briefly occupied Akobo

had killed three SPLM/A soldiers. He also said the armed men had destroyed part of the hospital and the church, and burnt down approximately 2,000 tukuls (grass huts).

In Darfur, we see a version of the same unwillingness to confront Khartoum. Instead of the humanitarian intervention that has been clearly dictated for over a year, the international response has been to provide only what humanitarian assistance Khartoum permits. The woefully inadequate African Union monitoring force of 2,000 under-equipped personnel constitutes the entire international response to the vast and urgent security needs of a region the size of France. Whether we look to the UN, the European Union, the US, or the AU itself, there has been such a consistent lack of willingness to confront Khartoum over its intransigent pursuit of genocidal counter-insurgency policies in Darfur that we can hardly be surprised by the regime's willingness to threaten humanitarian operations by means of its *Janjaweed* militia proxy.

West Darfur has been relatively quiet in recent months. But this is now the region within Darfur where fighting is concentrated. Khartoum has seen the AU deploy its highly limited resources in North and South Darfur, and as a consequence has simply shifted the military front, thereby eluding a great deal of whatever scrutiny the thinly deployed AU might provide.

Reuters reported in March 14 and 16, 2005 dispatches on the fighting between Khartoum's forces and the National Movement for Reform and Development, a third Darfuri rebel movement, in the Jebel Moon area of West Darfur. The Darfur Relief and Documentation Center (DRCD) (Geneva) has also reported in detail on intense fighting in the same area, and gives a much fuller sense of the impact of fighting on humanitarian operations. Portions of their March 14, 2005 report follow,

Lawlessness, banditry activities, violence and the threat of violence are rampant in the region with serious implications on the situation of food security in many affected areas especially in the Jabal Marra massive and Jabal Moun in West Darfur. Banditry activities and growing security risks are leading to suspension of relief operations and delivery of food and other lifesaving material to thousands of internally displaced persons and vulnerable host communities.

Fighting and violence are also causing more displacement and casualties among the civilian populations. DRDC received reports of fighting and intensive unrest in the Nertiti, Wadi Azoum, Habilla and Seleia areas (West Darfur) since the beginning of March 2005. As a direct result the UN declared these areas as No-Go Zones.

Threat of violence by militiamen forced UN agencies in West Darfur to withdraw their personnel from the countryside into El-Geneina town since 10th March 2005. Other humanitarian organisations followed the UN and are withdrawing their workers into the town from the countryside.

DRDC is concerned that most of the attacks and banditry activities were carried out in areas controlled by the government of Sudan, and in some cases the army and police were visibly present. The indiscriminate targeting of humanitarian organisations and relief workers appears to be a calculated attempt to cause starvation among the internally displaced populations.

The UN Security Council remains paralyzed, unable to reach consensus on even a mildly threatening sanctions regime. This is so despite the urgent call for humanitarian intervention from 15 distinguished UN human rights experts in "UN Human Rights Experts Call for Urgent, Effective Action on Darfur," a March 16, 2005 IRIN dispatch from Geneva,

We are gravely concerned about the ongoing violations of human rights and humanitarian law in the Darfur region of Sudan . . . and we call upon the international community to take effective measures to end the violations on a basis of utmost urgency. . . . Despite efforts by the international community to commit troops and assistance to the region, the violence continues virtually unabated in a context of wholesale impunity, and the threat of famine is looming.

The violations in Darfur have been staggering in scale and harrowing in nature. . . . If the vow that the international community will "Never Again" stand idly by while crimes against humanity are being perpetrated is to have any meaning, now is the time for decisive action. . . . A robust international solution is urgently needed, as the Secretary-General affirmed when he called upon the Security

Council, on 16 February 2005, "to act urgently to stop further death and suffering in Darfur, and to do justice for those whom we are already too late to save."

But instead of humanitarian intervention, with all necessary military support, Jan Egeland despaired in a March 7, 2005 Reuters dispatch, " '[T]he world is only putting an expensive humanitarian plaster on the open wound in Darfur.' "

This substitution of humanitarian relief for humanitarian intervention ultimately reflects an unwillingness to address the Darfur crisis honestly, to confront Khartoum directly over its genocidal ambitions. It reflects an international inability to speak honestly about the massive shortcomings of the African Union as a source of civilian protection. This in turn reflects a dishonest accommodation of the views of such African leaders as Nigerian President and AU Chair Obasanjo, Libyan President Ghaddafi, and Egyptian President Mubarak – views that would substitute the slogan "African solutions for African problems" for a meaningful response to genocide in Darfur.

Meanwhile, the humanitarian crisis continues to deepen. The UN World Food Program's disingenuous claims of a 33% increase in food deliveries in February 2005 over January 2005 deliveries mask a greater truth. The average monthly food delivery for January and February 2005 to 1.4 million recipients is actually 100,000 less than the December 2004 total of 1.5 million recipients. Moreover, there is little chance for the significant increases that are necessary to help the 2.4 million people described as "conflict-affected" by the UN in its January 1, 2005 *UN Darfur Humanitarian Profile No. 10*. As the WFP acknowledged in its March 2-8, 2005 Situation Report on Darfur,

> WFP is reaching the limits of its Cooperating Partners' capacity on the ground in the three [Darfur] States, an issue that requires attention in the course of this month.

In other words, the capacity of those humanitarian organizations that enable the WFP to reach intended beneficiaries has reached its limits – at a level more than 1 million human beings below what is currently required.

This statistical/logistical reality is clear if we consider the food-distressed populations in rural areas that are presently inaccessible and not likely to reach camps, either for security reasons or because they are waiting until all coping mechanisms and food-stocks are exhausted. A March 4, 2005 USAID Darfur fact sheet noted,

> Some nongovernmental organizations have voiced concerns that potential [food] beneficiaries may not seek food assistance until their coping mechanisms are exhausted and no food-stocks remain. Relief agencies report that registrations are increasing in supplementary and therapeutic feeding centers, confirming the fact that additional communities are beginning to lack sufficient food.

The ominous gravity of the food stock situation was underscored by the Chief AU envoy for Darfur, Baba Gana Kingibe, in a March 17, 2005 Reuters dispatch. "There was a two-month food security gap before. Our estimates now are giving us a four-month food security gap," [Kingibe] said.

Additionally, WFP is reporting a serious current break in the food pipeline for "pulses," or legumes, essential for a healthy human diet. Other non-cereal shortcomings are also in evidence. The current curtailment of humanitarian operations in West Darfur also poses an extremely serious risk to belated efforts by WFP to pre-position food in West Darfur prior to the rainy season, which affects West Darfur the most. This is the context in which to assess Khartoum's use of the *Janjaweed* to threaten and obstruct humanitarian relief efforts in West Darfur. There is precious little evidence that sufficient honesty will obtain in that assessment.

November 13, 2005 – African Solutions for African Problems – Will the World Fail Darfur as it Failed Rwanda?

The ghosts of Rwanda are stirring ever more ominously in Darfur. Differences in geography, history, and genocidal means do less and less to obscure the ghastly similarities between international failure in 1994 and the world's current willingness to allow ethnically-targeted human destruction to proceed essentially unchecked. To be sure, the Hutu génocidaires in

Rwanda accomplished their frenzied destruction of perhaps 800,000 Tutsis and moderate Hutus in approximately 100 days; the génocidaires in Khartoum's National Islamic Front have been more patient, more calculating, more willing to accomplish their goals through genocide by attrition. But their savage equivalent to the Hutu Interahamwe – Arab tribal militias known as *Janjaweed* – are no less efficient or relentless in their human destruction. And as the death toll in Darfur now likely exceeds 400,000, with human mortality poised to increase significantly in coming weeks and months, there is no clear evidence that Rwanda's unspeakable slaughter will not eventually be surpassed.

In 1994 the international community knowingly abandoned the clear targets of genocidal destruction, leaving in place only a hopelessly inadequate remnant of the UN Assistance Mission for Rwanda (UNAMIR), led heroically in failure by Lieutenant General Roméo Dallaire. Dallaire's *Shake Hands with the Devil: The Failure of Humanity in Rwanda*, an unsparing account of this international failure, gives us what is in many ways the most relentlessly insightful chronicle of the decisions, equivocations, mendacity, and cowardice that left hundreds of thousands of innocent civilians to die by machetes, small arms, and innumerable other acts of individual and collective savagery.

In Darfur, we are witnessing an equivalently dishonest and cowardly failure. The international community has expediently chosen to rely exclusively on an African Union observer force to provide human security amidst violence that has never been controlled and is once again accelerating. The AU is no more capable of halting the ongoing destruction of primarily African tribal populations than Dallaire was able to halt the Interahamwe or deter the Hutu extremists of the Rwandan government and military.

Dallaire's account of the actions and calculated inaction of the UN, including those of Kofi Annan, then head of UN peacekeeping operations, the Clinton administration in the US, France, Belgium, and other international actors makes for excruciating reading. But a recent series of detailed, independent reports on the African Union Mission in Sudan (AMIS) makes powerfully clear that current international failure to protect innocent civilians in Africa is distinguished only by different forms of unctuous pronouncement, a more ingenious expediency, a greater sophistication in dishonesty.

Any accurate history of the world's response to Darfur, more than two and half years into genocidal conflict, will need to take careful account of extensively researched reports released by Refugees International and the Brookings Institution/University of Bern. In conjunction with a recent series of authoritative reports from the International Crisis Group, these assessments strip away all means of obscuring how fundamentally the AU in failing in Darfur, and how deeply complicit in this failure the international community has become.

The November 2005 report from Refugees International is the most aptly titled, *No Power to Protect: The African Union Mission in Sudan.* Moreover, this report makes the most essential point on its opening page, "Darfur civilians have only the African Union Mission in Sudan to protect them right now; this is a choice that has been made by the entire international community." It is essential that any critical assessment of the AU – and such assessment must perforce be harsh – be seen also as an assessment of the international community that has, with full knowledge of what is occurring on the ground in Darfur, chosen to leave the security of Darfuri civilians, as well as international humanitarian organizations, exclusively in the hands of the AU.

The November 2005 report from the Brookings Institution/Bern University, *Protecting of Two Million Internally Displaced: The Successes and Shortcomings of the African Union in Darfur,* also makes a critical point, bearing directly on the nature of international failure to uphold commitments made on September 16, 2005 in the UN World Summit "Outcome Document," paragraphs 138-139,

> The world's heads of state endorsed the emerging norm of a "Responsibility to Protect" from genocide, war crimes, ethnic cleansing, and crimes against humanity, in the "Summit Outcome Document" at the September 2005 United Nations General Assembly.

Darfur, in less than two months time, has demonstrated just how far this "emerging norm" is from governing in any meaningful way the actions of the UN and the world's most powerful nations. But despite the implicit indictment of the international community contained in all these reports, detailed attention must be devoted primarily to the failings of the AU itself.

For these are not accidental shortcomings or peripheral deficiencies: they are fundamental failings – military, political, diplomatic, and moral. And the failure only compounds itself, allowing genocide in Darfur to continue, with the terrifying specter of massive human destruction in coming weeks and months if the tenuous humanitarian lifeline is severed because of insecurity. Even without accelerating human destruction, the catastrophe in Darfur gives all signs of being perpetuated by uncontrolled violence. As the International Crisis Group declared on page 14 in its July 2005 report, *The AU's Mission in Darfur: Bridging the Gaps*,

> Disturbingly, the daily death and suffering [in Darfur] is already becoming "status quo" for some relief agencies, and the situation has the potential to become another never-ending "low intensity" conflict in which the international community spends large sums each year keeping Internally Displaced Persons and refugees alive but otherwise fails to protect civilians and address the underlying political causes.

This is an all too apt description of "genocide by attrition" in Darfur. For of course the ambitions of Khartoum's NIF regime, overwhelmingly dominant in the new "Government of National Unity," are clearly to preserve violent conflict, even at lower levels, in order to change the fundamental demographic, economic, and political realities in Darfur – this as a means of ensuring that Darfur poses no threat to NIF power and control of national wealth in Khartoum.

The ambition to "change the demography" of Darfur is declared explicitly on page 8 in a document cited by the November 2005 Brookings Institution/Bern University Report (hereafter Brookings Report),

> The [Khartoum] government's objective in this [military] campaign is clear. A document seized from a *Janjaweed* official that appears to be genuine orders all commanders and security officers in Darfur to: "Change the demography of Darfur and make it void of African tribes." The document goes on to encourage "killing, burning villages, farms, terrorizing people, confiscating property from members of African tribes and forcing them from Darfur."

Many such documents have been seized or obtained, by the AU, Human Rights Watch, and Darfuris. Nicholas Kristof's February 23, 2005 *New York Times* article, "The Secret Genocide Archive," catalogues but a small selection. The author has also received scanned and translated versions of a number of these documents. Such documents serve as powerful, if ultimately gratuitous, corroborating evidence of genocidal intent on the part of the NIF and its *Janjaweed* militia proxy.

As all reports make clear, the challenges to the AU mission are manifold, complex, extremely difficult, and yet also unsurpassably urgent. They also serve to highlight a point made on page 6 in the November 2005 Brookings Report,

> The African Union could not have chosen a more daunting conflict for such an [intervening] operation. Darfur is as large as France, with few passable roads, [and] rudimentary communications systems.

There is a significant distortion in the Brookings Report title, insofar as it seeks to define these challenges as "Protecting Two Million Internally Displaced." For the crisis in Darfur demands much more than the protection of well over 2 million internally displaced persons (IDP), leaving aside the more than 200,000 refugees in eastern Chad who are again vulnerable to *Janjaweed* predations during the dry season.

To be sure, protecting this enormous population, in widely scattered areas, is a massive task unto itself. The UN estimated in August 2005 that there are 338 locations for IDP Gatherings and Affected Populations throughout Darfur. It will require extraordinary efforts to secure the camps with Civilian Police (CIVPOL), a capacity in which the African Union mission is exceedingly weak. It will also require equally extraordinary military efforts to secure the camp environs, where civilians – especially women and girls searching for firewood, water, and animal fodder – remain terrifyingly vulnerable to *Janjaweed* assaults.

Additionally, humanitarian corridors and convoys must be protected, along with humanitarian workers and operations. There are over 12,000 humanitarian workers in Darfur, including over 1,000 international aid workers. They are increasingly the targets of attacks by the *Janjaweed*, insurgency groups, opportunistic armed gangs, as well as "banditry" orchestrated by Khartoum's intelligence services. This disturbing trend is highlighted by Juan Méndez, UN special advisor on the prevention of genocide, in paragraphs 19 and 23 of his *Report of the Special Adviser on the Prevention of Genocide - visit to Darfur, Sudan 19-26 September 2005.*

Because of rampant insecurity, in late September 2005 the UN put non-essential personnel in el-Geneina, the capital of West Darfur, on notice for evacuation because of rising insecurity. The ability of all humanitarian workers to travel on any of the roads leading out of el-Geneina has been severely curtailed by growing attacks, putting hundreds of thousands of needy civilians beyond humanitarian reach. Half of all South Darfur is presently inaccessible to humanitarian operations, and aid workers on the ground speak of increasingly restricted access.

Notably, there have also been quiet withdrawals of expatriate staff. Refugees International speaks on page 2 in their November 2005 report of "witnessing the site director for one of the [humanitarian organizations] sending three of her staff home to Europe." Such withdrawals are of course unpublicized for a variety of reasons, the notable exception being the public withdrawal of Save the Children/UK in 2004 following the deaths of three staff members in separate incidents. But these decisions to withdraw must be understood in the context of an unsparing assessment of deteriorating security throughout Darfur offered by Jan Egeland, UN humanitarian coordinator, in a September 28, 2005 Associated Press dispatch,

> "My warning is the following: if [insecurity] continues to escalate, if it continues to be so dangerous on humanitarian work, we may not be able to sustain our operation for 2.5 million people requiring life-saving assistance," said Jan Egeland, head of the United Nations Office for the Coordination of Humanitarian Affairs. "It could all end tomorrow – it's as serious as that."

Violence against humanitarians has increased ominously in the intervening six weeks from September to November 2005.

The security challenges in Darfur also include protecting large and acutely vulnerable rural populations that are still not internally displaced. There is strong evidence that food deliveries to more remote areas are becoming increasingly endangered, as signaled recently by the International Committee of the Red Cross (ICRC). A November attack on an ICRC convoy increases concern on this score, given the ICRC's leading role in rural food deliveries.

Additionally, any civilians attempting to return to their land and villages must have especially effective security if they are not to be attacked by the relentlessly lurking *Janjaweed*; militia attacks on initial returnees would have a profoundly chilling effect on those remaining in camps, seeking to assess whether safe returns are possible.

Indeed, vigorous, widespread security will be required if displaced persons are to reclaim their land and villages. As the Brookings Report notes on page 9,

> An enormous transfer of wealth has occurred. [The *Janjaweed*] have stripped two million people of their assets in an already desperately poor place. Prime farmland, seed and farming utensils have been seized from people whose survival depends on farming and now must rely on assistance from the international community. Livestock especially is central to the wealth of many Darfurians, yet experts estimate that the non-Arab population has lost 50 to 90% of its animals to government forces.
>
> Some fear that the government plans to remove the farmers of Darfur from their land forever. A Sudanese law that allows the government to take over land that has been abandoned for more than a year has never been applied before in Darfur. If this law is applied, millions could lose their land and fuel a cycle of revenge and violence, plus permanent dependence on international charity. This would cement the ethnic cleansing that a UN official maintains was the primary objective of the Khartoum government.

The Brookings Report also noted on page 7 that "approximately 75% of all villages in Darfur were burned by February 2005, leaving precious little remaining to destroy; many experts believe this is the reason that large-scale violence subsided in early summer 2005 and not from any change in policy or sudden government beneficence or, in fact, AU intervention."

At the center of all security issues is the ongoing military viability of the *Janjaweed*, and its role as a proxy force for Khartoum's NIF. All recent reports on the AU in Darfur reiterate what has long been known about the intimate relationship between the *Janjaweed* and Khartoum's regular military forces. The Brookings Report underscores this on page 2 when it states,

> This study will show that it is precisely the government of Sudan and the *Janjaweed* militias acting under its command and control or with its acquiescence who present the greatest danger to the approximately two million IDPs in Darfur.

And the November Refugees International November 2005 Report amplified the Khartoum regime - *Janjaweed* relationship on page 1,

> The Government of Sudan armed, trained, and equipped Arab militias to fight as their proxy force in the [Darfur] region.

The July 2005 International Crisis Group's report *The AU's Mission in Darfur* on pages 3-4 characterizes Khartoum's ongoing support for its proxies,

> Most disturbing is the [Khartoum] government's continued use of proxy militias and incitement of ethnic violence. Rather than disarming its allies, the *Janjaweed* militias, as it has pledged numerous times, it continues to recruit, train, financially support, and arm ethnically-based militias and polices forces.

Disarming the *Janjaweed*, demanded of Khartoum in July 2004 by UN Security Council Resolution 1556, is the central task in providing security in Darfur, despite Khartoum's obduracy. None of the reports cited offers the slightest evidence that the AU contemplates, or has the means for addressing the root cause of insecurity in Darfur. This fundamental failing makes all civilian and humanitarian protection tasks inordinately more difficult.

In fact, only the International Crisis Group has the political courage to be fully explicit about the need to target the *Janjaweed* militarily when it argues on page 9,

> The best way to provide security [in Darfur] would be prudent but deliberate application of force against those directly responsible for the insecurity and atrocities.

Although those directly responsible would also include elements of the insurgency movements and lawless elements, the most obvious and significant target would be the *Janjaweed* militia. Skirting this basic fact vitiates a great deal of commentary on the security crisis in Darfur.

Despite these extremely daunting security demands, the African Union Peace and Security Council committed to the Darfur mission with considerable – if wholly unjustified – confidence. Moreover, even as AU shortcomings became increasingly clear following initial deployment of 60 military observers and a force of 300 soldiers to protect the observers in July 2004, this confidence did not abate. The November 2005 Brookings Report cites on page 16 a November 29, 2004 article from *The New York Times* in which senior AU political official Jean-Baptiste Natama said,

> "If the situation is getting worse, we are not going to pack our luggage and leave Darfur. . . . We are going to have a robust mandate to make sure we are not here for nothing. We should be able to bring peace, or impose peace."

The utter failure of the AU to secure a "robust mandate" from Khartoum is the most consequential feature of what remains a monitoring rather than protection mission; and the manifest inability either to bring or impose peace in Darfur is a reality that even now the AU seems perversely unwilling to acknowledge – a prideful reticence that betrays the people of Darfur in deepest consequence.

Nor does the glibly disingenuous insistence on "African solutions for African problems" come only from AU officials. Refugees International's Report on page 1 notes that leaders of AU member states have been equally insistent, including President Obasanjo of Nigeria and President Mbeki of South Africa,

As South Africa's President Thabo Mkeki explained, "We have not asked for anybody outside of the African continent to deploy troops in Darfur. It's an African responsibility, and we can do it."

Mbeki is right only in declaring the AU has not asked troops from outside Africa. But genocide, whether in Darfur or anywhere in the world, is an international responsibility; the response to genocide must never be rendered parochial or we have lost completely the commitment embodied in the 1948 UN Convention on the Prevention and Punishment of the Crime of Genocide, as Article 1 emphatically declares,

> The Contracting Parties [to the Genocide Convention] confirm that genocide, whether committed in time of peace or in time of war, is a crime under international law which they undertake to prevent and to punish.

Mbeki's insistence that genocide in Darfur is an African responsibility, and that African forces can halt the violence, is powerfully refuted by an overwhelming body of evidence, assiduously assembled, in all the reports under consideration. Moreover, Mbeki is indulging in spectacular hypocrisy here, given South Africa's reneging on its commitment to provide 700 CIVPOL, one of the most critically deficient areas in the AU Darfur mission.

Understanding the transparent dishonesty of Mbeki's claim that the AU "can do it" entails first understanding how profoundly the AU has failed politically. For the character of the AU military mission in Darfur is ultimately a reflection of political failure – the unwillingness of AU leadership to confront Khartoum in any meaningful way on the essential issues of mandate for the mission, force and material requirements for the mission, and the NIF's own complicity in Darfur's genocide, including support for the *Janjaweed* militias most responsible for insecurity and ethnically-targeted human destruction.

By way of understanding how politically diffident the AU has been in its dealing with the NIF, we should note that at present not one of the 53 member states in the AU has objected to the next AU summit taking place January 2006 in Khartoum. By protocol, the host nation succeeds to the role of chair of the AU. This will make the NIF génocidaires the leaders of the very organization charged with providing security in Darfur and negotiating a peace agreement. That members of the AU cannot find the political courage to change this outrageous prospect is perhaps the best measure of how abysmally the AU is failing Darfur.

But the failure to demand of Khartoum a mandate for civilian protection – let alone the peacemaking mandate the AU's Natama spoke confidently of securing ("We should be able to bring peace, or impose peace") – is most defining of current AU limitations, and deserves particular scrutiny.

The initial decision by the AU to settle for a monitoring, rather than civilian protection, mission grew out of the "Humanitarian Cease-Fire Agreement on the Conflict in Darfur" negotiated between Khartoum and the insurgency movements in N'Djamena, Chad, April 8, 2004. Notably, the AU did not insist that the *Janjaweed* be a party to the "cease-fire," a state of affairs that continues to the present, creating a highly asymmetrical negotiating situation. Without including the *Janjaweed* – indisputably a critical military ally of Khartoum – discussions of troops dispositions, military stand-down, separation of forces, and a general cease-fire are hopelessly inadequate from the insurgents' perspective.

To be sure, the deployment of only 360 personnel in July 2004 dictated the initial nature of the AU mission: such a force could do little more than observe, and as quickly became apparent, mere observing had virtually no effect on the actions of the *Janjaweed*, Khartoum, or the insurgents. But when the AU Peace and Security Council agreed on an expanded mission in Darfur on October 20, 2004, there was still no political will to demand of Khartoum a civilian protection mandate. Though the enhanced mission would eventually consist of 3,320 personnel – 2,241 military, including 450 military observers, and 815 CIVPOL – there was only the very narrowest provision for the actual protection of civilians. In fact, the mission virtually abdicated responsibility for civilian protection when it stipulated in Point 7 of the AU Peace and Security Council Communiqué, October 20, 2004,

[AU forces can] protect civilians whom it encounters under imminent threat and in the immediate vicinity, within resources and capability, it being understood that protection of the civilian population the responsibility of the government of Sudan

There could no longer be any mistaking the crippling trade-off the AU was willing to make in enlarging its mission in Darfur. It would ask Khartoum for no strengthening of its mandate, thereby creating many of the weaknesses currently conspicuous even with a still larger deployment – 6,700 personnel as of late October 2005. As the Brookings Report notes on page 17, "Sudanese officials have adamantly insisted that any increase in troop numbers be allowed only if the mandate does not change." So long as the AU has no mandate to protect civilians or humanitarian workers, so long as the AU cannot confront or preempt the *Janjaweed* in its brutal predations, Khartoum will not object to larger numbers of personnel.

There is brave talk in some quarters within the AU about creating an expanded mandate *de facto*, and to a certain extent some troops on the ground have "interpreted" their governing mandate "creatively," in the words of Baba Gana Kingibe, AU ambassador for Darfur. But this has had only limited effect, though appropriately celebrated by all the reports here under review, if notably without any truly meaningful quantitative benchmarks or terms of reference.

The fundamental military reality remains what it has been from the beginning: AU forces cannot possibly serve as a deterrent to actions by either the *Janjaweed* or Khartoum's regular military. Moreover, the relatively lightly armed AU mission can always be intimidated in a particular encounter with hostile elements. As Refugees International points out on page 13, "the Government of Sudan forces (and the other groups to a lesser extent) have weapons with much greater capabilities than the small arms carried by [the African Union]."

And even those military and transport capabilities the AU does have are frequently compromised by Khartoum, which has systematically denied reliable fuel resources for AU helicopters, and burdens helicopter pilots with gratuitously burdensome restrictions. This is crucial, since helicopters are typically the only means by which the AU forces can move rapidly over the great distances of Darfur. Refugees International's report details on page 13 the obstacles Khartoum creates for the hapless AU pilots,

> The AU is often unable to use its helicopters because the Government imposes severe flight restrictions on [the AU mission]; in addition, the Government permits only civilian pilots. Refugees

International was told that the Government requires AU pilots to travel to Khartoum to re-certify their domestic flight credentials every two months.

The decision by the AU in March 2005 to increase the Darfur force level to 7,731 – 5,583 military and 1,198 CIVPOL – was again made without any commitment to secure from Khartoum a meaningful mandate for civilian or humanitarian protection. This has sent an unmistakable message to the NIF regime. The AU lacks the political will to demand what all recognize is essential for human security in Darfur. Thus it should hardly be surprising that Khartoum has refused to grant entry to the 105 critically needed armored personnel carriers delivered by Canada to Senegal in June 2005. The Refugees International report notes on page 14,

> Even the equipment that is being donated or loaned is not getting to Darfur because the Government of Sudan. In June 2005, Canada loaned 105 Grizzly Armored Personnel carriers (APCs) to the AU; they first went to Dakar, Senegal so that [AU] troops could be trained on them. The Grizzlies would provide solid protection from even 12.7mm bullets for the five soldiers that can fit inside of them. They also come with their own 12.7mm machine gun [.50 calibre Browning] on top and thus would be a huge boost to the [AU] combat capacities. However, the Government has been standing in the way of the Grizzlies' delivery. Only in October 2005 has it agreed to allow 35 of these APCs to enter the country.

There is no evidence that even now the 35 APCs have actually been delivered and deployed.

Khartoum has been emboldened to the point of denying such critical equipment because the AU has demonstrated it has no political will to confront the génocidaires. Here it is important to be clear that in the case of the Canadian APCs, the issue is not, in the eyes of senior Canadian government officials, a bilateral one between Canada and Khartoum, but rather an issue between the AU leadership and one of its member states.

In turn, the past weakness and lack of resolve on the part of the AU are increasingly likely to produce violent attacks against AU forces on the ground by emboldened military elements on all sides, as the Refugees International report notes on page 21,

> With the growing number of attacks on the [AU mission] over the past few months, it appears that [the AU] is being tested by the armed factions to see if it is a force to be ignored or respected. As [the AU mission] is tested and found ineffective due to resource, training, and mandate constraints, their deterrence factor will decline and they will more often become targets, as will civilians under their protection.... Unless this situation is remedied, the violence will thus likely grow in Darfur with more and more civilian and AU casualties.

In this context, it should be noted that the attack that killed six AU personnel on October 8, 2005 – the first such casualties in the mission – has been declared by AU investigators to be the responsibility of "Arab tribesman," an increasingly used euphemism for the *Janjaweed*. Initially the AU had blamed the rebel SLA/M, but on the basis of further investigation and additional witnesses, investigators revised their assigning of responsibility as a November 7, 2005 Reuters dispatch has detailed ("AU changes verdict on killings of troops in Darfur").

Such attacks on AU forces, operating without an appropriate mandate or adequate equipment and manpower, will almost certainly increase in the near term. Ominously, as AU failures become more conspicuous, and frustration over AU impotence builds throughout the African tribal communities of Darfur, the insurgency movements are also more likely to target the AU. However misconceived, the sentiments of Mohamed Saleh, leader of the JEM splinter group that kidnapped an entire AU patrol of 18 men on October 9, 2005, are increasingly representative. An October 10, 2005 Reuters dispatch offers a blunt quote from Saleh,

> "The AU have become part of the conflict. We want the AU to leave and we have warned them not to travel to our areas"

NATO this week issued an unprecedented expression of alarm over Darfur, even as it signaled pointedly that it could do no more until the AU found the political courage to ask for greater help, including NATO troops. Reuters reported from Brussels on November 10, 2005 that,

> NATO joined a growing chorus of alarm over rising violence in Sudan's Darfur region on Wednesday but insisted it did not have a mandate for military intervention to help over-stretched AU troops. "The AU is not as well equipped as a Western army might be. But there is no political will for any intervention force," said a NATO official who requested anonymity. He added that he meant the requisite will did not exist in either Sudan, Africa or the international community. "NATO is doing what it has been asked to do – no more or less. There is no scope to do any more," he said, referring to current agreements with Sudan and the AU on its role.

The real question for Western leaders, then, is whether belatedly to push the AU to accept its desperate need for assistance in halting genocide in Darfur. But judging by the tenor of comments coming from US Deputy Secretary of State Robert Zoellick during his trip to Sudan, this is a question that has already been answered. ABC Online quoted Zoellick on November 9, 2005 as saying,

> "It's a tribal war," Zoellick said. "And frankly I don't think foreign forces want to get in the middle of a tribal war of Sudanese."

Even leaving aside the highly problematic characterization of conflict in Darfur, we must be struck by how Zoellick conveniently elides the fact that those really in the middle of tribal war are the millions of extraordinarily vulnerable Darfuri civilians who desperately need international protection. Zoellick evidently believes, illogically, that it would be impossible for the US and its allies to protect these defenseless people at the same time it seeks to improve the chances for successful peace negotiations. As ABC Online continued,

> "I don't think we can clean it [the crisis in Darfur] up because it's not just a question of ending violence, it's a question of creating the context for peace," Zoellick said.

Ending violence and creating the context for peace are indeed the essential tasks. But accepting Zoellick's perverse and disabling logic in speaking of their mutual necessity ensures a continuation of the genocidal status quo, and makes terrifyingly clear that the only lesson of Rwanda is that there is no lesson. The transparent determination to avoid international humanitarian intervention, and the corresponding willingness to allow the AU to fail in Darfur, stir the most obscene ghosts of 1994. We have learned nothing.

September 24, 2006 – UN Impotence: Darfur Security Remains Solely with AU. Khartoum's Génocidaires Triumph

Despite glib talk in various quarters of a partial or temporary success this past week in renewing the African Union mandate for Darfur, the UN's refusal to move toward urgent deployment of the Darfur protection force contemplated in the August 31, 2006 Security Council Resolution 1706 marks a moment of abject international failure. There has been no significant movement to assemble, let alone deploy the 22,500 troops and civilian police specified in the Resolution. The robust language defining the mandate of the force attaches to nothing. In the face of obdurate and defiant claims of national sovereignty by National Islamic Front President Omar al-Bashir, the world's most powerful nations have decided to allow the protection of some 4 million vulnerable civilians in Darfur and eastern Chad to remain in the hands of the African Union – notionally as preparation for a follow-on UN force. But in fact al-Bashir and other senior members of the NIF regime continue adamantly in their refusal to accept a UN force under any circumstances, and remain equally insistent that security continue to be provided solely by the African Union.

This weak, under-manned, under-equipped, and badly demoralized force remains, then, the only source of protection for humanitarians and humanitarian operations in Darfur, upon which the vast majority of Darfur's conflict-affected populations are increasingly dependent. UN promises of modest additional resources and logistical support cannot transform or even change in significant fashion this failing operation. Recently announced Africa Union conditions for UN support further undermine the prospects for adequate civilian protection.

Certainly the AU has fully demonstrated that it cannot protect humanitarian operations, which continue to contract amidst intolerable levels of insecurity. Aid organizations have already withdrawn from large and growing areas of Darfur, even as the need for food, clean water, shelter, and medical assistance grows relentlessly. After more than three and a half years of devastating violence and ethnically-targeted destruction, the vast majority of conflict-affected populations have no food reserves, no opportunity for significant agricultural production, and no security allowing them to deploy their superb coping skills. They grow more, not less dependent upon humanitarian assistance. And yet further significant humanitarian withdrawals and evacuations are now inevitable. As Undersecretary for Humanitarian Affairs Jan Egeland warned in his August 28, 2006 briefing of the UN Security Council,

> Our entire humanitarian operation in Darfur – the only lifeline for more than three million people – is presently at risk. We need immediate action on the political front to avoid a humanitarian catastrophe with massive loss of life. . . . If the humanitarian operation were to collapse [because of insecurity], we could see hundreds of thousands of deaths. In short, we may end up with a man-made catastrophe of an unprecedented scale in Darfur.

Egeland's desperate plea – "We need immediate action on the political front to avoid a humanitarian catastrophe with massive loss of life" – made no difference. There has been no meaningful political action, merely an increase in rhetorical volume.

Egeland continued in his August 28, 2006 briefing,

> Attacks against humanitarians are at an all-time high, with 9 humanitarian workers killed in the month of July alone. More than 25 UN or NGO vehicles have been ambushed or hijacked in the last two months, with one organization losing three vehicles to hijackings in a two-day period. If this continues, one organization after the other will be leaving Darfur because we cannot expose our staff to such unacceptable risks to their lives.

> [Humanitarian NGOs] in North Darfur are largely confined to
> the capital [el-Fasher]. Again, key organizations feel paralyzed and
> have raised the prospect of full withdrawal. Hundreds of thousands
> would then be left without any humanitarian assistance.

The massive North Darfur military offensive by Khartoum, long in conspicuous preparation, but beginning in earnest the very day that Egeland
spoke to the Security Council, has already killed and displaced many thousands of civilians, and placed many tens of thousands further beyond
humanitarian reach. Egeland concluded his Security Council briefing by
making clear that his words marked the culmination, not the inauguration,
of the direst possible warning,

> In the past months I have repeatedly called for attention to the dete-
> riorating situation in Darfur. As you have heard today our warnings
> have become a black reality that calls for immediate action: insecu-
> rity is at its highest levels since 2004, access at its lowest levels since
> that date and we may well be on the brink of a return to all-out war.
> This would mean the withdrawal of international staff from Darfur,
> leaving millions of vulnerable Darfuris to suffer their fate without
> assistance and with few outsiders to witness.
>
> [The humanitarian gains of the past two years in Darfur] can all
> be lost within weeks – not months. I cannot give a starker warning
> than to say that we are at a point where even hope may escape us and
> the lives of hundreds of thousands could be needlessly lost. The
> Security Council and member states around this table with influence
> on the parties to the conflict must act now. Hundreds of humanitar-
> ian organizations from around the world are watching what you will
> be doing or may refrain from doing in the coming weeks.

This is the context for last week's international acquiescence before self-
serving claims of national sovereignty by a cabal of génocidaires.

Two weeks after Egeland's terrifying warning, and two weeks after
Khartoum launched its massive and long-anticipated military offensive in
North Darfur, Egeland declared in a Reuters dispatch of September 12, 2006
that humanitarian operations in Darfur were "in free fall." And in the face of

conspicuous and ongoing inaction, Egeland could not have been more explicit about what was urgently required, declaring in a September 15, 2006 Associated Press dispatch, "we need this UN force to avoid a collapse."

These are the realities to which the international community has responded with various upticks in rhetoric, bluster, and bluffing – all understandably dismissed by Khartoum after many months of similar posturing by the various international actors who might ensure that Security Council Resolution 1706 is more than mere exhortation. Khartoum rightly feels diplomatically victorious, and the regime's enthusiastic welcoming of the three-month AU extension – indeed, its urging of an even greater extension of the AU mission – serves as a grimly ironic measure of the incompetence and manipulability of the AU force. Khartoum's génocidaires, despite factitious threats to expel the AU, never had any intention of doing so; the regime discerned all too clearly that such expulsion, and the complete security vacuum in Darfur that would have ensued, was the only possible catalyst for international action. Absent that catalyst, Khartoum was confident – and deservedly so – that there would be no more than further exhortation, even in the face of the most outrageous defiance.

In understanding the implications of Khartoum's continuing obduracy, we must bear in mind that a pattern of increasing violent human destruction, displacement, and humanitarian need has been clearly in evidence for over a year – a period of time during which security for humanitarian operations in Darfur has steadily deteriorated, even as Khartoum has continued with a pattern of obstruction, harassment, and intimidation of humanitarian workers.

Beyond this yearlong pattern of deterioration, a precipitous rise in violence occurred following the signing of the deeply flawed Darfur Peace Agreement by Khartoum and one faction of the Sudan Liberation Movement (SLM) in Abuja, Nigeria on May 5, 2006. The August 2006 military offensive launched by Khartoum's regular forces and the *Janjaweed* in North Darfur, and increasingly in Eastern Jebel Marra in West Darfur, was many weeks in the making, and was conspicuously obvious to all observers. The failure of Khartoum to meet in meaningful fashion any of the key security deadlines stipulated in the Darfur Peace Agreement should also have signaled to even the most optimistic believers in the agreement that the regime's genocidal military ambitions were far from extinguished.

The United Nations and the international community as a whole – in failing to act despite the clear evidence of many months – have continued to preserve the genocidal status quo in Darfur. The African Union mission in Darfur is a force that is deteriorating rapidly in the field, offers painfully little protection to civilians and humanitarian operations, and is powerless to halt or even report adequately on Khartoum's widening military offensive, which entails the ongoing, indiscriminate bombing of civilian targets.

Instead of moving to deploy as rapidly as possible the authorized UN protection force of 17,300 troops, 3,300 CIVPOL, and 16 Formed Police Units, the UN has offered the African Union very modest equipment and logistical support. It is extremely unlikely that this offer will produce any significant or timely augmentation of AU capabilities. We should also recall the fate of 105 armored personnel carriers offered to the AU by Canada in summer 2005: they languished from July to November in Senegal because Khartoum refused to allow their entrance into Darfur, and then admitted them only without their key armament, .50 calibre Browning machine guns. And given Khartoum's relentless history of obstructing the AU, imposing curfews, restricting flying time, denying fuel to AU aircraft – indeed, commandeering AU fuel for its own military aircraft – there is simply no reason to believe that the AU force will change in character.

Moreover, although the AU has promised to strengthen its mandate, there is no evidence that the organization has the ability to absorb first-world military aid beyond a rudimentary level to make good on this promise. A September 24, 2006 Associated Press dispatch from Khartoum brought this sad fact home,

AU peacekeepers also intend to broaden their rules of engagement so they can protect civilians more efficiently in Darfur. Under their new "concept of operations," peacekeepers would not only monitor violence and investigate incidents, but also actively interfere to prevent attacks on civilians by the multiple rebel groups and pro-government militias that plague the region.

The AU's spokesperson in Sudan, Nouredinne Mezni, said these new operational rules would enable peacekeepers to better implement the Darfur Peace Agreement signed in May between Khartoum and the main rebel group. "With our current resources, we don't

really have the means to fully implement the peace agreement,"
Mezni said.

While the absence of a meaningful mandate for civilian protection has certainly been one of the most conspicuous features of the AU mission, this
reflects more than anything a lack of resources, trained troops and civilian
police, adequate equipment, communications and intelligence capacity,
and leadership. Words alone will not change the overall ability of an overwhelmed and demoralized AU force. Only a much larger, more cohesive,
better trained and better-equipped force – guided by a much more effective
intelligence capacity – could begin to take on the mandate defined by
Security Council Resolution 1706,

> Acting under Chapter VII of the Charter of the United Nations, [the
> Security Council] . . . [a] decides that the UN Mission in Sudan
> (UNMIS) is authorized to use all necessary means, in the areas of
> deployment of its forces and as it deems within its capabilities,
>
> to protect United Nations personnel, facilities, installations and
> equipment, to ensure the security and freedom of movement of
> United Nations personnel, humanitarian workers, assessment and
> evaluation commission personnel, to prevent disruption of the
> implementation of the Darfur Peace Agreement by armed groups,
> without prejudice to the responsibility of the Government of the
> Sudan, to protect civilians under the threat of physical violence, in
> order to support early and effective implementation of the Darfur
> Peace Agreement, to prevent attacks and threats against civilians, to
> seize or collect, as appropriate, arms or related material whose pres-
> ence in Darfur is a violation of the Agreements and the measures
> imposed by paragraphs 7 and 8 of Resolution 1556 [July 2004], and
> to dispose of such arms and related material as appropriate.

It should be emphasized that the refusal to accept deployment of this critically needed UN force is not one made by Sudan's notional "Government of
National Unity" (GONU). It is a refusal that reflects only the fears and
genocidal ambitions of the ruling National Islamic Front (National
Congress Party). The Government of South Sudan, including President

Salva Kiir, who is First Vice President in the GONU, has strongly and unambiguously supported UN deployment. Yasir Arman, perhaps the most distinguished member of the Sudan People's Liberation Movement (SPLM) to serve in the GONU, in a September 17, 2006 UN Mission in Sudan SITREP from Khartoum, "confirmed the formal [SPLM] decision to support a UN operation focused on protection and humanitarian aid delivery [in Darfur]."

Support for UN deployment also comes from the only rebel faction to sign the ill-fated, ill-conceived Darfur Peace Agreement (DPA) of May 5, 2006 – the SLA/M of Minni Minawi. Minawi, who is nominally the fourth-ranking individual within the Presidency of the GONU, has not yet been consulted in any meaningful way on the issue of UN deployment to Darfur, although such consultation is explicitly stipulated in the DPA. His strong support for UN deployment is in any event quite meaningless. The NIF regime's security cabal retains full and ruthless control of all policy decisions concerning Darfur; it is a shameful and expedient fiction to suggest otherwise.

The threatened people of Darfur – those most directly at risk from accelerating violence and diminishing humanitarian access – are of course unanimously and desperately in favor of UN deployment, as are the rebel factions that have not signed the Darfur Peace Agreement.

Many other voices, including African voices, have spoken out in support of UN deployment, some even arguing for non-consensual deployment if Khartoum continues its adamant refusal. Reuters reported on September 19, 2006 from New York that Liberian President Ellen Johnson-Sirleaf "hinted at UN intervention without the consent of Khartoum." Johnson-Sirleaf continued in a September 20, 2006 UN News Service dispatch,

> "The world must not allow a second Rwanda to happen," [Johnson-Sirleaf] said, referring to the genocide that claimed the lives of more than 800,000 people in less than 100 days during 1994. "My Government therefore calls on this General Assembly and the Security Council to exercise the Chapter VII authority to restore peace, security and stability to Darfur," Johnson-Sirleaf said, referring to the UN Charter provision allowing for enforcement measures to deal with threats to peace and security.

Nobel Prize-winning Nigerian writer Wole Soyinka, the conscience of Africa, gave an unsparing account of Darfur's realities in a September 20, 2006 Paris speech noted in a *Business Day* article from South Africa,

> [Soyinka said] the *Janjaweed*, the militia accused of waging campaigns of ethnic cleansing in the Darfur region, are the "arrowhead of a state policy of ethnic cleansing," who have a "naked language of racial incitement" with "claims of race superiority, complemented by the language of contempt and disdain for the indigenous African."

Soyinka had nothing but scorn for the insistence that there could be no UN deployment without the consent of Khartoum's génocidaires,

> "When a deviant branch of that family of nations flouts, indeed revels in the abandonment of, the most basic norms of human decency, is there really justification in evoking the excuse that protocol requires the permission [for UN deployment of force] of that same arrogant and defiant entity?"

The *Irish Independent* reported on September 18, 2006, [in "Rwanda begs world to bring an end to genocide in Darfur"]

> Survivors of the 1994 Rwandan genocide yesterday marched through the streets of Kigali, calling for the world to take action to end the slaughter in Darfur.

An extraordinarily courageous open letter, *Arab NGOs Call Upon the Sudanese Government to Accept the Deployment of the UN Forces*, from 31 Arab human rights organizations in 10 Arab countries, published on September 18, 2006 in Cairo on the Human Rights Education Associates website, urged,

> the Sudanese government to support the arrangements necessary for transferring the peacekeeping and civilians protection missions to the UN, in execution of the Security Council resolution No. 1706 and calling upon the international community and the Arab governments

to exercise pressures on the Sudanese government to approve the resolution, together with the necessity to support the African Union troops
in the province until its mission is transferred to the UN.

The Arab NGO open letter complements another letter, *International
Human Rights, Humanitarian and Conflict Prevention Organizations Con-
demn the Recent Violence Launched by the Government of Sudan in North
Darfur and Call for Stepped up Diplomatic Pressure and Planning for the
Rapid Deployment of a Robust UN Peacekeeping Force*, published September
14, 2006 on the Physicians for Human Rights website.

The signatories – including Larry Cox, Executive Director Amnesty
International USA, Ken Bacon, President Refugees International, Osman
Hummaida, Director Sudanese Organization Against Torture, Physicians
for Human Rights, Aegis Trust (UK), Africa Action, Human Rights First,
Urgence Darfour (France), Genocide Watch, and the Montreal Institute for
Genocide and Human Rights Studies – concluded,

> In summary, we call on the international community to significantly
> intensify diplomatic efforts with the Government of Sudan while
> concurrently planning for the rapid deployment of an adequately
> funded and well-equipped UN force to protect the people of Darfur
> regardless of the acquiescence of the Sudanese Government.

A number of US senators have also spoken out forcefully on the need for
urgent UN deployment, including Russ Feingold, Barack Obama, and
Patrick Leahy (D-Vermont). Senator Leahy argued explicitly that the world
must be prepared to consider non-consensual deployment to Darfur in a
September 19, 2006 statement from Senate floor,

> Finally, in circumstances like this, the United Nations should be
> empowered to deploy troops to prevent the mass murder of civilians,
> irrespective of the stubborn, self-serving opposition of the govern-
> ment of the country.

French Foreign Minister Philippe Douste-Blazy became the first senior
French official to declare realities in Darfur to be genocide, and pushed for

serious consideration of non-consensual deployment as a September 15, 2006 *Spiegel* Online dispatch reported,

> France's Foreign Minister Philippe Douste-Blazy has raised the possibility of sending UN peacekeeping troops to Darfur, even in the face of resistance from Sudan. "We don't have a right to let these women and children die," said Douste-Blazy. "Do we go there [Darfur], in spite of [Khartoum's refusal to accept a UN force]?" Douste-Blazy told reporters [September 6, 2006]. "That's not on the table, nobody has asked the question like that. But it's a real question."

Many other voices have been raised, including an increasing number of prominent editorial pages calling for non-consensual deployment of the UN force authorized by Security Council Resolution 1706. The *Chicago Tribune* published such an editorial on September 18, 2006. *The New York Times* on September 19, 2006 weighed in with this editorial,

> [The] message [to Khartoum] would be even stronger if Mr. Bush said the US would take the lead in soliciting troops for the UN and recommended making NATO planners available to help draw up contingency plans for a possible forced entry.

The authority and prospects for such non-consensual intervention have been subject to a good deal of ill-informed and tendentious commentary, particularly by British writers in *The Guardian*. So it is especially useful that Ian Davis, in *The Guardian Online* on September 16, 2006, clears away much of the smug foolishness embodied in commentators such as Jonathan Steele, Daniel Davies, and Simon Jenkins (the latter infamously wrote in 1994 an essay for *The Times of London* entitled "Leave Rwanda Alone"),

> The 2005 [UN] World Summit outcome document endorsed the "responsibility to protect civilians" concept, and in April 2006, the UN Security Council unanimously adopted resolution 1674 on the protection of civilians in armed conflict. Resolution 1674 contains the historic first official security council reference to the responsibility to protect: it "reaffirms the provisions of paragraphs 138 and 139

of the World Summit Outcome Document regarding the responsibility to protect populations from genocide, war crimes, ethnic cleansing and crimes against humanity."

Paragraph 139 of the UN World Summit "Outcome Document" could not
be more explicit in declaring that the international community must be,

> prepared to take collective action, in a timely and decisive manner,
> through the Security Council, in accordance with the UN Charter,
> including Chapter VII, on a case by case basis and in cooperation
> with relevant regional organizations as appropriate, should peaceful
> means be inadequate and national authorities manifestly failing to
> protect their populations from genocide, war crimes, ethnic cleans-
> ing, and crimes against humanity and its implications, bearing in
> mind the principles of the Charter and international law.

If these words have no compelling force in Darfur today, then the very
notion of a "responsibility to protect" civilians at risk has been stillborn.

Precisely because international obligations to act non-consensually in
Darfur are so clear and compelling, there is enormous incentive for
various international actors to indulge the fiction that the African Union
can somehow, in sufficiently timely fashion, be made into an adequate
security presence in Darfur. It simply cannot, given extremely high levels
of security affecting humanitarian operations and the more than 4 million
human beings the UN estimates are affected by violence in Darfur and
eastern Chad.

Although recently elided from virtually all news coverage of the Darfur
crisis, eastern Chad and its 350,000 conflict-affected civilians continue to
experience severely deteriorating security. Humanitarian operations face
the same high levels of insecurity as their counterparts in Darfur, as
various armed groups surge back and forth across the Chad-Darfur border.
The Chad rebel group FUC continues to be supported by Khartoum
inside Darfur.

The proposal for augmenting the AU includes a modest commitment
from the UN to provide equipment, logistics, and a very few personnel;
faint encouragement from NATO; and an AU commitment to increase its

manpower in Darfur. Some details were reported in a September 24, 2004 Associated Press article from Khartoum,

> AU leaders are finalizing a decision to add some 1,200 new troops to the existing 7,000-strong force, [AU] officials said. Even more soldiers could come if NATO provides adequate material support, and if the Arab League and other international donors secure funding, the AU officials said.

The notion that 1,200 additional AU personnel – of unknown quality or potential for integrating with the current force – represent a significant change in the potential effectiveness of the AU is perverse in the extreme. For even this increase would still leave the AU force at approximately one-third of what normal peacekeeping guidelines dictate for a crisis of this magnitude; and Darfur's extreme levels of violence, as well as its remoteness and size, argue for a figure at least as large as the proposed UN force of approximately 22,500 troops and security personnel.

The November 2005 Brookings Report, page 25, recognized and forth-rightly articulated an important roadblock to efforts to expand force size using AU resources,

> As [the African Union mission in Darfur] expands, along with demands placed on the AU from other peacekeeping operation in South Sudan, Congo, and Somalia, combined with security crises at home (Nigeria, Ethiopia), it will become increasingly difficult to maintain [troop] quality [at higher AU force levels].

This problem has not in any way diminished; indeed, given the outlook on Darfur in Rwanda and in some quarters in Nigeria, it is difficult not to conclude that the problem has become even more severe in the past ten months. Certainly confidential assessments of AU personnel have continued to be scathingly, even contemptuously critical. Publicly, on the other hand, tact and expediency have combined to credit the AU with far more than it deserves.

This is certainly not to say the AU deployment has been useless or has not saved a great many lives; and many AU personnel have served with great distinction and courage. But too many have not. Too many have simply hunkered down in the face of an uncertain future and a very dangerous present, in which AU forces increasingly find themselves targeted by combatants. And as the AU has come to be perceived as having taken sides in the conflict, with the Khartoum regime or Minni Minawi's forces, violent attacks have increased, and the contempt, even hatred for the AU in camps for displaced persons has also risen. These desperate civilians realize quite well that the AU is serving as the international presence in Darfur, and that it is a force woefully inadequate to urgent security tasks.

The African Union force is defined by critical shortcomings in leadership, logistics, communications equipment, transport capacity, intelligence-gathering abilities, timely payment for troops, and administrative capacity in Addis Ababa. There is exceedingly little operating cohesion within this force. Assembled as it was on an *ad hoc* basis, this is the first peacekeeping task the fledgling African Union Peace and Security Council has taken on. It is only in recent months that AU leadership has acknowledged how completely out of its depth it is in Darfur. Moreover, in the field, the AU continues to be treated with utter contempt by Khartoum's military forces. For example, the commandeering of AU aviation fuel has become a routine occurrence, as both *The New York Times* and *Washington Post* have reported from el-Fasher military air base in North Darfur.

This force simply cannot be turned around, or converted into a success story in Darfur, even as it is clear the AU is – and should be – the future of peacekeeping in Africa. What is even more certain, however, is that Darfur must not be held hostage to AU political sensibilities and pridefulness.

Many in the AU are of course quite aware of their limitations and Khartoum's manipulations, and speak with great frustration. IRIN reported from Tawilla, North Darfur September 5, 2006,

Simply the lack of fuel and vehicles, as well as a mandate limited to monitoring ceasefire violations, hampers even routine work. "We are too few and not well equipped – it makes me furious. We just patrol, show our faces, and we come back to our base," an AU commander said. "This is my ninth mission, but I have never worked in a situation like this, in terms of mandate, equipment, and procedures. We only investigate and report when something happens, but we don't do anything about it."

The current and future character of the force was described bluntly by a senior AU official in a September 5, 2006 Reuters dispatch datelined Khartoum,

> One senior AU official, who declined to be named, said: "They will drag it out until the end of the year . . . but this is no way to run a peace-keeping operation." "Morale is low, we cannot pay our troops and the government makes sure we are unable to do our job."

Here it is important to realize that deployment of the authorized UN force to Darfur faces very substantial non-African political obstacles. Russia and China both continue to cleave to their previously articulated insistence that Khartoum must first accept UN deployment, even in the face of adamant refusal by a regime that has launched a major military offensive with clear genocidal features – an offensive that shows no sign of letting up. As Secretary of State Condoleezza Rice observed on September 22, 2006, and was reported the same day from Khartoum, "'Time is running out. The violence in Darfur is not subsiding, it is getting worse.'" Of course the notion that only now is it clear that time is running out is obscenely disingenuous, given the reports that have been available to Rice for many months now.

Besides Russia and China, the Arab League has continued to side unrelentingly with Khartoum in its refusal to accept the UN force authorized by Security Council Resolution 1706. To be sure, it proved expedient for Egyptian President Hosni Mubarak, while in Washington, to accept an account of his meeting with President Bush that "expressed a strong commitment to effecting a transition [from an AU force] to a UN force," as Agence France-Presse reported from Washington on September 20, 2006. But comments from Egyptian foreign policy officials, as well as from an Arab League that is content to serve as an extension of Egyptian policy views, were clear in their insistence that Khartoum's consent was essential prior to UN deployment. Mubarak himself is reported as giving this assurance directly to Khartoum's President Omar al-Bashir during his visit to Cairo, as the *Sudan Tribune* reported in a September 22, 2006 dispatch,

Mubarak told Bashir that Egypt supported Sudan's position on Darfur, underlining that a possible deployment of UN forces could only be conducted with consent from the Sudanese government.

This is the context in which to understand why the African Union continues to defer to Khartoum. Moreover, the AU leadership's insistence on AU military command and troop majority in any follow-on UN force creates potential new difficulties and clashes with the UN Department of Peacekeeping Operations, inevitably time-consuming and retarding the urgent planning required. A September 24, 2006 Associated Press dispatch from Khartoum underscored this,

> Alpha Oumar Konare, the head of the AU, said last week that UN troops were necessary in Darfur, but said they should come with the consent of the government of Sudan and under African leadership.

The *Sudan Tribune* reported even more fully from Paris on September 23, 2006,

> "[Alpha Oumar Konaré said the transition to the UN force] has to be done with the Sudanese government's approval and we have clearly said that even if the UN was to come, the bulk of the troops would be AU forces; the command would be African and the AU political leadership will be there."

Konaré outlines an arrogant formula for further disaster, especially given the acute limitations in AU troop availability, the lack of cohesiveness that would come with any substantial increase in force levels, and the disastrous leadership – military and political – that has dogged the AU mission in Darfur from the beginning. In this latter respect, Nigerian general and former overall commander Festus Okonkwo represents only the most extreme case of incompetence. Of course there can be no disputing the importance of troops from African, and Muslim countries; at the same time, to hold the threatened people of Darfur hostage to ethnic, religious, and political sensitivities is intolerable.

There is an irreducible truth in the present historic moment. The UN force authorized by UN Security Council Resolution 1706 could save hundreds of thousands of innocent lives if rapidly deployed with adequate resources for military and security personnel. This force has been blocked by the same handful of NIF génocidaires that has for three and a half years relentlessly, systematically, and savagely targeted the African tribal populations of Darfur as a means of crushing the insurgency that emerged in February 2003. The ethnically-targeted nature of this well-orchestrated destruction has been documented in numerous human rights reports, assessment missions, and by a wide range of journalists and humanitarian workers. Amnesty International, Human Rights Watch, the International Crisis Group, Physicians for Human Rights, and others have made overwhelmingly clear that civilian destruction has been deliberate, systematic, and that in countless instances such destruction has been based solely on the ethnicity of those targeted.

Such destruction continues to this very day in the form of indiscriminate aerial bombardment of villages that are predominantly those of the non-Arab or African tribal groups perceived as supporting the non-signatory SLA/M factions, in particular the Fur. A September 22, 2006 Associated Press dispatch from Geneva reported,

> "Civilians in villages in North Darfur are forced to flee due to indiscriminate aerial bombardment by government aircraft waging a military campaign against rebel groups," said Jose Diaz, spokesman for UN human rights chief Louise Arbour. Diaz, citing clashes in the locality of Tabarat that led some 400 people to arrive recently in a Darfur camp, said "the military campaign against rebel movements in North Darfur that have not signed on to the peace agreement continued through the first two weeks of September." . . .
>
> Diaz cited reports from UN monitors in Sudan in making the accusations against Khartoum. He said some of the airstrikes have reportedly been carried out by forces dropping bombs from the back of a white plane(s) – appearing to corroborate a claim made earlier this month by Human Rights Watch that the government was indiscriminately attacking villages.

This regime is unwilling to accept any responsibility for such actions – past, present, or future. Instead, it lashes out viciously, blaming "Zionist Jews," Israel, and human rights organizations for Darfur's catastrophe, as a Reuters dispatch from the UN/New York reported on September 19, 2006,

> "The main purpose [of UN peacekeeping deployment to Darfur] is the security of Israel. Any state in the region should be weakened, dismembered in order to protect the Israelis, to guarantee the Israeli security," [President Omar al-Bashir] said. Asked about Sunday's [September 17, 2006] Darfur peace rallies from Rwanda to San Francisco, Bashir said they were "invariably organized by Zionist Jewish organizations."

The Associated Press on September 20, 2006 from the UN/New York reported more of al-Bashir's hateful allegations,

> Sudan's president claimed that human rights groups have exaggerated the crisis in Darfur to help their fundraising.

But beyond this preposterous mendacity, the génocidaires in Khartoum share with Macbeth, one of Shakespeare's greatest figures of evil, individually and collectively, the sense that,

> I am in blood
> Stepp'd in so far that, should I wade no more,
> Returning were as tedious as go o'er.

Such men will not be deterred from further genocidal crimes by the threat of sanctions, targeted or otherwise; they will never allow themselves to be seized by the International Criminal Court. And they live in no fear of an inevitably dilatory and incompetent deployment of some additional AU personnel. These men will not yield. If the world continues to defer to this defiance of international will, as represented in UN Security Council Resolution 1706, hundreds of thousands of innocent civilians in Darfur and eastern Chad will die.

This is what's happening in Darfur 2002-2003

These photos show civilians killed by *janjaweed* militias in Darfur. They were taken by conscience citizens and passed them to us in confidence.
Darfur Diaspora Association, Toronto.

Darfur's Civilians

It is of course the civilian populations that have suffered most from the crisis in Darfur. Although the victims of the conflict are mainly black Africans from the Fur, Massalit, and Daju ethnic groups, millions of people, both Arab and non-Arab, have been forced to flee their homes and face starvation.

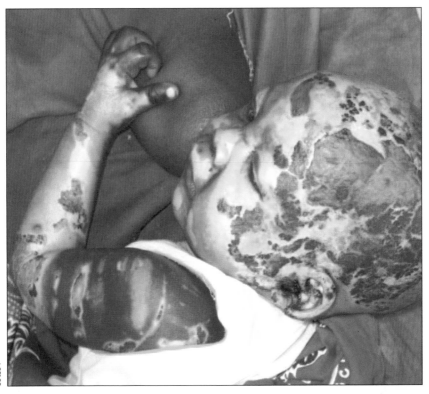

IRIN

Baby burnt during a bombing raid in Darfur, Sudan, 11 December 2003. Daily bombing raids on villages in Darfur are injuring and killing hundreds of civilians, causing thousands more to flee across the border.

Women displaced
by militia attacks
in Kalma camp,
outside Nyala,
southern Darfur,
13 April 2004.

IDPs loading
their property
onto trucks at
Al-Mustaqbal
school, West
Darfur, October 9
2004.

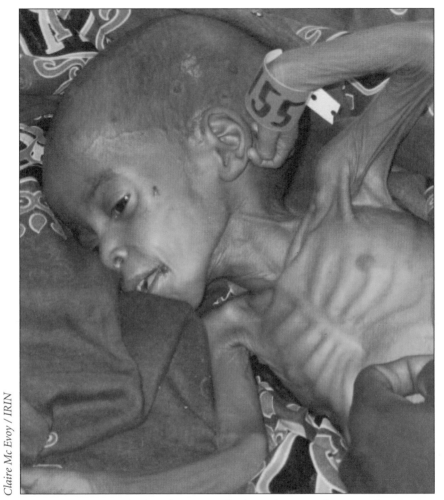

Claire Mc Evoy / IRIN

Severely malnourished girl in MSF feeding clinic in al-Junaynah, Western Darfur, 9 July 2004.

Lining up for water at Cariari refugee camp on Chad-Sudan border

One sector of Cariari camp.

Aerial view of a burned-out village in Darfur.

Destroyed market in Furawiya, Darfur

Destroyed home, Furawiya, Darfur

The destroyed village of Terbeba in West Darfur

A woman crossing a river in Chad

Boy at a refugee camp in Chad

Photos this page by Michael Wadleigh. © gritty.org for Physicians for Human Rights

Aerial view of an intact village in Chad

Cooking at a refugee camp in Chad

Refugee camp, Chad

Adult education at a refugee camp in Chad

School for women at a refugee camp in Chad

Woman at a refugee camp, Chad

4

GENOCIDE BY ATTRITION

April 30, 2004 – World Community Fails Darfur. Will Tens or Hundreds of Thousands Die?

DESPITE ALL EVIDENCE demanding humanitarian intervention, despite a searing moral clarity, Khartoum's genocidal war on the African peoples of Darfur has now fully precipitated a massive and irreversible humanitarian crisis. There can no longer be anything approaching an adequate humanitarian response in present circumstances. The vast scale of the crisis forces the grimmest of questions: Will the death toll in Darfur over the next 12 months be measured in tens of thousands of deaths? Or will it be measured in hundreds of thousands?

Honesty and moral decency demand that we first accept that this ghastly question has become inevitable. No actions can now avert catastrophe. But a most urgent, resourceful, and robust humanitarian intervention can prevent the present catastrophe from generating the cataclysmic numbers that defined the Rwandan genocide. The international community has waited too long, the words have come too late – and the actions that such words now demand are even more belated. War in Darfur, as deliberately and relentlessly conducted by Khartoum's regular forces and *Janjaweed* militia allies, has now so fully compromised food production, has so deeply disrupted humanitarian relief efforts, has so traumatized the agriculturally productive civilians of the African tribal groups, that famine is inevitable.

Their deaths will come not from machetes, but from the far more agonizing death of starvation – starvation that will typically entail parents watching their children slowly, painfully die. And then they will die themselves. Others will die from cholera, measles, and a host of water-borne diseases that will proliferate uncontrollably with the onset of the rains, especially in overcrowded concentration camps lacking all sanitary facilities. These same rains will sever the ground transport arteries for foodstocks and medical supplies. Presently prepositioned supplies are not remotely adequate for the more than 1 million people already dependent on international aid, even as the vast majority of these people are beyond any humanitarian access. Access remains impossible both because of Khartoum's continuing obstructionism and travel-permit denials, and because the regime has not controlled or disarmed the *Janjaweed*.

These increasingly brutal militias, working in close concert with Khartoum, are clearly not respecting in any meaningful way the cease-fire Khartoum signed in N'Djamena, Chad on April 8, 2004. Refugees fleeing from the predations of the *Janjaweed* continue to stream into Chad. Numerous reports, from highly reliable sources – in Darfur and along the Chad-Sudan border – confirm that insecurity remains extreme throughout Darfur. The same assessment is offered by UN and humanitarian officials in private communications. Indeed, on the basis of very considerable evidence, Amnesty International's April 30, 2004 Public Statement reported that despite the cease-fire that was to have taken effect on April 12, 2004,

> civilians continue to suffer human rights abuses and are in a desperate humanitarian situation. Attacks on villages continue; indiscriminate and deliberate killings of civilians continue; looting continues and rapes continue. Most detainees imprisoned because of the conflict have not been released. . . .
>
> Most villages in Darfur have now been destroyed and the population hardly dares to leave the displacement camps. The Janjawid (government-supported militia) block the roads and even invade the

camps. In Ardamata camp for displaced people near al-Jeneina town, Janjawid are reported to enter openly and choose women to rape.

Furthermore, the conflict is in danger of spreading. On 28 April [2004] Sudanese planes bombed Kolbus village in Chad and the Janjawid attacked refugees and Chadian civilians across the border.

Senior UN officials, US officials, humanitarian workers, and others are also indicating that Khartoum has not begun to disarm the extremely heavily armed *Janjaweed* – forces originally armed by Khartoum and still clearly doing Khartoum's savage military work.

As a consequence of the insecurity created by the *Janjaweed*, there is now simply no chance that the African tribal groups of Darfur will be able to plant in time before the onset of the rains. Such planting must be accomplished in the next few weeks, and yet the areas to which these people would have to return to plant remain *Janjaweed* killing fields. As a result, there will be no significant harvest next fall. It is this that ensures famine, and the terrible conclusions of the USAID's *Projected Mortality Rates in Darfur, Sudan 2004-2005.*

The key assumptions guiding the assembly of these data continue to hold: highly constrained humanitarian access and a critical planting season missed because of insecurity. The presumed vulnerable population recently stood at 1.2 million; this number continues to grow. Thus the grim arithmetic – next December, when the consequences of famine are at their peak, people will be dying at a rate of 20 people per day per 10,000 in this vulnerable population. Put more starkly, 2,500 people will starve, or die from increased vulnerability to disease, every day.

They will be dying in agony, and too many will have endured the unfathomable agony of watching their own children starve to death. Vast human destruction, produced by extraordinary levels of global acute malnutrition, will continue through April of 2005, when USAID's *Projected Mortality Rates in Darfur, Sudan 2004-2005* predicts that, "Crude Mortality Rate will decrease as people die or migrate out; the cumulative death rate would be approximately 30% of the vulnerable group over a nine-month period." The grimmest statistical conclusion here is that more than 300,000 people will die.

We have permitted this. We can no longer stop the famine Khartoum has engineered. The genocide has been accomplished. What can be done now? We must first of all recall the words of Mukesh Kapila, UN humanitarian coordinator for Sudan, uttered urgently in a March 22, 2004 IRIN report over a month ago – when there was still a slim chance of averting catastrophe,

> "The only difference between Rwanda and Darfur now is the numbers involved" [said Kapila].

The only difference. . . . "now."

> [Conflict in Darfur] is more than just a conflict, it is an organised attempt to do away with a group of people.

These words are now, belatedly, registering. But the urgent dispatch by *New York Times* columnist Nicholas Kristof, written from the Chad-Sudan border March 31, 2004, posed a test that has already been failed,

> Darfur is not a case when we can claim, as the world did after the Armenian, Jewish and Cambodian genocides, that we didn't know how bad it was. Sudan's refugees tell of mass killings and rapes, of women branded, of children killed, of villages burned – yet Sudan's government just stiffed new peace talks that began last night in Chad.
>
> This is not just a moral test of whether the world will tolerate another genocide. It's also a practical test of the ability of African and Western governments alike to respond to incipient civil wars while they can still be suppressed. Africa's future depends on the outcome, and for now it's a test we're all failing.

We are not failing; we have failed. The verb tense has changed profoundly in the last month. The *Chicago Sun-Times* April 11, 2004 recorded the words of the US representative to the Geneva travesty that was the annual meeting of the UN Commission on Human Rights, Ambassador Richard Williamson,

> African countries and the entire world must decide if we will act to try to stop the genocide in Darfur or if we will respond with silence

and inaction as we did in Rwanda 10 years ago. To fail to act is morally indefensible.

But we have decided. We have failed to act, as we failed in Rwanda, and it is indeed morally indefensible. We have all too fully justified Samantha Power's recently expressed fear to the April 27, 2004 Rwanda hearing, International Relations Committee of the US House of Representatives, that "in 10 years we'll be sitting on a similar panel discussing Sudan's genocide."

It remains, then, first to accept our moral failure. But we must also do all that is possible to diminish the scale of the impending catastrophe. This catastrophe cannot be averted, but it can be substantially mitigated. The challenges are immense, however, even if we presume full international political resolve. There is no evidence to support such presumption.

Logistical challenges are many. With the onset of the May to September rainy season, road transportation of food supplies from central Chad to the Chad-Sudan border will shortly end. An authoritative assessment on this issue from Chad came to the author today,

Once the rainy season begins, the 650-kilometer road running east from N'Djamena, Chad's capital to Abeche, near the Chad/Sudan border, will be cut, as it is each year, as the "wadis," or the dry channels that fill with water during the rainy season are deepened by the floods that come with the rains. The 150-kilometer road from Abeche to the Chad/Sudan border is not at all good, even outside the rainy season. It presently takes five hours to cover this distance. The critical sections in this road are just to the east of Abeche, but there are wadis on north/south and northwest/southwest axes along the entire course of the road. This road will shortly be impassable.

Air transport has limits and challenges as well. There is a serviceable airstrip in Abeche along with a French military base with 200 troops. This airstrip can handle medium-sized air transport planes, but not the C-130 Hercules aircraft that are the backbone of any World Food Program airlift operation. These larger aircraft would have to fly from El Obeid in Kordofan Province in Sudan, well to the east of Darfur.

Some will imagine that airdrops of food are an alternative to ground transport. This is impractical for a number of reasons. There is first of all the prohibitive cost of airlifting food for 1 million people over as much as a year, given other humanitarian needs in the world. There is simply no money for such a massively expensive operation. Indeed, the present estimated costs of humanitarian response in Darfur, a response, which doesn't begin to contemplate such an unprecedented airlift operation, are far from receiving sufficient donor commitments.

Moreover, air transport of food is only in the most exceptional of cases simply the uncontrolled and unmonitored dumping of food from the air. Typically, food is airlifted to where there are humanitarian monitors and other personnel on the ground. But insecurity on the ground in Darfur makes this normal practice impossible. Indeed, so long as Khartoum continues to allow the *Janjaweed* its "reign of terror" – the phrase comes from an April 2004 UN human rights report on Darfur – food drops would simply be a means of feeding these deadly militias, and would make of the intended recipients more inviting targets. Neither road nor exclusive air transport are practicable, given present circumstances in Darfur. But we must not turn away from the shameful truth. Airlifting food aid has come to be seen as the only transport means available because we did not act in the urgent ways demanded by realities clearly in evidence months ago in Darfur.

May 17, 2004 - Stopping Genocide in Darfur – What Could Be Done Must Be Done

All reports from Darfur, public and confidential, make clear that the massive humanitarian crisis continues to deepen at an alarming rate. The region, including the border region inside Chad, is slipping further into a famine that will claim hundreds of thousands of lives. This is the predictable, indeed designed outcome of Khartoum's genocidal conduct of war in Darfur over many months, both with its regular forces and by means of its *Janjaweed* allies.

Notably, in a May 13, 2004 BBC interview following a recent meeting with British Foreign Minister Jack Straw, Khartoum's Foreign Minister Mustafa Ismail pointedly described the *Janjaweed* militia as in military "alliance" with the regime in conducting war in Darfur. Agence France-Presse (Cairo) on May 14, 2004 also reported Ismail asserting, "pro-government militias in strife-torn Darfur region would not be disarmed as long as weapons remained in the hands of rebel forces." It is of course the *Janjaweed* that are responsible for so much civilian destruction, for creating conditions of utter terror in the rural agricultural lands, and that have so willingly become the "Gestapo" forces in the ghastly concentration camps that continue to grow and multiply.

In a shameless, if unsurprising, contradiction, Ahmed Mohamed Haroun, National Islamic Front State Minister for Internal Affairs, said in a May 7, 2004 Reuters Dispatch, "the Darfur region was stable after the military quelled a revolt there and security would now be maintained by police."

The systematic denial of humanitarian access – the characterization is that of the UN and virtually all humanitarian organizations; the burning of thousands of villages; the destruction of foodstuffs, seeds, agricultural implements and donkeys; the dynamiting, bombing, and poisoning of wells and irrigation systems; the looting of herds of cattle; and the creation of what a UN human rights team recently called a "reign of terror" in the rural areas, precluding any planting prior to the rainy season, and thus ensuring that there will be no harvest in the fall: these are the weapons of genocidal war that are now taking a toll that is increasing daily. Without humanitarian intervention, the death rate will rise to between 2000 and 3000 civilians per day by December. Total casualties may exceed 400,000 human beings according to USAID's *Projected Mortality Rates in Darfur*, and USAID's Assistant Administrator Roger Winter's May 6, 2004 Testimony Before the Committee on International Relations – US House of Representatives, *Ethnic Cleansing in Darfur: A New Front Opens in Sudan's Bloody War*.

There is no longer any credible alternative to humanitarian intervention, given the paucity of pre-positioned foodstocks and medical supplies in Darfur and the impending June to September seasonal rains that will soon sever the road corridors in both eastern Chad and Darfur. There will be no harvest next fall and the likelihood of a fall planting for next spring depends wholly on the ability of the international community to disarm the *Janjaweed* and restore security to the rural agricultural areas. If there is no planting in the fall, hundreds of thousands of acutely vulnerable people will have their vulnerability extended for many months. There will be many, many more deaths.

An overland transport route capable of supplying humanitarian aid must be secured in the very near-term, as the dwindling foodstocks in Nyala and al-Fashir are almost exhausted. Air transport of food and supplies is really only a stopgap measure for a crisis of this magnitude, and is not practicable over the longer-term. Leaving aside diplomatic considerations of the sort that have done so much to obscure both the urgency of the crisis and the culpability of the Khartoum regime, and ignoring the callous inclinations and abysmal performance of the UN Security Council to date, the most obvious route from a logistical point of view is the rail line that runs from Port Sudan to Khartoum and on to Nyala via El Obeid. This presents a series of difficult problems – logistical, military, and of course diplomatic – even as it holds promise of fully adequate transport capacity.

But we can no longer avoid the necessity of deciding whether or not we will intervene to save the hundreds of thousands of lives that will be lost without robust action. As Gareth Evans, President of the International Crisis Group, courageously wrote in the May 14, 2004 *The International Herald Tribune*,

> The UN secretary general, Kofi Annan, has called it "ethnic cleansing." President George W. Bush has condemned the "atrocities, which are displacing hundreds of thousands of civilians." Others are starting to use the word genocide. Whatever you want to call what is going on today in Darfur, in western Sudan, the time for forceful outside intervention is unmistakably approaching.

Evans went on to make clear that in all likelihood it would be necessary for the UN Security Council to,

> authorise the application of military force on "responsibility to protect" principles and [provide] the necessary political will and military resources to hold [the Khartoum regime] comprehensively to account.

But while the Security Council must certainly be urged to act, and given a chance to act, such action is highly unlikely. That Pakistan is currently chairing the Security Council gives but an inkling of how long the odds are against any authorization of the application of military force that is opposed by Khartoum. But inaction by the United Nations must not mean that there is no international response, specifically on the basis of the responsibility to protect principles that Evans articulates in his analysis. Racially/ethnically animated slaughter and starvation in Darfur continue and must be stopped. But they can be stopped only with humanitarian intervention. This is the context in which we should note the growing urgency of the comparisons to Rwanda. The US Committee for Refugees recently added its voice to many others, declaring in a May 12, 2004 Washington, DC press release,

> In 1994 President Clinton failed to act to stop genocide in Rwanda when 800,000 people were slaughtered in 100 days. The world knew about Rwanda then and it knows about Darfur now. Visiting Rwanda in 1998, Clinton "apologized," saying we "did not immediately call these crimes by their rightful name: genocide." For the sake of his name in history, Mr. Bush must avoid ever having to make a similar apology over Darfur.

The moment of historical truth has arrived: either we act now to mitigate this growing catastrophe, or we will see the horrific mortality projections of the USAID realized. For the numbers at risk from genocidal destruction are not diminishing, despite the growing visibility of Darfur, but rather continue to grow. The UN recently raised its estimate of the number of Internally Displaced Persons (IDPs) in Darfur to over 1 million in Paragraph 13, *Report of the High Commissioner for Human Rights: Situation of human rights in the Darfur Region of the Sudan*, dated May 7, 2004. Refugees International has recently urged that the figure for refugees in Chad be revised upward dramatically from the UN figure of 110,000, a figure now over two months old, as refugees have continued to stream across the Darfur-Chad border at many points.

Refugees International reported in their May 11, 2004 release,

> The number of refugees who have fled to Chad to escape fighting in the Darfur area of western Sudan could be has high as 200,000, nearly double the official estimate of 110,000, Refugees International reports.

The sharply higher figure is based on the observations of Refugees International advocates in Chad, as well as informal estimates by the United Nations. UN officials in Chad told Refugees International that the number of refugees in Chad may be approaching 200,000, as violence and starvation in Darfur continue to drive refugees out.

Refugees International strongly urges the UN and aid agencies to revise their figures for Darfur refugees in Chad upwards to 200,000. Current UN planning is based on a figure of 110,000, and with the rainy season looming, failure to pre-position supplies based on the actual figure will leave refugees vulnerable to shortages of food and medicines in the coming months.

Christine Foletti of the International Committee of the Red Cross (ICRC) told an Australian news agency on May 16, 2004 that "over the past two weeks one refugee camp had grown from 7,000 to 24,000 people." But these frightening increases are being reported even as there is not nearly enough presently funded transport capacity to move existing refugee populations further into Chad and away from the dangerous border areas, or to provide these camps with food, water, and medical supplies. With the rains imminent, transport opportunities will shortly end.

Highly authoritative reports from within South and West Darfur reaching the author also indicate that more and more of those displaced within Darfur are being forced into concentration camps of the sort reported by the UN at Kailek on April 24, 2004. Unless control of these camps is very soon secured by international military intervention, tens of thousands of people will be exterminated through starvation, lack of water, disease, and executions. Moreover, a growing number of those seeking to report on the terrible conditions in Darfur are being imprisoned, as a May 10, 2004 Amnesty International report detailed,

Nureddin Mohammad Abdel Rahim, omda (mayor) of Shoba; Bahr al-Din Abdullah Rifah, omda of Jabalsi.

The two men named above, each of whom is the omda (mayor) of his village, were reportedly arrested in North Darfur state on 9 May [2004] after a meeting called by the International Committee of the Red Cross, where they had given information on burnt villages, killings and mass graves in a region where many villages have been destroyed and villagers killed in attacks by government aircraft and, particularly, by government-supported militias. The two have no access to lawyers or their families, and are at risk of torture or other ill-treatment.

Further, unless there is a humanitarian intervention, the increasingly explosive military situation along the Chad-Sudan border threatens to spark a full-fledged international conflict. Highly authoritative reports from the ground inside Chad suggest that a number of factors could dramatically escalate the violence already occurring on a regular basis. The destabilizing effects of such violence in Chad should be of considerable international concern. Of particular note, IRIN reported on May 14, 2004 about the growing numbers of *Janjaweed* incursions into Chad.

What are the advantages and the difficulties of a humanitarian intervention, including internationalizing the rail line from Port Sudan to Nyala?

Rail transport has huge capacity, and could easily manage even the vast quantities of food that will be required to avert major famine in Darfur over the next year or longer. Tens of thousands will die no matter what the international response, already shamefully belated. But hundreds of thousands of lives can be saved. Rail is also the cheapest form of transportation.

Distribution from Nyala to the camps nearby and to more outlying areas could be accomplished by overland routes where possible, using four-wheel-drive trucks, and by air where this is not possible. The existing rail line runs through El Obeid, site of a major air base and a location already being used by the UN's World Food Program (WFP). Air transport would be possible using even the largest of the WFP's transport planes, the Hercules C-130, the backbone of airlift operations in southern Sudan. Smaller capacity planes could use the airport in Nyala for more targeted airdrops. Such airdrops would require the presence of humanitarian personnel in places presently too insecure; consequently, there must be a sufficient military presence to protect all aid workers deployed throughout the region.

Securing the concentration camps and ensuring that they are safe havens for the displaced and imprisoned is of critical importance; this will save many thousands of lives, possibly tens of thousands of lives that are now at growing risk from starvation, lack of water, disease and execution –

risks set to increase dramatically with the onset of the seasonal rains. More broadly, security throughout the agricultural areas of Darfur is the only long-term solution to the region's food problems. But taking control of the camps is the first essential step in creating this security.

Over the longer term the international community must force Khartoum to disarm the *Janjaweed*, despite what Foreign Minister Ismail calls the regime's "alliance" with these murderous predators. If Darfur is to become self-sufficient in food, such disarmament is essential.

Internationalizing and securing the rail line from Port Sudan to Darfur, if Khartoum proves intent on militarily opposing this plan, will require considerable military resources. Military control will not be so much for security on board the trains themselves, but for preventing the rail lines themselves from being cut by explosives. Khartoum's regular and militia forces are both likely sources of opposition if the regime is determined to resist the transport of humanitarian supplies. Moreover, substantial amounts of rail line repair equipment and supplies must be on hand to minimize the impact of the rail line being cut at any point. Fast-moving aerial military resources, with sophisticated communications and "look-down" ability, will be essential in this task. Khartoum must also be put on notice that various of its unrelated military resources will be struck if the regime attacks, directly or by proxy, the rail line.

The rail line already needs substantial work between Ed Da'ein and Nyala. Moreover, the trains themselves are in critical need of American-made spare parts. These must be supplied on an urgent basis, requiring that President Bush exempt these parts from current US sanctions against Sudan. A detailed inventory of such parts must be kept and the parts themselves removed if the crisis in Darfur ends and Khartoum is still subject to US sanctions. Internationalizing the rail line must mean that it will be used only for humanitarian transport; no non-humanitarian items would be permitted on the trains.

The *Janjaweed* have been heavily armed by Khartoum, and could present a significant threat to humanitarian operations and personnel in Darfur. But there is also good reason to believe that the *Janjaweed* would cease military resistance quickly if confronted with a well-trained, appropriately armed, and sufficiently robust military contingent with forceful rules of engagement. Confrontations would be inevitable, but the *Janjaweed* are no match for a modern, organized military force. Disarming the *Janjaweed* as well as the interdiction of further armaments flowing from Khartoum should be a clear part of the mandate of any international military force stationed in Darfur itself.

Where would the necessary military resources come from? On May 17, 2004, *EU BusinessWire* reported one possibility: an emergency assembly of one of the "battle groups" that were approved May 17, 2004 by the European Union defense ministers. To be deployed to "international hotspots," these 1500-strong battle groups "would be deployable within 10 days and able to stay on the ground for a few months." Strikingly, an aide to EU foreign policy chief Javier Solana said,

> A typical scenario in which they would be deployed would be in response to a UN request, said an aide to Solana. "If the UN Security Council for example asked for support to protect a humanitarian mission in Darfur, Sudan, we would be ready to respond to the request."

Given the critical situation in Darfur, there must be urgent planning for an *ad hoc* creation of just such a battle group – of appropriate size, utilizing the EU military planning to date, with an emergency assembly of troops and equipment. And even if the UN Security Council fails in its moral assessment of what is demanded in Darfur, there are other possibilities for sponsoring multilateral humanitarian intervention.

There are other difficulties that will confront any form of humanitarian intervention. There are also alternative overland transport routes presently under consideration, from Libya, for example. But the logistical difficulties presented and the lack of adequate transport capacity present immense problems if the international community is determined to avoid hundreds of thousands of deaths. Given the human stakes, it is critically important that humanitarian need define political/military possibilities, and not the reverse.

And because present and impending deaths are so numerous, and because of the abstraction that attends so much discussion of how to respond to the crisis in Darfur, the question to the international community should be framed in two ways. Are we prepared to acquiesce in Khartoum's engineered famine – a massive episode in human destruction that is genocidal in nature? Have we really learned nothing from Rwanda?

More particularly, as *The Economist* asked on May 13, 2004,

Are we prepared to accept countless versions of the story of Kaltuma Hasala Adan?

Her children's bodies were rotting in the village wells, where Arab militiamen had thrown them to poison the water supply. But Kaltuma Hasala Adan did not flee her home. Leaving her crops and livestock would condemn the rest of the family to death, she reasoned. So she stayed put for four months, despite her government's strenuous efforts to terrorise her into flight.

Her village was first attacked in January. An air raid caught her unawares: as the bombs fell, she ran around in confusion. When [Khartoum's] bombers had completed their return pass, the horizon filled with dust, the ground shuddered, and a host of mounted militiamen charged through the village, killing all the young men they could find. During that first attack, Kaltuma's 18-month baby, Ali, was killed by shrapnel. Two weeks later, her oldest son, Issa, 15, was made to kneel in line with other young men before being shot in the back of the head. Her husband disappeared the same day.

For four wretched months, Kaltuma lived with both ears strained for the faint drone of bombers, poised to dash with her three surviving children to a hiding place in a dry river bed. Then the *Janjaweed* – an Arab militia that kills for the Sudanese government – rode up to finish the job. They razed her village entirely. She fled from the embers of her hut and trekked for four days through the desert.

The comparisons between Rwanda and Darfur are indeed being made more frequently, more urgently; but this only makes present inaction the more profoundly inexplicable. Certainly such comparisons by themselves are of little use to Kaltuma Hasala Adan, and the many hundreds of thousands who have also been forced to flee into the desert. If she could frame for us her one question, it would certainly be, "why will you not help me?" We are, shamefully, without an answer.

August 9, 2004 – Halting Genocide in Darfur, Preserving the North-South Peace Agreement: Both Require Removal of Khartoum's National Islamic Front from Power

As the UN Security Council and political leadership continue to prove wholly inadequate to the crisis in Darfur, as humanitarian capacity slips further behind rapidly expanding humanitarian need, and as the international community badly fumbles over how to respond to massive genocidal destruction, the Khartoum regime's remorseless engine of human death and suffering continues to function with terrifying efficiency. Though most of the 2,000 who now die daily are succumbing to disease and the effects of starvation, most of these invisibly, a recent and extraordinarily revealing report from the UN Special Rapporteur on extrajudicial executions gives us a much clearer view of Khartoum's direct involvement in violent mass human destruction.

Associated Press reported August 6, 2004 that UN Special Rapporteur Asma Jahangir, a lawyer from Pakistan, minced no words in her final report, *Report of the UN HR Commission on Extrajudicial, Summary or Arbitrary Executions in S. & W. Sudan*, or in her public comments,

> It is beyond doubt that the Government of the Sudan is responsible for extrajudicial and summary executions of large numbers of people over the last several months in the Darfur region, as well as in the Shilook [also Shilluk] Kingdom in Upper Nile State [southern Sudan]," said Asma Jahangir, the UN investigator on executions, in a report based on a 13-day visit to the region in June.
>
> Jahangir said there was "overwhelming evidence" that the killing was carried out "in a coordinated manner by the armed forces of the government and government-backed militias. They appear to be carried out in a systematic manner."

Jahangir also takes a larger view of the consequences for Darfur of what a previous UN human rights investigative team called a "reign of terror" as she continued,

> "The current humanitarian disaster unfolding in Darfur, for which the government is largely responsible, has put millions of civilians at

risk, and it is very likely that many will die in the months to come as a result of starvation and disease," said Jahangir, a Pakistani lawyer.

Jahangir's account of attacks on the African civilian populations of Darfur has a ghastly familiarity, echoing as it does so many other human rights reports on Darfur,

> [Jahangir said] the most often heard report was of villages being surrounded by military vehicles accompanied by Arab militia riding horses. The local population was plundered, looted, tortured, raped and often shot at in a random manner; however, adult men seemed often to be specifically targeted. Before leaving, the Arab militia would burn down the villages. In some cases, helicopters or Antonov airplanes were used to bomb or attack the villages or to provide cover for ground operations, including operations carried out by Arab militia.

Though Jahangir suggested that the Khartoum regime "appeared oblivious to the dramatic and disastrous proportions and the magnitude," we can be sure that appearances are deceiving. Khartoum is fully aware of the proportions of its genocidal assault on the African tribal populations of Darfur, and its actions are clearly fully governed by an intent to destroy these people. The systematic and widespread military actions and military coordination that Jahangir and many others have described are unmistakably the deliberate policies of Khartoum. Intent can be inferred with certainty from the countless actions that make up Khartoum's sustained military strategy in Darfur.

Moreover, this inference has been indisputably confirmed in a July 20, 2004 Human Rights Watch report,

> Human Rights Watch said it had obtained confidential documents from the civilian administration in Darfur that implicate high-ranking government officials in a policy of militia support. "It's absurd to distinguish between the Sudanese government forces and the militias – they are one," said Peter Takirambudde, executive director of Human Rights Watch's Africa Division. "These documents

show that militia activity has not just been condoned, it's been specifically supported by Sudan government officials."

The NIF regime so potently indicted here by UN Special Rapporteur Jahangir and Human Rights Watch nonetheless presently enjoys a 30-day window of opportunity, courtesy of a weak and finally inconsequential July 30, 2004 UN Resolution 1556. Just as troublingly, Khartoum is now strenuously resisting the deployment of any African Union (AU) troops that might have a peacekeeping mandate. The NIF regime will only permit forces with a mandate to protect the small contingent of AU cease-fire monitors, a military task that obviously does not require the 2,000 troops the AU recently authorized to respond to the Darfur crisis, as Reuters reported August 7, 2004. Interior Minister Abdel Rahim Mohamed Hussein, a particularly brutal member of the NIF regime responsible for "Darfur policy," declared in an August 6, 2004 Reuters dispatch,

"We will not agree to the presence of any foreign forces, whatever their nationality," Sudanese Interior Minister Abdel Rahim Mohamed Hussein said in an interview with London's Asharq al-Awsat newspaper published on Friday.

The insidiously deceptive Foreign Minister Mustafa Ismail indicated the basis on which Khartoum would block any truly meaningful African Union force, one able to protect civilians, in an August 7, 2004 Reuters dispatch,

"We have to make a distinction between three categories. The presence of observers, the presence of protection forces for those observers and the presence of peacekeeping forces," Ismail told reporters in Khartoum when asked whether Sudan would accept African peacekeepers. "We don't have a problem with either the first or the second categories. As far as the third category is concerned . . . this is the responsibility of the Sudanese forces."

Why is Khartoum so eager to keep out a meaningful African Union peacekeeping force? Why in the face of massive insecurity, directly threatening many hundreds of thousands of displaced civilians, as well as humanitarian assistance and access, is Khartoum so insistent that no significant troop presence be permitted? Because the genocide is not complete and Khartoum is determined to finish a task well begun; moreover, the regime is determined to obliterate as much evidence of these crimes as possible. The primary goal is precisely to prevent and eliminate all international presence in Darfur.

No matter that UN Special Rapporteur Jahangir is all too accurate in her global assessment of the crisis deriving from Khartoum's policies, including her blunt warning in an August 6, 2004 Associated Press dispatch,

> "The current humanitarian disaster unfolding in Darfur, for which the government is largely responsible, has put millions of civilians at risk, and it is very likely that many will die in the months to come as a result of starvation and disease."

In fact, Jahangir's figure here of "millions of civilians at risk" is very likely suggestive of current realities. Evidence continues to accumulate that perhaps as many as 1 million people have not yet been included in figures for Internally Displaced Persons and refugees. The overall level of destruction of African villages is extraordinary – well over 50% by most estimates, a reality that has been confirmed by partial satellite photographic coverage and analysis of the Darfur region. The current UN total for Internally Displaced Persons and refugees is approximately 1.5 million. But this doesn't begin to account for all those who have been displaced, given the high level of village destruction and a total African tribal population that may be very roughly estimated at 4 million. We may in fact be seeing a gross underestimation by the UN and other international actors of the sort that defined the crisis in eastern Congo in 1996-97.

Even so, Khartoum is prepared to continue with present policies, amply supported by the Organization of the Islamic Conference and by the Arab League's irresponsible refusal to assess the crisis honestly. A perverse August 7, 2004 spectacle in Cairo saw the foreign ministers of various Arab countries rally around Khartoum, demanding both more time for the regime and rejecting any possibility of a militarily supported humanitarian intervention. The Arab League summit, called by a confident Khartoum, has offered the regime precisely what it wants, and this no doubt ensures that pressure to respond to the UN resolution has significantly diminished. The most appropriate response to this travesty comes from Peter Takirambudde, executive director of the Africa division of Human Rights Watch in an August 7, 2004 Reuters dispatch, " 'Allowing the Sudanese government to hide its crimes behind Arab solidarity would be an insult to more than one million Muslim victims in Darfur.' "

Assured that there will be no meaningful UN action at the end of the 30-day time-frame contemplated by the Security Council Resolution 1556, and further reassured by the incompetently optimistic judgment of Jan Pronk, Kofi Annan's new special representative to Sudan, Khartoum may be feeling increased pressure, but no obligation to respond beyond engaging in an especially energetic effort of disingenuousness, prevarication, trimming, and reneging. The regime's participation in peace talks in Abuja, Nigeria will be dilatory, grudging, time-consuming, and uncompromising. The regime will simply calculate what it must do, however speciously, to provide China and Russia with something to point to when the Security Council resumes discussions of Darfur.

What is, and has long been, certain is that humanitarian intervention will not be authorized by the Security Council, despite the Chapter VII auspices under which the resolution has been passed. This fig leaf of "tough resolve" will blow embarrassingly away – and still the people of Darfur will suffer and die.

Though it is not possible to draw any clear larger statistical inference from Jahangir's finding that nearly every third or fourth family had lost a relative to the militias, such a finding strongly suggests that many scores of thousands have been killed violently in Darfur. Jahangir's statements about a staggering number of violent deaths certainly lend considerable support to the figure of at least 80,000 killed violently, a figure derived by the author, primarily from data on violent death generated by MSF. Combined with data on malnutrition, morbidity, and mortality, this strongly supports a total mortality figure of over 150,000.

It is important here that we understand fully the nature of the violent deaths that are being reported by the UN Special Rapporteur Jahangir on extrajudicial, summary or arbitrary executions. A terribly telling example was provided in an April 7, 2004 Amnesty International report,

Amnesty International has now obtained detailed accounts of the
168 people extrajudicially executed [in West Darfur]. The men were
taken from 10 villages in Wadi Saleh, in the west of Darfur near the
Chad border, by a large force which included members of the Sudan
army, military intelligence and Janjawid. They were blindfolded and
taken in groups of about 40, on army trucks to an area behind a hill
near Deleij village. There they were then told to lie on the ground and
shot by a force of about 45 members of the military intelligence and
the Janjawid. Two of those shot lay wounded among the bodies
before escaping and giving information to the outside world.

This is but one instance, on one day, in one small part of Darfur; it is clear
from Jahangir's account that this genocidal practice has continued, on a
concerted basis throughout Darfur, for over a year.

Even as it has been directly involved in such mass murder, Khartoum has
continued to impede, in various and highly consequential ways, humanitarian assistance to the civilian populations traumatized by such executions
and by the pattern of village destruction that Jahangir has confirmed. The
destruction of these displaced people is no less certain, even if now they are
dead or dying from disease and starvation. If men and older boys have been
the particular target of mass executions, young children will be the primary
victims of the disastrously poor conditions in the camps for the displaced
and in the rural areas, where uncounted hundreds of thousands, perhaps
more than a million survivors are without food or security.

Forced expulsions and relocation of displaced persons from the camps
has also continued as a policy of human destruction on Khartoum's part.
This policy will result in a huge number of civilian casualties, of a sort suggested by an August 8, 2004 dispatch from Nyala by *The Independent* (UK),

The Sudanese government has been accused of sending refugees back
into the hands of the murderous *Janjaweed* militia. *The Independent*
on Sunday has been given accounts of returnees being killed by
gunmen – sometimes, it is claimed, in collusion with security forces.
There is also evidence that the police have attacked village chiefs who
have refused to lead their communities back home from refugee
camps. Refugees also claim that [Khartoum's] official agencies that

have a part in distributing international aid are cutting back on rations in an effort to get inmates to leave the camps.

A telling example from the huge camp near Kalma, with over 70,000 people, offers a glimpse of the coercion and violence that are being used to implement the policy of civilian expulsions from the camps, as *The Independent* (UK) also reported,

> In the latest clash [at Kalma] last week, 42 people were arrested and one village sheikh, Abdullah Bashir Sabir, was severely injured. The authorities say he was attacked after he tried to get people from his village to go back. But, according to people in the camp he was shot because he refused to comply with the authorities' demands to take them home. His wife, Halima, said: "They shot him in the leg because he would not agree."

Here we should bear in mind the general warning that has been coming from humanitarian workers for the last month, as IRIN reported July 13, 2004,

> Humanitarian workers fear that a forcible mass return of some 1.2 million Internally Displaced Persons in Darfur could result in enormous fatalities.

Some have wondered why we don't hear more often directly from humanitarian personnel working in Darfur – why identities of sources are so often obscured. An especially revealing answer to this question comes in the form of a comment reported in the August 8, 2004 *The Telegraph* (UK) by a humanitarian worker, also director of emergency programs for a European humanitarian organization, who explains not only what he/she has seen, but why silence has until now been obligatory,

> Our people have seen at first hand what has gone on in Darfur. We have watched government planes and helicopter gunships passing overhead to bomb villages, hours before the *Janjaweed* militia moved in to burn them. We have seen government officials and *Janjaweed* working together near the border with Chad. We have heard the

testimonies from survivors. Have we become complicit by not speaking out? I hope not. The fact is that any aid agency publicly speaking out would be immediately expelled from Sudan.

Despite the agonizing deliberation of the writer, his/her conclusion is clear,

But something more needs to happen. Not only is the situation in the camps where we are able to work getting worse, but there are still large parts of Darfur that no aid agency has ever been able to access. These, predictably enough, are the areas controlled by the two rebel groups fighting the government in Darfur, and into which the Sudanese army will not allow aid convoys to pass. There is a large civilian population trapped inside those areas, living (or dying) in conditions we can only imagine. Many aid workers on the ground now see some kind of international intervention as the last hope for hundreds of thousands of civilians.

Inevitably, this prompts yet again a comparison to the Rwandan genocide,

The *Janjaweed* is the creation of Khartoum, every bit as much as Rwanda's Interahamwe was a creation of a murderous political elite.

Though UN rhetoric and variously announced "improvements" in the situation in Darfur work to suggest a crisis essentially humanitarian in nature, and susceptible of humanitarian amelioration, the reality – as made clear yet again by this aid worker, freed to speak the truth by virtue of anonymity – is that humanitarian intervention is necessary to save hundreds of thousands of lives. To entrust security in Darfur to Khartoum and the new *Interahamwe* is to offer up these desperate people to a final holocaust.

With compelling authority, Alex de Waal of Justice Africa wrote in the August 5, 2004 *London Review of Books* that there is in the end nothing surprising or unprecedented about Khartoum's deployment of a domestic security policy of genocide,

The atrocities carried out by the Janjawiid are aimed at speakers of Fur, Tunjur, Masalit and Zaghawa. They are systematic and sustained;

the effect, if not the aim, is grossly disproportionate to the military threat of the rebellion. The mass rape and branding of victims speaks of the deliberate destruction of a community. In Darfur, cutting down fruit trees or destroying irrigation ditches is a way of eradicating farmers' claims to the land and ruining livelihoods. But this is not the genocidal campaign of a government at the height of its ideological hubris, as the 1992 jihad against the Nuba was, or coldly determined to secure natural resources, as when it sought to clear the oilfields of southern Sudan of their troublesome inhabitants. This is the routine cruelty of a security cabal, its humanity withered by years in power: it is genocide by force of habit.

This tells us far too much about the nature of the Khartoum regime, and the fate of Sudan if the regime remains in power. The international community must move to end this reign of terror, a tyranny that threatens not only Darfur but other marginalized areas throughout Sudan. Moreover, nothing could now be clearer than the extreme threat Darfur poses to the arduously negotiated north-south peace agreement: this agreement, still incomplete, will be meaningless so long as the National Islamic Front remains in power. The executions in the Shilluk Kingdom that UN Special Rapporteur Jahangir notes, almost in passing, are a sign of how completely indifferent Khartoum is to its commitments in the various signed Protocols and the October 2002 cessation of hostilities agreement.

Nor is it at all clear how the Sudan People's Liberation Movement (SPLM), or any other southern party, can join ranks with the génocidaires in Khartoum. The SPLM cannot possibly become part of the government, in the midst of a genocide, without hopelessly compromising itself, and its declared commitment to all the marginalized people of Sudan. At the same time, Khartoum may perversely work to use this refusal as a sign of the SPLM's bad faith in negotiations.

For now, Khartoum has not only refused to move toward completion of a final peace agreement, including a comprehensive cease-fire and modalities of implementation for the various protocols, but continues to be in egregious violation of the October 2002 cessation of hostilities agreement. All peace talks have now broken off, and with Darfur looming as the sticking point, it is exceedingly difficult to see how they can be resumed. Rather,

a resumption of full-scale hostilities in the south is the more likely possibility, with Eastern Upper Nile, the Shilluk Kingdom, and Western Upper Nile
particularly threatening flashpoints. The current and conservative US State
Department mortality estimate for casualties in this north-south conflict is
2.2 million human beings.

The international community can respond accommodatingly, as is all
too likely, to Khartoum's continuing bad faith and its present genocidal
policies in Darfur. The international community can respond in the same
fashion, *seriatim*, to what will certainly be continued massive human rights
abuses, atrocities, bad faith, reneging, lying, and human destruction on the
part of the regime.

Or the international community can fashion a means of taking Sudan's
governance into receivership, ideally under UN auspices, but by whatever
means are necessary to halt this shamelessly persistent evil. The political,
diplomatic, and administrative challenges would be daunting no matter
what the auspices or the nature of the interim governing mechanism. But
the future of Sudan simply cannot be entrusted any longer to a regime of
génocidaires – men responsible for mass executions, deliberate and massive
civilian slaughter, and who bear overwhelming responsibility for engineering the present catastrophic humanitarian crisis in Darfur.

This would seem to be the implication of the high-minded words Kofi
Annan used in accepting the 2001 Nobel Peace Prize. At the time, as he had
earlier in opening the 1999 General Assembly session, Annan, in an August
8, 2004 Reuters dispatch, "warned that national sovereignty had its limits in
the face of flagrant human rights violations." Fine sounding words, but like
so many of Mr. Annan's pronouncements, hollow at the core.

Of one thing we may be sure, and this marks a key consideration in the
so-called doctrine of an international "Responsibility to Protect": the
present governance of Sudan simply cannot get worse. No doubt some,
guided by past diplomatic investments in this tyrannical regime, will likely
argue otherwise. But events have clearly revealed their error.

Others, coming late to Darfur with a mechanically prepared political
agenda, are already claiming that the entire Western response to Darfur is
somehow a power-play for oil. Though garnering surprising attention and
newspaper column space, this theory reveals a painful ignorance of both
the logic of the concession structure in place in southern Sudan that barely

reaches southernmost Darfur, as well as the seismic and geological data for the Muglad Basin that runs in a broad southerly belt from Chad to Ethiopia, indicating how very unlikely it is that there are significant oil reserves in Darfur.

And of course while the highly distorting shadow of Iraq falls heavily on the prospects for even discussion of such a policy of intervention in Sudan, we would do well here to consider the conclusion of that anonymous European humanitarian aid worker in Darfur who reported in *The Telegraph* (UK) August 8, 2004,

> But Darfur is not Iraq. The people dying are Muslims. Cutting the throats of women and children, chaining villagers together and burning them, are the acts of cowards. The majority of the population in Darfur would welcome the arrival of troops.

Let those who worry about fundamentalist Islamic hostility to militarily supported humanitarian intervention and the removal of the NIF regime conduct interviews with the terrorized refugees in Chad, or the mothers watching hopelessly as their children die in camps, or the fathers who have seen their daughters gang-raped by the *Janjaweed*, or the survivors of mass executions, or the children who have endured being thrown in fires set by the *Janjaweed*. Let us hear what the results of these interviews suggest about the resistance to infidel forces from these notably pious Muslim people who are being destroyed because they belong to African tribal groups. These people have lost everything to Khartoum and its *Janjaweed* allies, and hundreds of thousands will die before the killing stops. This is not fertile ground for the predicted resistance or hostility.

Certainly there will be reflexive opposition from various quarters – the Organization of the Islamic Conference, the Arab League, and a good portion of the African Union – and it will be intense. Opposition from Russia and China virtually guarantees that the UN will be unable to respond to the real historical challenges of the moment.

The odds are long against a change of regime in Khartoum, even as such change is now clearly all that can rescue Sudan from the monstrous consequences of the National Islamic Front's ongoing and ruthless survivalism. Indeed, the odds against such fully justified action are exceedingly long. But let us understand, then, that so too are the odds of physical survival for countless thousands of Sudanese – in Darfur, in the Nuba Mountains, in Southern Blue Nile, in the east, particularly among the Beja people, and in southern Sudan.

If in present circumstances Khartoum's grotesquely illegitimate claim to "national sovereignty" can trump the recently articulated international ideal of a "Responsibility to Protect" – in this case the acutely vulnerable populations of Sudan, victims of deliberate, ethnically-targeted human destruction – then this carefully cultivated and lavishly funded "ideal" is transparently vacuous. Humanitarian intervention in Darfur cannot wait for an end to UN dithering, but must commence immediately; Sudan as a whole cannot endure further rule by the National Islamic Front.

September 23, 2004 – Proposals for Responding to Genocide in Darfur – critique of the international community

Various voices within the international community have proposed a number of different responses to ongoing, massive genocidal destruction in Darfur. Whether motivated by shame, human rights commitments, political expediency, or humanitarian concerns, these proposals are now numerous enough and come from enough different sources that they require some critical assessment, both as to efficacy and practicability.

Dismayingly, a number of policy suggestions do not take sufficient cognizance of political realities in Khartoum or the present circumstances defining human destruction in Darfur. Nor is there sufficient understanding of Khartoum's oil sector, or other key features of the economy that the NIF regime has built over fifteen years of tyrannical rule. Moreover, there seems to be a good deal of ignorance about how Khartoum has acquired weapons in the past and how it intends to provision its armory in the future.

UN proposals, both as embodied in Security Council Resolution 1564 dated September 18, 2004 and in statements/reports from the Office of the Secretary-General, seem especially worrisome – both for their generally disingenuous character and their serious miscalculations about the means to provide human security in Darfur. The plan for creating "safe areas" in Darfur – designed by Jan Pronk, Kofi Annan's special representative to Sudan – seems particularly ill-considered.

Plans for humanitarian relief in Darfur too often fail to take a longer prospective view of the crisis, and typically don't articulate the larger consequences of the virtually total destruction of traditional African agricultural economy and society. There is no conceptual plan for the ongoing relief efforts that will certainly be required for more than a year, or an articulation of the means by which some portion of the traditional agricultural economy of the region can be rebuilt. African tribal groups must be allowed to return to their lands, with adequate provisions for beginning productive lives again, or they will simply be warehoused in camps for the displaced, or drift towards urban environments where their agricultural skills and knowledge will be useless. Understanding how difficult this task of return will be must define any meaningful plan for a long-term peacekeeping force.

All of these issues should come into consideration during international planning, and in coordination between humanitarian organizations, UN organizations, and responding nations. Human rights groups should do a much better job both in collating their findings and in articulating meaningful advocacy positions. Presently the two most powerful human rights organizations, Amnesty International and Human Rights Watch, are entirely too timid in making recommendations that are commensurate in power with their highly impressive research on the ground.

Three areas need to be considered when formulating a comprehensive humanitarian response to the genocide in Darfur.

The first facet of a comprehensive humanitarian response is an effective and robust AU peacekeeping force. A modestly large African Union peacekeeping force deployment is presently the default international policy response to security issues in Darfur. Such a force – discussed in terms of 3,000 to 5,000 troops – would supplement the roughly 300 troops presently deployed to protect the African Union cease-fire monitoring team of 120 observers. Such an increased deployment would be of considerable significance, and with an appropriately robust mandate, could make a substantial contribution to security in the camps.

But there are many obstacles to such deployment and many problems with such heavy dependence on an exclusively African Union force. Few of these have been addressed in comprehensive fashion. Certainly UN Security Council resolution 1564 is hardly an effective means by which to compel Khartoum to accept either a larger force or a change in mandate;

Paragraph 2 of Resolution 1564 merely "welcomes and supports the intention of the African Union to enhance and augment its monitoring mission." And Paragraph 3 "welcomes the Government of Sudan's willingness to accept and facilitate an expanded African UN mission."

The word "peacekeeping" never appears in Resolution 1564, and both Kofi Annan and Jan Pronk have studiously avoided an explicit call for a peacekeeping mandate. This, of course, disingenuously skirts the central issue. Khartoum has for two months now repeatedly, adamantly refused to countenance a peacekeeping mandate for any augmented African Union force. Simply eliding this difficult fact from discussions hardly removes the key obstacle. Moreover, there are no explicit calls for a peacekeeping mandate coming from other members of the international community – from US Secretary of State Colin Powell in his September 9, 2004 Senate testimony on Darfur, from the European Union, or from various other international actors. This convinces Khartoum that there is no will to make such a demand, evidently for fear of being rebuffed. Without much greater international pressure than is presently in evidence, the regime will continue to resist strenuously the deployment of peacekeepers.

There are also exceedingly few discussions of the logistical and transport requirements for 3,000 to 5,000 AU troops. We must remember that the AU has virtually no logistical or troop transport capacity of its own, and any augmented force would be deploying to one of the most remote and difficult environments imaginable. Logistical and transport problems for the approximately 400 troops and observers now in Darfur have proved thoroughly formidable. And Khartoum has easily managed to keep the observers grounded when necessary by denying fuel and creating other obstacles. Communication equipment is woefully inadequate as well, and this obliges the AU force to utilize helicopters to ferry reports and intelligence rather than concentrate on investigating atrocities.

A force ten times the size of the present one, deployed to multiple locations throughout Darfur, a region the size of France, would create substantial needs. In addition to transport and logistics, including an independently controlled fuel supply, the force would require food, water, spare parts, ammunition, engineering support, other provisions – and modern communications equipment. Breakdowns in transport vehicles and other equipment must be anticipated. The costs over many months of deployment will be large. To be sure, the willingness of the African Union is clear, as are declarations of support from the UN and various. But this by itself is not enough, as African Union Commission Chairman Alpha Oumar Konaré told the Associated Press in a September 22, 2004 dispatch,

> The African Union is ready to send 4,000 to 5,000 troops "very soon – within days, weeks," African Union Commission Chairman Alpha Oumar Konare [said]. But Konare said movement depends on logistical help from "Europe, America and the United Nations especially." So far, he said, there has been just talk about assistance.

Until there are formal financial and material commitments to a force that has a clear and robust peacekeeping mandate, the African Union solution to the Darfur crisis is merely notional. Moreover, even the 3,000 to 5,000 troops presently being discussed would fall short of constituting a force adequate to the desperate security needs for Darfur as a whole. Authoritative military assessments of what would be required to secure the camps, provide protection to humanitarian relief efforts, and begin to secure the rural areas are in the range of 50,000 troops. No one is talking about this kind of deployment, which is to say that even deployment of the presently contemplated number of African Union forces, with a yet-unsecured peacekeeping mandate, would be at best a very partial response to the larger security issues in Darfur.

The second facet of a comprehensive humanitarian response is economic and could encompass sanctions and embargoes to ensure compliance. Various and typically vague proposals have been made to threaten the intransigent Khartoum regime, which still gives no sign of reining in the brutal *Janjaweed* militia force or curtailing its own genocidal ambitions. Indeed, a September 21, 2004 Agence France-Press dispatch reported UN High Commissioner for Human Rights Louise Arbour confirming during her recent assessment trip to Darfur that the *Janjaweed* are now being recycled into the "police" forces for the camps, and the so-called "safe areas" that were negotiated by Jan Pronk, Kofi Annan's special representative to Sudan. Agence France-Presse reported that,

[Arbour] said that during a visit to North Darfur that refugees told her that among the police guarding their camps were former members of the *Janjaweed* militia that forced them to flee their homes. Arbour also accused the Sudanese government of failing to do enough to protect refugees. "There is a total sense of impunity," she said.

And while it is important symbolically that the UN High Commissioner for Human Rights travel to Darfur, Arbour found nothing that has not been repeatedly and authoritatively reported before. Her visit thus inevitably creates the impression of UN temporizing for lack of a more effective response. We might note that Arbour was accompanied by Kofi Annan's inneffective and irrelevant special adviser on the prevention of genocide, Juan Méndez. But lest the world think that the UN might be in the process of actually determining whether genocide is occurring, a September 20, 2004 UN News Centre (New York) dispatch dashed that notion when it reported,

> Annan stressed [that Arbour and Méndez] are not determining whether or not genocide has taken place.

But Darfur doesn't need additional human rights reporting for purposes of the most robust and urgent action. The evidence, including overwhelming evidence of genocide, is in hand. The nominal reason for the visit of Arbour and Méndez was "to examine how to shield beleaguered civilians there from further militia attacks," as the UN News Centre reported. But the answer has long been clear: a robust peacekeeping force with a mandate to protect civilians. Such investigative trips add nothing to our understanding of the tasks at hand, and indeed work to convince Khartoum that there are no real consequences for continuing human destruction and abuse.

Can the Khartoum regime be pressured into accepting a peacekeeping force? Are threats of an arms embargo or an oil embargo credible and efficacious? The answer is clearly not. An arms embargo, of the sort recently called for by Amnesty International and others, is particularly unlikely to change perceptions in Khartoum. First, we should note that Khartoum is now largely self-sufficient in the small and medium arms that have been provided to the *Janjaweed* in such great quantities. Dual-use production facilities, such as the giant GIAD complex outside Khartoum, have been constructed with petrodollars, and have had the benefit of extensive Chinese and Russian military engineering expertise. Arms production continues to grow rapidly, as former NIF ideological leader Hassan el-Turabi predicted in 1999. Even Russian model T-55 tanks are now produced by Khartoum using oil revenues.

The only real point of military import pressure might be for servicing of the helicopter gunships that have been used to such deadly effect in Darfur and southern Sudan. But the Russian companies that supplied the helicopters are committed contractually to service them, and Russia has recently made clear that it is actually intent on expanding arms sales to Africa, including Sudan, as *Defence News* reported on Defencetalk.com, September 22, 2004,

> Russia has been criticised for supplying warplanes to Sudan, where Arab militias are attacking African villagers in the Darfur region and displaced villagers say government aircraft have bombed their homes. Russia's arms export agency said it wanted to do more business with Sudan and other African nations. "One of the key points of the Rosoboronexport Corporation marketing strategy is the extension of the volumes, diversity and geography in defence sales to African nations," the agency said in a statement.

Moreover, long-time arms supplier China will certainly not observe an arms embargo and would veto any UN resolution proposing such an embargo. And there are other nations to pick up any unlikely slack including Bulgaria, Yemen, and Ukraine. An arms embargo is a proposal with only symbolic value, and has no chance of being implemented.

An oil embargo is another economic consideration. Certainly there can be no doubting its efficacy. Khartoum, with a huge level of external debt, is critically dependent on oil revenues provided by Asian state-owned oil companies: India's ONGC, Malaysia's Petronas, and China's China National Petroleum Corp. They are all currently operating in southern Sudan. But there is not a shred of evidence that any of these countries would participate in an embargo, or that a UN resolution authorizing an embargo would not be vetoed by China. Indeed, one only need consider the nature of China's investment in Sudan and its own growing dependency on foreign oil to see how thoroughly impracticable an oil embargo would be.

China controls between 40 and 50% of total oil operations in southern Sudan, including Western and Eastern Upper Nile. China imports huge quantities of oil for its rapidly growing economy, and its consumption increases 10% annually. Sudan is China's premier source of offshore oil production. Even if every other country in the world were to participate in an embargo, China alone could provide a market for all of Sudan's current total export production of approximately 270,000 barrels/day. But China has partners in Malaysia and India that are just as eager for oil, and just as willing to overlook massive human rights abuses. Malaysia in particular has proved as much in southern Sudan for years.

An oil embargo or "boycott" will not work, and it is disingenuous for world leaders like Secretary of State Colin Powell and various senior officials in the European Union to suggest otherwise. It is yet another example of an apparently tough position that is transparently meaningless as a means of increasing pressure on Khartoum.

A third tool for pressuring Khartoum to accept humanitarian intervention is targeted sanctions. In particular, sanctions directed against specific members of the National Islamic Front regime have been proposed by several organizations, including the International Crisis Group. While such sanctions – restricting travel abroad, freezing foreign assets, suspending commercial relations with businesses owned or controlled by the regime – would have some effect, it is doubtful that by themselves they would have a serious impact on thinking in Khartoum. Assets abroad have already been largely sequestered into inaccessible or invisible accounts, and this process would accelerate if targeted sanctions appeared imminent. And Khartoum's leaders have previously faced travel restrictions and Khartoum has not forgotten. Following the 1995 assassination attempt on Egyptian President Mubarak the UN established that the regime was deeply involved, and diplomatic sanctions were officially imposed. These were to have included travel restrictions, but observance quickly disappeared.

UN Security Council Resolution 1564, Paragraph 12 speaks of "an international commission of inquiry," a morally and historically essential task. But the resolution merely "calls on all parties [in the Darfur conflict] to cooperate fully with such a commission." Khartoum has heard, and ignored, many previous calls from the UN. There is no evidence that the regime will cooperate now. Rather, it will make symbolic gestures, but at the same time work relentlessly, as it has for many months, to obscure the sites of atrocities and mass executions. The regime is brutally intimidating those in Darfur who attempt to speak with outside investigators, and will continue to obscure evidence even as it stalls any meaningful work by a commission of inquiry. The regime rightly fears the findings of any such investigation, but this is not the same as feeling pressure to change its present genocidal course of action. On the contrary, the prospect of such a commission of inquiry provides incentive to accelerate the obliteration of evidence and to consolidate the effects of months of vast civilian destruction and displacement.

In a "Joint Communiqué" – signed by Kofi Annan and Khartoum on July 3, 2004 – the groundwork was laid for what has developed into a plan to create so-called "safe areas" in Darfur. The idea, broached in general terms in the Joint Communiqué, was formalized in the August 5, 2004 "Plan of Action," signed again by the Khartoum regime and by Jan Pronk, representing Kofi Annan.

According to the exceedingly brief, but immensely destructive "Plan of Action for Darfur,"

> The Government of Sudan would identify parts of Darfur that can be made secure and safe within 30 days. This would include existing IDP [Internally displaced Person] camps, and areas around certain towns and villages with a high concentration of local population. The Government of Sudan would then provide secure routes to and between these areas. These tasks should be carried out by Sudan police forces to maintain confidence already created by redeployment of the Government of Sudan armed forces. (text from Plan of Action for Darfur, August 5, 2004 [Khartoum]).

As became clear only with Secretary-General Annan's August 30, 2004 *Report* to the UN Security Council on Darfur, the "safe areas" in the Plan of Action were conceived as entailing "the securing and protection of villages within a 20-kilometer radius around the major towns identified."

What does this language mean on the ground in Darfur? Most ominously, the creation of safe areas not only threatens to consolidate, indeed institutionalize the effects of Khartoum's campaign of ethnic clearances and genocidal destruction, but it is being deliberately manipulated by Khartoum for offensive military advantage. Human Rights Watch reported September 1, 2004 in *Darfur: UN 'Safe Areas' offer no Real Security*, that,

> These safe areas could become a form of "human shield." This would allow the government to secure zones around the major towns and confine a civilian population that it considers to be supporting the rebels.

These safe areas are, as Human Rights Watch continued, "only a slightly revised version of the Sudanese government proposal in early July [2004] to create 18 'resettlement sites' for the more than 1.2 million displaced Darfurian civilians." We should be suspicious of any such plan emanating originally from the Khartoum regime. And we should be especially concerned about the nature of the security that underlies resettlement sites or safe areas.

For in fact, the police that have been deployed to the safe areas, nominally to replace redeployed regular military forces of the regime, are not the credible and respected police force the Joint Communiqué stipulates. Rather they are soldiers and other militarily trained personnel in the uniforms of police. And given the geographic latitude provided by the 20-mile radius stipulated in the Plan of Action, these police/paramilitary forces have been extremely active: not in securing the areas and protecting civilians but in consolidating and expanding areas under Khartoum's military control.

Civilians, already vulnerable to the ongoing predations of *Janjaweed* militia forces, have now – by virtue of these various UN negotiations – been made even more vulnerable to violence from those policing the safe areas. Moreover, as Amnesty International points out, the very notion of safe areas suggests that civilians not in these areas are somehow without protections. The entire plan is a ghastly error in judgment, deriving from a wholly unjustified willingness to believe that by demanding a credible and respected police force, Khartoum will somehow feel obliged to provide one.

The fact that these safe areas are little different from what Khartoum originally called resettlement sites suggests that what Khartoum is enforcing is a
permanent displacement and destruction of the agricultural way of life of
these African tribal peoples.

As Human Rights Watch declared in a September 13, 2004 press release
speaking to the Pronk/Annan plan for "safe areas,"

> The [Human Rights Watch] letter [to the UN Security Council] also
> charged that proposed "safe areas" could impede the return of civil-
> ians to their homes and consolidate forced displacement and "ethnic
> cleansing" initiated by [the government of] Sudan.

Put another way, the safe areas and the camps that define so many of them
are in danger of becoming what UN Undersecretary for Humanitarian
Affairs Jan Egeland recently referred to in a September 1, 2004 IRIN dispatch "as concentration-camp like areas." In fact, we must see this terrible
reality as already too fully realized. This assessment has been echoed by
Andrew Natsios, administrator of the USAID, who declared, "The displaced
people in Darfur told us repeatedly . . . that the cities and displaced camps
have become prisons, concentration camps."

Reuters reported September 23, 2004 from Khartoum that Jan Pronk
has declared Khartoum "is obliged to ask for international support if it
cannot protect the nearly 1.5 million people displaced [in Darfur]",

> "If you cannot do it (protect your population) . . . then you have to ask
> international support. It's an obligation," Jan Pronk told reporters in
> Khartoum. "Are you serious, are you sincere in requesting adequate
> international support?"

This recourse to moral exhortation, an urging of "obligations to protect," is
at this point in the crisis both shamefully disingenuous and deeply destructive of diplomatic credibility. All this should highlight the significance of a
genocide determination and the importance of communicating with
Khartoum in the context of such a determination. For what could be more
ludicrous than to urge upon Khartoum's génocidaires a moral obligation to

protect the very people the regime has been systematically destroying for well over a year, both by means of its regular armed forces, the *Janjaweed* militia, and the deliberate obstruction of humanitarian relief?

The hortatory strategy that Annan and Pronk are evidently following is one of engagement, with the implicit assumption that Khartoum can be engaged in good faith. This entirely unjustified assumption presumably accounts for Pronk's September 18, 2004 Reuters article declaration that a genocide determination in Darfur is "premature." For of course determining that genocide was being committed by Khartoum would make engagement with the regime transparently what it is – an expedient, weak, and dishonest refusal to confront Darfur's realities.

Human Rights Watch in its September 3, 2004 report *UN Darfur Deadline Expires: Security Council Must Act*, found it "startling" that Kofi Annan's report to the UN Security Council,

> fails to acknowledge what several UN agencies and scores of independent reports have documented: the government of Sudan is responsible for these attacks against civilians, directly and through the *Janjaweed* militias it supports.

But finally, given the course of expediency and engagement that Pronk daily makes more evident, there is nothing "startling" about this deliberate omission. It is essential to the Annan/Pronk strategy. And Khartoum knows precisely how to construe such expediency – for expediency offers the clearest signal that there is no real pressure available through the UN, which in responding to the Darfur crisis has become little more than a platform for exhortation. We catch a glimpse of Khartoum's contempt for such weakness in a September 23, 2004 Agence France-Press dispatch, which reported comments by NIF Secretary-General Ibrahim Omar,

> A top official from Sudan's ruling party says the Government will not disarm "Arab tribes" in the troubled Darfur region, saying they were not all members of the *Janjaweed* militia.

But this is simply nonsense. Nobody has declared that all Arab tribes are part of the *Janjaweed*. In fact, the consensus figure for the number of *Janjaweed* active in the Darfur genocide and coordinating militarily with Khartoum is roughly 20,000. But there can be no doubt that the *Janjaweed* exist, and that they are directly responsible, along with the Khartoum regime for destroying perhaps 75% of the villages in all of Darfur, for displacing 2 million human beings, and for the deaths of more than 200,000 innocent civilians. The *Janjaweed* are operating in concert with Khartoum, and more recently have increasingly filled the ranks of "police" in the camps.

But though Ibrahim Omar's comments may have nothing to do with the truth, they do reveal how far Khartoum is from responding to its various commitments to the UN, most conspicuously including the commitment made almost three months ago in a "Joint Communiqué between the Government of Sudan and the United Nations on the occasion of the visit of the UN Secretary-General," July 3, 2004 to "immediately start to disarm the *Janjaweed* and other armed outlaw groups," and "ensure that no militias are present in all areas surrounding IDP camps."

The ineffective international political response to the catastrophe in Darfur brings heightened pressure to bear on humanitarian operations. Present monthly humanitarian requirements for displaced persons in Darfur and refugees in Chad are well in excess of 40,000 metric tons of food and non-food items, including medicine, shelter, water purification supplies, cooking fuel. This exceeds by more than 100% present logistical and transport capacity. Moreover, funding for humanitarian operations has been shamefully laggard, and at least two breaks in the food pipeline are now forecast.

But most troublingly, humanitarian relief will have to continue for the foreseeable future, or the international community will be consigning hundreds of thousands of people to slow death from starvation. For agricultural production has come to a halt in Darfur. There was no spring planting, and thus is no fall harvest. No seeds have been culled for the next planting, and the prospect of yet another missed planting season in spring 2005 is all too distinct. The secondary planting season, which should already be underway in parts of Darfur, will almost certainly be missed, creating yet greater food dependency.

Looming over this entirely grim situation is the difficulty of seeing how African agricultural societies can be re-established in areas that have seen unspeakable genocidal violence, village destruction, and a breakdown in

African-Arab relations and patterns of co-existence. Given present emergency conditions, the absence of a reconstruction plan is entirely understandable. But the humanitarian community must soon begin to address the question of how aid can be sustained for the next six months to a year, and how the agricultural economy of Darfur can again become self-sufficient. The challenges can hardly be overstated.

The only response that can change the fundamental dynamic of ongoing human destruction is humanitarian intervention, in either a permissive or non-permissive environment, with all necessary military support. A non-UN consortium of nations, acting in concert with the African Union, must issue an ultimatum to Khartoum demanding that it allow the deployment of a substantial peacekeeping force, ideally of at least 20,000 troops initially, with more to follow. This will require nations such as the US, Britain, Sweden, Germany, Australia, New Zealand, Norway and others to commit the financial and material resources that will permit the African Union to deploy. Rwanda, Nigeria, and Tanzania have offered to commit the necessary troops, but they will require massive logistical and transport assistance, and very substantial materiel.

Perhaps Canada, so long disgracefully immobilized in responding to Sudan's crises, can also be brought along. To be sure, it is troubling that Prime Minister Paul Martin on September 22, 2004 baldly lied at the UN, declaring that the international community "should have intervened last June when Canada called for it." Canada made no such call. But it is encouraging that Mr. Martin is now so emphatic, even though his UN remarks contained no specifics about the nature of such intervention, or precisely how it would be guided by the notion of a "Responsibility to Protect," a Canadian-funded product that has so far had no impact on Canadian foreign policy in Africa.

But the broad goals of a humanitarian intervention are clear, and these in turn dictate the nature and mandate of any intervening military force, as well as the degree to which transport and logistical capacity must be enhanced. The situation on the ground will be determined to a very considerable extent by whether Khartoum decides to create a permissive or non-permissive environment for intervention. No environment will be completely "permissive" and in either event, deployed troops must have robust rules of engagement with the *Janjaweed*, "police" forces, other paramilitary forces, and Khartoum's regular army forces. Such goals would encompass the following tasks and commitments:

- Sufficient troops in an initial deployment to protect approximately 200 camps and vulnerable concentrations of displaced persons; all Khartoum's "police" and security forces, including the *Janjaweed*, must be removed from the camps and the camp environs;
- Concomitant deployment of sufficient troops to protect vulnerable humanitarian workers and key humanitarian transport corridors;
- Dedication of transport and logistical resources to bring monthly capacity for food and non-food items to 40,000 metric tons;
- A commitment to substantial repairs of the rail line running from Port Sudan to Nyala; the rail line should be internationalized, and dedicated exclusively to enhancing humanitarian transport capacity (without such augmented rail capacity, transport costs over the next year and more will be exorbitant);
- Secondary deployment of troops sufficient to begin to secure villages and farm-land that have been ravaged by the predations of the *Janjaweed* and Khartoum's regular military forces; the return of displaced persons must be voluntary, and robust protection must be provided to early returnees;
- Seeds, agricultural implements, donkeys, and sustaining food supplies must be provided to returnees.

This is but an outline of the international response demanded by Darfur's catastrophe. But even in outline, such a plan should oblige those proposing other responses to explain how they will achieve the goals articulated here – or why such goals can be allowed to go unmet. Humanitarian intervention is expensive, difficult, and politically risky. In the face of massive genocidal destruction, the world must ask if these are reasons enough for inaction.

March 30, 2006 – George Bush "genocide has to be stopped' in western Sudan, NATO should send a 'clear signal' "

In remarks that do far more to highlight US impotence and lack of resolve, President Bush went on to declare in a March 29, 2006 Deutsche Presse-

Agentur/South African Press Agency dispatch from Washington that, " 'this is serious business. This is not playing a diplomatic holding game. . . . When we say genocide, that means genocide has to be stopped.' "

Perhaps President Bush has forgotten that his administration made a formal genocide determination over a year and a half ago. On September 9, 2004 then-Secretary of State Colin Powell testified to the US Senate Foreign Relations Committee that "genocide has been committed in Darfur, and the government of Sudan and the Janjawid bear responsibility." The many hundreds of thousands of Darfuris who have subsequently perished, experienced violent displacement, rape, torture, and the misery of lives defined by fear and deprivation provide gruesomely abundant evidence that the genocide continues. These victims also make clear that the Bush administration does not really regard genocide in Darfur – and increasingly eastern Chad – as urgent or serious business. In fact, all evidence suggests that the administration is indeed playing precisely a diplomatic holding game.

Certainly if the President and his State Department think that a highly limited, ultimately nebulous commitment from NATO to provide transport and minimal logistics to an overwhelmed African Union (AU) force somehow sends a clear signal to Khartoum's génocidaires, then we can be in no doubt that disingenuousness and expediency continue to rule US policy on Darfur. And there should be no mistake about the highly limited nature of NATO's commitment. The word from NATO headquarters in Brussels was a strong re-assertion of previous declarations by NATO Secretary-General Jaap de Hoop Scheffer in a March 29, 2006 Reuters dispatch from Brussels,

> NATO said it had agreed to a request by UN Secretary General Kofi Annan to look at how it could provide support to troops there, but said there was no question of it intervening on the ground. "No one is discussing, planning or considering a NATO force on the ground in Darfur. That is not one of the options," NATO spokesman James Appathurai told a regular briefing. "We should look at this in the context of what NATO is already providing."

What NATO is already providing consists entirely of transport lift capacity, as well as very limited logistics and training. This is certainly nothing that will change the calculations in Khartoum about how to continue with its genocidal counter-insurgency strategy, or how the regime might politically consolidate the effects of previous genocidal actions. It sends no clear signal to Khartoum that it must halt the genocide, but only confirms the regime in its belief that the Western powers are content to substitute words for meaningful action.

Moreover, de Hoop Scheffer has made it clear that NATO will not act without UN authority, precisely the authority that the African Union has recently refused to request. Instead, the AU at its March 10, 2006 Peace and Security Council meeting in Addis Ababa spoke only of a future handover to the UN – in six months – and this only "in principle." Further, the just concluded Arab League summit, revealingly held in Khartoum, pointedly rejected any UN authorization or deployment unless requested by the génocidaires who make up the National Islamic Front regime. This is the context in which to understand NATO's position on Darfur, as Agence France-Presse reported March 6, 2006,

> [De Hoop Scheffer] ruled out . . . sending troops from the western military alliance to Sudan's strife-torn Darfur province. De Hoop Scheffer said he believed that NATO could help in the region during the transition phase from an African Union operation to one led by the UN but only with a clear UN mandate. "Then we can discuss a NATO role, which I do see in the enabling sphere and not the boots of troops on the ground," he told reporters on the sidelines of a meeting of EU defence ministers in Innsbruck, Austria.

President Bush's assertion that the involvement by NATO should send a clear signal to Khartoum, like his previous declaration that there should be NATO stewardship for the Darfur protection mission, is mere political expediency.

Here we should recall precisely what the President had earlier declared. The *New York Times* quoted President Bush as saying,

> President Bush declared this past Friday [February 17, 2006] that a security force for Darfur will require "NATO stewardship, planning,

facilitating, organizing, probably double the number of peacekeepers that are there now, in order to start bringing some sense of security."

A month and a half later, and after thousands of additional genocidal deaths, there is no sign of meaningful "NATO stewardship." Again, NATO itself has offered only minimal assistance, and anything more is contingent upon a UN takeover in Darfur that evidently won't occur for almost half a year – and which Khartoum is already actively working to forestall. The AU force currently on the ground in Darfur, desperately outmanned and out-gunned, is overwhelmed by the violence, and daily finds itself less and less able to respond to the insecurity that continues to attenuate the humanitarian lifeline upon which millions of human beings depend. Nonetheless, a March 10, 2006 African Union Peace and Security Council Communiqué failed to acknowledge these weaknesses, and refused to move toward an immediate UN handover. Moreover, the AU Communiqué is not only hedged by various contingencies and qualifications – so many as to make the document largely meaningless beyond a vague gesture toward a terminus date of September 30, 2006 – it refuses to acknowledge the central shortcoming of the AU mission: that it has no useful mandate to protect civilians or humanitarian operations.

This refusal is a function of the AU's having neither the manpower nor resources to fulfill such a mandate. As well, the AU's continued deference to Khartoum has allowed the AU force to increase in Darfur only on Khartoum's condition that the mandate not change. The official AU task remains the futile one of monitoring a non-existent cease-fire, one that, significantly, does not include the brutal *Janjaweed*. While de facto expansion of the mandate by some AU commanders on the ground has made a marginal difference in the protection of civilians and humanitarians, the overall and rapid deterioration of security is obvious to all observers.

Humanitarian workers speaking, necessarily on condition of anonymity, to the author, to a wide range of journalists, UN officials, and representatives of donor countries paint a terrifying picture of violent threats against themselves and their operations. Many thousands of square kilometers within Darfur, especially West Darfur and the Jebel Marra area, and in eastern Chad are completely inaccessible to humanitarian operations. And the size of these areas only grows. UNICEF in a March 17, 2006 UN News Centre dispatch reported that,

> increased insecurity has already prevented humanitarian agencies from teaching over half a million people [in Darfur]; if funding shortages continue, that number will only grow.

Insecurity in eastern Chad is too great to permit meaningful assessment, but at least 100,000 conflict-affected civilians – and very likely a great many more – are also beyond humanitarian reach.

Jan Egeland, the conscience on the UN, has also spoken explicitly in a March 13, 2006 Associated Press dispatch from the United Nations about the humanitarian realities following from growing insecurity,

> As a result of [deteriorating insecurity], Egeland said, UN relief offi-cials and relief organizations cannot reach more than 300,000 people on the Chad border in western Darfur and the central mountainous region of Jebal Marra because they are too dangerous. These unreachable areas, he said, "will soon get massively increased mortal-ity because there is nothing else but international assistance." He expected deaths to increase markedly within weeks.

Additional hundreds of thousands of civilians are inaccessible in South Darfur and North Darfur states. Egeland went on to declare that "Darfur is returning to 'the abyss' of early 2004 when the region was 'the killing fields of this world.' 'We're losing ground every day in the humanitarian operation which is the lifeline for more than 3 million people.'" Again, in aggregate, UN figures – including those from the UN High Commission for Refugees – suggest a total population in need of approximately 4 million people throughout the greater humanitarian theater of Darfur and eastern Chad.

This is the horrific context in which President Bush has chosen to posture about a NATO role in Darfur, evidently in response to the bur-geoning civil society movement in the US. This dishonesty works in effect to politicize the Darfur crisis – taking it from the realm of a moral impera-tive, accepted as such across the political spectrum, into the arena in which partisan management becomes the chief consideration. Comments from NATO officials in Brussels make the point clearly, if not quite explicitly in a March 30, 2006 United Press International dispatch from Brussels,

> Speaking on condition of anonymity, a NATO official told United Press International that the idea of the alliance dispatching ground troops to the troubled province was a "non-starter with the Africans, a non-starter with the United Nations and a non-starter with NATO." Officials in Brussels also criticized the US president for sending out confused messages about what he expects from the alliance. "Bush has been a little bit unclear in his language," said one, referring to the president's call for 20,000 peacekeepers to be sent to Darfur under NATO's command.

In fact, even when Bush spoke of "NATO stewardship" for a Darfur mission in February 2006, it was far from clear that there was any real commitment from within his administration. Notably, after the President spoke in February 2006, Pentagon spokesman Lt. Cmdr. Joe Carpenter declared in a February 17, 2006 *Washington Post* dispatch that it was "'premature to speculate' on potential increases in US troops." Privately, Bush administration officials make clear there is no intention of sending US troops to Darfur. The Pentagon comment comported precisely with a statement by US State Department spokesman Sean McCormack following a meeting several days earlier between Bush and UN Secretary General Kofi Annan. A February 13, 2006 Reuters dispatch from Washington DC reported McCormack as saying,

> "It's really premature to speculate about what the needs would be in terms of logistics, in terms of airlift, in terms of actual troops. And certainly in that regard, premature to speculate on what the US contribution might be."

"Premature" would seem a terrifyingly inappropriate adjective three years into the first great episode of genocide in the 21st century.

During the month of February 2006, when the US was President of the Security Council, Bush's Ambassador to the UN, John Bolton, was unable to garner support for even a provisional resolution authorizing a UN peace support operation in Darfur. This US inability was certainly not lost on the African Union during its deliberations in Addis Ababa prior to the crafting of its March 10, 2006 Peace and Security Council Communiqué, which simply reiterated its previous January 2006 commitment – "in principle" – to a UN handover, though with a time-frame that now extends to the end of September.

Nor does President Bush give any signs of appreciating the significance of Arab League support for Khartoum's continuing obduracy. Leaders gathered at the Arab League summit in Khartoum March 28, 2006, and as the Associated Press reported on March 29, 2006,

> affirmed their support for the AU peacekeeping mission in Darfur and underlined their rejection of deploying other troops there without permission of the Sudanese government, a reference to UN peacekeepers.

Emboldened by Arab League support, by AU deference, and by political support from China and Russia on the UN Security Council, Khartoum will not be made to change its genocidal ways by vague threats of a NATO role, threats that prove vacuous when examined with any specificity.

All evidence and analysis clearly suggest that, despite an increase in posturing by the US President, Khartoum feels unconstrained in its actions. As the International Crisis Group notes in an important March 17, 2006 report, *To Save Darfur*, the National Islamic Front regime remains committed to a policy of "strategic chaos,"

> Low-level violence remains the norm for much of Darfur and is spilling over into eastern Chad. It continues to be caused primarily by Khartoum's unwillingness to rein in the militias on which it relies for its counter-insurgency campaign. The rebel SLA shares responsibility for deteriorating security, however, as it seeks to consolidate its military position in South Darfur in blatant contravention of the ceasefire. Meanwhile, civilians – particularly women, children and the elderly – bear the brunt of the war, and the region's social fabric is in ruins.

The destruction of rebel support bases, both villages in Darfur and those provided by the regime of President Deby in Chad, remains central to the government's counter-insurgency strategy. Militias allied to Khartoum attack civilians and deny the rebels villages from which to operate, while Chadian rebels based in West Darfur carry out operations against Deby. Khartoum seeks to stoke the tribal dimensions of the conflict and transform what was once a politically-based insurgency into an increasingly tribal war.

The key recommendation from the ICG report appropriately focuses on the immediate security needs of civilians and humanitarian workers,

The US, the EU and others need, therefore, to act without delay on three fronts to:
[1] provide the necessary financial and technical assistance to the AU through at least September 2006, and to help AMIS implement the key recommendations for internal improvements outlined in the December 2005 Joint Assessment Mission report and affirmed by the AU on 10 March [2006];
[2] do the heavy diplomatic lifting to persuade the AU and the UN Security Council to authorise the immediate deployment of a stabil-isation force, ideally some 5,000-strong, as part of a phased transition to a UN mission to be completed in October 2006, to focus on mon-itoring the Chad-Sudan border and deterring major cross-border attacks, and on bolstering AU Mission's ability to protect civilians in the Tawila-Graida corridor [a highly populated corridor running down the center of Darfur from North Darfur State to south of Nyala, capital of South Darfur State]; and
[3] persuade the Security Council to authorise immediate planning for a UN peacekeeping force of at least double the present size of AMIS, equipped to fulfil a more serious military mission, provided with an appropriately stronger mandate, and ready to take over full responsibility on 1 October 2006. (from the Executive Summary)

As ICG well realizes, this proposal is far from ideal:

This is not ideal. Crisis Group has long contended that because the African Union Mission in Sudan [AMIS] has reached the outer limits of its competence, and a UN mission authorised today would not be fully ready to take over from it for some six months, a distinct and separate multinational force should be sent to Darfur to bridge that gap and help stabilise the immediate situation. We have argued, and continue to believe, that NATO would be best from a practical military point of view. Unfortunately, political opposition to this in Khartoum, within the AU and even perhaps within the Atlantic Alliance itself, means it is not achievable at this time.

What we now propose, therefore, is a compromise driven by the urgent need for a more robust force in Darfur. A militarily capable UN member state – France seems most promising since it already has troops and aircraft in the area – should offer to the Security Council to go now to Darfur, wearing blue helmets, as the lead nation in the first phase of the incoming UN mission. It could be joined from the outset by forces from one or two other militarily capable UN members (and would probably need to be if the desirable target of around 5,000 personnel for this force is to be achieved).

This stabilisation force would be a self-contained, separately commanded UN mission with identified functional or geographic divisions of responsibility that would work beside AMIS [African Union Mission in Sudan] and through a liaison unit at its headquarters until arrangements were in place for a 1 October [2006] transition to the full UN mission. That full mission would need to be recruited from the best AMIS elements as well as a wider circle of Asian and other member states – no easy task at a time when several large UN peacekeeping missions in Africa and elsewhere have exhausted the capabilities of many contribution candidates.

The US and other NATO states should respond generously and quickly to requests from it or AMIS to provide logistical help as well as regular access to satellite imagery, air mobility and close air support, especially to deter or react to egregious movements of men or heavy weapons in the border area.

If the Bush administration is at all serious about halting genocide in Darfur, it will accept the ICG proposal as, at the very least, a highly credible starting point in deliberations and planning. The proposal is tough-minded, both politically and militarily, even as it recognizes its limitations and the difficulties at the UN. Ultimately, if the UN Security Council insists on securing from Khartoum permission for deployment – permission that will never be granted – then the UN, or individual members states, must make the extraordinarily difficult decision to enter Darfur as a "non-permissive environment." The obligations under the 1948 UN Convention on the Prevention and Punishment of the Crime of Genocide give clear moral and compelling legal justification for such action. So, too, does the key Paragraph 139 from the UN World Summit document, unanimously adopted in September 2005,

> [all countries should be] prepared to take collective action, in a timely and decisive manner, through the Security Council, in accordance with the UN Charter, including Chapter VII [conferring enforcement authority], on a case by case basis and in cooperation with relevant regional organizations as appropriate, should peaceful means be inadequate and national authorities manifestly failing to protect their populations from genocide, war crimes, ethnic cleansing, and crimes against humanity and its implications.

If the Security Council refuses to accept these obligations, despite findings by multiple UN investigative bodies that confirm both that these crimes are occurring and the defenselessness of Darfur's civilian populations, then there is still certainly overwhelming moral justification, and finally obligation, for humanitarian intervention. As Jan Egeland, head of UN humanitarian operations, has rightly declared, Darfur is the "test case for the world for having no more Rwandas and no more massive loss of innocent lives." The world continues to fail the "Rwanda Test," and that failure is only compounded by the disingenuousness of the Bush administration

As ongoing "strategic chaos" proves a devastatingly effective weapon in the Darfur genocide, humanitarian organizations continue to provide us some of the means by which we can measure the ghastly human costs. The number of conflicted-affect persons in Darfur and eastern Chad is now approximately 4 million. *UN Darfur Humanitarian Profile No. 22*, reflecting conditions as of January 1, 2006, presents a figure of 3.6 million conflicted-affected persons in Darfur – a figure that has grown by at least 50,000 since the beginning of the year; at least another 220,000 Darfuris have fled to increasingly threatened refugee camps in eastern Chad; and the effects of genocidal warfare against the non-Arab or African tribal populations indigenous to eastern Chad further raises the total, almost certainly by well over 100,000.

In short, 4 million people have now been affected by Khartoum's genocidal campaign; the total pre-war population of Darfur was likely between 6 million and 6.5 million. This population is various in its humanitarian needs, but these needs grow relentlessly, even as humanitarian funding and access continue to diminish. These people are badly weakened in a great many cases by the cumulative effects of three years of annihilating war. UNICEF's Country Representative Ted Chaiban warned in a March 16, 2006 UN News Centre dispatch,

> Nearly 2 million children in Sudan's war-torn Darfur region are threatened by severe funding shortfalls, with only 11 per cent of the urgently needed $89 million either committed or pledged, the United Nations Children's Fund reported today. "Without significant and immediate funding, and given existing problems with security and access, the humanitarian crisis that was averted only last year will return," [Sudan] country representative Ted Chaiban said.

UNICEF in a March 17, 2006 press release spelled out some of the specific threats to children,

> UNICEF and its partners in Darfur are working to immunize half a million children still vulnerable to disease. But without additional resources to maintain cold chain systems and fund special campaigns, fewer children will be vaccinated, greatly increasing the threat to their health.
>
> If maintenance and expansion of water and sanitation infrastructures in rural areas were halted, millions of people could have limited or total lack of access to safe water and sanitation, leading to water-borne diseases that spread rapidly and lethally in close quarters.

Lack of resources will force schools to close and leave hundreds of thousands of children without access to education. Approximately 382,000 children have benefited from UNICEF education support, including the provision of education supplies and teacher salaries.

And this grim assessment does not take into consideration the threats to refugee children in eastern Chad or the Chadian children from the targeted non-Arab tribal populations.

The UN World Food Program (WPF), for its part, is explicit about the threat to civilian populations in Chad, where the humanitarian crisis grows rapidly by the day.

Mounting violence in eastern Chad, which aid workers say has forced thousands of Chadians from their homes, "could seriously impede" humanitarian relief efforts in the region, where aid groups are assisting nearly a quarter-million refugees from Sudan's Darfur conflict, the UN food aid agency said on Friday. The World Food Programme said in a communiqué that unrest is hindering efforts to evaluate how dire the situation is for families recently displaced by violence. "We are at an extremely delicate stage in Chad – right on the edge," said Stefano Porretti, Chad country director for WFP.

As a March 24, 2006 IRIN dispatch reported,

Violence from the Darfur conflict has repeatedly spilled over into eastern Chad, but the instability has increased in recent months with incursions by various armed groups . . . . One aid worker said at least 25,000 Chadians have been displaced by the latest unrest. And the UN refugee agency, UNHCR, said late last month that some Chadians were fleeing over the border into Darfur. WFP called the fresh population movements "worrying."

While the most recent harvest was a good one in this part of Chad, the March 24, 2006 IRIN dispatch continued, " 'there are very real fears that people would soon require essential humanitarian assistance,' WFP said, adding, 'it is difficult to assess the magnitude of needs because of current insecurity.' 'The longer the insecurity in the area persists, the more serious the situation will become,' Porretti said in the WFP statement. 'Most people affected by the recent violence have enough food for another month or two, but after that, things are far less certain.' "

In two months, the rainy season will have begun, coinciding with the traditional "hunger gap" between spring planting and fall harvest, and overland movement of humanitarian assistance into eastern Chad will come to a halt because of impassable roads.

John O'Shea, head of the Irish humanitarian organization GOAL, which has worked in Darfur for almost three years, framed the security crisis that is at the center of the humanitarian crisis in blunt terms. Invoking the specter of Rwanda-like human destruction, O'Shea declared in a March 22, 2006 GOAL Press Release,

> "It is clear that the International Community has been unable to stem the flow of deaths – and the aid community realises the time is fast approaching when the region may be deemed too insecure for relief activity." GOAL . . . was recently forced to abandon one of its major health programmes in the Jebel Mara district, due to fighting between rebels and *Janjaweed* militia. "We knew from day one that protection was needed in Darfur. But the International Community has failed to do its job." "The Security Council has not found the courage to take on the Sudanese Government nor face objections from Russia and China to deploy UN peacekeepers."

This is the perspective of many within the UN, as well. Juan Méndez, Kofi Annan's special advisor on the prevention of genocide, declared in a March 23, 2006 South African Press Association dispatch from Brussels that,

> "no one disputes that the situation on the ground is unraveling, it's getting worse," [Méndez said]. "The almost two million Darfurians who were vulnerable to human rights violations are more vulnerable now than they were a year ago.

Méndez went on to identify, in the same dispatch, the primary source of insecurity for civilians and humanitarian operations,

[Méndez] said the main problem was that the government in Khartoum had refused to respect a UN Security Council resolution demanding that it disarm local militiamen known as the *Janjaweed*. "If [the *Janjaweed*] are not armed, they are incorporated into the security forces to the point where you don't know whether they act as *Janjaweed*, or police, or military."

There are no signs that any of this matters enough to the Bush administration to commit more than words and humanitarian dollars. The latter are, to be sure, critical and reflect deeply meaningful national generosity. But the substitution of words for action is a pattern disturbingly long in evidence. Though Colin Powell declared forthrightly, if belatedly, on September 9, 2004 that "genocide has been committed in Darfur, and the government of Sudan and the Janjawid bear responsibility," he immediately went on to declare that nothing new in the way of US policy followed from this determination. In short, having referred a genocide determination to an obviously paralyzed UN Security Council, which has yet to impose a single sanction on any of the génocidaires indicted by Powell, the US asserted that it had fully discharged its responsibilities as a contracting party to the 1948 UN Convention on the Prevention and Punishment of the Crime of Genocide.

But Article 1 of the Convention declares that, "the Contracting Parties confirm that genocide, whether committed in time of peace or time of war, is a crime under international law which they undertake to prevent and punish." We must conclude that the US was and is prepared to take a minimalist view of its obligations to "undertake to prevent genocide." And it is in this context that we must understand the implications of President Bush's tough-sounding but ultimately hollow words March 29, 2006, " 'this is serious business. This is not playing a diplomatic holding game. . . . When we say genocide, that means genocide has to be stopped.' "

How will we stop genocide in Darfur, Mr. Bush? How? It is not enough to gesture vaguely toward NATO. It is not enough to invoke "NATO stewardship" or some unspecified involvement by NATO – the more so when NATO officials clearly have no intention of moving beyond present severely constrained assistance. What diplomatic and political capital have you expended, Mr. Bush, in securing NATO consensus for a more vigorous role in protecting civilians and humanitarians in Darfur? To date, there is no evidence of any meaningful such expenditure. What prevents you, Mr. Bush, from high-profile public diplomacy, laying out the case for international involvement of the sort outlined by the International Crisis Group? And if the ICG proposal is unsatisfactory, what prevents you from articulating your own detailed plan?

You are trying to respond to genocide in Darfur on the cheap, Mr. Bush – and the effect is only to make any meaningful response less likely. For your expediency is easily sniffed out not only in Brussels, but also in Khartoum. The National Islamic Front génocidaires have seen your Assistant Secretary of State for African Affairs publicly refuse to confirm your genocide determination; they have seen your senior State Department official working on Darfur lie conspicuously about the level of civilian destruction in Darfur. They have noted with pleasure the State Department website that continues to grossly underestimate human mortality in Darfur. They have heard your Deputy Secretary of State describe genocide in Darfur as "tribal warfare," Khartoum's own preferred characterization. They have seen your Secretary of State recently testify to Congress that while genocide continues in Darfur, there is – remarkably – no longer a nameable genocidal agent; and they have seen the blustery impotence of your UN Ambassador, who failed to secure any meaningful resolution on Darfur during the entire month the US held the Presidency of the Security Council.

Darfur must not become a partisan or political cause, or any hope for effective and widely supported US action is doomed. And yet the political expediency that so obviously governs your actions, Mr. Bush – and those of your State Department – works relentlessly to politicize; and partisans on both sides of the aisle are all too ready either to seize advantage or to become protectively defensive of your inaction. There is no further room for bluster, disingenuousness, or expediency, Mr. Bush. Khartoum has taken your measure and found you wanting; if this is to change, only deliberate, forceful actions – diplomatic, economic, and military – can effect the change.

You once declared that genocide in Africa would not occur on your watch. It is your watch. Genocide is occurring in Africa, it continues on a massive scale, and you have done nothing meaningful to stop it. History's judgment of your failure will be savage.

October 9, 2006 – Paralysis in Darfur: Khartoum's Diplomatic Success

With humanitarian operations now in free fall, the UN and the international community have abandoned commitment to the military and police force defined by the August 31, 2006 Security Council Resolution 1706, leaving in its place a still-notional "African Union-Plus" as the sole source of security in Darfur.

The final shape of Khartoum's diplomatic strategy in seeking to retain ultimate control over security arrangements in Darfur is now clearly in evidence; so, too, is the shameful success of this ruthless strategy. By insisting so vehemently that there be no deployment of a robust UN force in Darfur, despite the authorization of such a force by the Security Council, the National Islamic Front (innocuously renamed the National Congress Party) regime has forced upon the international community a choice between only two options – a choice sufficiently stark that these shrewdly calculating génocidaires are confident it will be made in their favor.

The first choice is the exceedingly difficult, and in many ways, risky non-consensual deployment of the preferably UN-sanctioned force required to protect the desperately embattled humanitarian operations upon which more than 4 million conflict-affected persons in Darfur and eastern Chad and many more in neighboring Central African Republic increasingly depend. A tremendous number of these civilians, numbering in the many hundreds of thousands, are now completely beyond humanitarian reach because of insecurity.

The second choice is the very modest international augmentation of an African Union mission in Darfur that is structurally weak and radically inappropriate for present security purposes. The AU mission is severely under-manned and badly demoralized. It is undertaking many fewer patrols per unit and is fatally hampered by critically inadequate communications and intelligence capacity. The AU mission is continually denied the ability to patrol because of Khartoum's appropriation of AU helicopter fuel and imposition of severely restrictive curfew terms. Sadly the AU mission is often poorly commanded, and suffers from an unsuitable command structure. Perhaps most consequentially, the AU is now a force that has extremely poor relations with the more than 2 million Darfuris in displaced persons camps, an immense population that almost universally regards the AU as having sided conspicuously with the signatories to the Abuja, May 2006 Darfur Peace Agreement – including the Khartoum regime, its military forces, and its Arab militia proxies in Darfur, the very men who have so energetically displaced and destroyed non-Arab/African civilians for the past three and a half years.

These are the terms and conditions Khartoum has engineered through its defiance of the UN, and because the regime enjoys diplomatic backing from China, Russia, and the Arab League, even the African Union. By refusing to accept a UN force – indeed, by relentlessly and obdurately refusing to accept the terms of UN Resolution 1706 – Khartoum has fashioned a choice that the regime rightly presumes will be simply too difficult for the militarily capable Western nations. On the one hand is an exceedingly difficult, militarily complex, and politically challenging effort – one justifiable, finally, in no terms other than saving many of the hundreds of thousands of African lives that will almost certainly be lost to ongoing genocidal destruction. On the other hand is an operation that is politically simple in its expediency, if transparently inadequate for the security needs of civilians and humanitarians – what has been designated "African Union-Plus."

Confronted with these stark options, Western and UN officials – despite ongoing politically expedient bluster – have chosen the "African Union-Plus," despite its acknowledged and radical limitations.

In short, all evidence suggests that Khartoum has succeeded in eliminating the political possibility of any timely deployment of UN forces with a mandate to protect humanitarians and civilians, regardless of whether or not the regime's génocidaires acquiesce. Instead, the UN and the international community have decided – explicitly in some quarters, implicitly in others – to support an incremental increase in the African Union force presently overwhelmed by the security crisis in Darfur, while augmenting AU resources on the ground in highly limited fashion. The AU proposal, accepted by the UN in default, calls for raising the current deployment of 7,200 troops, CIVPOL, and other personnel to approximately 11,000 personnel – a total force level still only approximately half the force contemplated in Security Council Resolution 1706, which proposes 17,300 troops, 3,300 CIVPOL, and 16 Formed Police Units – for Darfur, approximately 2,000 back-up security forces.

Currently planned UN augmentation of this force is exceedingly modest, extending to only about 200 personnel. A UN/AU letter of September 22, 2006, addressed to NIF President Omar al-Bashir, calls for: 23 UN mission support staff; 33 police advisors; 105 staff officers; and 25 additional civilian staff to work in a large range of complex tasks. Khartoum is assured in the letter that "UN staff deployed to Darfur as part of the support package for [the African Union mission] would be fully dedicated to support the AU operation and will operate under the operational control of [the African Union mission]."

Khartoum could hardly have asked for an easier UN imprimatur for preservation of the status quo. "African Union-Plus," as represented in this very small augmenting effort, is nothing short of capitulation to Khartoum's demand, explicitly declared such by an aide to the senior Khartoum official managing the Darfur genocide. An October 2, 2006 Reuters dispatch from Cairo reported,

> An official who is an aide to Mohamed al-Dabi, the Sudanese president's top Darfur representative, told Reuters by telephone that, . . . "The AU-Plus is a Sudanese demand."

We may be relatively sure that some of the failures to pay deployed AU forces, as well as some of the many logistical and communications problems, will be remedied by these approximately 200 UN personnel, and that some additional resources – transport, communications, and logistics – will be contributed by other international actors, including NATO in limited fashion. But no larger-scale change of character in the overall AU mission is discernible in present proposals. Moreover, any additional helicopters and other transport vehicles will be subject to the same manipulation of fuel supplies that has defined the entire course of AU deployment in Darfur.

Further, the contributions discussed to date suggest no truly significant increase in transport capacity on the ground, or any enhancement of firepower. The African Union will still be outgunned by, and necessarily deferential to, Khartoum's regular military forces, the Khartoum-backed *Janjaweed*, and the non-signatory insurgency forces. And in a development fraught with military implications, it is also now quite possible that the forces of SLA/Minni Minawi, the signatory faction of the rebel movement, may abandon its agreement with Khartoum, especially in light of a recent, apparently Khartoum-backed attack on SLA/Minni Minawi headquarters in Nyala. Even before the Nyala attack, SLA/Minni Minawi commanders on the ground in Darfur were speaking independently of forsaking partnership with a regime that was clearly continuing a genocidal assault on the African populations of Darfur.

The massive failure of the African Union is revealed in part by a survey of current violence throughout the region. In all three Darfur states and eastern Chad, there has been steadily escalating violence and displacement, and the AU has been completely unable to change the larger security dynamic. Seen from the perspective of the NGOs on the ground, continued exclusive reliance on the African Union or "African Union-Plus" will result in ever-expanding regions throughout Darfur that are simply inaccessible to those attempting to provide life-sustaining food supplies, clean water resources, medical care, and other key forms of human care. The most recent UN map of the vast areas largely or wholly inaccessible to humanitarian efforts is terrifying, and has grown every month since the signing of the ill-conceived and ill-fated Darfur Peace Agreement (DPA).

With no force on the ground to provide for the disengagement of forces, Khartoum's military actions continue to expand throughout all three Darfur states and inside eastern Chad. In South Darfur, the Buram area was the arena for what have very recently been revealed as large-scale assaults on the African populations of the region by Khartoum's Arab militia proxies. The October 6, 2006 *Fifth Periodic Report of the UN High Commissioner for Human Rights [UNHCHR] on the situation of human rights in the Sudan* suggests how much violence against civilians has gone unreported, and how useless the African Union force has become even in monitoring the ethnic targeting of civilians,

> From 28 August [2006] until the beginning of September 2006, militia groups from the Habbania tribe embarked on a brutal campaign in the Buram locality of South Darfur. The campaign, marked by widespread targeting of civilians from tribes that are locally referred to as being of African origin, wholesale burning of villages, looting and forced displacement, appears to have been conducted with the knowledge and material support of Government [of Sudan]

authorities. The attacks resulted in a death toll that could amount to several hundred civilians.

Furthermore, the large-scale attacks resulted in an extremely chaotic displacement, causing widespread separation of families and scores of missing children. Subsequent attacks on Internally Displaced Persons fleeing the fighting, carried out by militia from the government-allied Fallata tribe, caused the displaced population to scatter even further, hampering efforts to deliver aid to those affected.

In further evidence of genocidal intent, the UNHCHR *Report* continues,

Witnesses reported that the recent attacks were far more brutal towards civilians than previous attacks. Furthermore, if in April [2006] the SLA presence was significant in the area, all witnesses interviewed claimed that, during the recent attacks, armed resistance was either non-existent or minimal. Most of the villages attacked were under government control.

Reportedly, the area is currently deserted as the majority of the population has fled. Displacement of inhabitants from these villages may have been the ultimate objective of the recent attacks. According to several people from the area, the motive behind the attacks was to change the demography of the region before the arrival of international troops. This area was not the traditional homeland for tribes of African origin. The present conflict seems to be an attempt to remove the tribes of African origin and make it an entirely Arab tribe area. This was reportedly done with the assumption that any international troops would focus on maintaining the status quo in the area.

The savagery of the southern militia offensive, which began the same day, August 28, 2006, as Khartoum's regular military forces began their major offensive in North Darfur, is made clear at many points in the UNHCHR report, including its narrative of the attack on Tirtish,

Tirtish, about 40 kilometers southwest of Geweghina, was inhabited by a variety of tribes of African origin, namely Massalit, Misseriya Jebel, Tama, Birgit, Dajo, Abdarak, among others. Witnesses reported that the village was attacked on 28 August by hundreds of Habbania militiamen. At around 11:30 am, the perpetrators, many wearing khaki uniforms similar to those worn by government forces, arrived at the village on horse and camelback and were accompanied by several vehicles. The attackers possessed heavy weaponry, including machine guns; one witness also reported the use of rocket-propelled grenades.

A witness reported that the militia stormed into town, shooting at civilians and setting fire to dwellings and shops. Reportedly, women and children were thrown into burning dwellings as they attempted to flee. Children as young as three years old, including the daughter of an interviewee, were killed in this manner. A witness reported that he personally participated in the burial of 62 people killed in Tirtish that day (he himself later fled), and estimates the total civilian death toll in the village at between 80 and 90. He reports that at least 40 people in the village, including many children, are unaccounted for.

Such large-scale, ethnically-targeted, Khartoum-backed militia assaults defined the worst phases of the genocidal violence occurring in Darfur 2003-2004. Now, in late 2006, the African Union is completely and conspicuously powerless to control the resurgence of such violence.

The connection between the Habbania Arab militia force and the Khartoum regime is stressed in the UNHCHR report,

In nearly all of the attacks documented, victims and witnesses made reference to the presence of two Habbania leaders with ties to the Sudanese Armed Forces (SAF): Agid Ayadi and Umda Mohammed Musa. These two men were also believed to have been personally involved in directing the April [2006] Habbania militia attacks in the area. Several sources reported that on 25-26 August 2006, in Wad Hajum, Agid Ayadi and Umda Mohammed Musa organized a recruitment meeting for the upcoming attacks, for which the stated purpose was "removing Zurga [African tribes] from the area." Two witnesses recognized government officials (some in higher-ranking military uniforms) at the meeting . . . .

The Conclusion to the UNHCHR *Report* highlights Khartoum's complicity in these genocidal attacks,

> The attacks, spearheaded by Habbania militia, were massive in scale, involving a large number of villages, and were carried out over only a few days. Government knowledge, if not complicity, in the attacks is almost certain. In all the above cases, militia members wore khaki uniforms similar to those worn by government forces, carried heavy weaponry in most cases, and were accompanied by vehicles. Several interviewees noted that the Habbania militiamen themselves do not possess vehicles nor the kind of heavy weapons used during the attacks (such as Rocket-Propelled Grenades and vehicle-mounted machine guns).
>
> Furthermore, reports regarding participation of government officials in the Habbania meeting in Wad Hajum on 25-26 August 2006 also indicate previous government knowledge about the attacks. The attacks appeared to have been directed at civilians as reports indicate that the rebel presence in the area was not significant. The attacks appeared to have targeted civilians from tribes of African origin in what appeared to be an attempt to drive them from the Habbania homeland and therefore completely change the ethnic balance in the area.

If this report provides clear evidence that rural areas remain especially vulnerable because of African Union incapacity, camps for displaced persons are also highly vulnerable. The Sudan Organization Against Torture reported October 4, 2006 that *Janjaweed* militia forces attacked the vast Kalma camp for displaced persons near Nyala, South Darfur, killing two people and critically wounding a third. Such attacks are becoming more common and could easily become occasions for catastrophic violent human destruction.

Alarmingly, great areas of West Darfur have come under de facto governance of the *Janjaweed*, as Amnesty International has very recently reported in *Crying Out for Safety* (October 5, 2006),

> In large parts of West Darfur, the Janjawid have almost complete control and are gradually occupying the land which was depopulated

by the scorched earth campaign in 2003 and 2004. Hundreds of thousands of people – most of the original population – now live in camps for internally displaced persons (IDPs) or in refugee camps across the border in Chad. The Janjawid presence threatens attack on any IDP movement outside of the camps, making venturing outside extremely difficult and any return of the displaced to their homes impossible. The displaced are effectively imprisoned inside the camps. Even within them, the Janjawid commit killings, rapes, beatings and theft. Rape is a near certainty for women caught outside the camps, and women are sometimes abducted and enslaved in Janjawid households. Men venturing outside the camps are often beaten, tortured or killed.

The governing genocidal dynamic is captured in subsequent paragraphs of that same Amnesty International report,

The vast majority of the original residents of large areas of West Darfur, the Masalit, were targeted by the Janjawid attacks at the beginning of the conflict in 2003 and 2004. The Janjawid now have almost absolute control of large areas of West Darfur, where they drove hundreds of thousands of people from their homes. The displaced fled either to Chad or to the nearest urban centres, which quickly developed into massive IDP camps.

The land abandoned did not remain vacant. The Janjawid utilized the land of the displaced for their livestock, passing through villages, making use of the untended water points, taking what was left of the agricultural produce, and attacking any of the original inhabitants who attempted to return – effectively occupying the land. The displaced in the IDP camps in West Darfur and the refugee camps in Chad not only await an end to the fighting in order to return home, but also an end to the occupation of their land. Until the Janjawid are disarmed and have vacated their land, they cannot return.

Amnesty continued describing the character of the *Janjaweed*'s terrifying authority,

The Janjawid use their control of the camp occupants to assert their ownership of territory and the livestock in it [one woman reported].

"In October 2004 I went to a wadi [seasonal watercourse] with another villager [a man named Gandme, aged about 50] and our cattle. We came across a group of many Janjawid who beat me with rifle butts, breaking my right leg and left arm. Gandme was shot dead. The Janjawid told me: You are a Nuba [derogatory racial epithet for African tribal people] woman, daughter of a whore. You have no right to these cattle and they do not belong to you. They took away my cattle (seven cows and goats) and Gandme's cattle." [A Masalit woman aged in her fifties, originally from the village of Hajilija near Arara, in West Darfur.]

Enslavement of women, though less usual than rape, is also a threat. Numerous women who had fled the IDP camps in Darfur told Amnesty International that the Janjawid took women to serve in their households and to be "used" at will. Women survivors rarely describe in detail their enforced servitude in Janjawid households, but the abuses against them are widely understood to include rape.

A similarly grim picture is offered of eastern Chad, where genocidal violence is poised to explode with the onset of the dry season, which opens previously impassable cross-border routes:

In eastern Chad, directly across the border from West Darfur, attacks reminiscent of the first wave of Darfur's scorched earth campaign continue unopposed. Amnesty International has documented the cross-border attacks since late 2005, in which the Janjawid have killed and driven from their homes thousands of civilians, targeted according to their ethnicity, and looted whole communities' wealth.

The potential for vastly widening violence in eastern Chad, in response to Khartoum's continuing support for Chadian rebels and the *Janjaweed*, is perhaps the most ominous finding of Amnesty International's October 5, 2006 Report,

Since Chadian armed opposition groups based in West Darfur and supported by Sudan have become more active, Chad has been increasingly involved in the Darfur conflict. From late 2005 it has openly hosted and sometimes aided Darfurian armed opposition groups in retaliation for Sudan's increased support of the Chadian armed opposition.

To date this has been war by proxy, but the developments in south-eastern Chad, with large parts of the Chadian population drawn into the conflict, represents a new level of involvement. Amnesty International warned of the regional repercussions if the Janjawid were not checked. As a result of these attacks, the region's civilian population, previously largely removed from the Darfur conflict, is being drawn into active participation in it. Conscious of the role ethnicity has played in the targeting of certain communities in Chad, increasingly they see a common cause with the Darfurian armed opposition groups that ignores the nominal international border between Chad and Darfur.

There are now some members of the National Redemption Front [the main military and political coalition among non-signatory Darfuri rebels] with recruitment and training facilities in south-eastern Chad, and the flow of small arms into the region has increased. In Goz Beida, capital of Dar Silah region, members of the tribes most affected by the Janjawid attacks – most of them from the Dajo community – have begun to be recruited, armed and trained.

The implication of these developments will become apparent after the rainy season, when traditionally fighting resumes in the region. Ethnic polarization is on the rise, and the victims of the previous Janjawid attacks, no longer unarmed, may retaliate against other Chadian ethnic groups who aligned themselves with the Janjawid during these attacks.

With Chad's government neither willing nor able to protect rural populations, a massive increase in violence and civilian destruction seems both imminent and inevitable. Associated Press reported October 8, 2006 from N'Djamena, Chad that,

Sudanese soldiers crossed the border into eastern Chad to fight a group of Darfur rebels, leaving more than 300 people injured, an aid worker said Sunday.

IRIN reported October 9, 2006,

> For the first time, combat between Sudanese rebel groups and the government of Sudan has spilled across the border from the embattled Darfur region into eastern Chad, aid workers said on Monday [October 9, 2006]. Previously, such clashes had involved the Chadian army in pursuit of rebels seeking to oust Chadian President Idriss Deby.
>
> The weekend fighting signals an escalation of violence in eastern Chad, but aid agencies said on Monday that humanitarian operations would continue. "Violence in eastern Chad, violence in Darfur is problematic for all of us. We are having less and less access to a number of internally displaced people in that part of that world and it does concern us and other UN agencies operating in the region," Jean-Jacques Graisse, senior deputy executive director of the World Food Programme, told IRIN in Dakar on Monday.

Certainly even an "African Union-Plus" cannot begin to take on the tasks of monitoring events on the ground in eastern Chad or cross-border military incursions, although such tasks are explicitly part of the mandate for the UN force contemplated in UNSC 1706.

To the south of Chad, but with a significant border with Darfur and Bahr el-Ghazal Province, the Central African Republic (CAR) has also been drawn unwillingly into the Darfur conflict. The UN News Centre on September 29, 2006 reported,

> Almost a quarter of a million people in northern parts of the Central African Republic (CAR) have been forced to flee their homes in recent months because of "severe levels of violence" perpetrated by armed groups, including Government soldiers, the top United Nations aid official in the impoverished country said today, warning of the regional impact of this unrest.

The connection to Darfur's conflict is drawn explicitly as the UN News Centre report continued,

> Toby Lanzer, the UN Humanitarian Coordinator in the CAR, [said in New York], "So there is certainly a regional impact that the situation is having and paradoxically quite some concern that the situation in [neighbouring] Sudan and Chad – also very fragile, as you know – is having quite some bearing on the situation in the Central African Republic."

Nicholas Kristof of the *New York Times* in an October 1, 2006 account from Paoua, Central African Republic, reported on conditions in northern CAR and the role of Khartoum in destabilizing this terribly impoverished country. He begins with a grim overview,

> My purpose [in traveling to the Central African Republic was] to emphasize the urgency of ending the genocide in Darfur before it destabilizes even more of Africa. The malignancy has already spread to Chad, and now it is beginning to destroy the Central African Republic as well. .... Sudan has in effect invaded the Central African Republic with a proxy force of Chadians whom it armed and transported to a remote airstrip in Sudanese Antonov aircraft. Now those troops are living in caves in the northeast part of this country and recruiting local people to fight. When the dry season comes in another month or so, that force of 500 troops will presumably join a larger force of Sudanese puppets in trying to overthrow the government of Chad and perhaps of this country as well.

There can be little avoiding Kristof's conclusions,

> [This] kind of random violence is incredibly infectious, and the legacy of Darfur may be that all of Chad and the Central African Republic will collapse into Somalia-style anarchy. In an interview ..., President François Bozize of the Central African Republic offered an excellent suggestion, "With the deployment of UN peacekeepers to Darfur delayed indefinitely because of Sudan's defiance, post them in

the meantime in Chad and the Central African Republic – while still pushing to get them into Darfur itself."

There is currently no such urgent planning for deployment of substantial, well-equipped and -supplied UN forces to either the Central African Republic or Chad – merely disingenuous celebration of the "African Union-Plus" as a modest diplomatic victory, moving things in the right direction. It is neither; indeed, it is sheer pretense to suggest that the AU, in any augmented form, is an adequate response to the desperate security crisis facing well over 4 million human beings and the vast, highly dispersed humanitarian operations upon which these people grow more – not less – dependent.

How did Khartoum triumph in forestalling UN deployment of forces under Security Council Resolution 1706? There are many answers. But we would do particularly well to focus on the cowardice and incompetence of Jan Pronk, the UN Secretary General's Special Representative for Sudan. Pronk has a spectacular history of mistakes, poor judgment, and stubbornness in his present capacity, and is widely held in contempt, including by many within the UN.

Most consequentially, Pronk feels no obligation to abide by the terms of UN Security Council resolutions. When UNSC Resolution 1556 passed on July 30, 2004, it contained the only "demand" of significance that has been made of Khartoum to date, that the regime disarm the *Janjaweed* and bring its leaders to justice. Just days later, in early August 2004, Pronk in effect negotiated away, on his own authority, this critical demand; and he did so in order to secure Khartoum's agreement in the creation of "safe areas" in Darfur.

So ill-conceived was Pronk's plan – it immediately served to provide diplomatic cover for Khartoum's expanding military offensive in areas contiguous to the safe areas – that both Human Rights Watch and Amnesty International issued blistering critiques, *Darfur: UN 'Safe Areas' offer no Real Security*, Human Rights Watch, September 1, 2004, and Amnesty International (Index: AFR 54/131/2004) *Sudan: Civilians Still Under Threat In Darfur*, October 13, 2004.

Pronk's safe areas plan was quietly dropped by the UN in September

2004, but not before the terrible political and diplomatic damage had been done with respect to holding Khartoum directly accountable for the ongoing genocidal predations of the *Janjaweed*.

More than two years later, Pronk has extended his very long list of critical errors; his most recent is reliably reported as having earned him a severe chastisement by senior UN officials, although again, too late.

On September 29, 2006, the BBC reported on comments made by Pronk the preceding day,

> Mr Pronk has meanwhile told the Associated Press news agency he does not expect Khartoum to accept UN peacekeepers any time soon. "The international community should instead push for the African Union's mission to be prolonged and reinforced," Mr Pronk is quoted as saying. He said the AU force's mandate should be extended indefinitely to ensure relief continued to reach Darfur's refugees. Mr Pronk is quoted as saying he was certain Khartoum would allow the AU force to stay on in Darfur.

Just as Pronk gratuitously surrendered the UN Security Council "demand" that Khartoum disarm the *Janjaweed* and bring its leaders to justice, so with these widely reported words Pronk essentially signaled to Khartoum that the UN had abandoned efforts to press aggressively for deployment of the UN force called for in UNSC Resolution 1706. This was certainly how Pronk's words were heard by Khartoum's génocidaires, by numerous human rights and policy organizations, by vulnerable humanitarian workers and civilians on the ground in Darfur – and by UN officials, who berated Pronk after the fact for his weak and ill-informed surrender of 1706, confirmed to the author by two very well-placed sources. But as was the case in August 2004, so in October 2006: the damage had already been done.

Pronk was right only in asserting that Khartoum would allow the AU to stay in Darfur, since it presently serves as the means for avoiding a complete withdrawal of security forces, a potentially catalytic event for a morally torpid international community. But Khartoum has also recently insisted that the AU mandate in Darfur will not be extended indefinitely. Reuters reported in an October 2, 2006 dispatch from Cairo,

[A Khartoum] official, who is an aide to Mohamed al-Dabi, the Sudanese president's top Darfur representative, told Reuters by telephone [speaking on condition of anonymity] that Sudan would welcome a planned increase in AU peacekeepers for now. But he said, "Sudan agrees that the African Union troops stay until the crisis is over, but not indefinitely." He had been asked whether Khartoum would agree to an indefinite extension of AU troops in Darfur as a way of breaking a deadlock over the deployment of UN peacekeepers there.

We may be all too sure that when international attention drifts from Darfur, when diplomatic pressure lessens, AU deployment and troop rotation will face growing challenges. Meanwhile, the AU will be obstructed, harassed, and impeded as mercilessly as it has for more than two years. Moreover, nothing reported in recent days suggests that the AU has been able to secure an independent and reliable fuel source for its helicopters and ground vehicles; nothing suggests that highly constraining curfews will be lifted, or that onerous requirements and certifications of various sorts have been abandoned by Khartoum.

And why should Khartoum feel any need to offer more than a few further modest concessions to an "African Union-Plus"? Diplomatic pressure is diminishing, after cresting during NIF President Omar al-Bashir's trip to the UN in New York for the opening of the General Assembly. To be sure, there's much tough talk from US Secretary of State Condoleezza Rice, quoted as saying "Khartoum must choose cooperation or confrontation," but no consequences have been spelled out if the regime continues to cleave to the genocidal status quo by means of the "African Union-Plus."

Europe is no better, only quieter in its accommodation of genocide. And in speaking about the "African Union-Plus" there is a clear willingness to pretend that this force has implications it clearly does not, as Reuters reported October 2, 2006 in a dispatch from Cairo,

In Finland, EU foreign policy chief Javier Solana said he understood that Bashir was close to accept[ing] the AU-Plus presence in Darfur, citing such a step as progress toward a genuine UN force in the region.

In fact, the "African Union-Plus" represents Khartoum's strategy for preventing, precisely, progress toward a genuine UN force in the region.

British lame-duck Prime Minister Tony Blair, with his legacy evidently much on his mind, is reported to be ordering plans drawn up for a force of "at least 1,000 troops to play a core role in an international protection force," as *Scotland on Sunday* [UK] reported on October 8, 2006,

> The Prime Minister has signalled his intention to back up his demands for international intervention to prevent "genocide" in Darfur by sending a large British force to help protect the black African population.
>
> Blair is continuing to press for the move as a gesture of intent, particularly amid the continuing failure of the international community to agree on a multi-national force – and the Sudanese government's refusal to accept any intervention.

But we have seen pointless saber-rattling from the Blair government several times before; as the author noted almost five months ago in an article in *The Guardian Online*, May 15, 2006, "International powers are talking about urgent action to enforce peace. But where are the troops?"

> It's easy for Tony Blair to declare that a non-existent peacemaking force must have "sufficient firepower" to guarantee the feeble accord signed last week in Abuja, and that "Britain and the US, with other NATO partners, [are] looking at the issue urgently to see what more could be done." But an assertion of "urgency" seems a cruel joke almost two years after General Sir Mike Jackson declared that the British army could field a brigade (5,000 troops) for a humanitarian mission to Darfur.

For his part, President Bush in February 2006 made the politically expedient promise that there would be "NATO stewardship" for a Darfur mission. But this promise was not only expedient, it was predictably vacuous as there was no firm commitment of troops or even a mandate.

There continue to be suggestions in various quarters that somehow Darfuris don't really want international humanitarian intervention, consensual or nonconsensual. This is simply untrue. There is indisputable and overwhelming consensus among the Darfuris who have been targeted for genocidal destruction for many years, as well as among Darfuris in the diaspora: "we are desperate for international intervention."

There are also declarations that any international deployment would find itself in the midst of an Iraq-like quagmire of ethnic violence and factional strife – precisely the threat that is so continually wielded by National Islamic Front leaders. But how likely is it that the African populations of Darfur, perhaps 65% to 75% of the total pre-conflict population, would not energetically assist in any intervention made for their own security and that of critically required humanitarian assistance? How likely is it that a non-Darfuri jihadist campaign would take root in this highly remote region, where non-Darfuris are thoroughly conspicuous?

There can be no denying that nonconsensual deployment would be dangerous and risky in many ways. Moreover, the extraordinary logistical difficulties of deployment, consensual or nonconsensual, bear repeated emphasis. Critically, any such intervention must take into primary consideration the task of preventing reprisals by Khartoum and the *Janjaweed* against humanitarian organizations and civilians, especially those concentrated in camps for displaced persons. Clear, extremely robust, and fully plausible threats must be issued, forcing as much of a military stand-down by all combatants as possible. There are other very difficult political, diplomatic, military, and economic issues that would present themselves. But it is also important to bear in mind as well that intervention at this point in the crisis will be much more difficult precisely because of earlier inaction, when genocide first was recognizable and immense impending human destruction was clearly visible. As the author wrote in a *Washington Post* Op-Ed, "Unnoticed Genocide," February 25, 2004,

> Immediate plans for humanitarian intervention should begin. The alternative is to allow tens of thousands of civilians to die in the weeks and months ahead in what will be continuing genocidal destruction.

The difficulties of intervention have continued to increase rapidly over the past 32 months, and will continue to do so, even as human mortality has climbed to approximately 500,000. And this already staggering total is clearly poised to explode upwards, as Jan Egeland, head of UN humanitarian operations, warned the Security Council on August 28, 2006,

> Our entire humanitarian operation in Darfur – the only lifeline for more than three million people – is presently at risk. We need immediate action on the political front to avoid a humanitarian catastrophe with massive loss of life. . . . If the humanitarian operation were to collapse [because of insecurity], we could see hundreds of thousands of deaths. In short, we may end up with a man-made catastrophe of an unprecedented scale in Darfur.

Egeland went on to put the Security Council on notice:

> Hundreds of humanitarian organizations from around the world are watching what you will be doing or may refrain from doing in the coming weeks.

Certainly there are hundreds of humanitarian organizations from around the world watching what the Security Council has, and has not done. But more than five weeks have passed since Egeland's briefing, and there is no meaningful plan for improving security in Darfur, merely expedient and specious efforts to pretend that an "African Union-Plus" force marks a serious response to the rapidly escalating security crisis throughout Darfur, as well as eastern Chad and the Central African Republic. Humanitarian operations continue, in Egeland's phrase of September 12, 2006, "in free fall."

Kofi Annan's monthly report on Darfur to the UN Security Council, September 26, 2006 covering August 2006, speaks with characteristic duplicity – on the one hand acknowledging in Section VIII Paragraph 58 that,

> Darfur is at a critical stage. Insecurity in this troubled region is at its highest levels and humanitarian access is at its lowest levels since 2004. Unless security improves, the world is facing the prospect of having to drastically curtail an acutely needed humanitarian operation.

But at the same time, refusing to demonstrate the leadership that might pressure Khartoum to accept the UN force specified in UNSC Resolution 1706, Annan continued in Section VIII Paragraph 61,

> As the Security Council has recognized, the transition to a United Nations operation will not be possible as long as the Government of Sudan refuses its consent. Once again, therefore, I urge the Government of Sudan to . . . to give its consent to the transition, and commit itself to the political process . . .

Nothing could embolden Khartoum more than the sense that it faces only further urgings. That neither the Arab League nor the African Union is prepared to do more than urge Khartoum to accept the UN force outlined in Resolution 1706 only further encourages the regime to believe in the ultimate success of its strategy. Thus the dismaying authority of the comment by the distinguished and courageous Suleiman Baldo of the International Crisis Group in an October 8, 2006 statement reported from Khartoum,

> "I don't think diplomatic pressure of any kind will make Khartoum accept a UN peacekeeping mission," said Suleiman Baldo, a Sudan expert at the US-based International Crisis Group.

But this diplomatic outcome has not been of necessity, certainly not if Khartoum were to have faced the clear and unavoidable prospect of non-consensual deployment in failing to accept a UN force; rather, Baldo's conclusion speaks to the self-fulfilling prophesy of people like Jan Pronk and others who encourage Khartoum's obduracy by means of their own cowardly acquiescence. These are the same people who fail to see Khartoum's determination to complete its genocidal task, and who as part of this exercise in blindness and deafness pretend that an "African Union-Plus" response is somehow a temporarily acceptable response to the desperate people of this tortured region.

The world has made it clear that it has no inclination to hear pleas from villages such as Amoodh Al-Akhdar, whose inhabitants were the victims of the August 2006 assaults in the Buram region by Khartoum's military proxies – assaults, the UN High Commissioner for Human Rights reports, in which young children and the elderly were hurled into their burning homes,

> "Most of our people are hiding in the bushes. The only routes connecting inhabited villages pass through *Janjaweed* held areas, while other roads have been submersed by water because of the rain. There are injured and sick who were caught in the fighting. Many people have gone missing. People cannot leave the area without protection. We call for the international community to intervene immediately to help the civilians in the area."

The people of Amoodh Al-Akhdar call in vain.

LIST OF APPENDIXES

Appendix 1: Text of the 1948 UN Convention on the Prevention and Punishment of the Crime of Genocide

Appendix 2: United Nations Inter-Agency Fact Finding and Rapid Assessment Mission: Kailek Town, South Darfur

Appendix 3: UN Security Council Resolutions 1556 (July 30, 2004) and 1706 (August 31, 2006)

Appendix 4: Articles by Eric Reeves

[a] "Quantifying Genocide in Darfur": Current data for total mortality from violence, malnutrition, and disease"
In two parts, April 28, 2006 and May 13, 2006,

[b] "Report of the International Commission of Inquiry on Darfur: A critical analysis,"
In two parts, February 2 and February 6, 2006

[c] "Ghosts of Rwanda: The Failure of the African Union in Darfur,"
In two parts, November 13 and November 20, 2006

[d] "Unnoticed Genocide."
February 25, 2004 *Washington Post* op-ed

APPENDIX 1

Convention on the Prevention and Punishment of the Crime of Genocide

Adopted by Resolution 260 (III) A of the United Nations General Assembly on 9 December 1948.

Article 1: The Contracting Parties confirm that genocide, whether committed in time of peace or in time of war, is a crime under international law which they undertake to prevent and to punish.

Article 2: In the present Convention, genocide means any of the following acts committed with intent to destroy, in whole or in part, a national, ethnical, racial or religious group, as such:

(a) Killing members of the group;
(b) Causing serious bodily or mental harm to members of the group;
(c) Deliberately inflicting on the group conditions of life calculated to bring about its physical destruction in whole or in part;
(d) Imposing measures intended to prevent births within the group;
(e) Forcibly transferring children of the group to another group.

Article 3: The following acts shall be punishable:

(a) Genocide;
(b) Conspiracy to commit genocide;

(c) Direct and public incitement to commit genocide;
(d) Attempt to commit genocide;
(e) Complicity in genocide.

Article 4: Persons committing genocide or any of the other acts enumerated in Article 3 shall be punished, whether they are constitutionally responsible rulers, public officials or private individuals.

Article 5: The Contracting Parties undertake to enact, in accordance with their respective Constitutions, the necessary legislation to give effect to the provisions of the present Convention and, in particular, to provide effective penalties for persons guilty of genocide or any of the other acts enumerated in Article 3.

Article 6: Persons charged with genocide or any of the other acts enumerated in Article 3 shall be tried by a competent tribunal of the State in the territory of which the act was committed, or by such international penal tribunal as may have jurisdiction with respect to those Contracting Parties which shall have accepted its jurisdiction.

Article 7: Genocide and the other acts enumerated in Article 3 shall not be considered as political crimes for the purpose of extradition. The Contracting Parties pledge themselves in such cases to grant extradition in accordance with their laws and treaties in force.

Article 8: Any Contracting Party may call upon the competent organs of the United Nations to take such action under the Charter of the United Nations as they consider appropriate for the prevention and suppression of acts of genocide or any of the other acts enumerated in Article 3.

Article 9: Disputes between the Contracting Parties relating to the interpretation, application or fulfilment of the present Convention, including those relating to the responsibility of a State for genocide or any of the other acts enumerated in Article 3, shall be submitted to the International Court of Justice at the request of any of the parties to the dispute.

Article 10: The present Convention, of which the Chinese, English, French, Russian and Spanish texts are equally authentic, shall bear the date of 9 December 1948.

Article 11: The present Convention shall be open until 31 December 1949 for signature on behalf of any Member of the United Nations and of any non-member State to which an invitation to sign has been addressed by the General Assembly.

The present Convention shall be ratified, and the instruments of ratification shall be deposited with the Secretary-General of the United Nations. After 1 January 1950, the present Convention may be acceded to on behalf of any Member of the United Nations and of any non-member State which has received an invitation as aforesaid. Instruments of accession shall be deposited with the Secretary-General of the United Nations.

Article 12: Any Contracting Party may at any time, by notification addressed to the Secretary-General of the United Nations, extend the application of the present Convention to all or any of the territories for the conduct of whose foreign relations that Contracting Party is responsible.

Article 13: On the day when the first twenty instruments of ratification or accession have been deposited, the Secretary-General shall draw up a proces-verbal and transmit a copy of it to each Member of the United Nations and to each of the non-member States contemplated in Article 11. The present Convention shall come into force on the ninetieth day following the date of deposit of the twentieth instrument of ratification or accession. Any ratification or accession effected subsequent to the latter date shall become effective on the ninetieth day following the deposit of the instrument of ratification or accession.

Article 14: The present Convention shall remain in effect for a period of ten years as from the date of its coming into force. It shall thereafter remain in force for successive periods of five years for such Contracting Parties as have not denounced it at least six months before the expiration of the current period. Denunciation shall be effected by a written notification addressed to the Secretary-General of the United Nations.

Article 15: If, as a result of denunciations, the number of Parties to the present Convention should become less than sixteen, the Convention shall cease to be in force as from the date on which the last of these denunciations shall become effective.

Article 16: A request for the revision of the present Convention may be made at any time by any Contracting Party by means of a notification in writing addressed to the Secretary-General. The General Assembly shall decide upon the steps, if any, to be taken in respect of such request.

Article 17: The Secretary-General of the United Nations shall notify all Members of the United Nations and the non-member States contemplated in Article 11 of the following:

(a) Signatures, ratifications and accessions received in accordance with Article 11;

(b) Notifications received in accordance with Article 12;

(c) The date upon which the present Convention comes into force in accordance with Article 13;

(d) Denunciations received in accordance with Article 14;

(e) The abrogation of the Convention in accordance with Article 15;

(f) Notifications received in accordance with Article 16.

Article 18: The original of the present Convention shall be deposited in the archives of the United Nations. A certified copy of the Convention shall be transmitted to all Members of the United Nations and to the non-member States contemplated in Article 11.

Article 19: The present Convention shall be registered by the Secretary-General of the United Nations on the date of its coming into force.

APPENDIX 2

United Nations Inter-Agency Fact Finding and Rapid Assessment
Mission: Kailek Town, South Darfur

Source: United Nations Resident Coordinator (UN RC)
Date: 25 Apr 2004

1. INTRODUCTION

A United Nations Inter - Agency fact-finding and humanitarian needs assessment
mission was carried out to the town of Kailek in South Darfur on Sunday 24 April
2004. The mission - team consisted of technical staff from UNICEF, WHO, FAO
and OCHA (lead). One member from the HAC in Nyala escorted the mission.
UNSECOORD cleared the road to Kailek on 17 April 2004. This is the first United
Nations humanitarian assessment mission to the location and surrounding areas.

Objectives

The key objective of the mission was to assess the security and humanitarian conditions in Kailek town, with the intention of soliciting a concrete plan of action
from the local authorities to alleviate the situation of the IDPs in that location.

Numerous reports obtained in recent weeks have revealed deplorable humanitarian and security conditions in the location, including a report submitted by
CARE International in early April, the findings of which have been continuously
contested by the GoS.

Background on Kailek

Kailek town is located some 64 kms South West of Kass town in the Administrative Unit of Shattaya inside the Kass locality. The original population of Kailek was some 5,000 persons. As the campaign to cleanse the entire Kass - Shattaya - Kailek triangle of its mainly Fur population progressed, villagers sought towards Kailek after other locations were destroyed by GoS and Jenjaweed forces, at times backed by GoS aerial bombardment (e.g. Shattaya on 10 February 2004). The 23 Fur villages in the Shattaya Administrative Unit have been completely depopulated, looted and burnt to the ground (the team observed several such sites driving through the area for two days). Meanwhile, dotted alongside these charred locations are unharmed, populated and functioning 'Arab' settlements. In some locations, the distance between a destroyed Fur village and an 'Arab' village is less than 500 meters.

Kailek town itself was attacked and burned with considerable force by Jenjaweed and GoS forces on several occasions between mid-February and 08 March 2004. Today, Kailek is completely destroyed with virtually no complete buildings left in the entire town area. All items of value have been stolen and personal possessions are scattered all over the place, bearing a somber testimony to the swiftness and violence with which people were attacked and dislocated.

Security

There is a strong and visible presence of the Jenjaweed in the entire region between Kass and Kailek, as well as between Kass and Abruminoa, the last village before Shattaya. Upon entry into Kailek town, a considerable number of armed Jenjaweed fighters approached the mission, accompanying the GoS police formally in charge of security in the town. While the tone between the UN and Jenjaweed/GoS was cordial, there were a number of well-armed young boys displaying a very belligerent attitude towards the IDPs despite the presence of the mission. Observing interactions between IDPs and the Jenjaweed fighters / GoS police officers, the IDPs are clearly under physical threat, and not in a benign and trusty relationship with their so-called protectors. The general atmosphere in town was that of aggression, anxiety and insecurity.

Methodology

Information was obtained using rapid assessment techniques, meeting with key-informants and several male and female representatives of the IDP community, semi-structured interviews and direct observation.

9. CONCLUSION

The team members, all of whom are experienced experts in humanitarian affairs were visibly shaken by the humanitarian state and conditions in which we found the caseload of IDPs in Kailek.

The clear presence of the Jenjaweed, and the inability to distinguish between them and the GoS police officers when carrying out their 'duties' in town call for the circumstances of the IDPs in Kailek to be described as imprisonment. With a under five child mortality rate of 8 - 9 children per day due to malnutrition, and with the GoS security representatives permanently located in the town without having reported this phenomena to the UN despite it having taken place for several weeks also indicate a local policy of forced starvation.

The team unilaterally recommends the immediate relocation of the IDP caseload to a location of their choosing, primarily Nayla or Kass, for the instant release from their current ordeal.

Furthermore, and in accordance with the explicit and informed advice of the IDPs themselves, the team recommends that neither food nor any other hard assistance are provided to the caseload in their current circumstances due to the complete lack of protection mechanisms.

The team does recommend that an emergency team of health/nutrition experts is being dispatched to the location for the urgent stabilization of the group of severely malnourished children, thereby ensuring their survival during the transport away from Kailek.

In addition to this, the UN team wishes to raise its concern regarding the following:

The numerous testimonies collected by the team, substantiated by the actual observations on the ground, particularly the longstanding prevention of access to food, alludes to a strategy of systematic and deliberate starvation being enforced by the GoS and its security forces on the ground.

Information and findings obtained from Kailek IDPs in Kass and Kalma, as well a CARE International assessment report from early April 2004 all contain information which confirms the findings in the present report have been persistently refuted by the GoS when presented by the UN Nyala team for clarification.

Following the CARE report, the UN continued to press the GoS for clearance to visit Kailek town and to follow up on the findings from the CARE erport but to no avail. UNSECOORD was only allowed access on 17 April after having been 'advised' not to visit the area after the ceasefire, while the GoS has consistently informed that there was no problems of security and assistance in Kailek and that the IDPs in the location were free to go.

Therefore, in light of this, a first conclusion by the mission team is that the GoS has deliberately deceived the United Nations by repeatedly refuting claims to the seriousness of the situation in Kailek as well as having actively resisted the need for intervention by preventing the UN access to the area. The fact that GoS' own security forces have monitored the deteriorating humanitarian situation in Kailek due to their constant presence on the ground only helps to underscore this fact.

Secondly, numerous, independent references have been made by both IDPs and security forces to a decree issued by the Commissioner of Kass which explicitly instructs GoS security forces to prohibit, by any means necessary, any civilian movement out of Kailek town.

If this is the case, the GoS has willfully breached its responsibilities as signatory to the Geneva Convention and additional protocols, International Humanitarian Law and Human Rights Law, by, amongst other things, deliberately preventing human beings their right to life, liberty and security of person and the freedom of movement, directly resulting in the preventable deaths and suffering of highly vulnerable persons in need of explicit protection under these legal instruments.

As this report is being prepared, the United Nations in Nyala is working with the GoS to secure the immediate relocation of the IDPs in Kailek. However, despite having been directly informed of the grave findings made by the UN mission in Kailek, the GoS continues to stall any concrete actions related to this urgent relocation. Thus, the UN continues to await confirmation that the rapid relocation of the IDPs will commence, having in the meantime dispatched a joint WHO/MSF-H team to Kailek to commence the emergency stabilization of the severely malnourished children in the location.

It is a grave concern to the United Nations team in Nyala that Kailek is but one of several locations where civilians are living under similar conditions without having been able to communicate their ordeal to the humanitarian community.

APPENDIX 3

United Nations Security Council
Resolution 1556 (2004)

Adopted by the Security Council at its 5015th meeting, on 30 July 2004

The Security Council,
Recalling its Statement by its President of 25 May 2004 (S/PRST/2004/16), its resolution 1547 (2004) of 11 June 2004 and its resolution 1502 (2003) of 26 August 2003 on the access of humanitarian workers to populations in need, *Welcoming* the leadership role and the engagement of the African Union to address the situation in Darfur and *expressing* its readiness to support fully these efforts,
Further welcoming the communiqué of the African Union Peace and Security Council issued 27 July 2004
Reaffirming its commitment to the sovereignty, unity, territorial integrity, and independence of Sudan as consistent with the Machakos Protocol of 20 July 2002 and subsequent agreements based on this protocol as agreed to by the Government of Sudan,
Welcoming the Joint Communiqué issued by the Government of Sudan and the Secretary-General of the United Nations on 3 July 2004, including the creation of the Joint Implementation Mechanism, and acknowledging steps taken towards improved humanitarian access, *Taking note* of the Report of the Secretary-General on Sudan issued 3 June 2004 and welcoming the Secretary-General's appointment of a Special Representative for Sudan and his efforts to date,

Reiterating its grave concern at the ongoing humanitarian crisis and widespread human rights violations, including continued attacks on civilians that are placing the lives of hundreds of thousands at risk,

Condemning all acts of violence and violations of human rights and international humanitarian law by all parties to the crisis, in particular by the Janjaweed, including indiscriminate attacks on civilians, rapes, forced displacements, and acts of violence especially those with an ethnic dimension, and expressing its utmost concern at the consequences of the conflict in Darfur on the civilian population, including women, children, internally displaced persons, and refugees, *Recalling* in this regard that the Government of Sudan bears the primary responsibility to respect human rights while maintaining law and order and protecting its population within its territory and that all parties are obliged to respect international humaniarian law,

Urging all the parties to take the necessary steps to prevent and put an end to violations of human rights and international humanitarian law and underlining that there will be no impunity for violators,

Welcoming the commitment by the Government of Sudan to investigate the atrocities and prosecute those responsible,

Emphasizing the commitment of the Government of Sudan to mobilize the armed forces of Sudan immediately to disarm the Janjaweed militias, *Recalling* also in this regard its resolutions 1325 (2000) of 31 October 2000 on women, peace and security, 1379 (2001) of 20 November 2001, 1460 (2003) of 30 January 2003, and 1539 (2004) of 22 April 2004 on children in armed conflict, and 1265 (1999) of 17 September 1999 and 1296 (2000) of 19 April 2000 on the protection of civilians in armed conflict,

Expressing concern at reports of violations of the Ceasefire Agreement signed in N'Djamena on 8 April 2004, and reiterating that all parties to the ceasefire must comply with all of the terms contained therein,

Welcoming the donor consultation held in Geneva in June 2004 as well as subsequent briefings highlighting urgent humanitarian needs in Sudan and Chad and reminding donors of the need to fulfil commitments that have been made,

Recalling that over one million people are in need of urgent humanitarian assistance, that with the onset of the rainy season the provision of assistance has become increasingly difficult, and that without urgent action to address the security, access, logistics, capacity and funding requirements the lives of hundreds of thousands of people will be at risk,

Expressing its determination to do everything possible to halt a humanitarian catastrophe, including by taking further action if required,

Welcoming the ongoing international diplomatic efforts to address the situation in Darfur,

Stressing that any return of refugees and displaced persons to their homes must take place voluntarily with adequate assistance and with sufficient security,

Noting with grave concern that up to 200,000 refugees have fled to the neighbouring State of Chad, which constitutes a serious burden upon that country, and expressing grave concern at reported cross-border incursions by Janjaweed militias of the Darfur region of Sudan into Chad and also taking note of the agreement between the Government of Sudan and Chad to establish a joint mechanism to secure the borders,

Determining that the situation in Sudan constitutes a threat to international peace and security and to stability in the region,

Acting under Chapter VII of the Charter of the United Nations,

1. *Calls on* the Government of Sudan to fulfil immediately all of the commitments it made in the 3 July 2004 Communiqué, including particularly by facilitating international relief for the humanitarian disaster by means of a moratorium on all restrictions that might hinder the provision of humanitarian assistance and access to the affected populations, by advancing independent investigation in cooperation with the United Nations of violations of human rights and international humanitarian law, by the establishment of credible security conditions for the protection of the civilian population and humanitarian actors, and by the resumption of political talks with dissident groups from the Darfur region, specifically the Justice and Equality Movement (JEM) and the Sudan Liberation Movement and Sudan Liberation Army (SLM/A) on Darfur;

2. *Endorses* the deployment of international monitors, including the protection force envisioned by the African Union, to the Darfur region of Sudan under the leadership of the African Union and *urges* the international community to continue to support these efforts, *welcomes* the progress made in deploying monitors, including the offers to provide forces by members of the African Union, and *stresses* the need for the Government of Sudan and all involved parties to facilitate the work of the monitors in accordance with the N'Djamena ceasefire agreement and with the Addis Ababa agreement of 28 May 2004 on the modalities of establishing an observer mission to monitor the ceasefire;

3. *Urges* member states to reinforce the international monitoring team, led by the African Union, including the protection force, by providing personnel and other assistance including financing, supplies, transport, vehicles, command support, communications and headquarters support as needed for the monitoring operation, and *welcomes* the contributions already made by the European Union and the United States to support the African Union led operation;

4. *Welcomes* the work done by the High Commissioner for Human Rights to send human rights observers to Sudan and *calls upon* the Government of Sudan to cooperate with the High Commissioner in the deployment of those observers;

5. *Urges* the parties to the N'Djamena Ceasefire Agreement of 8 April 2004 to conclude a political agreement without delay, notes with regret the failure of senior

rebel leaders to participate in the 15 July talks in Addis Ababa, Ethiopia as unhelpful to the process and calls for renewed talks under the sponsorship of the African Union, and its chief mediator Hamid Algabid, to reach a political solution to the tensions in Darfur and *strongly urges* rebel groups to respect the ceasefire, end the violence immediately, engage in peace talks without preconditions, and act in a positive and constructive manner to resolve the conflict;

6. *Demands* that the Government of Sudan fulfil its commitments to disarm the Janjaweed militias and apprehend and bring to justice Janjaweed leaders and their associates who have incited and carried out human rights and international humanitarian law violations and other atrocities, and *further requests* the Secretary-General to report in 30 days, and monthly thereafter, to the Council on the progress or lack thereof by the Government of Sudan on this matter and *expresses its intention* to consider further actions, including measures as provided for in Article 41 of the Charter of the United Nations on the Government of Sudan, in the event of non-compliance;

7. *Decides* that all states shall take the necessary measures to prevent the sale or supply, to all non-governmental entities and individuals, including the Janjaweed, operating in the states of North Darfur, South Darfur and West Darfur, by their nationals or from their territories or using their flag vessels or aircraft, of arms and related materiel of all types, including weapons and ammunition, military vehicles and equipment, paramilitary equipment, and spare parts for the aforementioned, whether or not originating in their territories;

8. *Decides* that all states shall take the necessary measures to prevent any provision to the non-governmental entities and individuals identified in paragraph 7 operating in the states of North Darfur, South Darfur and West Darfur by their nationals or from their territories of technical training or assistance related to the provision, manufacture, maintenance or use of the items listed in paragraph 7 above;

9. *Decides* that the measures imposed by paragraphs 7 and 8 above shall not apply to:
–supplies and related technical training and assistance to monitoring, verification or peace support operations, including such operations led by regional organizations, that are authorized by the United Nations or are operating with the consent of the relevant parties;
– supplies of non-lethal military equipment intended solely for humanitarian, human rights monitoring or protective use, and related technical training and assistance; and
–supplies of protective clothing, including flak jackets and military helmets, for the personal use of United Nations personnel, human rights monitors, representatives of the media and humanitarian and development workers and associated personnel;

10. *Expresses* its intention to consider the modification or termination of the measures imposed under paragraphs 7 and 8 when it determines that the Government of Sudan has fulfilled its commitments described in paragraph 6;

11. *Reiterates* its support for the Naivasha agreement signed by the Government of Sudan and the Sudan People's Liberation Movement, and *looks forward to* effective implementation of the agreement and a peaceful, unified Sudan working in harmony with all other States for the development of Sudan, and *calls on* the international community to be prepared for constant engagement including necessary funding in support of peace and economic development in Sudan;

12. *Urges* the international community to make available much needed assistance to mitigate the humanitarian catastrophe now unfolding in the Darfur region and calls upon member states to honour pledges that have been made against needs in Darfur and Chad and underscoring the need to contribute generously towards fulfilling the unmet portion of the United Nations consolidated appeals;

13. *Requests* the Secretary-General to activate inter-agency humanitarian mechanisms to consider what additional measures may be needed to avoid a humanitarian catastrophe and to report regularly to the Council on progress made;

14. *Encourages* the Secretary-General's Special Representative for Sudan and the independent expert of the Commission on Human Rights to work closely with the Government of Sudan in supporting independent investigation of violations of human rights and international humanitarian law in the Darfur region;

15. *Extends* the special political mission set out in resolution 1547 for an additional 90 days to 10 December 2004 and *requests* the Secretary-General to incorporate into the mission contingency planning for the Darfur region;

16. *Expresses* its full support for the African Union-led ceasefire commission and monitoring mission in Darfur, and *requests* the Secretary-General to assist the African Union with planning and assessments for its mission in Darfur, and in accordance with the Joint Communiqué to prepare to support implementation of a future agreement in Darfur in close cooperation with the African Union and *requests* the Secretary-General to report to the Security Council on progress;

17. *Decides* to remain seized of the matter.

United Nations Security Council
Resolution 1706 (2006)

Adopted by the Security Council at its 5519th meeting, on 31 August 2006

The Security Council,
Recalling its previous resolutions concerning the situation in the Sudan, in particular resolutions 1679 (2006) of 16 May 2006, 1665 (2006) of 29 March 2006, 1663 (2006) of 24 March 2006, 1593 (2005) of 31 March 2005, 1591 (2005) of 29 March 2005, 1590 (2005) of 24 March 2005, 1574 (2004) of 19 November 2004, 1564

(2004) of 18 September 2004 and 1556 (2004) of 30 July 2004 and the statements
of its President concerning the Sudan,

Recalling also its previous resolutions 1325 (2000) on women, peace and security,
1502 (2003) on the protection of humanitarian and United Nations personnel,
1612 (2005) on children and armed conflict, and 1674 (2006) on the protection of
civilians in armed conflict, which reaffirms inter alia the provisions of paragraphs
138 and 139 of the 2005 United Nations World Summit outcome document, as well
as the report of its Mission to the Sudan and Chad from 4 to 10 June 2006,

Reaffirming its strong commitment to the sovereignty, unity, independence, and
territorial integrity of the Sudan, which would be unaffected by transition to a
United Nations operation in Darfur, and to the cause of peace, *expressing its determination* to work with the Government of National Unity, in full respect of its sovereignty, to assist in tackling the various problems confronting the Sudan and that
a United Nations operation in Darfur shall have, to the extent possible, a strong
African participation and character,

Welcoming the efforts of the African Union to find a solution to the crisis in Darfur,
including through the success of the African Union-led Inter-Sudanese Peace Talks
on the Conflict in Darfur in Abuja, Nigeria, in particular the framework agreed
between the parties for a resolution of the conflict in Darfur (the Darfur Peace
Agreement), *commending* the efforts of the signatories to the Darfur Peace
Agreement, *expressing* its belief that the Agreement provides a basis for sustained
security in Darfur, *reiterating* its welcome of the statement of 9 May 2006 by the
representative of the Sudan at the United Nations Security Council Special Session
on Darfur of the Government of National Unity's full commitment to implementing the Agreement, *stressing* the importance of launching, with the African Union,
the Darfur-Darfur dialogue and consultation as soon as possible, and *recognizing*
that international support for implementation of the Agreement is critically
important to its success,

Commending the efforts of the African Union for the successful deployment of the
African Union Mission in the Sudan (AMIS), as well as the efforts of Member
States and regional and international organizations that have assisted it in its
deployment, and AMIS' role in reducing large-scale organized violence in Darfur,
recalling the decision of the African Union Peace and Security Council of 10 March
2006, and its decision of 27 June 2006 as outlined in paragraph 10 of its
Communiqué that the African Union is ready to review the mandate of AMIS in
the event that the ongoing consultations between the Government of National
Unity and the United Nations conclude on an agreement for a transition to a
United Nations peacekeeping operation, *stressing* the need for AMIS to assist
implementation of the Darfur Peace Agreement until transition to the United
Nations force in Darfur is completed, *welcoming* the decision of the African Union
Peace and Security Council of 27 June 2006 on strengthening AMIS' mandate and

tasks, including on the protection of civilians, and *considering* that AMIS needs urgent reinforcing,

Reaffirming its concern that the ongoing violence in Darfur might further negatively affect the rest of the Sudan as well as the region, in particular Chad and the Central African Republic, and *stressing* that regional security aspects must be addressed to achieve long lasting peace in Darfur,

Remaining deeply concerned over the recent deterioration of relations between the Sudan and Chad, calling on the Governments of the two countries to abide by their obligations under the Tripoli Agreement of 8 February 2006 and the agreement between the Sudan and Chad signed in N'djamena on 26 July 2006 and to begin implementing the confidence-building measures which they have voluntarily agreed upon, welcoming the recent re-establishment of diplomatic relations between the Sudan and Chad, and calling upon all States in the region to cooperate in ensuring regional stability,

Reiterating its strong condemnation of all violations of human rights and international humanitarian law in Darfur, and *calling upon* the Government of National Unity to take urgent action to tackle gender-based violence in Darfur including action towards implementing its Action Plan to Combat Violence Against Women in Darfur with particular focus on the rescission of Form 8 and access to legal redress,

Expressing its deep concern for the security of humanitarian aid workers and their access to populations in need, including refugees, internally displaced persons and other war-affected populations, and *calling upon* all parties, in particular the Government of National Unity, to ensure, in accordance with relevant provisions of international law, the full, safe and unhindered access of relief personnel to all those in need in Darfur as well as the delivery of humanitarian assistance, in particular to internally displaced persons and refugees,

Taking note of the communiqués of 12 January, 10 March, 15 May and 27 June 2006 of the Peace and Security Council of the African Union regarding transition of AMIS to a United Nations operation,

Taking note of the report of the Secretary-General on Darfur dated 28 July

Determining that the situation in the Sudan continues to constitute a threat to international peace and security,

1. *Decides*, without prejudice to its existing mandate and operations as provided for in resolution 1590 (2005) and in order to support the early and effective implementation of the Darfur Peace Agreement, that UNMIS' mandate shall be expanded as specified in paragraphs 8, 9 and 12 below, that it shall deploy to Darfur, and therefore invites the consent of the Government of National Unity for this deployment, and *urges* Member States to provide the capability for an expeditious deployment;

2. *Requests* the Secretary-General to arrange the rapid deployment of additional capabilities for UNMIS, in order that it may deploy in Darfur, in accordance with the recommendation contained in his report dated 28 July 2006;

3. *Decides* that UNMIS shall be strengthened by up to 17,300 military personnel and by an appropriate civilian component including up to 3,300 civilian police personnel and up to 16 Formed Police Units, and *expresses its determination* to keep UNMIS' strength and structure under regular review, taking into account the evolution of the situation on the ground and without prejudice to its current operations and mandate as provided for in resolution 1590 (2005);

4. *Expresses* its intention to consider authorizing possible additional temporary reinforcements of the military component of UNMIS, at the request of the Secretary-General, within the limits of the troop levels recommended in paragraph 87 of his report dated 28 July 2006;

5. *Requests* the Secretary-General to consult jointly with the African Union, in close and continuing consultation with the parties to the Darfur Peace Agreement, including the Government of National Unity, on a plan and timetable for transition from AMIS to a United Nations operation in Darfur; *decides* that those elements outlined in paragraphs 40 to 58 of the Secretary-General's report of 28 July 2006 shall begin to be deployed no later than 1 October 2006, that thereafter as part of the process of transition to a United Nations operation additional capabilities shall be deployed as soon as feasible and that UNMIS shall take over from AMIS responsibility for supporting the implementation of the Darfur Peace Agreement upon the expiration of AMIS' mandate but in any event no later than 31 December 2006;

6. *Notes* that the Status of Forces Agreement for UNMIS with the Sudan, as outlined in resolution 1590 (2005), shall apply to UNMIS' operations throughout the Sudan, including in Darfur;

7. *Requests* the Secretary-General to take the necessary steps to strengthen AMIS through the use of existing and additional United Nations resources with a view to transition to a United Nations operation in Darfur; and *authorizes* the Secretary-General during this transition to implement the longer-term support to AMIS outlined in the report of the Secretary-General of 28 July 2006, including provision of air assets, ground mobility package, training, engineering and logistics, mobile communications capacity and broad public information assistance;

8. *Decides* that the mandate of UNMIS in Darfur shall be to support implementation of the Darfur Peace Agreement of 5 May 2006 and the N'djamena Agreement on Humanitarian Cease-fire on the Conflict in Darfur ("the Agreements"), including by performing the following tasks:

(a) To monitor and verify the implementation by the parties of Chapter 3 ("Comprehensive Cease-fire and Final Security Arrangements") of the Darfur Peace Agreement and the N'djamena Agreement on Humanitarian Cease-fire on the Conflict in Darfur;

(b) To observe and monitor movement of armed groups and redeployment of forces in areas of UNMIS deployment by ground and aerial means in accordance with the Agreements;

(c) To investigate violations of the Agreements and to report violations to the Cease-fire Commission; as well as to cooperate and coordinate, together with other International Actors, with the Cease-fire Commission, the Joint Commission, and the Joint Humanitarian Facilitation and Monitoring Unit established pursuant to the Agreements including through provision of technical assistance and logistical support;

(d) To maintain, in particular, a presence in key areas, such as buffer zones established pursuant to the Darfur Peace Agreement, areas inside internally displaced persons camps and demilitarized zones around and inside internally displaced persons camps, in order to promote the re-establishment of confidence, to discourage violence, in particular by deterring use of force;

(e) To monitor transborder activities of armed groups along the Sudanese borders with Chad and the Central African Republic in particular through regular ground and aerial reconnaissance activities;

(f) To assist with development and implementation of a comprehensive and sustainable programme for disarmament, demobilization and reintegration of former combatants and women and children associated with combatants, as called for in the Darfur Peace Agreement and in accordance with resolutions 1556 (2004) and 1564 (2004);

(g) To assist the parties, in cooperation with other international actors, in the preparations for and conduct of referendums provided for in the Darfur Peace Agreement;

(h) To assist the parties to the Agreements in promoting understanding of the peace accord and of the role of UNMIS, including by means of an effective public information campaign, targeted at all sectors of society, in coordination with the African Union;

(i) To cooperate closely with the Chairperson of the Darfur-Darfur Dialogue and Consultation (DDDC), provide support and technical assistance to him, and coordinate other United Nations agencies' activities to this effect, as well as to assist the parties to the DDDC in addressing the need for an all-inclusive approach, including the role of women, towards reconciliation and peacebuilding;

(j) To assist the parties to the Darfur Peace Agreement, in coordination with bilateral and multilateral assistance programmes, in restructuring the police service in the Sudan, consistent with democratic policing, to develop a police training and evaluation programme, and to otherwise assist in the training of civilian police;

(k) To assist the parties to the Darfur Peace Agreement in promoting the rule of law, including an independent judiciary, and the protection of human rights of all people of the Sudan through a comprehensive and coordinated strategy with the aim of combating impunity and contributing to long-term peace and stability and to assist the parties to the Darfur Peace Agreement to develop and consolidate the national legal framework;

(l) To ensure an adequate human rights and gender presence, capacity and expertise within UNMIS to carry out human rights promotion, civilian protection and monitoring activities that include particular attention to the needs of women and children;

9. *Decides* further that the mandate of UNMIS in Darfur shall also include the following:

(a) To facilitate and coordinate in close cooperation with relevant United Nations agencies, within its capabilities and in its areas of deployment, the voluntary return of refugees and internally displaced persons, and humanitarian assistance inter alia by helping to establish the necessary security conditions in Darfur;

(b) To contribute towards international efforts to protect, promote and monitor human rights in Darfur, as well as to coordinate international efforts towards the protection of civilians with particular attention to vulnerable groups including internally displaced persons, returning refugees, and women and children;

(c) To assist the parties to the Agreements, in cooperation with other international partners in the mine action sector, by providing humanitarian demining assistance, technical advice, and coordination, as well as mine awareness programmes targeted at all sectors of society;

(d) To assist in addressing regional security issues in close liaison with international efforts to improve the security situation in the neighbouring regions along the borders between the Sudan and Chad and between the Sudan and the Central African Republic, including through the establishment of a multidimensional presence consisting of political, humanitarian, military and civilian police liaison officers in key locations in Chad, including in internally displaced persons and refugee camps, and if necessary, in the Central African Republic, and to contribute to the implementation of the Agreement between the Sudan and Chad signed on 26 July 2006;

10. *Calls upon* all Member States to ensure the free, unhindered and expeditious movement to the Sudan of all personnel, as well as equipment, provisions, supplies and other goods, including vehicles and spare parts, which are for the exclusive and official use of UNMIS in Darfur;

11. *Requests* the Secretary-General to keep the Council regularly informed of the progress in implementing the Darfur Peace Agreement, respect for the ceasefire, and the implementation of the mandate of UNMIS in Darfur, and to report to the Council, as appropriate, on the steps taken to implement this resolution and any failure to comply with its demands;

12. Acting under Chapter VII of the Charter of the United Nations:

(a) *Decides* that UNMIS is authorized to use all necessary means, in the areas of deployment of its forces and as it deems within its capabilities:

– to protect United Nations personnel, facilities, installations and equipment, to ensure the security and freedom of movement of United Nations personnel, humanitarian workers, assessment and evaluation commission personnel, to prevent disruption of the implementation of the Darfur Peace Agreement by armed groups, without prejudice to the responsibility of the Government of the Sudan, to protect civilians under threat of physical violence,

– in order to support early and effective implementation of the Darfur Peace Agreement, to prevent attacks and threats against civilians,

– to seize or collect, as appropriate, arms or related material whose presence in Darfur is in violation of the Agreements and the measures imposed by paragraphs 7 and 8 of resolution 1556, and to dispose of such arms and related material as appropriate;

(b) *Requests* that the Secretary-General and the Governments of Chad and the Central African Republic conclude status-of-forces agreements as soon as possible, taking into consideration General Assembly resolution 58/82 on the scope of legal protection under the Convention on the Safety of United Nations and Associated Personnel, and *decides* that pending the conclusion of such an agreement with either country, the model status-of-forces agreement dated 9 October 1990 (A/45/594) shall apply provisionally with respect to UNMIS forces operating in that country;

13. *Requests* the Secretary-General to report to the Council on the protection of civilians in refugee and internally displaced persons camps in Chad and on how to improve the security situation on the Chadian side of the border with Sudan;

14. *Calls upon* the parties to the Darfur Peace Agreement to respect their commitments and implement the Agreement without delay, *urges* those parties that have not signed the Agreement to do so without delay and not to act in any way that would impede implementation of the Agreement, and *reiterates* its intention to take, including in response to a request by the African Union, strong and effective measures, such as an asset freeze or travel ban, against any individual or group that violates or attempts to block the implementation of the Agreement or commits human rights violations;

15. *Decides* to remain seized of the matter.

APPENDIX 4

Articles by Eric Reeves

[a] Eric Reeves, "Quantifying Genocide In Darfur: April 28, 2006: Current data for total mortality from violence, malnutrition, and disease." In two parts, April 28, 2006 and May 13, 2006, at
http://www.sudanreeves.org/Article102.html
http://www.sudanreeves.org/Article104.html

[b] Eric Reeves, "Report of the UN International Commission of Inquiry on Darfur: A critical analysis." In two parts, February 2, 2005 and February 6, 2006, at
http://www.sudanreeves.org/Sections-article489-p1.html
http://www.sudanreeves.org/Sections-article488-p1.html

[c] Eric Reeves, "Ghosts of Rwanda: The Failure of the African Union in Darfur." In two parts, November 13 and November 20, 2006, at
http://www.sudanreeves.org/Sections-article535-p1.html
http://www.sudanreeves.org/Sections-article534-p1.html

[d] "Unnoticed Genocide"
By Eric Reeves
Published in the *Washington Post*, Wednesday, February 25, 2004; Page A25

In the remote Darfur region of western Sudan, a human disaster is accelerating amid uncontrolled violence. The United Nations' undersecretary general for humanitarian affairs has called it probably "the world's greatest humanitarian catastrophe." Doctors Without Borders has observed "catastrophic mortality rates." And yet, so far as most of the world is concerned, it isn't even happening.

There have been what Amnesty International calls "horrifying military attacks against civilians" throughout Darfur by the Sudanese government and its militias. The government has sent bombers to attack undefended villages, refugee camps and water wells. The United Nations estimates that 1 million people have been displaced by war and that more than 3 million are affected by armed conflict.

Yet Darfur has remained practically a non-story in international news media. One big reason is the fact that the central government in Khartoum, the National Islamic Front, has allowed no news reporters into the region and has severely restricted humanitarian access, thus preventing observation by aid workers. The war in Darfur is not directly related to Khartoum's 20-year war against the people of southern Sudan. Even so, military pressure from the Darfur insurgency that began a year ago has been instrumental in forcing the regime to commit to peace talks with the south.

But there are now signs that these talks have been viewed by Khartoum only as a way to buy time to crush the insurgency in Darfur, which emerged, inevitably, from many years of abuse and neglect. Despite efforts by the regime to stop it, a widening stream of information is reaching the international community, from tens of thousands of refugees fleeing to Chad (which shares a long border with western Sudan), and according to accounts from within Darfur. Amnesty International has led the way in reporting on Darfur; one of its recent releases speaks authoritatively of countless savage attacks on civilians by Khartoum's regular army, including its crude Antonov bombers, and by its Arab militia allies, called "Janjaweed."

An especially disturbing feature of these attacks is the clear and intensifying racial animus. This has been reported by Amnesty International, the International Crisis Group and various U.N. spokesmen. The words "ethnic cleansing" have been used by U.N. officials and diplomats. This term, which gained currency during the breakup of Yugoslavia, is another description for genocide. But whatever they are called, the terrible realities in Darfur require that we attend to the ways in which people are being destroyed because of who they are, racially and ethnically – "as such," to cite the key phrase from the 1948 U.N. Convention on Genocide.

Darfur is home to racially and ethnically distinct tribal groups. Although virtually all are Muslim, generalizations are hard to make. But the Fur, Zaghawa, Masseleit, and other peoples are accurately described as "African," both in a racial sense and in terms of agricultural practice and use of non-Arabic languages. Darfur also has a large population of nomadic Arab tribal groups, and from these

Khartoum has drawn its savage "warriors on horseback" – the Janjaweed – who are most responsible for attacks on villages and civilians.

The racial animus is clear from scores of chillingly similar interviews with refugees reaching Chad. A young African man who had lost many family members in an attack heard the gunmen say, "You blacks, we're going to exterminate you." Speaking of these relentless attacks, an African tribal leader told the U.N. news service, "I believe this is an elimination of the black race." A refugee reported these words as coming from his attackers: "You are opponents to the regime, we must crush you. As you are black, you are like slaves. Then the entire Darfur region will be in the hands of the Arabs." An African tribal chief declared that, "The Arabs and the government forces . . . said they wanted to conquer the whole territory and that the blacks did not have a right to remain in the region."

There can be no reasonable skepticism about Khartoum's use of these militias to "destroy, in whole or in part, ethnic or racial groups" – in short, to commit genocide. Khartoum has so far refused to rein in its Arab militias; has refused to enter into meaningful peace talks with the insurgency groups; and, most disturbingly, has refused to grant unrestricted humanitarian access. The international community has been slow to react to Darfur's catastrophe and has yet to move with sufficient urgency and commitment. A credible peace forum must be rapidly created. Immediate plans for humanitarian intervention should begin. The alternative is to allow tens of thousands of civilians to die in the weeks and months ahead in what will be continuing genocidal destruction.

BIBLIOGRAPHY

A Note About The Bibliography

This bibliography is unusual in several respects, and particularly in its heavy reliance on news wire services, especially Reuters, Agence France-Presse, Associated Press, Deutsche Presse-Agentur, and the UN Integrated Regional Information Networks (IRIN). If news reporting is the "first draft of history," these historians are of varying quality, and their use in these pages calls for a brief explanation. I have sought always to use those wire reports, and newspaper dispatches, with a dateline of either Darfur or Khartoum. At other times, of course, other datelines in Africa, Europe, and the United States have been more relevant. Inevitably I have come to trust certain journalists more than others. Some are extraordinarily talented, insightful, and courageous: Lydia Polgreen of the *New York Times*, Opheera McDoom of Reuters (Khartoum-based), and Alfred de Montesquiou of Associated Press (Khartoum-based).

But the on-site reporting by many other journalists has been indispensable in rendering timely accounts of Darfur's evolving realities, which the National Islamic Front regime has worked so assiduously to obscure. At times there has been no possibility of selecting from different dispatches reporting on key news developments. UN IRIN has frequently been exceptionally useful, particularly in providing detailed overview accounts, and in offering authoritative information unavailable from any other news source.

The "second draft of history" is represented in the many human rights reports I have so frequently cited, including those coming from Human Rights Watch,

Amnesty International, Physicians for Human Rights, and the International Crisis Group. The latter has also provided indispensable policy analyses that have done much to guide my thinking, even as there are significant differences in our current assessment of what pressures must be brought to bear on the regime in Khartoum if the international community is to secure access for a meaningful international protection force in Darfur.

I have spoken of my confidential sources in the *Introduction* to this book, and will say again how deeply indebted I am to a host of such sources, and how deeply I admire their courage in communicating as much as they have, and their trust in doing so with someone often unknown to them except by virtue of what I have previously written. I am especially indebted to those who have communicated with me from the ground in Darfur.

Reports

Non - Governmental Organizations

Amnesty International Press Release. *Sudan: Humanitarian Crisis in Darfur Caused by Sudan Government's Failures.* November 27, 2003.

Amnesty International. *Darfur: 'Too many people killed for no reason.'* February 2004.

Amnesty International. *Public Statement.* April 30, 2004.

Amnesty International. *Press Release (AFR 54/064/2004).* June 8, 2004.

Amnesty International. *Memorandum to the Government of Sudan.* June 9, 2004.

Amnesty International. *Sudan, Darfur: Rape as a Weapon of War.* July 19, 2004.

Amnesty International AFR 54/131/2004. *Sudan: Civilians Still Under Threat In Darfur.* October 13, 2004.

Amnesty International. *No One to Complain to: No Respite for the Victims, Impunity for the Perpetrators.* December 2, 2004.

Amnesty International Report. *Crying Out for Safety.* October 5, 2006.

Coalition for International Justice. *Documenting Atrocities in Darfur.* September 2004.

Coebergh, Dr. Jan. *Sudan: Genocide has Killed More Than the Tsunami.* UK Parliamentary Brief Vol. 9, No. 7, February 2005.

Committee on Conscience. *Report on Sudan: "Genocide Warning."* October 2000.

Darfur Humanitarian Workers to UN Resident and Humanitarian Coordinator. *A Briefing Paper on the Darfur Crisis: Ethnic Cleansing.* March 26, 2004.

Human Rights Watch. *Darfur Destroyed: Ethnic Cleansing by Government and Militia Forces in Western Sudan.* May 6, 2004.

Human Rights Watch. *A Human Rights Watch Briefing Paper - Darfur Documents Confirm Government Policy of Militia Support.* July 20, 2004.

Human Rights Watch. *Janjaweed Camps Still Active.* August 27, 2004.

Human Rights Watch. *Darfur: UN 'Safe Areas' Offer no Real Security.* September 1, 2004.

Human Rights Watch Report. *UN Darfur Deadline Expires: Security Council Must Act.* September 3, 2004.

International Commite Croix Rouge (ICRC). *Darfur: A Deteriorating Situation.* February 9, 2005.

International Crisis Group (ICG). *Sudan: Towards an Incomplete Peace.* December 11, 2003.

International Crisis Group (ICG). *Ethnic Cleansing in Darfur: A New Front Opens in Sudan's Bloody War.* May 6, 2004.

International Crisis Group (ICG). *End the Slaughter and Starvation in Western Sudan.* May 16, 2004.

International Crisis Group (ICG). *Sudan: Now or Never in Darfur Africa Report No. 80.* May 23, 2004.

International Crisis Group (ICG). *Darfur Deadline: A New International Action Plan.* August 23, 2004.

International Crisis Group (ICG). *The AU's Mission in Darfur: Bridging the Gaps.* July 2005.

International Crisis Group (ICG) Report. *To Save Darfur.* March 17, 2006.

Letter from 31 Arab Human rights Organizations. *Arab NGOs Call Upon the Sudanese Government to Accept the Deployment of the UN Forces.* September 18, 2006.

Doctors Without Borders/Médecins Sans Frontières (MSF) Press Release. *The Health of Hundreds of Thousands of Displaced People Worsens Dramatically.* April 28, 2004.

Doctors Without Borders/Médecins Sans Frontières (MSF). *On the Brink of Mass Starvation in Darfur.* May 20, 2004.

Doctors Without Borders/Médecins Sans Frontières (MSF) Study. *Emergency in Darfur, Sudan: No Relief in Sight.* June 21, 2004.

Doctors Without Borders/Médecins Sans Frontières (MSF)-Holland. *Persecution, Intimidation and Failure of Assistance in Darfur.* October 2004.

Doctors Without Borders/Médecins Sans Frontières (MSF) Study. *The Crushing Burden of Rape: Sexual Violence in Darfur.* March 8, 2005.

Physicians for Human Rights. *Evidence of Intentional Destruction of Livelihoods in Darfur.* February 2005.

Refugees International. *Sudan: Food Shortages Spreading Beyond Conflict Areas.* February 16, 2005.

Refugees International. *No Power to Protect: The African Union Mission in Sudan.* November 2005.

Save the Children. *Sudan Emergency Statement.* December 10, 2003.

Government Agencies

US Agency for International Development (USAID). Report and Chart. *Projected Mortality Rates in Darfur, Sudan 2004-2005.* December 2003.

US Agency for International Development (USAID), Assistant Administrator Roger Winter. Testimony Before the Committee on International Relations – US House of Representatives. *Ethnic Cleansing in Darfur: A New Front Opens in Sudan's Bloody War.* May 6, 2004.

US Agency for International Development (USAID). *Darfur: Humanitarian Emergency.* June 4, 2004.

US Agency for International Development (USAID). *Darfur - Humanitarian Emergency.* August 20, 2004.

US Congress. Congressman Frank Wolf et al. Letter to UN Secretary-General Kofi Annan. June 4, 2004.

United Nations

Report of the International Commission of Inquiry on Darfur to the United Nations Secretary-General - Pursuant to Security Council Resolution 1564 of 18 September 2004. January 25, 2005.

UN Secretary-General Kofi Annan. *Action Plan to Prevent Genocide.* April 7, 2004.

UN Secretary-General Kofi Annan. *Report of the Secretary-General pursuant to ... Security Council Resolution 1556.* August 30, 2004.

UN Secretary-General Kofi Annan. *Report of the Secretary-General pursuant to UN Security Council Resolutions, 1556, 1564, and 1574. (S/2004/947).* December 3, 2004.

UN Secretary-General Kofi Annan. *Report of the Secretary-General Pursuant to Security Council Resolution 1556.* February 4, 2005.

UN. Louise Arbour. *Report of the Commission of Inquiry document (S/2005/60).* January 25, 2005.

UN. *Darfur Humanitarian Profile No. 6.* September 1, 2004.

UN. *Darfur Humanitarian Profile No. 10.* January 1, 2005.

UN. *Darfur Humanitarian Profile No. 14.* May 1, 2005.

UN *Darfur Humanitarian Profile No. 22.* January – February 2006.

UNHCHR Supressed Report. *Report of the Office of the High Commission for Human Rights Mission to Chad, April 5-15, 2004.*

UN Integrated Regional Information Networks (IRIN). *SUDAN: Special Report on the Impact of a Future Peace Agreement on Refugees and IDPs.* November 11, 2003.

UN Integrated Regional Information Networks (IRIN). *UN Human Rights Experts Call for Urgent, Effective Action on Darfur.* March 16, 2005.

UN Office for the Coordination of Humanitarian Affairs. *Briefing by Jan Egeland, Under-Secretary-General for Humanitarian Affairs and Emergency Relief Coordinator, On the Humanitarian Situation in Darfur.* August 28, 2006.

UN Special Rapporteur Asma Jahangir. *Report of the UN HR Commission on Extrajudicial, Summary or Arbitrary Executions in S. & W. Sudan.* August 2004.

Juan Méndez. *Report of the Special Adviser on the Prevention of Genocide - Visit to Darfur, Sudan 19-26 September 2005.*

Tom Vraalsen, the UN Secretary-General's Special Envoy for Humanitarian Affairs for Sudan, Note to the Emergency Relief Coordinator. *Sudan: Humanitarian Crisis in Darfur.* December 8, 2003.

UN. *Report of the High Commissioner for Human Rights: Situation of human rights in the Darfur Region of the Sudan.* May 7, 2004.

UN. *Report: A UN Inter-Agency fact-finding and humanitarian needs assessment mission, Kailek, South Darfur.* April 24, 2004.

UN. World Food Program and Center for Disease Control and Prevention. *Emergency Nutrition Assessment of Crisis Affected Populations, Darfur Region.* September 2004.

UN. *Fifth Periodic Report of the UN High Commissioner for Human Rights [UNHCHR] on the Situation of Human Rights in the Sudan.* October 6, 2006.

Articles and Studies

Africa Confidential. February 18, 2005, Volume 46, No. 4.

Ateem, Eltigani Seisi. Former Governor of Darfur and chairman of the Darfur Union in exile in Great Britain. *Email.* March 24, 2004.

The Financial Times (London). "Thousands Die as World Denies Genocide." July 6, 2004.

Brookings Institution/Bern University. *Protecting of Two Million Internally Displaced: The Successes and Shortcomings of the African Union in Darfur.* November 2005.

Gingerich, Tara, JD, MA and Jennifer Leaning, MD, SMH. *The Use of Rape as a Weapon of War in the conflict in Darfur, Sudan.* USAID/OTI. Auspices of the Harvard School of Public Health and the Francois-Xavier Bagnoud Center for Health and Human Rights.

Gourevitch, Philip. *The New Yorker,* "The Genocide Fax." May 11, 1998.

Kristof, Nicholas. *New York Times,* "The Secret Genocide Archive." February 23, 2005.

Massaleit Community in Exile. *Dispatch.* Confirmed by Darfurians in exile with contacts inside Darfur. May 5, 2004.

de Waal, Alex. Article. *London Review of Books.* August 5, 2004.

Other

Appeals Chamber of the International Tribunal for Violations of International Law in the former Yugoslavia, Review of *Prosecutor v. Radislav Krstic Case No. IT-98-33-T.*

Books

Dallaire, Roméo A. Lieutenant-General. *Shake Hands with the Devil: The Failure of Humanity in Rwanda.* Toronto: Random House Canada. 2003.

Johnson, Douglas. *The Root Causes of Sudan's Civil Wars.* Oxford, England: James Currey publishers. 2003.

Mandell, Gerald et al. *Principles and Practice of Infectious Diseases.* 2 Vol. London: Elsevier Churchill Livingstone. 2005.

Power, Samantha. *"A Problem from Hell": America and the Age of Genocide.* New York: Harper Perennial. 2003.

de Waal, Alex and Julie Flint. *Darfur: A Short History of a Long War.* London: Zed Books. 2005.

Media: Magazines, News Agencies, Newspapers, Online News, Radio, Television

Agence France-Press
Associated Press
Al-Ayam (Khartoum)
BBC
BBC/Public Radio International
Business Day
The Chicago Sun-Times
CNN
Defence News – www.defencetalk.com
Deutsche Presse-Agentur
The Economist
EU BusinessWire
The Financial Times (London)
The Globe and Mail
The Guardian Online
The Guardian (UK)
The Independent (UK)
Inter Press Service
The International Herald Tribune

London Review of Books
The New York Times
New Yorker
National Public Radio
Public Broadcasting System (PBS)
Reuters
Scotland on Sunday (UK)
Spiegel Online
Sudan Tribune
The Telegraph (UK)
United Nations News Centre
UN Integrated Regional Information Networks (IRIN)
United Press International
Voice of America
Wall Street Journal
Washington Post
Xinhuanet

INDEX

355